OVERCOMING EMPIRE IN POST-IMPERIAL EAST ASIA

Published:
Women and Democracy in Cold War Japan, Jan Bardsley
Christianity and Imperialism in Modern Japan, Emily Anderson
The China Problem in Postwar Japan, Robert Hoppens
Media, Propaganda and Politics in 20th-Century Japan,
The Asahi Shimbun Company (translated by Barak Kushner)
Contemporary Sino-Japanese Relations on Screen, Griseldis Kirsch
Debating Otaku in Contemporary Japan, edited by Patrick W. Galbraith,
Thiam Huat Kam and Björn-Ole Kamm

OVERCOMING EMPIRE IN POST-IMPERIAL EAST ASIA

Repatriation, Redress and Rebuilding

Barak Kushner,

University of Cambridge

and

Sherzod Muminov,

University of East Anglia

BLOOMSBURY ACADEMIC

LONDON · NEW YORK · OXFORD · NEW DELHI · SYDNEY

BLOOMSBURY ACADEMIC
Bloomsbury Publishing Plc
50 Bedford Square, London, WC1B 3DP, UK
1385 Broadway, New York, NY 10018, USA

BLOOMSBURY, BLOOMSBURY ACADEMIC and the Diana logo
are trademarks of Bloomsbury Publishing Plc

First published in Great Britain 2020

A catalogue record for this book is available from the British Library.

A catalog record for this book is available from the Library of Congress.

ISBN: HB: 978-1-3501-2705-0
         ePDF: 978-1-3501-2706-7
         ePub: 978-1-3501-2707-4

Typeset by Integra Software Services Pvt. Ltd
Printed and bound in Great Britain

To find out more about our authors and books visit www.bloomsbury.com
and sign up for our newsletters.

CONTENTS

LIST OF ILLUSTRATIONS

Figures

Tables

CONTRIBUTORS

CHANG Chihyun

Chang Chihyun received his doctorate from the University of Bristol, with a thesis on the Chinese Maritime Customs Service, focusing on Chinese nationalism and the foreign colonial presence in China. In 2010 he joined the Center for Geographic Information Science and in 2011 the Institute of Modern History at Academia Sinica as a postdoctoral fellow, where he continued his study of modern China and imperial maritime customs and trade. He later accepted the offer of a research fellowship from the Department of History at Shanghai Jiao Tong University in Shanghai. He has published *Government, Nationalism and Imperialism in China* (2013) and *The L. K. Little Diaries, 1943–1954: The Witness of Chinese Revolutions and Wars* (2016).

Arnaud DOGLIA

Arnaud Doglia is currently a postdoctoral research fellow in the Department of East Asian Studies at the University of Geneva, Switzerland. He is interested in contemporary Japan and East Asia. He received his MA (East Asian studies) and his PhD (Japanese studies) from the University of Geneva. His first book, published by Peter Lang, is entitled *Japanese Biological Warfare, 1880–2011: Historical Realities and the Anatomy of Memory* (2016). His current research, *Japanese Medical Atrocities: Narratives of Reconversion of Former War Criminals in Postwar Japan*, seeks to analyze in depth the network of scientists and physicians who participated in medical experiments until 1945, equally discussing their profile, reconversion and responsibility. Other topics of interest include the birth of bioethics in Japan, Japanese war crimes and their memories in East Asia, the Second World War and Cold War atrocities as well as social history and popular culture during the Allied Occupation and in postwar Japan.

Koji HIRATA

Koji Hirata is a research fellow of Emmanuel College, Cambridge. His research centers on the history of industry, city, empires, and globalization in modern China. His current book project, "Steel Metropolis: Industrial Manchuria and the Making of Chinese Socialism, 1917–1975," examines the development of state-owned enterprises, the concepts and practice of urban planning, and the politics of everyday life among workers in twentieth-century China. Methodologically, his research combines examination of economic activities informed by the literature on political economy, a cultural history analysis of the language used in historical texts, and a transnational history approach to the movement of ideas, goods, and people across national boundaries. His dissertation makes use of archival documents in Chinese, Japanese, English, and Russian as well as oral history interviews.

Matthew D. JOHNSON

Matthew D. Johnson is an associate fellow of the Global Diplomatic Forum, an independent political analyst, and a higher education consultant. Previously, he was Executive Dean of the Faculty of Arts and Social Sciences at Taylor's University, Malaysia, and served on the board of the Malaysian-American Commission on Educational Exchange. He is a co-founder and director of the PRC History Group (http://prchistory.org/) and board member (at-large) of the Historical Society for Twentieth-Century China. His publications include *Maoism at the Grassroots: Everyday Life in China's Era of High Socialism* (co-edited with Jeremy Brown, 2015) and a forthcoming chapter on PRC responses to US cultural diplomacy and global strategy during the Kennedy administration.

Yukiko KOGA

Yukiko Koga is Associate Professor in the Department of Anthropology at Hunter College at the City University of New York, CUNY Graduate Center, and Associate Research Scholar at the Weatherhead East Asian Institute at Columbia University. She is the author of the award winning *Inheritance of Loss: China, Japan, and the Political Economy of Redemption after Empire* (2016), which explores how the introduction of the market-oriented economy in China created new dynamics concerning the contested yet under-explored past for both the Chinese and Japanese. Whereas *Inheritance of Loss* is set within the burgeoning economic sphere of Northeast China to explore the generational transmission of unaccounted for pasts stemming from Japanese imperialism in China, her book-in-progress takes place within a transnational legal sphere. She is currently completing a book entitled *Post-imperial Reckoning: Law, Redress, Reconciliation*, which is an ethnographic, historical, and legal exploration of a new moral landscape for imperial reckoning that has emerged through a series of collective lawsuits filed by Chinese victims of Japanese imperial violence against the Japanese government and corporations since the 1990s.

Barak KUSHNER

Barak Kushner is Professor of East Asian History at the Faculty of Asian & Middle Eastern Studies, University of Cambridge. He has written three monographs, most recently *Men to Devils, Devils to Men: Japanese War Crimes and Chinese Justice* (2015). Barak also recently co-edited, with former *Asahi Newspaper* editor-in-chief Funabashi Yoichi, a volume on Japan's lost decades entitled, *Examining Japan's Lost Decades* (2015) and completed a large translation project, *Media, Propaganda and Politics in Twentieth-Century Japan* (2015). In March 2013 Barak launched a six-year European Research Council-funded project, "The Dissolution of the Japanese Empire and the Struggle for Legitimacy in Postwar East Asia, 1945–1965," examining the impact of the fall of the Japanese Empire in East Asia. The first volume of that project, edited with Sherzod Muminov, was *The Dismantling of Japan's Empire in East Asia: De-imperialization, Postwar Legitimation and Imperial Afterlife* (2017).

Shi-Chi Mike LAN

Shi-chi Mike Lan (PhD, Chicago, 2004) teaches in the Department of History, National Chengchi University, Taiwan. He was Visiting Professor at the University of Tokyo, Japan, in 2010, and a research associate at Rikkyo University, Japan, in 2015. His research interests cover modern East Asian history, empire and nation, the Second World War, and historical memory. His recent publications include: "'Crime' of Interpreting: Taiwanese Interpreters as War Criminals of the Second World War," in Kayoko Takeda and Jesús Baigorri, eds., *New Insights in the History of Interpreting* (2016); "In Pursuit of Equality and Liberty: Taiwan's Indigenous Political Movement in the 1920s," in Jun-Hyeok Kwak and Koichiro Matsuda, eds., *Patriotism in East Asia* (2015); and "(Re-)Writing History of the Second World War: Forgetting and Remembering the Taiwanese-native Japanese Soldiers in Postwar Taiwan," *positions: asia critique*, vol. 21, no. 4 (Fall 2013).

Hyun Kyung LEE

Hyun Kyung Lee is a Research Associate in the division of International Studies, Hankuk University of Foreign Studies and CRASSH (Centre for Arts, Social Sciences, and Humanities), University of Cambridge. Her research interests include difficult heritage (colonial/Cold War heritage) in East Asia, trans-national heritage networking, the role of UNESCO programmes in East Asia, and peace-building. Her latest book *Heritage, Memory, and Punishment: Remembering Colonial Prisons in East Asia*, written in collaboration with her Taiwanese colleague Shu-Mei Huang, is forthcoming from Routledge. She is also the author of *Difficult Heritage in Nation Building: South Korea and Post-conflict Japanese Colonial Occupation Architecture* (Palgrave Macmillan, 2019).

Sherzod MUMINOV

Sherzod Muminov is Lecturer in Japanese History at the University of East Anglia, where he teaches courses on the histories of Japan, the Cold War, the Soviet Union, and POW and internment camps. His research is based on multilingual sources and views modern Japan within international and transnational contexts, specifically in competition and cooperation with the Soviet Union. Sherzod is co-editor, with Barak Kushner, of *The Dismantling of Japan's Empire in East Asia: Deimperialization, Postwar Legitimation and Imperial Afterlife* (2017), and his articles have been published in *Cold War History, Situations: Cultural Studies in the Asian Context, Gunji shigaku,* and other journals. He is currently working on a history of the Siberian internment of Japanese servicemen in Soviet forced labor camps, forthcoming.

Meredith OYEN

Meredith Oyen is Assistant Professor in history at the University of Maryland, Baltimore County. She received her doctorate in history at Georgetown University, and has held Fulbright and NSEP Boren Fellowships. Oyen specializes in the history of US foreign relations, Sino-American Relations, and Asian immigration history. She has published articles in *Diplomatic History,* the *Journal of Cold War*

History, and *Modern Asian Studies.* Her first book, *The Diplomacy of Migration: Transnational Lives and the Making of U.S.-Chinese Relations in the Cold War,* was published in 2015.

Samuel PERRY

Samuel Perry is Associate Professor of East Asian Studies at Brown University. His research brings together the fields of modern literature, translation, and cultural history as he seeks to understand the strategies by which marginalized people have contested dominant cultures in East Asia. His recent work includes the monograph *Recasting Red Culture in Proletarian Japan: Childhood, Korea and the Historical Avant-garde* (2014) and *Five Faces of Japanese Feminism: Crimson and Other Works by Sata Ineko* (2016). He is currently writing a monograph about Japanese literature at the time of the Korean War.

Dick STEGEWERNS

Dick Stegewerns is Associate Professor at the University of Oslo, where he conducts research and teaches courses on modern and contemporary Japanese history, international relations, politics, society, culture, and film. The Japanese translation of his monograph *Adjusting to the New World – Japanese Opinion Leaders of the Taishō Generation and the Outside World, 1918–1932* will be published by Tokyo University Press in 2019. At present, he conducts projects on postwar Japanese war films, a century of democracy in Japan, the visualization of Japanese history in film, *manga* and *anime*, the discourse on the dichotomy of Eastern and Western civilization (*Tōzai bunmeiron*), the Japanese film director Naruse Mikio, and a postwar global history of the Japanese fermented drink sake.

INTRODUCTION: OVERCOMING EMPIRE

Sherzod Muminov

In May 1942, as the Japanese troops took the Philippines and Burma by overpowering the Allies in the whirlwind battles of the Pacific War, three Japanese critics—Kamei Katsuichirō, Kawakami Tetsutarō, and Kobayashi Hideo—invited a group of leading thinkers to a symposium with a grand mission. Their goal, broadly defined, was to discuss Japan's struggles with the modern world. Ten eminent scholars, scientists, composers, and thinkers accepted the invitation, and the symposium, ambitiously titled *Overcoming Modernity* (*Kindai no chōkoku*), opened in the sweltering Tokyo of late July 1942.[1] Over two days of lively debates, the participants discussed such diverse issues as the clash between modernity and tradition, religion and spirituality, the need for imperial loyalty, Japan's place vis-à-vis the West and its responsibility to take on the cultural leadership of Asia. The discussions also had a practical side, perhaps best summarized by the philosopher Shimomura Toratarō, "to criticize what, how, and how much we have received from the modern West," and what to make of these lessons in the new order that was dawning on Asia under Japan's tutelage.[2] The participants clearly equated "modernity" with the West; "what is called 'modern,'" wrote the Kyoto School philosopher Nishitani Keiji, "means European."[3] Time was ripe for Japan's intellectual elite, represented by symposium participants, to decide what of Western culture to abandon and what to keep for the service of the empire. The time had come to overcome the West not only on battlefields but also in people's minds.

There was a contradiction hidden in how dispassionately many participants separated Japan from the West. In their criticism of the latter the discussants

The editors would like to thank the European Research Council for its support with a six-year grant (2013–2019) to conduct the research, workshops, and conferences with funds to draw together an excellent cohort of scholars as part of the project, "The Dissolution of the Japanese Empire and the Struggle for Legitimacy in Postwar East Asia, 1945–1965" (DOJSFL 313382). We would also like to thank Dr. Casper Wits for his efforts to compile the bibliography for this volume.

"refused to acknowledge that Japan's course of modernization, with its nearly fifty-year history of colonial acquisition, already represented a certain fulfillment of modernity."[4] In other words, while they challenged Western modernity, the symposium participants were oblivious to the fact that their gathering too had been enabled by Japan's empire, and was thus in some ways a manifestation and byproduct of Western—and now Japanese—modernity. Japan's pursuit of empire had been part of its quest for modernity; as Robert Eskildsen observed in his study of Meiji Japan's early attempts at imperialism, "the selective appropriation of Western civilization and the projection of Japanese military force abroad contributed to the formation of modern identity in Japan."[5] Moralizing pronouncements of symposium participants notwithstanding, territorial expansion and subjugation of Asia had become integral components of Japan's imperial modernity well before the start of the Second World War. Japan was as guilty of crimes against the peoples of Asia that the *Overcoming Modernity* participants attributed exclusively to European imperial powers. Thus the vision of Japan they advocated was as impossible as the utopian Japan touted by the imperial propaganda to unite the eight corners of the world under one roof. Conference participants extolled fantasies that spoke more of a negation of the West than an affirmation of Japan.

It did not take long for these chimeras to crash into the hard reality of the war. However earnest their intentions and dispassionate their methods, the reflections of the Japanese visionaries on overcoming Western influences and setting on the road to a quintessentially Japanese modernity were clearly premature. The gathering, after all, coincided with a turning point in the Pacific War. Even as they were preparing their notes for the July symposium, the Japanese new order was dealt a decisive blow in the June 1942 Battle of Midway. With hindsight, the Japanese Empire, having "come to full bloom" in 1942, had already started on its three-year downward spiral toward defeat and destruction.[6] Its hold over parts of Asia had been much shorter than the duration of European empires in whose footsteps Japan quickly followed shortly after the Meiji Restoration, starting in the 1870s with the annexation and colonization of the nearby islands of Okinawa and Hokkaido. Nevertheless, Japan's empire had expanded with lightning speed in the first four decades of the twentieth century, multiplying its territory and augmenting its influence across the eastern and southern parts of the Asian continent. In retrospect, we know that the meteoric rise of the empire was about to peak around the time of the *Overcoming Empire* symposium; the symposium participants could perhaps be forgiven for predicting a long life for the imperial undertaking. Hindsight also shows that the assertion "a successful conclusion of this war means the completion of the very task of constructing the new order of greater East Asia," made by the wartime Prime Minister Tōjō Hideki to the leaders of collaborating groups at the November 1943 Greater East Asia Conference in Tokyo, spoke more of desperation in the face of successive defeats than of any hope for success.[7] In August 1945, when the empire found its end in the mushroom clouds of Hiroshima and Nagasaki and the Manchurian blitzkrieg of the Soviet Red Army, hope in the new order the participants of the *Overcoming Modernity* symposium espoused had long ceased to exist. Now the Japanese Empire itself had to be overcome, both by the Japanese colonizers and the colonized subjects across Asia. It is these processes of overcoming the legacies of Japan's empire in Asia that the chapters in this volume analyze.

In Japan, the demise of the empire touted as the liberator of Asia from Western tyranny drew a collective sigh of relief mixed with voices of desperation. The lofty rhetoric of "eight corners of the world under one [Japanese] roof" (*hakkō ichiu*) almost instantly gave way to the earthly concerns of a populace long-exhausted by wartime exertions. The empire was abandoned quickly by the people who a few months earlier were ready to sacrifice their lives for it. To borrow a description from the Japanese historian Kawashima Shin, the Japanese people "rather limply accepted decolonization, that is to say, the separation of Japan's colonies and dependencies from the former empire."[8] Understandably, the end to the imperial frenzy of the recent past was greeted with weary optimism for the immediate future, despite the early deprivations caused by food shortages, chaotic repatriations of compatriots from imperial outposts, and the uncertainties of imminent occupation by yesterday's enemy. In November 1946, a little over a year after the empire's collapse, a poll conducted by the Japanese national daily *Mainichi shimbun* found that over 90 percent of respondents approved of the new constitution proposed by the postwar Yoshida Shigeru government but drafted by the US Occupation Administration.[9] The new charter was to replace the Imperial (Meiji) Constitution of 1889 that set in stone the emperor system. While the empire collapsed in convulsions, its constitutional foundation was quickly left behind in the new, US-occupied Japan.

In Japan's former colonies and occupied territories, the imperial collapse was greeted with a mixture of elation, indignation, and uncertainty about what the future held. While liberation put an end to years and in some cases decades of colonial subjugation, the victorious Allies' neglect for the colonized peoples' claims for justice and redress understandably gave rise to frustration. The plight of Koreans in both the newly liberated Korean peninsula and the Japanese home islands in the postwar order is illustrative in this regard. Recent research on Korean attempts to challenge the verdict of the International Military Tribunal for the Far East (IMTFE, or Tokyo Trial) shows how the subaltern's voice remained suppressed even after the withdrawal of the imperial master from the scene.[10] In Taiwan, Japan's oldest colony, the Japanese defeat and departure meant the local populations of ethnic Chinese and indigenous peoples had to welcome new masters from the mainland. The discontent of the locals at unjust treatment by Chinese Nationalist forces spilled over into the February 28, 1947 Incident, and the Nationalists' flight from the mainland following defeat in the Chinese Civil War (1945–1949) turned Taiwan into a new battleground of the Cold War. These select examples illustrate how post-imperial attitudes and reactions of people in former colonies were as diverse as the unique circumstances in these places.

The exasperation of the "liberated" peoples at being left out of major decisions concerning their future was compounded by the burning need to secure new-found sovereignty and to ensure legitimacy on the international stage in an environment of intense competition. This contest often resembled a race to take new positions and secure footing in the that is new world. Clambering for status, authority, and resources, powers great and small risked conflict only months after the global conflagration subsided, plunging their peoples into war once again. Japan's short-lived but expansive empire had left vacuums in its distant corners that these new powers were eager to fill. In some cases, such as in postwar China, internal competition culminated in a protracted civil war that was a closing act of at least two decades of intra-China conflict between Chiang Kai-shek's Kuomintang (KMT) and the Chinese Communist Party (CCP) led by Mao Zedong, put on hold during the Second World War only by the need to resist the Japanese conquerors. In liberated Korea, by contrast, the contest for power took some time to take off, as the legacies of colonialism and world war spawned the first major conflict of the Cold War era, the Korean War (1950–1953). Aftershocks of empires' collapse, even when situated in the same geographical region, had varying timelines that depended on the interplay of local conditions and the impending superpower struggle. This collapse left a legacy of divided postwar nations—Korea, China, Vietnam, and others—whose internal struggles soon came to mirror the global Cold War confrontation over ideology and influence.

Competition for legitimacy and authority occurred not only on battlefields but also in courtrooms, in government offices, on pages of newspapers, and over airwaves used for disseminating propaganda. Tribunals set up in the wake of the Japanese surrender were of paramount importance for those in charge; besides their original purpose of punishing the perpetrators of war crimes, they served a symbolic function of affirming the new status quo. The vanquished Imperial Japanese Army was there to be adjudicated by its victorious enemies and former victims, as was the expansive civilian bureaucracy that had worked hand in hand with the military in conquering, expanding, and controlling overseas colonies and dependencies. Since the Western Allies oversaw the service of transitional justice in the wake of the Second World War, they also set the tone of the many trials of the Japanese military and civilian officials suspected of war crimes. As seen already in the case of Korean grievances with transitional justice, the most extensive and concerted Allied exercise to bring the Japanese to justice, the Tokyo Trial, was also the best indication of the Allies' prioritization of their own interests. "For all of its lofty aims, and there were many, the Tokyo Trial was fundamentally Western oriented and centered on adjudicating the start of the war against the Western Allies with the attack on Pearl Harbor and crimes against Western soldiers in POW camps."[11] As argued by historian of China Hans van de Ven, China's victory in the war against Japan was not a triumph in the Clausewitzian sense; being on the side of victors did not give the Chinese Nationalist Party the authority to impose its will or its version of a new global order on the vanquished party, Japan.[12] Moreover, attempts to achieve justice in post-Second World War East Asia were at times so chaotic and violent that the term "transitional justice" does not accurately describe the immediate postwar era: "no one at the time knew what they were transitioning from or toward."[13] The traditional paradigm of a relatively orderly transition from wartime to postwar, overseen by benevolent victors whose aim was to achieve justice, not vengeance, rarely accounts for the destabilizing and sometimes destructive upheavals often within the same ethnic groups, such as the February 28 Incident in Taiwan or the 1948 Jeju Island Incident in South Korea. This transition does not address the complex social changes in the postwar societies that led to the eventual acceptance of or disagreement with Allied justice. Barak Kushner suggests that a new paradigm based on the idea of "competition for justice" is necessary to fully account for the chaos and uncertainty of the initial attempts to administer the law. Such a paradigm emphasizes the role and agency of Asian governments and peoples in the above attempts. It also challenges the idea, inherent in the word "transition" itself, which presupposes a complete settlement of all issues once the period of transition is over. The chapters in this volume demonstrate that the "competition for justice" in East Asia, initiated in the wake of Japanese Empire, did not end when the Allies decided they had settled all accounts of the war. In fact, it continues to this very day.[14]

Moreover, as seen in the example of Chinese nationalists' lack of influence in the postwar order, even alliances forged in the battles against the Axis powers proved ephemeral as the Cold War confrontation took shape on the horizon. The fact that even the victorious Soviet Union was largely dissatisfied with the outcome of the Tokyo Trial demonstrated the hollowness of Allied attempts to put into practice the lofty rhetoric of joint proclamations such as the Potsdam Declaration. Since every party contributing to disassembling the Japanese Empire was acting first and foremost in its own narrowly defined interests, the outcomes of this dismantling were also defined by the myriad goals of the victorious powers. Extending the age-old metaphor of the Tower of Babel is helpful here; the confounded parties who took on the task of taking apart the Japanese imperial structure often found it difficult to reach an understanding and made away with sundry pieces of the building, which they would try to devote in the most fitting way to the task of rebuilding their own countries.

Allied attempts to ensure that Japanese militarism did not rise from the ashes were not confined to the Tokyo Trial, but they could not have dealt with every feature and outcome of Japan's colonial empire. The empire, moreover, would not be easily dismantled even through concerted and agreed attempts to take down, brick by brick, the edifice. Unlike the British Empire, which, according to the nineteenth-century historian John Robert Seeley, had "conquered and peopled half the world in a fit of absence of mind," Japan's imperial project always had a preordained quality to it.[15] Though much of its expansion was engendered by spontaneous, risky, in hindsight even reckless, decisions (for example, the 1931 Manchurian Incident and the 1937 Marco Polo Bridge Incident), on the level of the everyday the Japanese Empire employed at all levels institutions, mechanisms, and practices of control that were effective in consolidating its hold over conquered territories.[16] While the empire collapsed much more quickly than its rulers and subjects had envisioned, taking with it most of its institutions and practitioners, the silent machinery that had run the affairs on the ground as well as the persistent practices of empire building could not have been removed or effaced as quickly. As the sections in this volume demonstrate, in many post-imperial territories the aforementioned competition for legitimacy meant that this machinery and these practices were required *not* to be deleted so quickly but, rather, called to serve new purposes in the postwar era. As a result, the empire silently lived on for a period of time, longer in some places and shorter in others.

The history of the empire's immediate aftermath in Japan and its erstwhile colonies has been relatively well documented, especially with the recent growth of interest in the empire's mechanisms of control and the legacies it left behind. Historians have investigated the construction, expansion, and collapse of Japan's empire, starting from classical works to new innovative histories.[17] The significant moment of Japan's defeat, heavy with implications for both the inhabitants of the Japanese home islands and those in the colonies, has attracted attention not only from scholars but also from members of creative professions as well as in countless memoirs, as I emphasize later. Japan's successful return to Asia as an economic hegemon in subsequent decades—the reward it earned for becoming the US partner in the Cold War order in East Asia—has been well studied, most recently by Louise Young, who wrote of Japan's "privileged access to Asian markets within the American bloc, becoming at once a client state and a client empire."[18] But there are still questions that await scholarly attention, partly because the majority of works on the Japanese Empire rarely venture beyond the empire's collapse. When they do so, they often limit their gaze to the unit of the nation-state. As a result, what once was a multinational, multiethnic undertaking is often analyzed only through the historical lens of national history, that is, through the histories of the empire's byproducts—the postwar Japanese state, the two Koreas, the People's Republic of China and Republic of China (Taiwan), and others. Few, if any, works continue to conceive of the Japanese Empire *after* its collapse in the same terms and using the same tools as when analyzing the period when it still existed. To put it simply, contemporary understanding of the Japanese Empire has been limited by the fixation, on the side of historians but also scholars of international relations, with the nation-state and its environment—the Cold War anarchic system where the nation-state is the main unit of analysis. To be sure, recent scholarship has posited "nation and empire as compatible political forms, rather than representing a linear progression where empires break up into nations or nations develop into empires."[19] The argument for compatibility, applied to the Japanese nation-state as successor to empire, further supports the need for continuity between prewar and postwar, and for examining the components of the empire that survived its collapse. The national focus that I have in mind is more a product of the Cold War international system than of the nineteenth-century national roots of Japan's empire. Another side effect of this Cold War national focus was that it hindered research by keeping archives out of the reach of researchers from other nations, especially those on the other side of the Iron Curtain or the Bamboo Curtain. However, even after these barriers were lifted, research has taken too long to catch up, making obvious the need for multilingual, transnational histories of how the many former colonies dealt with the aftermath of the world war in East Asia.

Partly as a result of this fragmentation of thinking along national lines, national histories of war and empire in East Asia are still in disagreement on many issues and interpretations.[20] Unlike in postwar Europe, where the warring nations have achieved some measure of reconciliation and redress, the nations of Asia continue to disagree on a plethora of issues: legal claims related to compensation for the empire's victims, particularly slave laborers and women forced into "sexual servitude," known as the comfort women; unresolved disputes over territory, such as the Diaoyutai/Senkaku Island dispute; and controversies over commemoration of war victims and perpetrators, seen most clearly in the Chinese or South Korean reaction to visits of Japanese officials to the Yasukuni Shrine that commemorates Japan's war dead. In other words, the competing East Asian versions of history, through militant attempts to safeguard the borders of the nation and the sanctity of national sacrifice, have led national leaders to prescribe the ways to "correctly" commemorate the disputed past to nationals of rival countries. Put simply, the issue of memory has invaded and dominated discussions of history in East Asia, where memories of victims and perpetrators alike have been recruited into identity and memory politics. Historian Timothy Snyder's warning that, "To be enlisted posthumously into competing national memories, bolstered by the numbers of which your life has become a part, is to sacrifice individuality" is paid little heed in contemporary East Asia.[21]

If we adopt a broader, transnational perspective to the post-imperial processes in East Asia, several tentative questions emerge. What happened once the dust of war settled in East Asia and the reality of a new era slowly sank in? How did the Japanese and their former colonial subjects deal with the sudden freedom from war and oppression visited upon them by the Allied victory? What became of the remainders of Japanese expansion, both tangible and intangible, that carried on to the new period? Once the elegies were pronounced and dirges performed—in Japan for the hopeless dream of a pan-Asian empire and in the colonies for those who gave their lives for independence—how did the peoples of Asia rebuild their livelihoods, economies, and nations? Initial answers to these questions reveal that attempts to overcome the empire in Asia remain unknown to the Anglophone readership. Despite the millions of human lives that it involved in postwar East Asia, the topic of post-imperial reconstruction, of what came after the empire exited the scene both as a political entity and a fashionable object of study, remains under studied.

Two sets of circumstances have conditioned knowledge on Japan's empire and its aftermath in the English language. The first concerns the near complete absence of the empire from the postwar narratives in Japan, which in their turn heavily influenced the Anglophone scholarship on and understanding of the Japanese Empire. At least in Japan, the "imperial hangover … [that can] be cured and forgotten," of which Ian Nish wrote in 1980, indeed seems to have been alleviated and exorcised from the collective minds of the Japanese people. The German historian Sebastian Conrad diagnosed this further when he wrote more recently about "a clinical separation of Japan from its empire." [22] With hindsight, this does not seem surprising; for the postwar society it was more convenient to consign the empire to the past in a future-oriented, economically successful Japan. Just how successful are these efforts, conscious or otherwise, to leave the empire behind is evident from a 2015 survey conducted by NHK, Japan's public broadcasting corporation, on Japanese attitudes toward the seven postwar decades. Of the 2,635 respondents, 85 percent evaluated Japan's postwar era as a "good period." Asked to choose one word that represented most accurately their impression of the postwar period, the largest group (37 percent) chose "peace" (*heiwa*); and an overwhelming majority of 87 percent described the Japanese society as "a peaceful society where there is no war."[23] From these responses, it is easy to come to conclusions about the general feeling among Japanese citizens concerning the postwar period. "Empire," which for half a century occupied the hearts and minds of the Japanese people, is hardly present in contemporary Japan. Yet seventy years is a long time and Japan has changed beyond recognition from the bombed out ruins of the world war, so it is hardly surprising that people look on the bright side. Less intelligible, however, is the long reluctance in Western scholarship to evoke the Japanese Empire and to scrutinize its many vestiges from the multiple possible vantage points.

To be sure, the Japanese Empire's crashing end as a result of defeat in the Second World War coincided with the twilight of empires, at least in the traditional European sense of the term. Winston Churchill may have famously proclaimed "I have not become the King's First Minister to preside over the liquidation of the British Empire," but Britain's hold over its colonies was not to last much longer than that of Japan.[24] The end of the British Empire was of course ushered forward by the Japanese, whose military undertakings that started with the February 1942 Battle of Singapore, through to the Battle of Imphal in 1944, and until the very end of the war in the Pacific, contributed much to shattering the British sense of invincibility and willingness to hold on to faraway colonies. The end of the Second World War also marked the beginning of the end for European colonial empires in Asia; though the victorious British, Dutch, and French succeeded in holding on to their overseas territories for a few years longer than the defeated Japanese, European colonialism was clearly a legacy of the old order, not a feature of the new Cold War system. However, there is a pronounced difference in the way the European Allies and the defeated Japanese commemorate their empires that deserves mention here. We have just seen that in the Japanese public sphere in the second half of the twentieth century empire was not a prominent presence. In contrast, in some Allied nations that lost their colonial empires after the Second World War, memories of empire have been made out of a potent mixture of victorious pride and melancholic loss. In Britain, for example, both components continue to survive largely in public debates as nearly irreproachable paradigms on which the nation's postwar memories and identity are partly hinged. In some cases, the hagiographic terms in which the Allied victory in the Second World War is portrayed in domestic societies has led to badly disguised nostalgia for empire, as in the controversy surrounding an Oxford University research project titled *Ethics and Empire*, where over 170 academics condemned the university for "backing apologists for Britain's colonial legacy."[25]

The second circumstance that conditioned understanding of the Japanese Empire was that, in Japan, where postwar narratives of empire were present they often acquired the attributes of a traumatic loss and victimhood, overshadowing the victimizing role and the loss inflicted on Asian peoples by the empire-building processes. Empire, when it was evoked, almost exclusively populated the narrow sliver of time in which it collapsed. Japanese memories of the war, while diverse, have been dominated by the recollections of its end. This is true of both Japanese narratives and those in Asian countries that suffered at Japanese hands during the war. August 15, 1945, when the "jewel voice" of Emperor horse-back Hirohito announced Japan's acceptance of defeat, continues to attract the lion's share of attention. In April 1982, it was designated the Day for Mourning of War Dead and Praying for Peace in Japan. Starting from early August each year, public and private media companies in Japan roll out a plethora of programs, investigative reports, special issues, and other products devoted to war experiences of the Japanese people, and sometimes of their former enemies and victims. At the secular National Memorial Service for War Dead held in Tokyo's Budōkan Hall, a stone's throw from the Imperial Palace, both the prime minister and the emperor deliver speeches commemorating the victims of the "last war." Both pronouncements are eagerly awaited and scrupulously analyzed by Japan's nearest neighbors and wartime victims, most importantly China and South Korea, who use the speeches as a barometer of Japanese official attitudes toward the disputed past. In other words, during the hot August week that coincides in Japan with the O-bon Festival, when the spirits of deceased ancestors are commemorated, the attention of millions of people outside Japan is turned to the ritual utterances and carefully orchestrated posturing of the Japanese leadership. August 15 has been securely established as a marker of eras, separating war from postwar; at least in Japan, it has also come to symbolize national sacrifice and loss and anti-war feeling, having shed over the decades much of its controversial attributes. In some ways, the existence of this marker and the attention surrounding it has made it easier for the inheritors of Japan's empire to elude responsibility for anything that happened *after* the empire collapsed.

The current preoccupation, present also in the Anglophone literature, with Japanese victimhood at its empire's end has left in the shadows some of the very important questions concerning post-imperial lives. In other words, the focus until recently on the Japanese people's post-imperial reckoning (*hansei*) has pushed scholars of Japan both within the country and around the world to devote less attention to post-imperial repatriations, redress, and reconstructions in various forms across Asia. The Cold War US–Japan Alliance necessitated a narrative that emphasized Japanese people's losses over those of their victims, while the economic growth and subsequent affluence "provided closure to the popular narrative of the war that claimed Japan's defeat and loss were necessary for its peace and prosperity."[26] As memories of war and empire increasingly evoked Japanese victimhood and losses, it became easier to disown both the empire and its consequences as a mistake of history.

As the research in this volume demonstrates, in many cases the empire's collapse did not put an end to violence. On the contrary, it often marked the start of a new phase of the struggle for power, legitimacy, and compensation. Besides the competition for recognition mentioned earlier, for years and even decades after the Japanese Empire exited the stage many of the newly formed or re-established governments and political groups struggled to overcome the aftereffects of processes initiated during the imperial times. Nish's phrase "imperial hangover" thus applies not only to the former imperial metropole, Japan, but also—and perhaps more so—to the many lands and peoples the Japanese Empire had conquered during its half-century of rule. Liberation from imperial rule may have come with the war's end, but it would take the former colonies years to free themselves completely from the empire's hold. Some of its vestiges are present even today, causing continuing disputes among governments, interest groups, and even individuals in East Asia. While there have been attempts to analyze the empire's aftereffects on Japanese society, what it left behind in former colonies requires more investigation and scrutiny. Such histories of overcoming Japanese Empire in colonized Asia will inject diversity into the study of the imperial phenomenon that was subsumed into the Cold War. Chapters compiled here scrutinize the liminal period when those liberated from imperial rule took their tottering steps toward independence before the superpower standoff incorporated them into the Cold War bipolar international system.

* * *

This collection of chapters suggests alternative perspectives to the study of East Asia after the demise and dismantling of Japan's Asian empire. The authors gathered here investigate endeavors in Japan and its former Asian colonies to overcome the collapse and impact of Japan's empire. Contributions open new fertile ground for research and discussion of the empire's aftermath, bringing to the limelight some of the hitherto understudied phenomena across East Asia. The volume is built on the premise that the Japanese Empire was a multi-ethnic, multinational entity that hardly conformed to one-size-fits-all frameworks; hence, the study of its legacies and incarnations requires more versatile, adaptable approaches. At the risk of stating the obvious, empire deserves imperial approaches, not the fragmented, national thinking through which it is largely understood these days. Furthermore, while East Asia remains perhaps the single region where Cold War legacies are most conspicuous, these legacies should not hinder the study of alternative connections, those not born of and bound by the thinking in Cold War terms. Put simply, as Japan's prewar and wartime history was closely intertwined with that of Asia, its postwar should also be viewed in larger Asian contexts. Japan's "invisible Asia" should be brought to the fore in order to have a fuller understanding of empire, of Japan, and of the postwar.

The perspectives adopted by the authors in this volume are threefold and favor a flexible, fluid, and complex approach to the diverse experiences of Asian nations following the Second World War. First, contributors shift the scholarly attention away from frameworks that focus solely on the nation and toward broader contexts that encompass a variety of actors. Examples of these actors examined here, besides the newly formed post-imperial nation-states, include international organizations such as the United Nations Relief and Rehabilitation Administration (UNRRA), the nominally national but in reality multi-imperial agencies such as the Chinese Maritime Customs Service (CMCS), conglomerates that rode the wave of imperial expansion, such as the Mitsui Mining Corporation, and those that were reborn in various forms, such as the Anshan Iron and Steel Works, a Chinese state-owned enterprise. These agencies had different, sometimes clashing, interests and goals, and they all had varying lifespans; some, such as UNRRA, were created after the imperial collapse to help alleviate the war damage, while others traced their origins to imperial times, often founded to make good use of the opportunities created by the empire. Some, like the CMCS, continued to exist and even maintained traces of their original structure even as empires that had founded and operated them departed the scene one after the other. Thus, when the Japanese Empire was no more, these latter institutions and agencies had to be repurposed, renamed, and reorganized. These processes of picking through imperial wreckage in search for resources, practices and meanings illuminate not just the empire and its mechanisms, but also what came after the empire in the new, chaotic but hopeful Asia.

Second, as seen in the varying lifespans of the actors and institutions mentioned earlier, a study of overcoming the empire requires alternative temporal frameworks. The carving up of the post-imperial field happened not only in the spatial but also temporal dimension. Put simply, if empire disappeared into many nation-states, which concealed the complex relations of power between the metropole and colonies by turning both into legally equal nations (e.g., Japan and South Korea), the periodization of the post-imperial time also served to obscure the empire's continuing impact. We have seen this briefly in the way August 15 became a watershed moment that marked a change of eras and thus consigned the preceding era to posterity. Work in this volume operates in varied timeframes; some of it deals with the immediate postwar period, while other sections examine legacies and afterlives that are in existence even today. This diversity of temporalities shows that empire's effects continued to persist throughout the postwar period. This research also demonstrates how in Cold War Anglophone scholarship on Japan the moment of the war's end in Asia was invariably tied to Japan; even when other regions of Asia came into the frame, they often served as starting points for journeys that inevitably finished in Japan. Thus, decoupling Japan and defeat requires focusing not only on other regions but also other timelines. It also requires favoring other vectors of movement, those leading from Japan to other places in Asia and around the world, and even those that do not include Japan at all, such as the odyssey of Taiwanese former imperial subjects.

Finally, thinking about post-imperial Asia in new ways requires shifting our gaze toward previously neglected entanglements, relations, and exchanges, away from the long-established connections. The US–Japan alliance, which still dominates many issues of Japan's foreign policy and some aspects of its domestic life, is a good example of such traditional entanglements. Another instance of such relations can be the inter-governmental ties dictated by the changing Cold War interests and influences—for example, relations formalized in the 1951 San

Francisco Peace Treaty between Japan and a number of nations, the 1965 Treaty on Basic Relations between Japan and South Korea, or even the 1978 Treaty of Peace and Friendship between Japan and the PRC. Instead of overcoming the bitter legacies of colonialism and war that marred relations between Japan and its former colonies and enemies, these treaties papered over disagreements in favor of temporary consensus on immediate issues. In other words, instead of resolving the legacies of empire, these Cold War-era treaties made the resolution of these legacies more difficult, in addition to creating a plethora of new issues. Essays in this volume, particularly Samuel Perry's examination of Japanese narratives of the Korean War and Yukiko Koga's analysis of Japan's imperial debt toward China, show how after the end of the Cold War the legacies of these agreements continued to obscure the imperial vestiges inherited by contemporary East Asian citizens from their parents' and grandparents' generations. These elements also fanned the flames of nationalist and right-wing sentiment in many of the nations concerned, making the attainment of genuine understanding and reconciliation on the issues of history increasingly difficult in the region.[27]

Important as they are in pointing out unresolved imperial legacies, the entanglements dictated by the Cold War are not helpful to analyses of how East Asian nations overcame these legacies. The perspective adopted by the contributors to this volume does not revolve either around Japan or its relations with the superpowers. In many of the essays, Japan does not occupy the center stage; while its subjugation of Asian territories left indelible marks on the ground, studies of Japanese Empire will not always involve Japan itself. In other words, the Japanese Empire is not Japan; the Japanese home islands (*naichi*), while occupying the empire's core, were but a part of it, just like the overseas territories (*gaichi*). The Japanese Empire left traces that developed into new forms and took on lives of their own well after the Japanese troops and citizens had withdrawn to their home islands. In this regard, it is possible to talk not only about the empire's legacies themselves but also their mutations over time and generations. Many of the processes described and evaluated in this volume fall into this category, seen, for example, in the postwar identity of collaborators such as Chang Hyŏkchu (Chapter 3), who denounced his Korean upbringing to become Japanese, thus transforming his status as an imperial subject to citizenship in the narrowly defined postwar Japanese nation-state. Or in the transformation of Ōkunoshima Island (Chapter 10), the site of wartime production of chemical weapons, into a popular resort perhaps better known these days as Rabbit Island. When they abandoned the imperial project as defeat loomed large, the Japanese leadership could not have anticipated the shapes and forms into which their creation would morph with time and under the influence of various circumstances. Overcoming the empire was never straightforward, and compromises had to be made. The ironic outcomes of these compromises were sadly lost, both to the former imperialists who were happy to put the empire behind them and many of those who were faced by myriad contingencies and interests and could not always be attentive to paradoxes of history.

* * *

This volume is organized around three major themes that correspond to the broad post-imperial contexts and processes in East Asia. The essays in the first theme analyze the web of human movement necessitated by the sudden loss of imperial protection, livelihood, or occupation. While the fates of over 6.6 million Japanese residents in the imperial outposts have resulted in a number of histories in recent years, those of millions of non-Japanese former imperial subjects left behind, or of foreign citizens who found themselves in limbo following the imperial collapse, have not received the attention they deserve.[28] In Chapter 1, "Trapped between Imperial Ruins: Internment and Repatriation of the Taiwanese in Postwar Asia-Pacific," Shi-chi Mike Lan analyzes the circuitous journey of the overseas Taiwanese, once Japanese imperial subjects, back to Taiwan by way of Hong Kong and Australia after the Japanese Empire's collapse left them stranded in its distant corners. By looking at individual cases of Taiwanese families but also recreating the broader context of post-imperial repatriation of non-Japanese former subjects, Lan emphasizes that the treatment the Taiwanese received was completely different from that meted out to Japanese citizens. Continuing the theme of displacement, in Chapter 2, "China's Refugees: Postwar 'Foreigners' and the Attempt at International Aid, 1945–1956," Meredith Oyen investigates the plight of four groups of individuals who found themselves in postwar China during the Second World War: the displaced overseas Chinese who had returned to China after the Japanese invasion of Southeast Asia; Central European Jews who had escaped the Nazis from Europe; White Russians; and Russian Jews.

The second theme concerns the creation of narratives following Japan's surrender that filled the vacuum of the very vocal imperial propaganda before and during the war. The transition from wartime to postwar, imperial to national narratives is another topic that is largely understudied in the context of post-Second World War East Asia. The diversity of these narratives and the media through which they found expression is seen in the variety of phenomena the authors analyze and is evident, among other things, in the image on the cover of this volume. It shows a 1950 Chinese propaganda leaflet on which General Douglas MacArthur is pushing the Japanese toward China, while the Chinese rally against remilitarization. In Chapter 3, "Early Narratives of Japan's Korean War," Samuel Perry analyzes the cultural reconstruction of Japan in the postwar period through the lens of Japanese perceptions of the conflict on the Korean peninsula. In his analysis of postwar Japanese cultural works, Perry focuses on the narratives of the Korean War as a "window onto processes of post-World War II cultural reconstruction." In Chapter 4, "Reconstructing Architectural Memories of the Japanese Empire in South Korea," Hyun Kyung Lee traces in painstaking detail the post-imperial afterlives of colonial structures in post-liberation Seoul through the example of two important buildings—the Seodaemun Prison and the Grand Shrine of Joseon. Her analysis demonstrates the unique phenomenon of shifting perceptions attached to seemingly immutable, tangible structures that were built by the colonizers but took on a life of their own once the Japanese withdrew from Korea. In Chapter 5, "The Cinematic Reconstruction of East Asia in Postwar Japanese War Films," Dick Stegewerns investigates how the new, decolonized East Asia found its reflection in postwar Japanese war films. As an influential format of postwar popular culture, the silver screen registered the many guises in which Asia re-entered the Japanese collective mind in the post-imperial period, after Japan left behind its Asian empire. Matthew D. Johnson in Chapter 6, "Anti-Imperialism as Strategy: Masking the Edges of Foreign Entanglements in Civil War-Era China, 1945–1948," seeks to question the ruptures and continuities between the wartime and the immediate postwar by analyzing propaganda and political warfare during China's domestic conflict. Johnson argues that postwar political groups utilized many of the same methods and means of influencing and controlling popular opinion used during the war, but with a newly necessary engagement with superpower interests.

The four chapters organized under the final theme of this volume address the empire's living traces seen in a variety of realms. In Chapter 7, "From the Ashes of Empire: The Reconstruction of Manchukuo's Enterprises and the Making of China's Northeastern Industrial Base, 1948–1952," Hirata Koji investigates, based on multilingual sources, the remaking of industrial enterprises of the former Japanese puppet kingdom of Manchukuo. For Hirata, these state-owned enterprises formed the basis for northeast China's industrial development in the first decade after Japan's defeat. In a chapter that traces the transition from empire to nation-state through the example of an important institution—maritime customs—Chang Chihyun (Chapter 8, "Empires and Continuity: The Chinese Maritime Customs Service in East Asia, 1950–1955") once again draws attention to the equivocal balance between fracture and continuity separating the empire from its aftermath. These traces of the past, left on the skins of former forced laborers and on the pages of secret documents, have miraculously avoided the furnace at empire's end. These themes are also the subject of Yukiko Koga's Chapter 9, "Inverted Compensation: Wartime Forced Labor and Post-Imperial Reckoning." In her poignant analysis of the difficult vestiges of wartime exploitation of colonial subjects, Koga lifts out of obscurity the relations of debt between the colonizer and the colonized, the exploiter and the exploited. Finally, in Chapter 10, "Japan, Chemical Warfare, and Ōkunoshima: A Postwar Overview," Arnaud Doglia takes the reader to a resort island in Japan's inland sea, affectionately known among contemporary visitors as Rabbit Island, to reveal its dark past as a site where chemical weapons were produced during the wartime and to trace its remarkable transition to a postwar, peaceful site of amnesia.

Seen together, these contributions chart a relatively new territory, aiming to add a new dimension to the international and transnational histories of imperial aftermath in East Asia. These histories, gaining popularity in recent decades, have thrown new light on the empire's under-investigated facets and questioned some of the facile assumptions about it that have miraculously survived the end of the Cold War. The chapters in this volume will also be an addition to the ever-expanding shelf of recent works that invert the relationship between metropole and colonies. The goal here is *not* to diminish the importance of Japan as the imperial core, or as a successor too ashamed of imperial baggage that it abandoned the empire in the postwar. The aim here is to train the historical viewfinder on the chaos, confusion, and competition that ensued after the empire's seeming demise. Perhaps the historic episodes and processes analyzed here will demonstrate that while the empire's many inheritors thought they had overcome it, its traces continued to resurface from the depths of oblivion from time to time. Some of these traces haunt East Asia to this day.

Notes

1   Richard F. Calichman, ed. and trans., *Overcoming Modernity: Cultural Identity in Wartime Japan* (New York: Columbia University Press, 2008).
2   Ibid., p. 111.
3   Ibid., p. 51.
4   Ibid., p. ix.
5   Robert Eskildsen, "Of Civilization and Savages: The Mimetic Imperialism of Japan's 1874 Expedition to Taiwan," *The American Historical Review* 107, no. 2 (April 2002), pp. 388–418, this quote p. 388.
6   The phrase about the empire coming "to full bloom" is from Ian Nish, "Regaining Confidence – Japan after the Loss of Empire," *Journal of Contemporary History* 15 (1980), pp. 181–195, this quote p. 181.
7   Tōjō Hideki, "Inaugural Address to the Greater East Asia Conference," in *Sources of Japanese Tradition, Volume Two: 1600 to 2000, Abridged, Part Two: 1868 to 2000*, Second Edition, compiled by W. M. Theodore de Bary, Carol Gluck, and Arthur E. Tiedemann (New York: Columbia University Press, 2006), p. 316.
8   Kawashima Shin, "'Deimperialization' in Early Postwar Japan: Adjusting and Transforming the Institutions of Empire," in *The Dismantling of Japan's Empire in East Asia: Deimperialization, Postwar Legitimation and Imperial Afterlife*, ed. Barak Kushner and Sherzod Muminov (Abingdon: Routledge, 2017), p. 31.
9   *Mainichi shimbun*, "Sengo 70 nen: Since 1945 dai 5 kai nihon kenpōhō wa doko e," available online: http://mainichi.jp/feature/afterwar70/since1945/vol5.html, accessed March 23, 2018.
10 Chong Young-Hwan, "The Tokyo Trial and the Question of Colonial Responsibility: *Zainichi* Korean Reactions to Allied Justice in Occupied Japan," *International Journal of Korean History* 22, no. 1 (February 2017), pp. 77–105.
11 Barak Kushner, *Men to Devils, Devils to Men: Japanese War Crimes and Chinese Justice* (Cambridge, MA: Harvard University Press, 2015), pp. 6–7.
12 Hans van de Ven, *China at War: Triumph and Tragedy in the Emergence of the New China* (Cambridge, MA: Harvard University Press, 2018).
13 Barak Kushner (Gu Ruopeng), "Chuli zhanhou de shengli: guomindang, riben yu gongchandang duiyu zhengyi de lichang" (Chen Kuan-jen fanyi) *Guoli zhengzhi daxue lishi xuebao* (Taiwan), di 50, November 2018, pp. 143–174.
14 Ibid.
15 John Robert Seeley, *The Expansion of England: Two Courses of Lectures* (New York: Cosimo Classics, 2005), p. 8.
16 For innovative analyses of these mechanisms of controlling other peoples and maintaining hierarchical relations in the Japanese colonial empire, see Christopher P. Hanscom and Dennis Washburn, *The Affect of Difference: Representations of Race in East Asian Empire* (Honolulu: University of Hawai'i Press, 2016).
17 For example, Ramon H. Myers and Mark R. Peattie, eds., *The Japanese Colonial Empire, 1895–1945* (Princeton, NJ: Princeton University Press, 1984); Peter Duus,

Ramon H. Myers, Mark R. Peattie, and Wanyao Zhou, eds., *The Japanese Wartime Empire, 1931–1945* (Princeton, NJ: Princeton University Press, 1996); Louise Young, *Japan's Total Empire: Manchuria and the Culture of Wartime Imperialism* (Berkeley: University of California Press, 1999).

18   Louise C. Young, "Rethinking Empire: Lessons from Imperial and Post-imperial Japan," in *The Oxford Handbook of the Ends of Empire*, eds. Martin Thomas and Andrew Thompson (Oxford: Oxford University Press, 2017), available online: www. oxfordhandbooks.com/view/10.1093/oxfordhb/9780198713197.001.0001/oxfordhb-9780198713197-e-13, accessed March 23, 2018.

19   Young, "Rethinking Empire."

20   Hiro Saito, *The History Problem: The Politics of War Commemoration in East Asia* (Honolulu: University of Hawai'i Press, 2016).

21   Timothy Snyder, *Bloodlands: Europe between Hitler and Stalin* (London: Vintage, 2011), p. 407.

22   Nish, "Regaining Confidence," p. 194; Sebastian Conrad, "The Dialectics of Remembrance: Memories of Empire in Cold War Japan," *Comparative Studies in Society and History* 56, no. 1 (2014), pp. 4–33, this quote p. 22.

23   Aramaki Hiroshi and Kobayashi Toshiyuki, "Yoronchōsa de miru nihonjin no 'sengo': 'sengo 70 nen ni kansuru ishiki chōsa' no kekka kara," *Hōsō kenkyū to chōsa* (August 2015), pp. 2–17, available online: www.nhk.or.jp/bunken/research/yoron/pdf/20150801_4.pdf, accessed March 21, 2018.

24   Churchill is quoted in John Darwin, *After Tamerlane: The Rise and Fall of Global Empires, 1400–2000* (London: Penguin, 2008), p. 435.

25   Richard Adams, "Oxford University Accused of Backing Apologists of British Colonialism," *The Guardian*, published online December 22, 2017, available online: www.theguardian.com/education/2017/dec/22/oxford-university-accused-of-backing-apologists-of-british-colonialism, accessed July 13, 2018.

26   Yoshikuni Igarashi, *Bodies of Memory: Narratives of War in Postwar Japanese Culture, 1945–1970* (Princeton, NJ: Princeton University Press, 2000), p. 17.

27   For a recent analysis of the so-called "history problems" in East Asia, see Saito, *The History Problem*.

28   Lori Watt, *When Empire Comes Home: Repatriation and Reintegration in Postwar Japan* (Cambridge, MA: Harvard University Asia Center, 2010); Mayumi Itoh, *Japanese War Orphans in Manchuria: Forgotten Victims of World War II* (New York: Palgrave Macmillan, 2010); Yoshikuni Igarashi, *Homecomings: The Belated Return of Japan's Lost Soldiers* (New York: Columbia University Press, 2016).

Chapter 1

Trapped Between Imperial Ruins: Internment and Repatriation of the Taiwanese in the Postwar Asia-Pacific

Shi-chi Mike Lan

On February 13, 1946, the British vessel *S.S. Suncrest* departed from Stanley, a fishing village on the south side of Hong Kong Island, and headed toward Keelung, Taiwan.[1] On board, a local newspaper reported, were "183 Japanese and Formosan [Taiwanese] soldiers, and some women and children."[2] Among the travelers were Mr. and Mrs. Lin Jun-ying and their three young children, including an infant.[3] Three weeks later, on March 6, and thousands of miles away, a decommissioned Japanese naval destroyer named *Yoizuki* left the harbor of Sydney, Australia. This vessel was also carrying Taiwanese people—several hundred of them, including many women and children.[4] Among them were Mr. and Mrs. Kwee Thiam Ting and their five children, all below the age of twelve.

The Lins and the Kwees came from different social backgrounds in Taiwan and had traveled abroad at different times before the Second World War broke out in 1941; but both families ended up being interned as a result of the war. The Lins and the Kwees were just two families among thousands of Taiwanese civilians who had been interned under British authorities in Hong Kong for more than six months and under Dutch/Australian authorities first in the Dutch East Indies (DEI, present-day Indonesia) and then in remote locations across South Australia, New South Wales, and Victoria for more than four years. In 1946, both families, together with other Taiwanese internees, were forcefully repatriated to Taiwan. As the Second World War ended in 1945, a colossal number of Japanese, numbering roughly 7 million, were outside of the Japanese home islands. The massive scale of moving these people back to their homeland was a major postwar issue for Japan as well as the Allies. In recent years, Japanese and Western scholars have devoted significant effort to studying the condition and process of repatriation of overseas Japanese subjects after the end of the Second World War. Little attention, however, has been paid to the immediate postwar condition of overseas colonial subjects of the Japanese Empire—primarily Taiwanese and Korean—people who at least in name were Japanese subjects when they went to China, Southeast Asia, and other foreign destinations before or during the war.

During postwar repatriation, former colonial subjects of the Japanese Empire received completely different treatment from Japanese citizens. Stripped of their Japanese "status" at the end of the war, their identity—or rather legitimacy as "citizens"—was then called into question and debated in the postwar reconstruction of the East Asian order. This chapter aims to study the postwar internment and repatriation of overseas Taiwanese; it will focus in particular on those who returned from Hong Kong and Australia, as they offer an interesting contrast of the ways in which the Taiwanese were defined and redefined among the Allied nations, Japan, and the postwar sovereign states to which they eventually belonged in the immediate postwar period.

Internment, repatriation, and the postwar Japanese Empire

When the Second World War in Asia ended with Japan's defeat in August 1945, the Allied countries and Japan began the long process of postwar resettlement. Among the many issues to be dealt with was the repatriation of overseas Japanese, known as *hikiagesha* (overseas returnees) in postwar Japan. This issue was particularly significant, as Lori Watt points out, because "repatriates were defined in the crucible of imperialism, colonialism and decolonization."[5] By the end of the war, 3.2 million Japanese civilians and 3.7 million Japanese soldiers were outside of the Japanese home islands. An estimated 2 million Koreans and 35,000 Taiwanese lived in mainland Japan;[6] and many more live abroad in China and Southeast Asia by the end of the war. After the war ended, the Japanese were sent back to Japan, the Koreans to Korea, and the Taiwanese to Taiwan. However, before their repatriation, many of them were first put into internment by the Allied authorities. Therefore, the problem of repatriation was closely connected to the issue of internment.

While most discussion of civilian victims in Asia from the Second World War has focused on Allied civilians who were interned under the Japanese military occupation, it is important to note that the Japanese, Korean, and Taiwanese civilians interned by the Allied countries underwent similar experiences and suffered no less during and after the war.[7] Some of the better-known cases of Japanese internment and repatriation are the imprisonment of Japanese-Americans—many were US citizens—from 1942 to 1945, Japanese children left behind in Manchuria at the war's end and subsequently adopted by Chinese parents, and the internment of 600,000 former Japanese soldiers in Siberia between 1945 and 1956.

As this chapter will demonstrate, in the discussion of internment and repatriation of civilians during and after the Second World War, experiences of the Taiwanese should be distinguished and further examined. Within the larger context of the number of Japanese *hikiagesha*, the internment and repatriation of the Taiwanese was hardly a major event in the Second World War, or for that matter, the collapse of the Japanese Empire. However, the very unique status of the Taiwanese—from Japan's colonial subjects to a redefined postwar identity—helps to shed new light on the postwar reconstruction of East Asia.

Overseas Taiwanese

When the war ended, an estimated 150,000 Taiwanese remained overseas throughout Japan's former empire, mostly in China and Southeast Asia.[8] These Taiwanese—most of them civilians—had traveled outside of Taiwan by their own choice during the Japanese colonial period and were regarded both by imperial Japanese and imperial authorities in the host societies as "Japanese subjects." After the war, while Japan ceased its control of Taiwan, these overseas Taiwanese continued to be regarded by the Allied authorities as "Japanese subjects" in the immediate postwar period and were therefore put into internment, similar to most overseas Japanese, before being repatriated.

The issue of the internment and repatriation of overseas Taiwanese has received some attention from researchers, and more archival materials have been made available in recent years. But most studies have placed the postwar internment and repatriation of overseas Taiwanese in the postwar political and social context of China.[9] A handful of studies have looked into the Taiwanese situation in Southeast Asia, but they have relied mostly on archival materials from the Republic of China (ROC) government.[10] I would like to rebalance this situation and emphasize that the postwar internment and repatriation of the overseas Taiwanese should be placed and understood in the larger *transnational* context of postwar repatriation that involved Japan and the Allied powers such as the United States, Great Britain, and Australia. To more fully understand the context of postwar internment and repatriation of the Taiwanese in Hong Kong and DEI/Australia, this chapter will first delineate the situation of the Taiwanese in these places before 1945. It will then analyze the conditions of postwar internment and repatriation of the Taiwanese as former colonial subjects when the Japanese empire left them behind.

Taiwanese in Hong Kong before 1945

Hong Kong was a British colony from 1841 to 1997. Having been developed into a major port in southern China, Hong Kong continued to attract foreign visitors, including the Taiwanese, in pursuit of various interests. A small number of Taiwanese had worked in or relocated to Hong Kong in the nineteenth century, and more did so after Japanese rule began in Taiwan in 1895. Annual statistics compiled by the Japanese authorities showed that between 1916 and 1926, the number of Taiwanese in "British-ruled Hong Kong" remained rather stable, between forty-four and eighty-five.[11] The Taiwanese population in Hong Kong seems to have come from the higher echelons of society: a 1930 report by the Japanese Consulate in Hong Kong noted that the larger portion of the Taiwanese population in Hong Kong comprised, "businessmen, school teachers, doctors on ships with high social status, education, and assets."[12] The report added that even though the Taiwanese were subjects of the Japanese Empire since Japan's takeover of Taiwan in 1895, the Taiwanese in Hong Kong seemed to keep their distance both from the Japanese authorities and people:

There seems to be very little contact between people from the mainland (of Japan) and the Taiwanese *seikimin* (Taiwan-registered people) … At the same time, however, Taiwanese *seikimin* in Hong Kong only need to make connection with the majority local population of the Chinese in their relevant profession and business.[13]

This passage indicates that the Taiwanese in Hong Kong tended to rely on their own efforts and abilities—and, notably, their good relations with the local population—rather than seeking to benefit from the second-hand power or influence of the Japanese Empire or indeed Japanese people. Among those Taiwanese in Hong Kong, the aforementioned Lin Jun-ying (1910–1991) is a good example.

A graduate of the Taipei Technology School, Lin went to Hong Kong in 1934, at the age of twenty-four, and took up a job with a local trading company. In less than a year, he set up his own trading company, importing automobile parts, and established partnerships with the local business community. Lin's relations with the local Chinese population enabled him to continue his business throughout the 1930s, in spite of the growing anti-Japanese sentiment in Hong Kong as a result of the Japanese military confrontation with China from 1937. During this period, Lin lived in the high-end residential district at Kennedy Road in the Wanchai area of the Hong Kong Island, where a large Western population lived at the time.

With the start of the Pacific War in 1941, however, this situation changed radically. Japanese forces launched their attack on Hong Kong on December 8, 1941, and the British authorities surrendered on December 25. Thereafter, until the end of the war, Hong Kong was under Japan's military occupation, or what was later colloquially known as the "three years and eight months" period.[14] During the occupation period, the composition of Taiwanese in Hong Kong underwent a significant change. As Japan's war and occupation progressed, the Japanese recruited and dispatched more Taiwanese from Taiwan to Hong Kong, to serve in various capacities. Some Taiwanese served as interpreters, as they were capable of speaking Japanese and various Chinese dialects. Since most of these Taiwanese newcomers served in the Japanese forces, they and the Taiwanese in general came to be seen by Hong Kong's local population as playing a supporting role to the Japanese Empire, and sometimes even as acting on behalf of the Japanese occupiers.[15] A considerable amount of the growing animosity and hatred felt toward Japan's military action, occupation, and oppression gradually rubbed off on the Taiwanese as a whole.

Taiwanese in Hong Kong after the war

After Japan's surrender, the British returned to take over Hong Kong at the end of August. Admiral Cecil Harcourt, the Military Governor of the Colony, established a British Military Administration in Hong Kong. On August 30, he issued an order that "all Japanese troops and Japanese nationals were to be evacuated out of the island of Hong Kong to Kowloon by 1600 on the next day, Saturday, September 1."[16]

At this point, the British authorities had not specified how to deal with the Taiwanese in Hong Kong. For the next few days, the status of Taiwanese in Hong Kong hung in a gray zone. Then on September 4 the situation took a critical turn. Hong Kong's Chief Justice, Sir Atholl MacGregor, issued a statement, through Chief Censor D. J. Sloss, confirming that the Formosan "is still an enemy national."[17] As quoted in the local English newspaper *South China Morning Post and the Hong Kong Telegraph*, the Chief Justice explained his rationale in great detail:

> Japan has been soundly beaten in the field, but we are not yet formally at peace with her. She has surrendered, but in law the war is not yet at an end. In due course the Allies will formally negotiate with Japan a Treaty of Peace, and in that document the status of Formosa will be decided and the Island will once again become part of the Republic of China. Even then the legal status of Formosans born in Formosa during the Japanese tenure of the Island will present difficulties, which doubtless will be settled by the Peace Treaty. Until that day comes the Formosan is still an enemy national.[18]

This statement is interesting on several accounts. First, it shows that the British authorities in Hong Kong had now made clear the distinction between the Taiwanese and the Japanese, which was in fact the reason for issuing the statement that specifically addressed and clearly delineated "the Formosan issue." Secondly, it shows the rationale behind the decision to define and treat the Taiwanese as "enemy national" was based on a continued link between the Taiwanese and the war that had been conducted by the Japanese Empire. A certain consciousness of the unusual if not contradictory status of Taiwanese people seems to be acknowledged in the sub-heading of the newspaper article: "[An] Interesting Problem."

The British military administration put its words into practice the very next day, taking immediate and systematic action to treat the Taiwanese as enemy subjects and putting all of them—men, women, and children—into internment camps in Hong Kong. As reported in the *South China Morning Post and the Hong Kong Telegraph*, at the very center of the front page, under the heading of "Enemy Nationals: Formosans and Koreans to Report to Police: Public Responsibility," a police notice was issued on September 5 concerning the Taiwanese.[19] This police order, demanding compliance with the government's internment policy, was quoted in full in the newspaper:

> All Formosans and Koreans including women and children on Hong Kong Island will report at the Japanese Primary School, Kennedy Road, between noon and 3 p.m. September 7th, 1945, taking with them any arms or ammunition in their possession and will deposit these with the officer in charge there. They will also take with them hand baggage, personal effects, Japanese ration cards and sufficient food for 24 hours. Before vacating their houses they will arrange for a responsible person to take charge of their property and premise.[20]

Conspicuously, as the British administration undertook various measures to dismantle the Japanese Empire at the end of the war, it reinforced—intentionally or not—the Japanese colonial structure, as it considered and treated the Taiwanese (and Koreans) using policies applied to the Japanese, such as compulsory reporting and consequently forced internment.

In the next few days, *South China Morning Post and the Hong Kong Telegraph* reported on the handling of the Taiwanese as well as public hostility against the Taiwanese. Under the title of "Public Animosity: Formosans and Koreans Concentrated in Kowloon: Weeding Out,"[21] the newspaper reported the "dispatch of Koreans and Formosans to Kowloon by ferry" on the afternoon of September 7. The news article described, in great detail, the process of transport and the scenes in which the locals came out to witness the removal of these unwanted persons and to demonstrate their condemnation of them. The report further delineated the route the trucks took to transport the Taiwanese, starting from the compulsory reporting point of the Japanese Primary School, which was located on Kennedy Road near Happy Valley/Causeway Bay, through Des Voeux Road Central to Pedder Street, and finally on to Blake Pier. All along the route, the Chinese crowd gathered and reacted with violence toward the procession of trucks ferrying Taiwanese. As the procession moved, the article reported:

> The crowd surged forward to meet it and, to the accompaniment of shouting, waving of sticks and hurling of bricks, the vehicles made their way to the entrance of the pier. Even wet red earth from a pile on the roadway nearby the seawall was thrown at the lorries.[22]

Such reactions from the crowd showed that the hostility toward the Taiwanese was widespread and deep-rooted among the locals in Hong Kong. Eventually, one report recounted, the situation got so violent that at one point "it was necessary for the police to draw their revolvers." The scenes at the embarkation point of Blake Pier were equally tense, with a strong law enforcement presence and, again, with overt displays of hostility against the Taiwanese or rather the "enemy nationals": "Among the crowd, the more youthful members were armed with sticks. Police officers, British marines and sailors kept them well away from where the enemy nationals were assembling on the wharf prior to embarkation." The report described the crowd's reaction to the departure of these internees in an almost jocular, mocking way: "The small wharf between Blake Pier and Douglas Wharf formed a ringside seat for the onlookers and there were intermittent bursts of cheers and jeers as they watched the Koreans and Formosans boarding the ferry-launch."[23]

The strong sense of animosity, violent hatred, and desire for physical retribution evidenced by the reactions of the local population toward the Taiwanese is all too clear in the report. This postwar attitude of the local population was a stark contrast to the friendly relationships between the locals (Chinese in particular) and the Taiwanese in the prewar years. So what explains the change of attitude toward the Taiwanese before and after the Japanese occupation of Hong Kong and the outburst of animosity against the Taiwanese after the war?

After the war, several eminent Chinese in Hong Kong wrote about their encounter with the Taiwanese during the Japanese occupation. One veteran journalist wrote:

> Taiwanese serving in the Japanese spoke the southern Fujian dialect and limited Cantonese dialect, (but) they enjoyed all privileges and collaborated with local Chinese traitors and bullies, assisted the devil and committed all kinds of crimes, (they) were more terrifying than the Japanese.[24]

This perception of the Taiwanese—an unequivocally negative image—was widely accepted among the local population in Hong Kong, and it can be found in the recollections of many Hong Kong residents, who repeatedly stressed the close ties between the Taiwanese and the Japanese occupiers.[25] The previously cordial, even close, relations between the Taiwanese and the local population in Hong Kong turned decidedly sour after 1941. As the war progressed, this animosity grew deeper and stronger and after the war ended in 1945 it erupted into the open.

After reporting to the British authorities on September 7, all Taiwanese were interned against their will and subsequently transferred to Kowloon and put into indefinite internment. According to one newspaper report, more than 18,000 Japanese, Koreans, and Taiwanese were interned in Kowloon.[26] They were sequestered in the Whitefield Barracks (and the surrounding area) in the Tsim Sha Tsui area.[27] After more than a month of internment in Kowloon, the British authorities decided to move all internees—including the Taiwanese—to Stanley, located in the southern end of the Hong Kong Island, starting from the end of October; the process was not completed untill the end of November.[28]

It is worth noting that throughout the relocation process, the Taiwanese were handled separately from the Japanese. Relocation of the Japanese to Stanley started much earlier, from October to the early part of November, and repatriation started as early as November. However, most Taiwanese remained in Kowloon in late November; in an article in the local Chinese newspaper *Sing Tao Daily* (Xing Dao Ribao), the director of the Kowloon camp was quoted saying: "there are around 2,000 Taiwanese and Koreans in the compound, about 1800 of them are Taiwanese, 200 were Koreans, men make up half of it and women and children make up the other half." If this is correct, it meant that roughly 1,000 Taiwanese women and children were still imprisoned in Kowloon's internment camp toward the end of November.[29]

In November 1945, the British authorities started the repatriation of internees; and similar to the earlier relocation process, the Taiwanese were separated and treated differently from the Japanese. Throughout the month of November, there were several rounds of repatriation of the Japanese.[30] After that, the British authorities continued to make arrangements to send the Japanese back to Japan; by January 1946, as reported in the newspapers, more than 10,000 Japanese soldiers and civilians had left Hong Kong.[31] In contrast, the Taiwanese, after being transferred to Stanley, remained in internment. The British policies concerning the relocation and repatriation of internees demonstrate a conspicuous contradiction in the postwar dismantling of the Japanese Empire and the handling of its subjects: while the Taiwanese were held equally liable for the empire's war and consequently forced into internment like the Japanese, at the same time they were recognized by the British authorities as different from the Japanese and categorically separated from the Japanese in the subsequent relocation and repatriation process. This contradiction concerning the status of the Taiwanese living abroad perfectly exemplifies the complexity of re-defining the postwar international order in East Asia.

Things did not change for another two months, until February 1946, when the British authorities finally made the decision to repatriate all the Taiwanese internees back to Taiwan. Notably, no choice was given to the Taiwanese to stay in Hong Kong. As a result, those Taiwanese—such as the Lin family—who had worked and lived in Hong Kong long before the war had begun were forced to leave Hong Kong and return to Taiwan. After he reported to the police on September 7, 1945, Lin lost almost everything he had earned and established in Hong Kong since he first went there in 1934. They were fortunate to return safely to Taiwan on February 15, 1946.

While the internment of the Taiwanese in Hong Kong occurred after the war ended in 1945 and took place in a territory previously occupied by Japan's wartime empire, some Taiwanese living abroad were interned immediately after the war began in December 1941 in places that were not yet occupied by the Japanese military. Recent scholarly works have looked into the internment of the Taiwanese by the British authorities in India (having been captured in and transferred from Malaya and Singapore) from December 1941 to May 1946.[32] This chapter will further examine the internment of Taiwanese in Australia in roughly the same period.

From the Dutch East Indies to Australia

The internment of the Taiwanese civilians in Australia was more complicated than that of the Taiwanese in Hong Kong, as it commenced long before the war ended and, in fact, started *outside* Australia.

The most comprehensive records of the wartime (and postwar) internment of "Formosans" in Australia is held in the National Archives of Australia in Canberra. For each of the Formosan (Taiwanese) internees in Australia, a record was created, using the "Service and Casualty Form" of the Australian Military Forces. According to these records, some Taiwanese interned were "prisoners of war" who had served in the Japanese military and then captured by the Allied forces in battlefields across the Pacific; but many Taiwanese interned in Australia were indeed civilians, categorically identified as "internees" on their records.

During the Japanese colonial period, the Dutch East Indies was a major immigration destination for the Taiwanese. Aside from China, the largest number of Taiwanese living abroad was found in the Dutch East Indies. Annual statistics compiled by the Japanese authorities showed that in 1916, the number of Taiwanese living in the Dutch East Indies was 146. Their number continued to climb year after year; in 1926, it reached 391.[33] These statistics show that a sizable Taiwanese population was living in the Dutch East Indies before the Second World War broke out.

Immediately after Japan's declaration of war against the Netherlands following the attack on Pearl Harbor in December 1941, the Dutch authorities took swift action to intern all the Japanese nationals—Taiwanese included—across the Dutch East Indies. Soon after that, the Dutch made an arrangement with the Australian authorities and transferred all internees to Australia. Their numbers were between 1,000 and 2,000, and they were kept in several different camps across Australia and were not freed or repatriated till March 1946.

While these Taiwanese from the Dutch East Indies had no prior conflict with the Australian government, they were nevertheless considered "enemy aliens" because of their Japanese identity. During the Second World War, the Australian government put thousands of "enemy aliens" into internment, including Japanese, Germans, and Italians. All of them were considered potential threats to national security after the war broke out at the end of 1941.[34] In addition to "local internees" —those "enemy aliens" living in Australia when the war broke out—Australia also received thousands of "enemy aliens" who were interned by its Allies in "Britain, Palestine, Iran, the Strait Settlements, the Netherlands East Indies, New Caledonia, and New Zealand."[35] In other words, "overseas internees," who had originated in internment camps in other countries, constituted a significant portion of Australia's wartime internment.[36] One study states that out of a total of 15,000 civilians interned in Australia during the war, 8,000 had originally been "detained overseas."[37] Those Taiwanese who were originally interned in the Dutch East Indies constitute part of the "overseas internees" in Australia. Therefore, the internment of the Taiwanese should be understood as part of the larger and coordinated action taken by Australia and its Allies after the outbreak of the Pacific War in dealing with civilians from enemy countries.

Profile of the Taiwanese civilian internees

The Australian archival records reveal that the arrests and the subsequent internment of the Taiwanese civilians by the Dutch and later the Australian authorities were carried out without consideration of age or gender. As the war broke out, Taiwanese living in the Dutch East Indies—young and old, men, women, and children—were detained without distinction and sent to Australia, where they were interned until the war ended. At least sixteen Taiwanese were aged sixty or older (born in 1882 or before) when they were interned in 1942; another fifty were between the age of fifty and fifty-nine (born between 1883 and 1892). Some of these elderly Taiwanese did not survive the internment. For example, the widow Shi Chin Ang was aged sixty-eight when she was sent to the Tatura camp in February 1942, and she died in the camp before the war ended.[38]

It is also worth noting that among the Taiwanese internees, there were a significant number of children. At the time of internment in 1942, at least fifty-five Taiwanese children were six years of age or younger (born in and after 1936). And between 1942 and 1946, at least eighteen Taiwanese were born in internment camps. These numbers indicate that a good number of Taiwanese families with young children were interned in Australia. Take the aforementioned Mr. Kwee as an example: he and his wife, together with their four children, were detained in Wadjah Malang in the Dutch East Indies in December 1941, and subsequently sent to the Tatura No. 4 camp in Victoria, Australia, in February 1942. During their internment, the Kwee family had their fifth child, a daughter born on December 28, 1942.[39]

The end of internment and the Yoizuki, *March 1946*

After the war ended, most Taiwanese internees continued to be held in camps for more than half a year. It was not until March 1946 that the Australian authorities took action to repatriate these Taiwanese. However, quite unexpectedly, the repatriation of Taiwanese internees turned into a major controversy for the Australian as well as the Allied authorities.

On March 6, 1946, the Australian military put hundreds of Taiwanese internees—including women and children—on board the ship *Yoizuki*, which had been prepared to embark from Sydney Harbour. The ship had originally been a destroyer in the Japanese Imperial Navy, taken over by the Allied forces after Japan's surrender. As the Australian authorities were planning to repatriate the Taiwanese interned in Australia, the *Yoizuki* was chosen to carry out the mission.

But what seemed like a routine transport mission, which was part of the "repatriation" of millions of subjects of the former Japanese Empire, unexpectedly became headline news in Australia. Australian newspaper articles reported "panic-stricken Formosans protesting vigorously against being driven on board" and particularly of one "sobbing Formosan, aghast at the thought of boarding the vessel of his masters, [who was] dragged screaming towards the gangway by provosts."[40] It was widely reported in local newspapers that these Taiwanese were being "forced aboard," and that there had been "one attempted suicide and an attempted sit-down strike" on the site.[41]

Other newspapers further reported that Australian Army officers had refused to allow hundreds of Taiwanese women and children to board the ship, claiming that the "conditions on the destroyer were so cramped that it would be certain death for some of the women and children." The Taiwanese "cannot speak or write Japanese," and they "looked at the destroyer and her Jap [Japanese] crew with fear in their eyes."[42] Based on these newspaper reports and information collected from the Taiwanese internees but only published in recent years, we find two major reasons behind the Taiwanese protest and refusal to board the *Yoizuki*.[43] The first is the poor condition of the ship. Secondly, the destination of the voyage had not been specified to the Taiwanese; to make the situation even more perilous, the *Yoizuki*, originally a Japanese ship, was still manned by a Japanese crew. Therefore, (some) Taiwanese internees suspected that the ship was taking them to Japan; they refused to follow the order to board, and some even pleaded to return to the internment camp and remain in Australia.[44] In addition, as an Australian news article pointed out at the time of the *Yoizuki* controversy, most of these Taiwanese internees originally came from the Dutch East Indies.[45] However, as the postwar repatriation process began, the Taiwanese were ordered to return to Taiwan and had not been given the choice to return to the Dutch East Indies, where they had lived for decades before the war. This condition of "forced repatriation," which is also seen in the aforementioned case of Taiwanese in Hong Kong, may also have contributed to the Taiwanese protest at Sydney Harbour.

Most attention was given to the plight of the Taiwanese women and children who were being repatriated on this vessel. Every major newspaper in Australia featured extensive reports on the repatriation of Taiwanese on the *Yoizuki*. Many articles had emotive headlines such as "Hundreds Herded into Jap Destroyer" and "Children Weep," and often featured highly emotional photographs: "One hundred Formosan women and 112 of their children, a sobbing wretched procession, were forced aboard the Japanese destroyer *Yoizuki* today," one article ran.[46] Another report, also with a vivid photograph, stated:

> With one infant in her arms and another on her back, this mother was one of the 100 Formosan women compelled to travel in the Japanese "hell-ship" *Yoizuki*, which is returning them to their homeland.[47]

Public opinion in Australia was whipped up into a storm of pity. On the one hand, there was a great sense of sympathy toward the Taiwanese; on the other hand, there was strong criticism of the government's handling of their repatriation. One newspaper in Sydney reported that immediately after learning what happened on board *Yoizuki* on March 6, "many organizations and individuals in Sydney yesterday joined in condemning the crowding of Formosan women and children into the *Yoizuki*" and demanded that the government "bring the ship back."[48] It appears that in some quarters the criticism was very forceful: the "Sydney University Women Graduates' Association," it was reported, had sent "a telegram of protest to the Prime Minister asking that the Formosan women be transferred to another ship." Members of the Association were quoted in a newspaper article, saying that "for a supposedly Christian country it was an unparalleled disgrace." Sir Samuel Walder, president of the Australian-Chinese Association, was also quoted as saying: "It is hard to think that the Government could have been guilty of such an outrage" and "I want to protest with all the vigor I can command."[49] One newspaper headline stressed the indignity that the *Yoizuki* controversy had brought to Australia with a headline "Disgrace Inflicted on Australia."[50]

It is worth noting that amidst the emerging public sympathy toward the Taiwanese and criticism against the Australian authorities, the Australian public began to redefine the status of the Taiwanese as Chinese rather than as enemy aliens or as Japanese. The aforementioned Sydney University Women Graduates' Association asserted categorically, "(T)he women are Chinese, not Japanese, and were terrified of the ship's (Japanese) crew." Mr. E. V. Elliott, general secretary of the Seamen's Union, stressed that, "Every hour aboard endangers these Chinese nationals, particularly the women." Scholarly authority was even consulted on the matter: Professor A. P. Elkins, Professor of Anthropology at the University of Sydney, was quoted as saying: "These people were not enemies in the real sense of the term and should not be shipped along with Japanese." Sir Samuel Walder stressed, on the contrary, that the Taiwanese should be regarded as Australia's ally: "the treatment is bad enough for any group of nationals, but it is even more distressing for a people who are Australia's allies."[51]

Once regarded by the Australian government as "enemy aliens," these Taiwanese internees were now suddenly considered by the Australian public worthy of sympathy and redefined as Chinese and friendly subjects of an ally country. Furthermore, the ship *Yoizuki*—with its Japanese crew on board—was seen by many in Australia as a "Japanese-manned destroyer."[52] By designating this ship as the vessel to repatriate the Taiwanese, Australian officials were considered to have placed (or even forced) Taiwanese internees into the hands of the (enemy) Japanese, "on a ship where they will be wholly under Japanese control."[53] Now that the Taiwanese were redefined as (ally) Chinese, this was unacceptable.

Among those who raised their voices to redefine the Taiwanese, the most notable was the Chinese community in Australia. The Chinese Seamen's Union, acting "on behalf of the Chinese community in New South Wales," issued a rather staunch statement:

> We wish to enter a most strenuous protest against the means adopted, by the Australian Army authorities to repatriate Formosan prisoners of war and internees. We fought this war to free such people from the Japanese yoke, now the Australian Army authorities seek to subject these people further to Japanese domination. Their action is an insult to the Chinese people and to the Chinese nation.[54]

In response to mounting criticism and public (media) outrage, the Australian government took what should have been a routine repatriation (of the Taiwanese) as a serious national matter. Immediately after the *Yoizuki* controversy, Premier William McKell of New South Wales was quoted in a newspaper as having "denied any responsibility for conditions under which Formosan women were alleged to have been shipped on the *Yoizuki*." Furthermore, "if Press reports of the conditions were correct they indicated a deplorable state of affairs."[55] Members of the Legislative Assembly, from both the ruling Labor party and the opposition, also demanded that the government "make a searching investigation into conditions on the vessel." One Labor member went so far as to declare that "Australia should stand appalled at the disclosures."[56]

At this point, it seems that the controversy was centered on the inhospitable condition of the *Yoizuki*; thereby, Premier William McKell, to appease the public, was disavowing responsibility for the condition of the ship, but not for the decision to use the ship for repatriation. However, the matter only continued to escalate, and several days later Prime Minister Ben Chifley personally announced that the Australian government had officially appointed and sent four officials to conduct an investigation of the *Yoizuki* at its next port of call at Rabaul; the investigation would be led by Justice Simpson, of the Australian Capital Territory Supreme Court, and Brigadier F. G. Galleghan, deputy director of the Commonwealth Investigation Branch, N.S.W.[57] A report was presented to the House of Representatives, two weeks after the *Yoizuki* controversy occurred, which found that 1,005 individuals were on the ship when it left Sydney on March 6, exceeding its capacity limit of 800 persons.[58] As a result of this investigation, it became clear that the use of the *Yoizuki* was a mistake as the ship did not even have the capacity for the mission, and the decision to allow the ship to sail became the point of contention.

The matter finally culminated in a confrontation between the Australian government and the Supreme Commander for the Allied Powers (SCAP). Shortly after the incident was reported in the media, Australian authorities tried to place the blame on SCAP. Australia's Minister for the Navy, Norman Makin, asserted that the Australian government was simply following "instructions given" by "the Supreme Allied Commander in Japan" to repatriate the Taiwanese, "of whom Australia was only the custodian."[59] But the very next day, SCAP refuted the Australian assertion and placed the blame squarely on the Australian government. Under the headline of "MacArthur disclaims onus for Jap ship scandal," a radio message by SCAP was reported, which indicated an "outright denial that Allied authorities in Japan were responsible" for the *Yoizuki*, and that "local authorities were responsible" for "crowding of women and children" on the ship.[60] While denying SCAP's responsibilities for the *Yoizuki*, the radio message further stated that:

> Gen MacArthur immediately requested the Australian military and naval authorities to disembark all women and children with the males of their families at Rabaul … and arranged for the Japanese hospital ship *Hikawa Maru*, a former 11,000 tons NYK liner, to carry them the rest of their journey.[61]

Amidst the heated negotiation between SCAP and Australia over the repatriation of Taiwanese, hundreds of Taiwanese were finally returned to Taiwan in March 1946, more than four years after their initial internment in the Dutch East Indies and subsequent internments in camps across Australia.

Conclusion

My account of these returnees' experiences reveals several issues concerning the postwar reconstruction of East Asia.

The first is the conspicuous absence of Japanese authorities in the process. Both in Hong Kong or Australia, when Taiwanese were being interned and subsequently repatriated, there were Japanese nationals who were undergoing the same process. When the Taiwanese were interned, whether during or after the war, they were detained for the reason of being "Japanese." But neither in the handling of the Taiwanese internees nor in their eventual repatriation was there any trace of involvement from the Japanese government. Further studies are needed to confirm this, but preliminary findings show that as former imperial/colonized subject, the Taiwanese were left unnoticed and unattended by any Japanese authorities when the empire disintegrated.

In contrast, the postwar government in Taiwan, the newly established Republic of China (ROC) authorities, did play a role in the Australian case. Soon after the *Yoizuki* incident, it was reported that the Chinese Legation in Australia held meetings with Prime Minister Chifley and Minister for External Affairs Herbert Vere Evatt, and subsequently issued a statement confirming that it had "confidence that the Australian Government would induce Gen (General) MacArthur to take action necessary to protect the safety and health of Formosans on the Japanese destroyer *Yoizuki*."[62] When the *Yoizuki* was directed to dock at Rabaul, a representative from the Chinese Legation in Australia was tasked to fly to Rabaul to be present as a representative of the Chinese government; this person was regarded as the sole member of the party from Australia able to speak the Formosan dialect and the only person able to carry out actual first-hand interviews with those Taiwanese on the *Yoizuki*.[63]

The great contrast between the conspicuous absence of the Japanese authorities in the repatriation of the Taiwanese from Hong Kong and Australia, and the presence of Chinese authorities in the repatriation of the Taiwanese from Australia, suggests that in the postwar reconstruction of East Asia, the Chinese (ROC) government was engaged and eager to take opportunities to assert its sovereignty (over the Taiwanese as its newly claimed subjects) and establish itself on the international stage as a lawful and responsible player. This repositioning of the ROC, and the recriminations that flew back and forth between Australia and SCAP in dealing with the *Yoizuki* incident, should be understood in the larger context of negotiation and (re-)balancing of power in postwar East Asia. What was at stake in the repatriation of the Taiwanese and the *Yoizuki* incident was not just the fate of hundreds of ordinary Taiwanese; rather, it was the international legitimacy of different Allied authorities, and at the same time the denial by the Allies of Japan's postwar legitimacy and/or the disavowal by Japan of its postwar responsibility in dealing with former subjects of its empire.[64]

The second issue was the definition and redefinition of Taiwanese identity. The case of Taiwanese in Hong Kong shows that before the war, while the Taiwanese were legally Japanese subjects, some Taiwanese were reluctant to be identified with and distanced themselves from the Japanese. This disengagement from the Japanese allowed the Taiwanese to maintain good relationships with the local population, mostly the Chinese. However, the outbreak of the Pacific War in 1941 and the subsequent Japanese military occupation made most people in Hong Kong resentful and hostile against all things and persons Japanese. As a result, in the eyes of Hong Kong people as well as the British, the Taiwanese were equally responsible for the war carried out by the Japanese. As the internment of the Taiwanese in September 1945 demonstrates, this perception against the Taiwanese continued well into the postwar era in Hong Kong.

The Taiwanese in Australia also experienced a process of having their identity redefined but with a very different result from their counterparts in Hong Kong. During the war, Taiwanese internees were transferred from the Dutch East Indies to Australia, and they were regarded as "enemy aliens," to be confined in internment camps across Australia. Immediately after the war, the internment of Taiwanese persisted it seemed that the Taiwanese continued to be seen as the "enemy," no different from the Japanese, as they awaited repatriation. However, the *Yoizuki* controversy in March 1946 redefined the Taiwanese in the eyes of the Australian public. Before the Taiwanese went on board the vessel on March 6, 1946, they were seen simply as Japanese people waiting to be repatriated; after the media reported their condition before and after boarding the *Yoizuki*, they were redefined as subjects worthy of sympathy, Australia's ally, and as Chinese rather than Japanese.

The contrast between Hong Kong and Australia in the postwar handling of Taiwanese internment and repatriation leads us to the third issue, the effect of wartime experiences, or war memories, in the postwar reconstruction of East Asia. The cases of Hong Kong and Australia show that the wartime experiences of the host society played a fundamental role in shaping postwar perceptions of the Taiwanese and determining the fate of the Taiwanese internees. The British authorities and the people of Hong Kong, having lived through the defeat and occupation at the hands of the Japanese, clearly held a much stronger and longer-lasting sense of resentment against anything—and anyone—Japanese, and to them this designation included the Taiwanese. In contrast, the Australian public was more sympathetic toward the plight of the repatriated Taiwanese: they were inclined to see the Taiwanese as citizens of the ROC, a community that was on their side.

One major reason why postwar attitudes toward the Taiwanese among the people of Hong Kong and Australia were so different was that while the former had close contact and a certain amount of conflict with the Taiwanese during wartime, the latter had no direct contact with the Taiwanese during the war. Most Taiwanese interned in Australia were not previously residents in Australia and moreover were confined to certain selected internment camps. While the Taiwanese interned in Australia were considered "enemy aliens," the lack of direct interaction between the Taiwanese and the local communities—and thus the lack of conflict and possibilities for resulting resentment—made it much easier for the people of Australia to overturn and overcome wartime animosity once the war ended.

Regardless of the condition of their internment and repatriation in Hong Kong and Australia, the lives of these Taiwanese were deeply and permanently affected by the war, the collapse of the Japanese Empire and the subsequent postwar reconstruction of East Asia. In his journal Lin Jun-ying summed up his departure from Hong Kong, after nearly twelve years of living and working there, simply as "February 13, left Hong Kong." He and his family were forcefully interned and repatriated back to Taiwan on that date in 1946. Until his death in 1991, he never spoke to his children about his life in Hong Kong and perhaps that silence best sums up the ambivalence many Taiwanese had toward the empire and their role within it.

Notes

1   *South China Morning Post and the Hong Kong Telegraph* (Hong Kong) (hereafter as *SCMPHKT*), "Hong Kong Shipping: Formosan Internees On Board Suncrest," February 12, 1946, Morning edition, p. 7.

2   *SCMPHKT*, "Formosans Leave," February 14, 1946, Morning edition, p. 4.

3   Mr. Lin, Jun-ying was born on October 14, 1910, and passed away on April 18, 1991. The account of Mr. Lin as quoted in this article was based on his personal notes (not dated, private collection); I would like to thank Mrs. Lan Lin, Shingjy, the daughter of Mr. Lin, for her generous assistance and support in providing these materials.

4   *The Daily News* (Australia), Wednesday, March 6, 1946.

5   Lori Watt, *When Empire Comes Home: Repatriation and Reintegration in Postwar Japan* (Cambridge, MA: Harvard University Press, 2009), p. 14.

6   Ibid., p. 2.

7   For Japanese internment of Allied civilians, see Bernice Archer, *The Internment of Western Civilians under the Japanese, 1941–45, A Patchwork of Internment* (London: RoutledgeCurzon, 2004); Greg Leck, *Captives of Empire: The Japanese Internment of Allied Civilians in China, 1941–1945* (Bangor, PA: Shandy Press, 2006); Kevin Blackburn and Karl Hack, eds., *Forgotten Captives in Japanese-Occupied Asia* (London: Routledge, 2007).

8   Tang Shi-Yeoung (Tang Xiyong), "Huifu guoji de zhengyi: zhanhou luwai Taiwanren de fuji wenti, 1945–1947" [Establishing of Nationality of Overseas Formosans and Their Problems, 1945–1947], *Renwen ji shehuikexue jikan* [Journal of Social Sciences and Philosophy], 17, no. 2 (2005), p. 401.

9   For the situation in China, see Zhongyang yanjiuyuan jindaishi yanjiusuo koushu lishi bianji wenyuanhui [Oral History Committee, Institute of Modern History, Academia Sinica, *hereafter* Zhongyang yanjiuyuan], ed., *Koushu lishi diwuqi: Riju shiqi Taiwanren fu dalu jingyan zhuanhao zhiyi* [Oral History 5: Taiwanese Experiences in Mainland China during the Japanese Occupation] (Taipei: Zhongyang yanjiuyuan jindaishi yanjiusuo, 1994); Zhongyang yanjiuyuan, ed., *Koushu lishi diliuqi: Riju shiqi Taiwanren fu dalu jingyan zhuanhao zhier* [Oral History 6: Taiwanese Experiences in Mainland China during the Japanese Occupation] (Taipei: Zhongyang yanjiuyuan, 1995); Chang Chien-Chiu (Zhang Jianqiu), "Tianyuan jiangwu hubugui? zhanhou Guangzhou diqu Taibao chujing ji fanji wenti" [Why Don't They Go Back Home? Research on the Situation of Taiwanese in Canton after the War and the Issue of Their Return], *Taiwanshi yanjiu* [Taiwan Historical Research], 6, no. 1 (1999), pp. 133–166.

10 Tang, "Huifu guoji"; Tang Shi-Yeoung (Tang Xiyong), "Fenghuo hou de tongxiangqing: zhanhou Dongya Taiwan tongxianghui de chengli, zhuanbian yu jiaose" [Establishment of Native Place Associations of Overseas Formosans and Their Functions, 1945–48], *Renwen ji shehuikexue jikan* [Journal of Social Sciences

and Philosophy], 19, no. 1 (2007), pp. 1–49; Chang Chien-Chiu (Zhang Jianqiu), "Tiaotiao guixianglu: zhanhou Gang Ao diqu Taibao fanji shimo" [A Long Way Home: The Process of Taiwanese Returning from Hong Kong and Macao after the War], in *Gang Ao yu jindai Zhongguo xueshu yantaohui lunwenji* [Edited Volume of Papers Presented at the Hong Kong Macao and Modern China Conference] (Taipei: Academia Historica, 2000), pp. 549–580.

11 Statistics compiled from Gaimushō tsushōkyoku [International Trade Bureau, Ministry of Foreign Affairs], *Benshō fukkokuban – Kaigai kakuchi zairyū honbōjin shokugyōbetsu jinkōyō: Daiichikan Meiji 40 nen – Taishō 13 nen,* and *Dainikan Taishō 14 nen – Shōwa 4 nen* [Edited and Reprinted Version: Table of Occupations of Overseas Japanese, vol. 1, Meiji 40 – Taishō 13, and vol. 2, Taishō 14 – Shōwa 4] (Fuji shuppan, 2002). Unless otherwise noted, all Japanese titles are published in Tokyo.

12 Consulate General of Japan in Hong Kong, *Taiwan sekimin kankeijikō chōsa* [Investigation of Registered Taiwanese] (1930), in *Riben ren fang Gang jianwenlu – 1898–1941, xia juan* [Records of Visit to Hong Kong by the Japanese — 1898–1941, vol. 2], ed. Chan Cham-Yi (Chen Zhanyi) (Hong Kong: Sanlian shudian, 2005), pp. 268–269.

13 Ibid., p. 268.

14 This is a common reference to the Japanese occupation; see Tse Wing-Kong (Xie Yongguang), *Sannian ling bageyue de kunan* [Suffering of the Three Years and Eight Months] (Hong Kong: Mingpao Publishing, 1994).

15 Tse Wing-Kong (Xie Yongguang), *Zhanshi Rijun zai Xianggang de baoxing* [Wartime Atrocities by the Japanese Military in Hong Kong] (Hong Kong: Mingpao Publishing, 1991), pp. 16, 114; Tse, *Sannian ling,* p. 235.

16 Private Paper of Admiral Cecil Harcourt Relating to the British Military Administration of Hong Kong, 1945–46, Record number: HKRS 951.2504 Har, Hong Kong Public Record Office.

17 *SCMPHKT,* "Formosans Enemies: Legal Status Explained by Chief Justice: Interesting Problem," September 5, 1945, p. 2.

18 Ibid.

19 *SCMPHKT,* "Enemy Nationals: Formosans and Koreans to Report to Police: Public Responsibility," September 6, 1945, p. 1.

20 *SCMPHKT,* "Enemy Subjects: Time for Formosans and Koreans to Report," September 6, 1945, p. 2.

21 *SCMPHKT,* "Public Animosity: Formosans and Koreans Concentrated in Kowloon: Weeding Out," September 8, 1945, Morning edition, p. 1.

22 Ibid.

23 Ibid.

24 Tse Wing-kong (Xie Yongguang), *Zhanshi rijun zai Xianggang de baoxing* [Wartime Atrocities by the Japanese Military in Hong Kong], p. 16; my translation.

25 For example, see the memoir by a well-known medical professional, Li Shu Fan (Li Shufen, 1887–1966), *Xianggang waike yisheng liushinian huiyilu* [Memoir of Sixty Years by a Hong Kong Surgeon] (Hong Kong: The Li Shu Fan Medical Foundation Limited, 1965), pp. 128–131, 134.

26 *SCMPHKT,* "Japanese Killed: Fourteen Molested by Chinese Mob," September 11, 1945, p. 2.

27 Samejima Moritaka, *Xianggang huixiang ji – Rijun zhanlingxia de Xianggang jiaohui* [Hong Kong Reminiscence], trans. Gong Shusen (Hong Kong: Jidujiao wenyi chubanshe, 1971), p. 142; Tse, *Sannian ling,* p. 412.

28 *SCMPHKT*, "Japanese Prisoners: More Internees Transferred," November 3, 1945, p. 2; *Sing Tao Jih Pao (Xingdao ribao)*, "Moluo bingfang Rifu gai qianchu rijian lai Gang Yingjun jiang jinzhu" [Japanese Internees Moving out of Molou Soldiers' Quarters, British Soldiers to Hong Kong Moving in soon], November 28, 1945, p. 3.

29 *Sing Tao Jih Pao (Xingdao ribao)*, "Jizhongying Tai Xian ren, huifu ziyou buque, xianzai shangyou erqianyu ming" [Taiwanese and Koreans in Concentration Camps, Uncertain to be Granted Freedom, more than Two Thousand Remained], November 21, 1945, p. 3; my translation.

30 *Sing Tao Jih Pao (Xingdao ribao)*, "Qibai Rifu, zhoumo fan Ri" [Seven Hundred Japanese Internees, Returning to Japan This Weekend], October 31, 1945; *Sing Tao Jih Pao (Xingdao ribao)*, "Dierpi difu, zuo qiansong fan Ri" [Second Group of Enemy Internees, Sent back to Japan Yesterday], November 12, 1945, p. 3.

31 *Sing Tao Jih Pao (Xingdao ribao)*, "Sanqian Rifu, jinchen guiguo" [Three Thousand Japanese Internees, Returning Home This Morning], January 15, 1946, p. 3.

32 Chung Shu-Min (Zhong Shumin), "Erzhanshiqi Taiwanren Yindu jizhongying liuji" [Taiwanese Interned in India during the Second World War], *Taiwanshi yanjiu* [Taiwan Historical Research], 24, no. 3 (2017), pp. 89–140.

33 Statistics compiled from Gaimushō tsushōkyoku, *Benshō fukkokuban*, vols. 1–2.

34 See Joan Beaumont, Ilma Martinuzzi O'Brien, and Mathew Trinca, eds., *Under Suspicion: Citizenship and Internment in Australia during the Second World War* (Canberra, ACT: National Museum of Australia Press, 2008); Klaus Neumann, *In the Interest of National Security: Civilian Internment in Australia during World War II* (Canberra, ACT: National Archives of Australia, 2006); Yuriko Nagata, *Unwanted Aliens: Japanese Internment in Australia* (St. Lucia, Qld: University of Queensland Press, 1996); Margaret Bevege, *Behind Barbed Wire* (St. Lucia, Qld: University of Queensland Press, 1993).

35 Neumann, *In the Interest of National Security*, p. 13.

36 Beaumont, Martinuzzi O'Brien, and Trinca, eds., *Under Suspicion*, p. 3.

37 Neumann, *In the Interest of National Security*, pp. 2, 7.

38 National Archives of Australia, Prisoner of War/Internee: Ang, Shi Chin; Date of birth – August 26, 1874; Nationality – Formosan, MP1103/1, IJF50381, and MP1103/2, IJF50381.

39 National Archives of Australia, Prisoner of War/Internee; Kwee, Sioe Kim; Date of birth – December 28, 1942; Nationality – Formosan, MP1103/1 and IJF50448A.

40 "Formosan Protest at Ship's Side," *The Mercury*, March 8, 1946.

41 *The Daily News*, March 3, 1946; *The Mercury*, March 7, 1946; *The Mercury*, March 8, 1946.

42 *The Daily News*, March 6, 1946.

43 Major James T. Sullivan, an Australian officer who served as a guard commander at Camp 4 in Tatura internment camp, published a book in 2006 detailing his experiences and the stories of many he knew and kept correspondences after the war. In this book, the author discussed the *Yoizuki* controversy in detail; see Major James T. Sullivan, *Beyond All Hate: The story of a wartime internment camp for Japanese in Australia, 1941–1946* (Victoria, Australia: James T. Sullivan, 2006), pp. 365–378.

44 Sullivan, *Beyond All Hate*, p. 366.

45 *The Daily News*, Wednesday, March 6, 1946.

46 *The Mercury*, March 7, 1946.

47 "Homing," *The Mercury*, March 9, 1946.

48 "Authorities Missed Opportunity," *Sydney Morning Herald*, March 7, 1946.

49 Ibid.

50 "Disgrace Inflicted On Australia," *Sydney Morning Herald*, March 7, 1946.

51 "Authorities Missed Opportunity."

52 Ibid.

53 Ibid.

54 Ibid.

55 "Disgrace Inflicted On Australia."

56 "Jap Destroyer Unlikely to Be Recalled," *The Mercury*, March 8, 1946.

57 "Yoizuki to be examined at Rabaul," *Sydney Morning Herald*, March 11, 1946.

58 "Yoizuki Overcrowded by 205," *Sydney Morning Herald*, March 21, 1946.

59 "Jap Destroyer Unlikely to be Recalled."

60 "MacArthur Disclaims Onus for Jap Ship Scandal," *The Mercury*, March 9, 1946.

61 Ibid.

62 "Jap Destroyer Unlikely to Be Recalled."

63 "Yoizuki to be Examined at Rabaul."

64 For further discussion of ROC government's postwar pursuit of international legitimacy, see Barak Kushner, *Men to Devils, Devils to Men: Japanese War Crimes and Chinese Justice* (Cambridge, MA: Harvard University Press, 2015).

Chapter 2

CHINA'S REFUGEES: POSTWAR "FOREIGNERS" AND THE ATTEMPT AT INTERNATIONAL AID, 1945–1956

Meredith Oyen

On August 11, 1945, Rena Krasno recalled, she answered the phone in her family's modest Shanghai apartment to hear the words "Peace! Peace!" shouted at her down the line.[1] The Japanese had lost the war, and slowly the city's residents emerged from wartime occupation with visions of recreating the thriving, cosmopolitan metropolis of the prewar years. Shanghai's diverse international population had made it a famous destination in the jazz age, and its unique circumstances had turned it into a haven for refugees, many of them Jewish, as the Second World War escalated. After the war, the city would become the epicenter of international programs to aid displaced persons in China. Across China, the eight-year conflict created tens of millions of internal refugees who fled their homes in the wake of Japanese advances.[2] In addition to the internally displaced, four other categories of refugees in China would command particular attention from both the Chinese government and the newly formed United Nations. Two of these categories emerged out of the Second World War, including the displaced overseas Chinese who returned to China as the Japanese advanced on their homes in Southeast Asia and Central European Jews who fled Europe in the wake of the Nazi rise to power. The other two were remnants of the 1917 Bolshevik Revolution: White Russians and Russian Jews.

Though these four populations took vastly different paths to end up in China at war's end in 1945, they shared the postwar designation of externally displaced persons (or DPs), and their situation required transnational cooperation. The postwar refugee crisis facing the world in 1945 proved far wider in scope than any previous such documented episode in human history.[3] There are really only three options for any refugee: to repatriate (i.e., to return to the country of his or her citizenship); to remain in the country of asylum permanently, often with support to establish a home and occupation; or to resettle in an entirely new country that is neither the place they left nor their current residence. With an eye on the first two, even before the war had ended, the Allied powers created the United Nations Relief and Rehabilitation Administration, or UNRRA. Tasked not only with aiding refugees but also with rebuilding economies and infrastructure damaged by the war, the UNRRA operation in China proved "more extensive than any comparable effort ever previously undertaken on behalf of a single nation." During its short tenure, UNRRA spent approximately US $670 million in China, not including administrative costs.[4] The UNRRA program for DPs included relief in the form of food, clothing, and housing assistance, and aid with repatriation by facilitating transport and help with obtaining travel documents.

It became quickly evident in China as well as in Europe that repatriation and rehabilitation alone would not solve the larger postwar refugee crisis, and a new body tasked with facilitating resettlement of DPs was necessary. Member nations of the UN gathered again in 1945 to create the Preparatory Commission of the International Refugee Organization (or PCIRO) for the purpose of resettling the "last million" DPs from Europe to the United States, Australia, Canada, and any other countries willing to accept them. Between its formal launch in 1947 and its official closure in 1952, the IRO resettled, repatriated, or otherwise closed the cases of 1,208,586 DPs internationally. The numbers of externally displaced persons in China, at just under 30,000, were a fraction of those in Europe: 18,668 European DPs and 11,122 overseas Chinese.[5] As the IRO began winding down operations in 1950, the United Nations created the office of the United Nations High Commissioner for Refugees (UNHCR) to advocate for remaining postwar displaced persons after the IRO disbanded.

The broader story of the evolution of the modern international refugee regime from UNRRA to IRO to UNHCR has been widely explored by historians and political scientists. The consensus is that the IRO in particular played an important but underappreciated role in forging the political battle lines that hardened into the Cold War in Europe.[6] This is in large part due to geography, timing, and the means of its creation: the organization's constitution was enacted by vote on December 15, 1946, after months of debate over who would be included in the mandate, what the scope of the work would be, and how the IRO would be financed by the member governments. The countries of origin for many DPs were now behind the emerging "Iron Curtain," and as members of a newly forming Eastern Bloc they favored defining refugees narrowly and limiting the work to repatriation. The Western European states, by contrast, advocated for a more expansive definition of who would qualify and took issue with repatriating DPs nonvoluntarily to communist countries. Instead, they preferred to focus on resettlement.[7] By December 1946, the USSR, Byelorussian Soviet Socialist Republic (SSR), Ukrainian SSR, Poland, and Yugoslavia had all already voted against the IRO constitution, and Soviet officials suspected that the IRO would be operated as a tool to fuel American and Western goals of weakening and isolating the communist world.

In China, the IRO emerged against the backdrop of a completely different kind of crisis. The Republic of China joined the organization after much convincing and cajoling by the United States and Britain, both concerned about the Western-heavy population of member states without the USSR's participation. Still, Chinese leaders had their own reasons to consider membership: they wanted to assert their place in the postwar international order as well as to rebuild economically by reestablishing an important source of foreign exchange in the form of remittances from overseas Chinese still on the waiting list for repatriation.[8] Moreover, a backlash against a century of colonization contributed to an increased desire to resettle even long-term European residents outside of China and affected the ways in which Chinese officials cooperated with both UNRRA and the IRO. Even though the Nationalist government signed the IRO constitution and lost control of the mainland to the Chinese Communists in 1949, the IRO quietly continued its work well into the 1950s. Its task of resettling and repatriating DPs was as valuable to the new Chinese government as it had been to the old one. Indeed, the continuity experienced by the organization in operating before and after 1949 demonstrates the extent to which cooperation with the IRO on the movements of overseas Chinese, European Jews, and White Russians allowed both the Nationalist and Communist Chinese governments to address a humanitarian crisis, seek out legitimacy from the United Nations, and assert a new vision of China free from Western colonial influence.

Repatriating overseas Chinese

The "overseas Chinese" were ethnic Chinese who had long been resident outside China, mostly in Southeast Asia. As the Japanese swept through first China and then Southeast Asia in the late 1930s and early 1940s, thousands of overseas Chinese returned to China to protect family, guard financial interests, or avoid the invading army. Hu Cheong-on was one such migrant. Hu lived in Thailand before the war but returned to China sometime before 1942. In April 1947, a letter he wrote to UNRRA officials made clear that he was speaking as a representative of a group of fifty-eight overseas Chinese displaced persons who were being repatriated together. In a scant three paragraphs, his letter provides insight into the challenges inherent in the overseas Chinese repatriation project, including the scale and complexity of managing overseas transportation, the nature of relief efforts, and growing frustration with what many Chinese observers and participants perceived as unequal treatment between Chinese and European DPs.[9]

Immediately after the war, UNRRA officials divided China's DP problem into two categories: that of the internally and the externally displaced, the former being the larger group. Among the externally displaced persons, the overseas Chinese formed the largest category, with an estimated 1.5 million overseas Chinese seeking repatriation abroad, though many were able to facilitate their own travel, leaving 184,000 overseas Chinese registered with UNRAA by December 1945. At the outset of repatriation operations, shortly after the Japanese surrender, Chinese representative Li Choh-ming suggested that China would not require assistance repatriating overseas Chinese. Instead, the government would execute a series of bilateral agreements with the target nations to allow the return of ethnic Chinese former residents.[10] In the meantime, they established a clear division of labor: the Chinese National Relief and Rehabilitation Administration (CNRRA) would organize and operate DP camps that provided basic food, shelter, healthcare, and other necessary short-term relief, and UNRRA would arrange for transportation.[11]

Despite this early optimism, Hu's letter suggests that life in the CNRRA camp was not always pleasant–after first being in a camp in Nanjing at the end of the war, in 1947 he and his comrades were transferred to Shanghai, where they remained for three months. He complained about delays, limited information, and food shortages in the camp.

The Nationalist assumption that it would find easy solutions to the overseas Chinese problem rapidly proved incorrect. The first challenge was that the displaced were scattered across East and Southeast Asia. In addition to overseas Chinese in China hoping for repatriation abroad, there were Chinese left behind in the Philippines, Japan, and elsewhere who wanted to return to China.[12] As Shi-chi Mike Lan demonstrates in Chapter 1 of this volume, Taiwanese displaced in China, across the region, and as far away as Australia also needed a way to return to their newly decolonized home island. Only those migrants already located in Yunnan or Sichuan Provinces could reasonably travel overland to Burma or perhaps north Indochina. The rest had to be repatriated by ship, and passenger shipping was in desperately short supply.[13]

Beyond the logistical challenges, Southeast Asian governments often proved reluctant to accept former Chinese residents back. In some cases, anti-imperialist movements often targeted local overseas Chinese merchants as collaborators in European economic regimes. Newly independent regimes in Indonesia and the Philippines proved recalcitrant about allowing former Chinese residents to return at a time when domestic stability and postwar recovery were very much in question, and even British colonies not in rebellion proved reluctant to accept returnees. UNRRA stepped in and negotiated for whole groups of repatriates at a time, with mixed success.[14] By the time of Hu's voyage it was increasingly clear that despite the early optimism, the Nationalist Chinese government did not have the diplomatic influence necessary to convince or cajole Southeast Asian governments into accepting displaced overseas Chinese, and the problem was likely to linger on for some time.[15] In the case of Hu Cheong-on, his cohort of fifty-eight repatriates finally boarded the *S.S. Hupeh* for Hong Kong in mid-April 1947, a difficult voyage marked by limited food, sickness and contagion, and few warm or dry places to retreat. Upon landing, they prepared for the next stage of their journey to Thailand by making a series of requests to UNRRA for fresh clothing, better rations, assistance with immigration-related fees, and financial assistance "like other refugees get," likely a reference to the fact that aid to European refugees in Shanghai was often adjusted to their higher expectations, a source of great frustration and growing anti-foreign sentiment among the Chinese of the city.[16] By January 1946, CNRRA was already fielding complaints from the Chinese population in Shanghai that Europeans received better treatment (usually by way of better rations) than Chinese refugees.[17]

It was in the context of such mounting problems that the IRO came into being. As mentioned, in spring 1947, British and American officials went to work to convince a reluctant China to sign on to the program. Chinese reluctance was based on reasonable concerns, including the burgeoning civil war and the requirement that all member states make financial contributions to the organization's operating budget—something that a Chinese economy in free fall could scarcely afford. Two arguments ultimately convinced them, however: (1) that the IRO would continue the work of overseas Chinese repatriations along with resettling European refugees, and (2) that joining would bolster China's standing in the world and cooperation with the United States, something made even more necessary by the turning tide of the civil war.[18] Ideally, participation would both preserve the overseas Chinese as a source of foreign exchange and investment and would ensure continued international recognition for the Nationalist government in the face of the communist challenge. Either way, the Chinese Nationalists were still stuck with paying for a refugee problem, and IRO cooperation might hasten the resolution. China officially joined the IRO on April 29, 1947.[19]

The new organization existed as a Preparatory Commission (PCIRO) first, then when fifteen UN members ratified its founding constitution and subscribed 75 percent of the funds necessary for its operation, it formally came into being. The governments pledged what they could afford, with the United States unsurprisingly shouldering the lion's share of the burden (though one British diplomat noted sardonically that the United States could make a much more significant contribution by passing legislation admitting DPs to the United States, which it proved slow to do).[20] The IRO used the funds to maintain DP camps, to offer food and clothing aid to the destitute, to provide medical care to the elderly and infirm, and particularly to subsidize transport and visa fees for migrants able to resettle in a new country. Whereas the UNRRA focused on repatriation, the IRO would also work as an intermediary to convince governments to accept refugees as new immigrants.[21] As the IRO began work, some 11,000 European DPs remained in China, in addition to about 17,000 overseas Chinese awaiting repatriation.

The IRO had worked in China for just over two years when the Chinese Communists won the civil war and set up a new government. Though plans were already in place internationally to begin winding down operations in 1950, the Shanghai office not only survived the transition but remained in place several years thereafter. The overseas Chinese repatriation program formed a large part of the reason that the IRO office in China survived. Communist China had even less clout than the Nationalist government had enjoyed with Southeast Asian governments, which feared Chinese returnees might now bring communist revolutions with them. But even the inexperienced new Chinese government recognized that stopping repatriations might well damage overseas Chinese opinions regarding the new regime, and that the benefits from aiding this population could be transferred to the new state.[22]

China's stateless European problem

Overseas Chinese repatriations were a primary motivation for Nationalist and Communist Chinese governments to get behind the IRO, but eagerness to resolve the problem of stateless European refugees also played a role. In the aftermath of the Japanese defeat, this diverse population posed a unique problem for the

Chinese government. Although both the Chinese government and the personnel working under first UNRRA and then the IRO concerned themselves with a wide variety of Europeans in China, three groups stood out as posing unique challenges: Russian Jews, Central European Jews, and White Russians.

In the years prior to the war with Japan, China had become a haven for European Jews fleeing violence in Europe. During and after the Bolshevik Revolution, thousands fled pogroms and persecution in Soviet Russia by traveling across the Russo-Chinese border to settle in northern cities such as Harbin and Tianjin. As time went on, many migrated further south to Shanghai.[23] Rena Krasno's family was an example of this migration, as both of her parents fled Russia to meet in Shanghai, where Rena was born in 1923.[24] By the outbreak of the Second World War, approximately 4,000 Russian Jews resided in Shanghai, scattered throughout the city. Beginning in the 1930s, Central European Jews also began to trickle into Shanghai as the rise of the Nazi Party led some prescient individuals to seek new homes. After the Anschluss with Austria beginning in March 1938 and the arrests and attacks in Germany during Kristallnacht in November of the same year, the trickle grew to a stream as increasing numbers of German and Austrian Jews sought avenues of escape from Adolf Hitler's regime. In some cases, the only way to secure release from German concentration camps such as Buchenwald was to show Nazi officials proof of plans to emigrate in the form of tickets out of the country. Most destinations were closed to these late departures: the United States had long waiting lists and required elaborate paperwork to prove migrants had a relative financially able to sponsor them, and the British kept the doors closed on the best chance for mass migration, Palestine.

For around 20,000 desperate Central European Jews, Shanghai became a last-ditch option for survival. The city was divided into three sections: the International Settlement, the French Concession, and Greater China. Only the last of these sections fell under the jurisdiction of the Chinese government, and then only until the Japanese invaded the city in 1937 and seized control of this section. Until August 1939, no visa was needed to enter Shanghai. Arriving passengers could clear customs and simply enter the city, so Jewish refugees who could complete the complicated bureaucratic red tape necessary to leave Nazi territory and who managed to secure passage on an ocean liner could simply enter. As the refugees arriving swelled in numbers from the hundreds to the thousands, relief agencies joined with city leaders in calling for measures to partially close the open port. In August 1939, leaders of the three sectors agreed to ban the arrival of any additional Central European refugees (except those already en route); by October they had agreed on provisions governing who would be allowed to land going forward: only those who either held a landing permit issued by one of the three sectors or who were in possession of US$400 per adult and US$100 per child to ensure they would not become a public charge.[25] The outbreak of war in Europe further closed off the oversea routes to China, though a trickle of refugees continued to arrive through 1941 by way of the Trans-Siberian Railway.[26]

Russian Jews and Central European Jewish refugees experienced the Sino-Japanese War quite differently. While the former struggled under the privations of living in an occupied city beset with refugees, they remained in their homes and continued to work and attend schools. They occupied an unusual space in colonial Shanghai society, as they were neither citizens of the colonial powers that ruled the city nor were they part of Chinese society. Liliane Willens, a Russian Jew born in Shanghai to refugee parents, reflected, "From a very early age my friends and I looked down on the Chinese, whose main function we had observed was to serve us and all other foreigners. Little did I know then we were behaving as colonial racists did in other parts of the world."[27] Central European Jewish refugees recalled similar attitudes toward the Chinese. Gertrude Kracauer recalled, "In thinking back, I am ashamed to admit that we all copied the prevailing custom to call every male helper or servant 'boy,' the women *amah*, regardless of age."[28] As much as they did not assimilate with the Chinese residents, Ernest Heppner observed that the refugees' unique status also made them unpopular with the existing foreign settlements. "One factor was the 'loss of face' suffered by the white community with the arrival of destitute refugees," who broke with tradition and competed alongside Chinese for jobs in manual labor.[29] Few refugees learned any Chinese, recognizing that they were better served by learning English to communicate with the colonizers than by communicating with the colonized. For a time, the advantages of race trumped those of poverty, but Central European refugees became subject to a Japanese edict in 1943 that forced those scattered across the city's three sectors to relocate into a small section of Japanese-controlled Hongkou. They resettled in a small territory that would become known as the "Shanghai ghetto," and they were permitted to leave only with Japanese permission. By the end of the war, many had been made destitute, totally reliant on the aid of the American Jewish Joint Distribution Committee (JDC) that funded communal kitchens and provided very basic supplies.

After the defeat of Japan in August 1945, the Nationalist Chinese government sought to reassert control in Shanghai—not only in the Chinese sector but across the city. The Vichy French government had signed over control of the French Concession in 1943, and the United States and Britain signed agreements with China in 1942 relinquishing extraterritoriality, which also ceded control over the International Settlement. After eight years of war against an imperialist Japan and a century of de facto colonization under the "unequal treaties," the Nationalists were reasserting Chinese sovereignty. Stateless Jewish refugees found themselves in the crossfire.

In late 1945, the Chinese government issued a notice that all Germans, former Austrians, and German Jews would be repatriated to Germany, a suggestion that alarmed both the refugee community and UNRRA officials. In seeking clarification on the rule, Moses W. Beckelman of the Intergovernmental Committee on Refugees sought a meeting with Dr. Kan Nai-kuang and Wu Nan-ju, both of the Chinese Ministry of Foreign Affairs. According to Beckelman's report of the meeting, Wu commented that when the Central European refugees came to China in 1938 to 1941, "'advantage had been taken of China's inability at the time to enforce her rights,' that if application had been made to Chinese consular representatives at that time visas would not have been granted, that these refugees have had the opportunity of asylum in China for several years now and that they should leave as soon as they could."[30] Thus the future of these refugees became inherently tangled up with China's attempts to break free of its prewar neocolonial status, when Shanghai had been a "free port" only because the Chinese government had no control over it.

Still, the Chinese government's decision to lump Jewish refugees together with German citizens and even former Nazi Party members raised questions for those interested in refugee aid. While recognizing the rising tide of nationalism in China, Beckelman also suspected that the Jewish refugee population was also being used as a bargaining chip to ensure that UNRRA officials gave overseas Chinese repatriations proper attention:

> The countries to which externally displaced Chinese wish to return are for the most part under British or American control. Jewish refugees and their problems enjoy considerable sympathy in Great Britain and the United States. Hence, runs this speculation, the Chinese government hopes to trade the privilege of allowing refugees from Germany to remain in China against the extension of the right of the displaced Chinese to return to countries of pre-war residence.[31]

If this was a calculation, it badly overestimated the extent to which the United States could still influence the Philippines to accept returning Chinese and underestimated the degree of resistance to Chinese returnees in the British colonies. Moreover, it created a situation in which China was alone among the wartime United Nations in mandating refugee repatriation regardless of the wishes and desires of the migrants involved. By March 1946, the Chinese government agreed to a modification of its proclamation that allowed Jewish refugees to stay in China if their presence would benefit the Chinese, but otherwise only to remain until they could be repatriated by UNRRA or resettled by the Intergovernmental Committee.[32]

Before the Intergovernmental Committee could begin work in China, however, the newly established International Refugee Organization took over all refugee operations. When it was created, the IRO established in its constitution who qualified for aid as a "*bona fide* refugee." The list included refugees from Nazi Germany, Spanish Republicans, and anyone who was already considered a refugee before the outbreak of the Second World War. This last designation ensured that the IRO worldwide would accept responsibility for those displaced by the First World War or the Bolshevik Revolution. In China, this meant that thousands of Russian Jews and White Russians would be included in the IRO mandate, though this did not take formal effect until 1948, when Jennings Wong, the Chinese director of the Shanghai IRO office, determined that the funds were available to extend aid to displaced Russians.[33] Though the Chinese government made no immediate, formal objections to the expansion of the program in China, Wong commented to IRO Executive Secretary William Tuck, "there is probably little doubt that [Nationalist Chinese officials] do not regard our activities with any particular favor except perhaps in so far as we are successful in resettling [the Russians] and thereby getting them out of China."[34] China was, in fact, incredibly anxious for the resettlements to continue uninterrupted: to get the troublesome Europeans out as well as to aid the overseas Chinese.

The actual efforts on the ground to aid displaced Europeans in China experienced increasing challenges. The Chinese government through CNRRA balked at providing direct aid to European refugees, insisting that its greater obligation was to its own people.[35] And whether or not the Chinese government permitted refugees to stay, "not more than a few thousand [refugees] will be able to build an existence for themselves at Shanghai."[36] Indeed, few of the Central European refugees who had fled Nazi terror had ever considered Shanghai a long-term solution. In a survey conducted in early 1946 by the JDC, only 2.4 percent of the 13,475 Shanghai refugees receiving JDC aid gave remaining in China as their first choice for their future. By contrast, over 39 percent preferred emigration to the United States, with Australia and Palestine following as distant second or third choices. The rest hoped for repatriation or resettlement in another third country such as Canada, Britain, Argentina, or Brazil.[37] For stateless Russian Jews long resident or born in China, such as Rena Krasno, hopes divided between returning to familiar prewar life in Shanghai and making a new future elsewhere. Some were lifelong Zionists who anticipated making their way to Palestine as soon as transport and British regulations permitted.

Britain and other Western European countries accepted the first postwar wave of DPs as a part of rebuilding efforts but after that visas came predominantly from traditional countries of immigration: the United States first and foremost, but also Australia, Brazil, Canada, Argentina, and the rest of Latin America. All of these countries maintained either hard quotas or highly selective criteria for accepting refugees, so "hard cases" were left behind. For German Jews with access to the United States' large German quota, waiting for a spot to open up to emigrate took a year or two at most, after which a loan from the JDC (which received funding from both American Jews and directly from the IRO) made it possible to arrange passage across the Pacific to San Francisco. Lisbeth Epstein was Austrian (a country with a very small quota), but while in Shanghai she married a German Jew named Bruno Loewenberg. Their quota came up in 1948, which she recalls as "very late" because "the economy went down, and people started leaving in droves."[38] The IRO helped with travel documents and shipping details to allow the Loewenbergs and thousands of others to depart as the political situation in Shanghai grew increasingly uncertain.

The only option for many of the remaining refugees—including the "hard cases" whose age, health, or financial situation would not make them likely candidates for immigration visas elsewhere—was Israel. For the first ten months it was in operation, the IRO assisted with resettlement of DPs to Israel in small numbers, adhering to the limits set up by Britain as the Mandatory Power over Palestine. When war broke out in May 1948, the IRO suspended all such operations until hostilities ceased.[39] Starting in December 1948, a series of transports brought Jewish refugees from Shanghai to Israel, including Rena Krasno and her family in early 1949. The IRO reported resettling 9,175 refugees from Shanghai during its tenure, leaving only 1,700 Jewish refugees still in Shanghai by mid-1950.[40] Despite the challenges along the way, the shared goal of the IRO and the Chinese government to relocate displaced Jewish refugees experienced reasonable success. However, the IRO increasingly viewed the project through the twin lenses of humanitarian imperatives and emerging Cold War politics, while for the Chinese government it was part of a larger project to decolonize Shanghai. All three motivations clashed in the efforts to aid the third group of displaced foreigners targeted by the IRO, the White Russians.

The White Russian dilemma

White Russians in China posed a unique challenge for IRO officials and Chinese government representatives alike. First, the scope of the problem was vast: the UN High Commissioner for Refugees estimated that as of 1946, there were around 20,000 White Russians in Shanghai, Tianjin, Qingdao, and Beijing. Exact numbers for Manchuria were even harder to establish, though at their peak in 1935 there were at least 40,000 White Russian residents and likely many more.[41] Second, the Chinese civil war posed the greatest potential risk to these refugees, who had already fled communism once.[42] The refugees themselves experienced "great anxiety … that they might fall under communist jurisdiction, which in their case might mean forced repatriation to the USSR."[43] White Russians in China also had an unusual set of handicaps preventing them from easily obtaining visas for resettlement: a reputation of lawlessness in China, an unusually long period of exile, a large population unfit for manual labor (especially the aged and infirm), and, in some cases, USSR claims that they should be considered Soviet citizens. Postwar, some even faced charges as "*hanjian*," similar to the charges levelled against some Chinese as traitors, detailed in Yun Xia's research.[44] Instead of trying to process visas for every individual in the waning months of the civil war, the IRO opted to evacuate as many Russians from China as possible and then worry about sites of resettlement after they were safely out of Chinese territory.[45]

The British Foreign and Colonial Offices considered sending White Russians en masse to locations around their empire: Malaya, Singapore, North Borneo, Sri Lanka, and East Africa. Eventually, however, the solution came from American imperial ties instead: American servicemen helped the IRO convert a former US naval base near Samar Island in the Philippines into a makeshift DP camp. The Philippines remained reluctant to accept overseas Chinese repatriates from China, and the movement of some 5,000 White Russians to Samar in mid-1949 effectively closed the debate on that issue. Originally, IRO had a four-month deadline from the Philippine government, within which it needed to reprocess and ship out all of the refugees.[46] Though around 2,000 were accepted for emigration to Australia, and thousands more were slowly processed by the United States, completing the task was "like prying oysters off a rock," as the IRO Chief of mission in the Philippines described it.[47] It took three years to clear the camp, and even that only occurred after a direct hit from a typhoon.[48]

Even after emergency evacuations like the Philippines case and the mass transfer of Jews to Israel, thousands of Europeans remained in China, so between this and the ongoing overseas Chinese repatriations, the IRO stayed open through the founding of the PRC and the uncertain months that followed in late 1949. Communist China's reasons for tolerating and even cooperating with the IRO proved remarkably similar to those of the Nationalist government it had just defeated: it needed third-party help negotiating overseas Chinese repatriations, wanted to be rid of foreigners associated with the colonial era, and hoped that cooperation with a UN-founded international organization would lend credibility and legitimacy to the regime.[49]

M. C. Liang, who had worked as an eligibility officer and was promoted to director of the office in Shanghai, served as a diplomatic middleman between the new regime in China and the overwhelmingly British IRO representatives based in Hong Kong.[50] In 1951, Liang commented in a letter,

> Assimilation is obviously impossible, nor is it at all possible to place refugees into the local economy without the creation of special work-projects capitalized with IRO funds ... Our office is literally besieged by panic-stricken eligibles whose pathetic appeals were echoed to you in our two cables No. 277 and 285 of June 25 and 29, 1951, urging total evacuation.

He argued that the IRO, having taken responsibility for these people, needed to complete the task.[51]

Repatriating or resettling Russian refugees after 1949 revealed the increasingly politicized nature of IRO work. In the aftermath of the Second World War, the Soviet consulates in China announced an amnesty program in which White Russians were offered Soviet passports and encouraged to repatriate. As news trickled back of the hard life returnees faced, many White Russians-turned-Red Russians attempted to become "white" again by renouncing Soviet citizenship, becoming in the words of one such man, "pink."[52] After 1949, those newly pink Russians faced increased difficulty gaining permission to leave China for anywhere other than the Soviet Union.[53] The Soviet Union preferred that all Russians in China be repatriated and in 1954 announced a "right of return" that would ensure Russians in China would be universally accepted. For the next three years, it was difficult for Russians to obtain exit visas from the Chinese authorities for any destination other than the Soviet Union.[54]

Even before 1954, Chinese Communist officials sometimes limited or delayed exit permits for Soviet citizens attempting to depart for the West, but the IRO also rarely sent any refugee to an Eastern Bloc nation. By 1953, the PRC's Ministry of Foreign Affairs considered it so novel that the IRO would resettle someone to a new "People's Republic" they sent a special telegram to Shanghai asking for details about a White Russian woman moving to Czechoslovakia.[55] Chinese authorities questioned whether she or others like her might be spies planted by the American CIA, as detailed in one *People's Daily* article that cast the United States as the villain, treating the IRO as an unwitting dupe of Western imperialist trickery.[56] Resettling outside China or Russia came with a host of bureaucratic difficulties: to go to Brazil, as many White Russians did, meant first submitting pre-clearance materials to the IRO for communication with the Brazilian consulate in Hong Kong, as there was no Brazilian consul available on the Chinese mainland. Migrants then needed a medical exam, an exit permit, a quarantine certificate with vaccinations, and identity papers or travel documents. Upon exiting China into Hong Kong, a trip that in the early 1950s would be arranged through the quasi-state-run China Travel Service, they could go to the Brazilian consulate to complete the visa application. During their stay in Hong Kong, migrants would be transferred over to the care of UNHCR. Each new certification had a limited validity, so getting all the documents in order and timed perfectly proved an unexpected barrier to emigration for some DPs.[57]

What is remarkable throughout the post-1949 narrative of the IRO in China is the pragmatism with which both the IRO and the new Communist Chinese officials went about their work. Though the IRO's work in Europe became increasingly consumed by Cold War tensions that pitted American and British IRO officials against Soviet critics of their work, Communist China did not have substantially more disputes with the IRO than the Nationalists before it. The forces that pushed IRO work into a more political narrative largely came from the United States and the Soviet Union, and the IRO in Shanghai was at its most effective when it was able to ignore them both.

Those who remained

By 1956, when the IRO finally closed its doors in Shanghai, only a few hundred "hard cases" remained of European refugees under IRO care who had not successfully resettled or repatriated out of China. The JDC continued to work with cases involving Jews, usually by securing permission for them to travel to Israel, and other organizations such as the United Friends Service Committee and UNHCR advocated for non-Jewish Russians and Eastern Europeans to travel to whatever country would take them. Into the 1960s, British consular officials monitored a small trickle of migrants continuing to leave, and voluntary agencies in some cases provided funds for convalescent homes to those too elderly or ill to further contemplate departure.[58] The DP problem in China was never fully "solved" so much as it was overcome by subsequent events.

The record of the International Refugee Organization in China proved stronger than anyone suspected, given the domestic turmoil in China and international conflict in which it operated. Part of that success was due to its ability to occupy a liminal space suspended between China's ally status in the Second World War and the hardening of Cold War ideologies later in the 1950s. Both Chinese governments—the Chinese Nationalists and the Chinese Communists—pursued positive relations with the IRO for their own purposes. These were largely the same: the successful repatriation of the overseas Chinese, financial and resettlement aid to European refugees, and a desire to use cooperation with a UN organization as a means to bolster government legitimacy at a time when the claim to it was highly contingent. The IRO office finally closed its doors for good in 1956, with the Chinese People's Relief Association taking over relief payments to the remaining "hard cases."[59] As the office closed, a British consul in Beijing theorized that the urgent desire to effect the departure of the refugees demonstrated as early as 1945 by the Nationalist government continued a decade later, explaining that the PRC "[did] not seem to care which way refugees leave China as long as they do leave."[60]

Throughout the six years that the IRO operated under the Communist government, the latter showed a remarkable degree of flexibility in cooperating with the organization, prioritizing common interests over pressure from its Soviet ally and even their own anti-imperialist rhetoric. Though the position of the Shanghai office and its head, M. C. Liang, grew increasingly fraught as the Korean War raged and American and Nationalist Chinese propagandists started to make political hay out of the growing refugee crisis in Hong Kong caused by Chinese fleeing communist rule on the mainland, the work continued unabated. This suggests a different nature to the IRO position in the emergence of the Asian Cold War in comparison with the European. Instead of being one more weapon of the West to oppose the spread of communism, the IRO Shanghai office stood as an oasis amidst growing tensions, a rare space where opposing sides cooperated toward a common goal.

That said, the relationship between the various UN-affiliated organizations and both Chinese governments still often struggled to overcome the legacy of European and American colonialism in Asia. The presence of Europeans in Shanghai—even as displaced persons—raised concerns for Nationalist officials in 1945 that never abated. Consternation about unequal treatment for European and Chinese refugees proved consistent throughout the decade of operations. Decolonization also had a tremendous impact on the ability of the UNRRA and later the IRO to negotiate the return of displaced overseas Chinese to their former homes. Chinese sovereignty became the ultimate argument for closing the office when the time came, as the idea of having international forces managing Chinese affairs grew increasingly unpalatable. When the central modus operandi for cooperation between the PRC and these UN-based operations finally broke, it stayed that way until the United Nations finally admitted the People's Republic of China in 1971.

Notes

1 Rena Krasno, *Strangers Always: A Jewish Family in Wartime Shanghai* (Berkeley, CA: Pacific View Press, 2000), p. 198.
2 Based on contemporary estimates, an institutional history of the International Refugee Organization estimated that 20 million Chinese were displaced by the war, but a more recent study has suggested the number of internally displaced Chinese is closer to 80 million, and possibly as high as 100 million. See Louise W. Holborn, *The International Refugee Organization: A Specialized Agency of the United Nations:*

Its History and Work, 1946–1952 (New York: Oxford University Press, 1956), p. 15; Rana Mitter, *Forgotten Ally: China's World War II, 1937–1945* (Boston, MA: Houghton Mifflin Harcourt, 2013), p. 123.

3 The scope of the crisis was compounded by the addition of millions of displaced troops also requiring repatriation. Rotem Kowner, "The Impact of Surrendered Japanese Troops on the Postwar Recolonization and Decolonization of East Asia," in Barak Kushner and Andrew Levidis, eds., *In the Ruins of the Japanese Empire: Imperial Violence, State Destruction, and the Reordering of Modern East Asia*, Hong Kong: Hong Kong University Press (forthcoming); see also Araragi Shinzo, "The Collapse of the Japanese Empire and the Great Migration: Repatriation, Assimilation, and Remaining Behind," in *The Dismantling of Japan's Empire in East Asia: Deimperialization, Postwar Legitimation and Imperial Afterlife* (London: Routledge, 2017), pp. 66–83.

4 George Woodbridge, *UNRRA: The History of the United Nations Relief and Rehabilitation Administration* (New York: Columbia University Press, 1950), p. 371.

5 Holborn, *The International Refugee Organization,* p. 200.

6 See Gerard Daniel Cohen, *In War's Wake: Europe's Displaced Persons in the Postwar Order* (New York: Oxford University Press, 2012); Ben Shephard, *The Long Road Home: The Aftermath of the Second World War* (New York: Alfred A. Knopf, 2011); Gil Loescher, *The UNHCR and World Politics: A Perilous Path* (New York: Oxford University Press, 2001); Kim Salomon, *Refugees in the Cold War* (Lund: Studentlitteratur, 1991).

7 "International Refugee Organization," *International Organization* 1, no. 1 (1947), p. 137.

8 I have explored these arguments for joining in more detail elsewhere: Meredith Oyen, "The Right of Return: Chinese Displaced Persons and the International Refugee Organization, 1947–56," *Modern Asian Studies* 49, no. 2 (March 2015), pp. 546–571.

9 Hu Cheong On to Repatriation Branch Office, Hong Kong, April 30, 1947, S-1129–0000-0758 Repatriation of Chinese, UNRRA-China, Archives of the United Nations, New York, NY (hereafter UN Archive).

10 UNRRA Third Session of the Council, Subcommittee on Displaced Persons in the Far East, August 18, 1945, *UNRRA Standing Technical Committee on Displaced Persons, 1943–1946,* UN Archive.

11 Memorandum, Displaced Persons, August 15, 1945, S-0528–0009-0001 DP Operations, UNRRA-China, UN Archive.

12 In a December 1945 report, the China office of UNRRA summarized the main groups requiring their assistance for repatriation to include: non-Chinese foreigners (arriving both during and before the war), Koreans who took refuge in China, Chinese hoping to return to Taiwan, overseas Chinese returning to their homes overseas, displaced Chinese in the Philippines, and ex-prisoners of war in Japan seeking return to China. This list was not comprehensive, but it did demonstrate the complexity of the early operations directed at externally displaced persons. Six Month Report, UNRRA China Office, June 13 to December 13, 1945, China Office Reports, Record Group 67.059, UNRRA China Office, Records of UNRRA, United States Holocaust Memorial Museum (hereafter USHMM).

13 Pierce Williams to Myer Cohen, March 15, 1946, *UNRRA Standing Technical Committee on Displaced Persons, 1943–1946,* UN Archive.

14 DH Clarke, Dir Repat Branch Office, UNRRA HK, to Glen E. Edgerton, Maj Gen, USA, Dir UNRRA China offices, September 22, 1946, 370/77, Overseas Chinese Affairs Commission, Number Two Historical Archive, Nanjing, People's Republic of China; Feilubin waijiaobu dian fu zhongguo waijiaobu jujue huaqiao jingyou lianheguo shanhou jiuji zongshu zhu xianggang banshichu fagei lxing qianzheng

fanhui Fei jing, November 23, 1946, in *Repatriated Overseas Chinese After World War II: A Documentary Collection,* vol. 2 (Taipei: Academia Historica, 2004), pp. 303–304.

15 Washington Embassy to Nanjing MOFA, Telegram 4571, April 15, 1947, 642/0049, Guojinanminzuzhi zhinan, Archives of the Ministry of Foreign Affairs, Institute of Modern History, Academia Sinica, Taipei, Taiwan (hereafter MOFA Taipei).

16 In 1945, CNRRA established that it would only provide financial aid to the European DPs at a rate equal to that given to Chinese DPs, knowing "it was inadequate as far as foreigners were concerned but a matter of principle was involved," Memorandum of Conversation over dinner with T. F. Hsiang, Director General of CNRRA, November 6, 1945, S-1121–0000-0118 DPs – European, UN Archive.

17 T. Y. Hsiang to Benjamin H. Kizer, January 20, 1946, S-1132–0000-0047 DPs – European – Accounts, UN Archive.

18 Chinese National Relief and Rehabilitation Administration memo on the IRO, December 1, 1946, 642/0049, Guojinanminzuzhi zhinan, MOFA Taipei; Washington Embassy to Nanjing MOFA, Telegram 4571, April 15, 1947, 642/0049, Guojinanminzuzhi zhinan, MOFA Taipei.

19 Holborn, *The International Refugee Organization*, p. 767.

20 Aide Memoire, December 23, 1947, Foreign Office (hereafter FO) 371/107252, the National Archives of the United Kingdom (hereafter TNA).

21 Draft resolution on the problem of refugees and displaced persons in the Far East, May 19, 1947, 642/0055, Guojinanminzuzhi Zhinan, MOFA Taipei.

22 Huadong xun [Min zhewei] guanyu nanmin chuguo chuli banfa, September 20, 1950, 113–00125-01(1), Archive of the Ministry of Foreign Affairs, Beijing, People's Republic of China (hereafter MOFA Beijing).

23 David Kranzler, *Japanese, Nazis & Jews: The Jewish Refugee Community of Shanghai, 1938–1945* (Yeshiva University Press, 1976), pp. 57–58.

24 Krasno, 9.

25 "Entry of Refugees to Shanghai," *North China Daily News*, October 22, 1939, File 2972, Reel 4, Records of the Shanghai Municipal Archive, USHMM.

26 Kranzler, 86.

27 Liliane Willens, *Stateless in Shanghai* (Hong Kong: Earnshaw Books, 2010), p. 35.

28 Berl Falbaum, ed., *Shanghai Remembered: Stories of Jews Who Escaped to Shanghai from East Europe* (Troy, MI: Momentum Books, 2005), p. 121.

29 Ernest Heppner, *Shanghai Refuge: A Memoir of the World War II Jewish Ghetto* (Lincoln: University of Nebraska Press, 1995), p. 43.

30 M. W. Beckelman, Summary of Conversation at Chinese Ministry of Foreign Affairs, February 26, 1946, AJ43/699 File 55/2, Reel 3, RG043.048M Organization Internationale Pour Les Refugies, 1944–1955 (hereafter IRO), United States Holocaust Memorial Museum, Washington, D.C. (hereafter USHMM).

31 M. W. Beckelman to Herbert, January 27, 1946, AJ43/699 File 55/2, Reel 3, IRO, USHMM.

32 Text of Statement Agreed Upon Between M. W. Beckelman, Intergovernmental Committee on Refugess, and Mr. Wu Nan-Ju, Ministry of Foreign Affairs, for issue by Mr. Beckelman as a News Release, March 8, 1946, AJ43/699 File 55/2, Reel 3, IRO, USHMM.

33 Jennings Wong to Dr. George Yeh, June 2, 1948, 642/0058, Guojinanminzuzhi zhinan, MOFA Taipei.

34 Jennings Wong to William H. Tuck, August 5, 1948, FO371/72086B, TNA.

35 Memo to China Department, Foreign office, from Eleanor M. Hinder, May 10, 1948, Preparatory Commission of the International Refugee Organization (Far East): Russian Refugee Program in China, FO371/72086B, TNA.

36   Ed Egle to International Red Cross Committee, September 24, 1945, S-1121–0000-0118 DPs – European, UNRRA-China, UN Archive.

37   American Jewish Joint Distribution Committee, Statistical Analysis of 13,475 Refugees in Shanghai, China as of January 1 to March 31, 1946, AJ43/699 File 55/2, Reel 3, IRO, USHMM.

38   Hochstadt, 194.

39   Third Session, Report of the Director-General on Immigration into the Countries of the Middle East, December 22, 1948, AJ43/387 File VS/92/10, Reel 2, IRO, USHMM.

40   Note on Operations in China, June 24, 1950, AJ43/706 File 55/2, Reel 4, IRO, USHMM.

41   Letter to Kenneth H. Summers from L. Stumpf, September 11, 1953, CO 1023/119, TNA.

42   Minutes, Emergency Measures being considered for the evacuation of Jewish and White Russian DPs, FO 371/72086B, TNA.

43   M. A. Grimaud to Myer Cohen, November 29, 1948, AJ43/706 File 55/2, Reel 4, IRO, USHMM.

44   Meeting about special classes in Shanghai – White Russians, Jews, Indians, Stateless people, October 11, 1945, Q-127-8-284, Song Hu jingbei silingbu waishichu guanyu dui rijun tezhong qiaomin, bai'e, youtairen guanli banfa ji jingbeibu dierci waishi zuotan huiyi jilu deng, Shanghai Municipal Archive, Shanghai, China (hereafter SMA); Yun Xia, *Down with Traitors: Justice and Nationalism in Wartime China* (Seattle: University of Washington Press, 2017).

45   Fraser Newham, "The White Russians of Shanghai," *History Today* 55, no. 12 (December 2005), pp. 20–27; European Refugees and DPs, n.d., AJ43/700 File 55/2, Reel 3, IRO, USHMM.

46   IRO Executive Committee, 3rd Session, January 26, 1949; Telegram from Shanghai to Foreign Office, January 18, 1949, FO 371/78187, TNA; Holborn, *The International Refugee Organization*, pp. 423–425.

47   Frederick Thompson to Ernest Griegg, September 24, 1951, AJ43/1080, Reel 7, IRO, USHMM.

48   Thompson to Liang, December 19, 1951, 1951113099159–02(1) Guojinanminzuzhi shanghaizhi youguan qiansong dianhan, December 1951–January 1952, MOFA Beijing.

49   Huadong xun, guanyu diancha fu guojinanminsushi deng shi, July 25, 1950, 113–00125-01(1) Guojinanminjigou shentan woxin zhengfu de zhengce, zai woguo shantou, shanghai jieshu gongzuo ji qiansong nanmin qingkuang 1949, MOFA Beijing.

50   Joseph Liao to John Donald Kingsley, February 20, 1950, AJ43/700 File 55/2, Reel 3, IRO, USHMM. IRO was dominated by Americans in Europe, but not in Asia.

51   M. C. Liang to Frederick Thompson, n.d. 113–00077-01(1) Guanyu Guojinanminzuzhi tianjin banshichu jieshu gongzuo de qingkuang baodao, MOFA Beijing.

52   Marcia R. Ristaino, *Port of Last Resort: The Diaspora Communities of Shanghai* (Stanford, CA: Stanford University Press, 2001), pp. 253–254; Letter from H. W. Shaiditzhy to DP Commission, January 15, 1950, Shanghai Refugees, Box 53, RG 278, NACP.

53   A. M. Bagg, The Plight of Soviet Jews in China, June 25, 1956, FO 371/121166, TNA.

54 Laurie Manchester, "Repatriation to a Totalitarian Homeland: The Ambiguous Alterity of Russian Repatriates from China to the USSR," *Diaspora: A Journal of Transnational Studies* 16, no. 3 (December 2007), p. 359.

55 According to the writer, it was actually the first time that the IRO had ever resettled someone from Shanghai to a People's Republic other than repatriations to the USSR. Qingshi kefou chongxu suqiao oujeiko Helene chujing, February 10, 1953, 113–00177-01(1) Guanyu guojinanminzuzhi shanghaizhi qiansong suqiaomin fu balagui, jieke shi, MOFA Beijing.

56 "Meidi zai ruishi xunlian jiandie," January 9, 1950, *Renmin Ribao.*

57 Lang to China Travel Service, May 17, 1952, Q-368-1-806 Zhongguo luxingshe tianjin fenshe 1952 nian yu lianheguo guojinanminzuzhi shanghai banshichu deng laiwan wenshu, pp. 301–400, SMC.

58 See FCO141/14983 Singapore: The Movement of White Russian Refugees from China through Singapore, 1958–1959, TNA; FO 371/175955 White Russian Refugees in Sinkiang, 1964, TNA.

59 MOFA to Shanghai, telegram, May 22, 1956, 113–00287-01(1), Chuli he jieshu lianheguo guijinanminzuzhi shanghaizhi wenti, MOFA Beijing.

60 Letter to A. H. Campbell, British Embassy Peking, from R. T. D. Ledward, October 31, 1956, FO 371/121166, TNA.

Chapter 3

EARLY NARRATIVES OF JAPAN'S KOREAN WAR

Samuel Perry

It was June 1950 when a nineteen-year-old Korean man named Ch'oe Pyŏn-de first heard that North Korean leader Kim Il-sung had ordered his troops to invade South Korea. Ch'oe was working at the time on an American military transport ship, sailing between the South Korean port of Pusan and the US military port of Sasebo, Japan. Convinced that a full-scale war was imminent, he decided to desert ship once he had entered Japan on his temporary shore pass. Having spent much of his youth in Japan, Ch'oe had little difficulty finding friends in his former home with whom he could live under an assumed identity. Eventually he managed to obtain a visa from a sympathetic bureaucrat who wished to support a young Korean, newly determined to enter a Japanese university, and return to his homeland upon graduation to help rebuild his war-torn nation.[1]

The crossing of the Straits separating the main islands of Japan and the Korean Peninsula—a distance of some 200 km—was hardly an uncommon or particularly arduous journey, historically speaking. Once Japan had made Korea a Protectorate in 1905, and then annexed it in 1910, Japanese colonists and businessmen began pouring across the Straits onto the Korean peninsula for the next thirty-five years, while Koreans moved eastward toward Japanese cities in search of work and education. During its colonization by Japan, Korea also became one of the most important gateways to Japan's growing empire on the Asian continent, which only intensified this seafaring traffic. In 1945, when the Second World War ended, however, millions of Koreans and Japanese soon found themselves moving again in opposite directions, as the post-Second World War governments of Japan and Korea began facilitating a process whereby people "displaced" by the Japanese Empire were "put back" into their proper places.[2] The onset of the Korean War, which began in late June 1950, and ended only with an armistice in July 1953, precipitated yet another wave of wartime migration, largely from South Korea to Japan. Ch'oe Pyŏn-de's surreptitious, but successful, re-entry into Japan was one of the first to take place after the outbreak of the Korean War, with thousands following in his wake. Journalistic accounts published at the time, however, tended to narrate such wartime crossings as acts of "illegal entry" into Japan, and war migrants—when they were of Korean heritage that is—were subject to arrest, deportation, and even imprisonment. "Tales of escape" (dasshutsuki) from war-torn Korea to a peaceful, postwar Japan—on the part of both Japanese and Koreans alike—would also proliferate in the Japanese media in the early 1950s and slowly solidify into a more abiding narrative through which Japan came to see both its postwar history, and its changing relationship to the Korean people. As I argue here, such Korean War narratives in Japan, more generally speaking, became a means by which the Japanese came to relive Japan's Second World War memories and also, importantly, sought to articulate a new postwar identity.

In line with other contributions to this volume, this chapter seeks to explore the contours of the post-Second World War reconstruction of East Asia but does so with a particular focus on early Japanese narratives of the Korean War, which serve as a window onto processes of post-Second World War cultural reconstruction. Although filed away in the forgotten annals of Japanese history for several decades, Japan's connection to the Korean War was instrumental to the rebuilding of modern Japan and played a key role in the recreation of Japanese culture.[3] After five years of US Occupation, in June 1950, Japan became the headquarters for US efforts to plan and fight the Korean War. Almost overnight a defeated country seen as "a land of too many people, too little food," became a site of enormous strategic importance to the United States: a new "bulwark," as *Life* magazine put it, against the encroachment of communism in Asia.[4] The Korean War saw no fighting in Japan proper, but the war still had extraordinary consequences for the UN-occupied nation. American General Douglas MacArthur had already purged members of the Japanese Communist Party from government offices in Japan several weeks before the Korean War broke out, but with the onset of the war he expanded this "red purge" of both party members and fellow travelers to news organizations, publishers, film studios, and broadcasters in July 1950.[5] Japan's post-Second World War rearmament began shortly thereafter under the guise of a new national police reserves, ostensibly a police force, but equipped and employed like a paramilitary with .30 caliber rifles and military tanks. The Korean war witnessed a massive expansion of US military bases and troop levels in Japan, as well, and over the course of the Korean War billions of US dollars were injected into Japan's once formidable industrial-military complex—amounting to at least 25 percent of its export market. This had the effect of revitalizing Japan's depressed economy and restoring its population back to almost full-time employment. Before an armistice was signed in 1953, the terms "special procurement economy" (*tokujū keizai*) and Korean War boom (*Chōsen dōran būmu*) had already become the catch phrases used to describe the first years of a war which would flatten most of North Korea's cities, kill roughly one-eighth of the Korean population, and at the same time precipitate a remarkable upswing in Japan's economy.

This revitalization of Japan's economic base via the Korean War procurement industry had consequences for the refashioning of Japan's superstructure—which is to say that wide range of cultural practices by which a newly defeated Japan took measure of these material transformations.[6] Wolfgang Schivelbusch makes an argument relevant to a number of places around the world, which also applies to the case of twentieth-century Japan, that the reinvention of defeated nations involved a process of myth-making closely connected to efforts on the part of an elite to retain power.[7] Indeed, among the most enduring myths at the heart of twentieth-century Japanese history is the very notion of a "postwar" Japan itself: an era that came in the wake of Japan's imperial loss to the Allied Powers, who refashioned the former aggressor into a peace-loving and prosperous nation.[8] This postwar myth was not a historical inevitability. It took time for Japanese society to find ways of accommodating the contradictions of an ambiguously postwar Japan, whose 1947 US-imposed constitution had renounced both war and a standing army, but whose US Occupiers forced Japan to cooperate in the Korean War effort, rebuild its army, and reboot its military-industrial complex.[9] A history of Japanese activism certainly shows that collective inquiry and dissent were to some extent possible even during the Korean War, though information about the war was kept tightly under wraps in the press.[10] A wide variety of early narratives about the Korean War, which often played a role in reconstructing memories of the Second World War, also suggests the diversity of positions from which the Japanese people were reimagining the new identity of their nation in relation to the Korean Peninsula— once its closest colony, and the former home to millions of Japanese. The state of concurrent colonialisms in which occupied Japan found itself ensnared, however, placed specific pressures and limits on the production of Korean War narratives. In what had once been a formidable empire that had lasted almost eighty years —a country newly colonized by the United States and insufficiently decolonized of its imperial culture—narratives that were more likely to symbolically resolve these "postwar" contradictions than to foreground them enjoyed prominence in the mainstream Japanese press before and after US Occupation.

This chapter briefly explores the broader field of these contradictions, shedding light on a wide spectrum of voices that made it into print during the early years of the Korean War before turning more concertedly to the work of one writer in particular, a widely published ethnic Korean writer named Chang Hyŏk-chu, who legally became a Japanese citizen in 1952 as soon as it was possible to do so. Stories about the Korean War written by Chang became subsumed within a system of postwar myth-making, joining a body of writings that would soon eclipse those voices which were more critical in their assessment of Japan's postwar, and postcolonial, contradictions. The prominence given to writings of authors such as Chang not only contributed to the reinforcement of colonial bias against Koreans but also help demonstrate how the Korean War worked to impede rather than promote the decolonization process of postwar Japanese culture.

Perceived indifference in the Women's Democratic News

Many of the earliest and most vocal opponents to the Korean War were women. Pioneering Japanese feminist Hiratsuka Raichō, co-founder of the women's magazine *Blue Stocking* (Seitō) in 1911, was a leading voice of early protest against Japan's involvement in the Korean War. "We read over the Japanese constitution," Hiratsuka wrote in September 1950, referring to the legal document written in

1946 that had barred Japan from ever maintaining an army or engaging in war, "and invariably we think, 'How on earth could we have allowed things to come this far?' We can never forget the extraordinary sacrifices that we have already suffered."[11] Hiratsuka joined four renowned stateswomen in submitting to the US government one of the first official declarations against the Korean War, a declaration later printed in the *Women's Democratic News* (Fujin minshu shimbun), the official organ of the highly influential Women's Democratic Club, founded in 1946, with over twenty branches throughout Japan.[12]

Hiratsuka's anti-war sentiments were shared by many ordinary Japanese citizens. In a letter to the editor of the *Women's Democratic News*, published about one year before the end of Japan's occupation by US forces in April 1952, Tani Toshiko, an elementary school teacher in Japan's former colony wrote nostalgically about her time as a Japanese woman in Korea in an op-ed entitled, "My thoughts on Korea – the land where I was born." But as one of millions of recent Japanese "returnees" (*hikiagesha*) from the colony, she quickly turned her nostalgic reflections into an occasion for asserting the "evils" of colonization and a sense of guilt for her own support of armed conflict during the Second World War.

> Now I regret what I did. I wonder why, back then, I was not able to teach that "war is the most heinous of all crimes committed in the world." All I can do now is raise my voice as loudly as I can, and make an appeal to as many Japanese as possible: Let us cease this war that sacrifices so many blameless citizens in Korea, and work as hard as we can for the day when peace shall reign over all.[13]

The urgency of Tani's appeal was animated by a lament that so many of her fellow Japanese had become utterly "indifferent to the evils of foreign troops in Korea." Tani's voice was but one of many expressing the importance of peace in the women's newspaper. Journalists working for the *Women's Democratic News* often documented anti-war sentiments expressed not only by women but also by children. A February 1951 article, calling attention to new military procurement jobs available for working-class youth, finds in the country's teenagers a stubborn resistance to any participation in the military industrial complex. "I got no interest in making weapons used to fight wars with other countries," announced one boy preparing to graduate from Haginaka Middle School in Tokyo's Ota Ward. "There's not much I can do if they conscript me against my will, but if I had a choice, I'd never work in a place like that," declared another.[14] According to their guidance counselor, all of these children wished to find stable, long-term employment prospects and were uninterested in the higher-paying jobs offered by the procurement industries. If a truly "postwar" Japan existed in this moment of Japanese history, it certainly resided in the hopes and dreams of these Japanese middle-school students, who were unequivocal about their opposition to the Korean War—even if, as the journalist acknowledges, maintaining their postwar principles in a procurement-driven economy was likely to be impossible.

What Tani called "indifference" in 1951 on the part of her fellow Japanese was indeed a complicated affair. The impoverishment of Japanese families during the Second World War had led many people to make the practical decision of taking jobs in the Korean War procurement industry, tens of thousands of people making fabric for soldiers' uniforms and tents, but just as many others refurbishing military vehicles and manufacturing the kinds of weapons that had only a few years earlier incinerated their own family members—and would soon be used to burn the cities of North Korea to the ground.[15] If details about the US bombing of Japanese civilians during World War II were largely contained by the kinds of censorship mandated by Occupation authorities, those who had connections to people living in Tokyo, Hiroshima, and Nagasaki certainly knew of the unimaginable horrors that the US Armed Forces had inflicted in bombing raids during the Second World War.[16] If the Japanese people were "indifferent," as Tani Toshiko put it in the *Women's Democratic News*, this indifference was not a matter of individual apathy on the part of working people who had lived through those horrors but rather a structure of feeling hemmed in by the political and economic structures of abiding empire and occupation.

While the *Women's Democratic News* was prevented by Occupation-era regulations from disclosing the details of the fighting in Korea, the newspaper was consistent in its demand that the Korean War must end and that Japan must refrain from remilitarizing itself amidst Cold War tensions. The paper embraced its role in what it also saw as a broader cultural struggle to carve out the contours of a truly "postwar" Japan in the face of powerful institutional efforts to erase memories of Japanese wartime and colonial aggression, and even to celebrate its imperial achievements. Several days after the returnee Tani Toshiko published her op-ed article, for example, the *Women's Democratic News* offered details about a dispute between officials at Keio University and its teachers' union over a decision at one of its feeder schools to distribute Meiji era ethics texts to middle school students. These texts, written in the late nineteenth century by the patriot Fukuzawa Yukichi, urged the fledgling modern Japanese State to "build up its armed forces," insisted that Japanese "citizens not forget their obligation to fight Japan's sworn enemies in the effort to protect its existence," and demanded that "Japan's loyal subjects serve the chamber of the unbroken imperial line."[17] Another article published on the same day details the removal of a Fukuoka high school student from a speech contest when the anti-war theme of his talk was deemed too controversial by school officials. By documenting the experiences of individuals and communities across the country who struggled to inject a new postwar consciousness into the minds of Japan's youth, the *Women's Democratic News* attempted to make visible the residual influence of an ultranationalist elite, once loyal to the Second World War militarist government, which still proliferated in positions of authority throughout Japanese institutions in the final years of the US Occupation. The implication in their articles was that educational institutions —both public and private, which should have been committed to fostering the growth of a new, peaceful, democratic nation—had been insufficiently purged of an imperialist vision in their uppermost ranks. Equally upsetting to editors of the progressive newspaper was the conduct of their fellow editors at some of Japan's more renowned and influential publications, who often failed to make important connections between the Korean War and Japanese imperialism, and in some cases seemed happy to absolve Japan of any responsibility for the civil war that had recently broken out in its former colony.

Women's Review *and the forgetting of colonial history*

One case in point was the journal *Women's Review* (Fujin kōron), Japan's ostensibly "highbrow" women's magazine with a long and distinguished history, which offers a typical example of how the Korean War was reported in Japan's mainstream press during the US Occupation, effectively whitewashing Japan of its recent colonial history. It took the journal six months to offer much information at all about the Korean War, but in January 1951, it published a special section called "*Women's Review* travels to Korea." The short selection of articles was prefaced by a general piece on "international politics" by a hawkish diplomatic critic—Kase Shun'ichi—who insisted that Japan's remilitarization was the only way to ensure peace at a time when freedom was under threat from communism. Making comparisons between Japan and Western Germany, Kase placed Korea firmly within a Cold War framework, at the nexus of an epic battle between the light of democracy and the darkness of totalitarianism, his presentism effectively cutting off the Korean War entirely from Korea's earlier experience of colonization.

"Escaping the Chaos" (*dōran wo nogarete*) was the title of a round table discussion (*zadankai*) held at the journal's headquarters and published in this special section of the *Women's Review*. At a time when many Japanese feared the outbreak of a Third World War, and others sought to downplay the fierce fighting on the Korean Peninsula, a variety of terms was used to name what was going on in Korea in 1950: "incident" (*jihen*), "fighting" (*tatakai*), "chaos" (*dōran*), "battle fires" (*senka*), though rarely the term "war" (*sensō*) itself. The old-fashioned word "chaos" was a favorite however, and tended to perpetuate a fear that the instability of its war-torn Korean neighbor might well spill over to Japan itself. The roundtable conversation published in the *Women's Review* featured the editor in chief of the *Dong-a ilbo*, a leading newspaper in Korea, as well as several other prominent Koreans. But not surprisingly it was the voice of a young student, named Pak Imsuk, who became the privileged speaker in the highly edited roundtable talk. Pak Im-suk was given a chance to relate a terrifying tale of her flight through North Korea and her harrowing crossing into the South. But even in South Korea, Pak found that university students were quick to label her a "Commie," and she bemoaned the ideological nature of both North and South Korea. No one else in the roundtable discussion—even the editor of the *Dong-a ilbo*—was allowed to rebut the generalizations Pak offered, which are particularly compelling given the first-person narration of her experiences. Pak's personal story in fact echoed what was already evident in a steady stream of narratives relating the valiant efforts of Japanese women to "escape the North" in the aftermath of the Second World War as well as in the tales of former Japanese colonialists still trapped in communist North Korea.[18]

A second article in the January 1951 issue of *Women's Review* was written by former colonialist and historian of early Korean history Kamata Takuichirō, who attempted to explain Korea's Cold War division in terms of the nation's long history of internecine conflict, and what he called the Korean "fighting mentality" (*tōsō seishin*). Digging deep into the historiographical record, going back one thousand years, Kamata offered copious details on the factionalism rife in each period of ancient Korean history, reducing the Korean War to the inevitable consequence of a nation whose elite simply could not get along. Kamata's account is in fact remarkable for the derivative nature of its historical claims, which echoed decades of essentialist Korean histories written by Japanese scholars, whose conclusions usually worked to justify Japanese colonial rule over the Korean Peninsula. A final feature in this issue of *Women's Review* was a light-hearted account by a US journalist, the soon-to-be Pulitzer Prize winner Hal Boyle. With delightful detail, Boyle described interactions between US soldiers and the Korean children with whom they shared their meals, and related the embarrassing situation US troops often found themselves in when frisking Korean women, who were accustomed to baring their breasts when nursing children. This was a narrative of bashful young American boys doing their best to help the people of Korea despite cultural differences, a narrative consistent with the flattering portraits of US soldiers promoted by the US Occupying forces in Japan.

If the kind of reporting on the Korean War found in *Women's Review* dovetailed with classical orientalist discourse in that it largely ignored the experience of native laboring bodies in favor of the perspectives and feelings of their colonizers and their elite, even the Japanese historian of Korea refused to reflect on Korea's more recent history as a colony, and the crucial role that Japan played in helping to create the very conditions for Korea's partition. That each of the purportedly "diverse" opinions on the Korean War in *Women's Review*—Kase's diplomatic analysis, Pak's personal narrative of escape, Kamata's essentialist history, and the jovial tale spun by the embedded American journalist—all completely avoided the tragic conditions on the ground can in part be explained by pressures placed on journalists by the US Occupation. But they also circumvented any discussion of two related elephants in the room: the colonial origins of North Korea's leadership in guerrilla warfare against the Japanese and the pedigree of South Korea's military leadership, who had been trained in the Japanese Kwantung Army and remained almost entirely unpurged even after the Second World War. Any historically informed assessments of the postcolonial devastation of the Korean peninsula and the suffering of its people were replaced in this highbrow, intellectual journal by the epic abstractions of Cold War conflict, details of Korean antiquity, and descriptions of youthfully optimistic, benevolent actors—tender-hearted doughboys and resourceful Korean kids. The lack of a postcolonial consciousness in journals such as *Women's Review* was directly related to the state of concurrent colonialisms in Japan; it is but one example of how public discourse on the Korean War often worked to exacerbate Japan's historical amnesia, displacing questions of the more recent, colonial past.

In contrast to the more intellectual emphasis of *Women's Review*, narratives of the Korean War published in entertainment magazines such as the highly popular *King* (Kingu), *Fuji* (Fuji), and *Storytelling Club* (Kōdan kurabu) tended to linger on the pitiful experience of Japanese still trapped in Korea, on the Korean War refugees "stealthily entering" Japan by boat, and on the danger of Korean spies who now lived in Japan, apparently ready and willing to commit acts of terror.[19] These journalistic works lack the historical consciousness one might reasonably expect from a more serious journal such as *Women's Review*; they certainly fail to demonstrate the kind of commitment to pacifism we see across the pages of the more activist-oriented *Women's Democratic News*. At the same time, they can hardly be called indifferent. The magazines made money tapping into the emotional needs of their readers, resonating with their feelings about personal safety, their desires for romance and success, and their hope for being reunited with family and friends lost in the Second World War, as we shall soon see. After MacArthur's notorious red purge of leftists from the media and entertainment industries in the summer of 1950 all forms of media were also susceptible to the kinds of omissions and embellishments one might even under normal circumstances expect to find in such entertainment journals.[20]

The fiction of Chang Hyŏk-chu, a newly naturalized Japanese

Embodying a wide range of ideological positions, literary responses to the Korean War on the part of ethnic Korean residents in Japan (*zainichi*) came somewhat later than nonfictional and journalistic accounts. Their works suggest that broader social and political developments closely associated with the Korean War were also shaping, and being shaped by, works of fiction. The pioneering writer Kim Tal-su (1919–1997), for example, grew up in colonial Korea but had studied and was working in Tokyo when the Korean War broke out. After publishing for several years in the small Japanese-language journal *Democratic Korea* (Chōsen minshu), he had recently found support for his writing on the pages of a much more nationally prominent magazine, *New Japanese Literature* (Shin Nihon bungaku), run largely by members of the Japanese Communist Party. On July 15, 1950, three weeks after the outbreak of the Korean War, Kim wrote in the *Women's Democratic News* that he found himself unable to write because he was glued to the radio, listening every day to broadcasts from Pyongyang and Seoul, and all too frequently hearing about the deaths and suffering of civilians. "Having lived through the bombing of Japan during the Pacific War, I know and feel in my very bones the hideous effects of aerial bombing, and can't help but imagine the wretched scenes of people scrambling this way and that to escape these bomb attacks."[21] Going on to publish one of the first important postcolonial novels about colonial Korea titled *The Genkai Sea* (1952), and co-translating a North Korean postcolonial novel by writer Yi Ki-yong Kim felt pressed by the Korean War perhaps more than any other writer in Japan to ask his readers to reflect on the trauma inflicted on Koreans during Japanese colonial rule.[22] In the fall of 1952, eight months after the return of Japan's independence, but with no end to the Korean War in sight, he was invited by the *Women's Democratic News* to serialize a short story.

"Hye-sun Hope" (*Keijun no negai*) takes us through a series of trials that the eponymous high school student and her Korean family face as minorities in Japan during the period coinciding with the Korean War, and proposes ethnic solidarity and active protest as potential solutions to their many woes, which include patriarchal abuse, racism, unemployment, sexual harassment by US soldiers, threats of deportation from Japan, the ideological division of families, the closure of ethnic Korean schools, and the violence of militarized police against civilian protestors.[23] Although the story most closely follows Hye-sun experiences, the affective arc of Kim's narrative is closely connected to the changes Hye-sun sees in her delinquent brother, who transforms from an unfairly treated student—and now twenty-something hoodlum—into a protective brother and budding political agent, newly intent on learning more about his historical and legal status as an ethnic Korean living in Japan. Indeed, by the time this narrative was published, some six months after the Occupation ended, Koreans in Japan had only recently been stripped of the Japanese nationality that had been temporarily conferred upon them in 1946 by US authorities. Japan's largest minority population—mostly Koreans who had chosen not to repatriate after the Second World War—now effectively included at least half a million stateless "aliens."[24] Kim's short story suggests that the Korean War had serious consequences on the lives of Koreans who had made Japan their home decades earlier and decided not to return to the Korean Peninsula after the Second World War.

Often contrasted with the work of Kim Tal-su is that of Chang Hyŏk-chu also known as Noguchi Kakuchū. In 1932 Chang had made a name for himself in Japan by writing a work of proletarian literature for the journal *Kaizō*, which helped establish him as one of the first successful ethnic Korean writers to be read throughout the Japanese Empire.[25] He went on to produce voluminous amounts of Japanese propaganda during the Second World War.[26] While scholars have often assessed Chang's works on the basis of his collaboration with the Japanese Empire, John Treat claims his "sycophantic writings … and his effort to bury them under new themes after the war were the stuff of pathos."[27] Hated collaborator or pitiable sycophant, Chang's established position in literary circles gave him an important role to play during the Korean War, a role on which he did not fail to capitalize. He was indeed one of the few ethnic Koreans to whom the media could safely turn for an authentic, and importantly non-communist, voice when it came to stories about the Korean Peninsula. In the years following Japan's defeat in the Second World War, Chang successfully reinvented himself, as did many others, along more liberal lines, publishing what some refer to as "humanistic" works about the struggles of Japanese in the post-Second World War period as well as plenty of work related to his homeland—books such as *The Secret History of the Yi Royal Family* and translations of Korean fairytales like the "Tale of Simchŏng."[28] Before and during the Korean War, Chang also wrote a good deal of girls' fiction (*shōjo shōsetsu*) for children's magazines.

In stories such as "Urei wa harete" (Clearing the Clouds of Her Sorrows), for example, published in January 1949, Chang demonstrated his proclivities for identifying with his Japanese, rather than Korean, compatriots, as he sought to realign the articulation of Japanese identity within the new geopolitical landscape of US-occupied East Asia. Marketed as a "moving story" of heroic childhood,

Chang's preteen story tells of the delicate young Yoshiko, who seeks to clear her father's name and save him from certain execution as a war criminal for crimes that have been falsely attributed to him by an uncouth, uneducated non-commissioned officer.[29] Her college-educated father, in fact, had gone out of his way to increase the rations given to the American prisoners in his care, and he refused to mistreat them, saying that "prisoner cruelty is an abuse of international law." He later suffers the consequences of his good conscience, while his daughter Yoshiko later suffers the ridicule of her classmates as the daughter of an accused "war criminal," whose sense of helplessness is exacerbated by the fact that her mother is on her deathbed. On the advice of a girlfriend, Yoshiko writes to the Chief Justice of the court to insist on her father's innocence; she had witnessed her father's kind treatment of war prisoners—how he had found them extra rations and permitted them to celebrate the holidays around a Christmas tree. In the end Yoshiko succeeds in getting her father cleared of all charges.

It is easy to see in Chang's story how the figure of the innocent victimized girl helps to naturalize the redemption of Japan as an unjustly demonized wartime aggressor as well as to affirm the friendship between Japan and the occupying US forces, whose system of justice demonstrates its own benevolence by taking into account Yoshiko's appeal. Chang shifts whatever historical guilt there is to be reckoned with onto the backs of uneducated non-commissioned officers as well as a "professional military" in his story so that the oppressed innocence of his preteen protagonist works to absolve the Japanese middle class, in particular, of their support of wartime violence. One would be hard pressed to find a piece of fiction that more deliberately seeks to symbolically resolve postwar contradictions and to cement happy relations between well-bred middle-class Japanese and their US occupiers—something Chang accomplishes largely by turning a matter of wartime criminality into that of imperial largesse. The International Military Tribunal for the Far East (IMTFE, or Tokyo Trial) of Class A war criminals had adjourned only a couple months prior to the story's publication, and popular opinion in Japan would from this point on increasingly turn its attention—and sympathy—to lower-level war criminals—corresponding precisely to men in Yoshiko's father's position—for whom the Japanese government would soon seek a broad amnesty. It may be true that works of popular entertainment are rarely prepared to teach the lessons of war—never mind decolonization. As Yoshikuni Igarashi argues, Japan survived the Second World War's destruction in part because Japanese popular culture was able to express memories of its own wartime loss and devastation in spite of the state's interest in forgetting them.[30] But Chang's melodrama about a young girl who saves her unfairly demonized father was one of many works that helped lay down the foundation for a more enduring myth of unjustly denigrated war criminals in Japan, and helped to shift popular consciousness away from a deeper understanding of their own historical responsibility for empire.[31] Well before the Korean War ended, on June 12, 1952, Japanese war criminals would in fact be referred to in the Japanese National Diet as "national victims" and as "patriots who sacrificed their bodies [and lives]."[32] If anything, Chang's early postwar fiction proved that he could be counted on to hold a finger to the pulse of Japanese public opinion and was thus be very helpful in the reconstruction of a postwar Japanese culture and in tune with the important, and evolving, Japanese relationship with the United States.

In the two years that followed the outbreak of the Korean War, Chang wrote at least eight short stories and one long novel about Korea as well as numerous journalistic accounts of the conflict in major newspapers. He was one of very few writers from Japan to be given UN press credentials and to travel on the Korean Peninsula. By the fall of 1952 he was legally naturalized as Japanese—with letters of recommendations from such literary luminaries as future Nobel Laureate Kawabata Yasunari and former proletarian writer Aono Suekichi, heads of the Japanese PEN Club and the Japan Writers Association, respectively. "I feel a certain sadness in separating from my motherland," Chang explained to a reporter upon the conferral of his new citizenship, "but I see Japan as my fatherland."[33]

One of the underlying themes in much of his Korean War period work was already evident in his preteen melodramas: the use of women's experiences as a means of constructing a narrative of Japanese victimization. Policies of assimilation that had encouraged intermarriage between Japanese and Koreans during the late colonial period left Chang with plenty of material as a writer to work with, including the stories of a large population of Japanese women who, having married Korean men, now found themselves stuck in war-torn Korea. Many of these women had children they wished to take back to Japan to escape the fighting; many were simply war widows, left to make a living by whatever means they could. The figure of a disheveled, determined, and often sexually contaminated woman returning from the continent had been something of a stock figure in postwar news accounts in the wake of the 1945 mass migration of colonialists out of Korea and back to the islands of Japan.[34] As war broke out on the Korean peninsula in 1950, this pattern of migration repeated itself, especially in narrative form, and Chang made Japanese women trapped in Korea a staple of both his reporting and his fiction.[35] After one encounter with several Japanese women who had remained in Korea with their Korean husbands, he wrote, "My dear readers, these women had forgotten how to speak Japanese. They had to go to great pains to recall the Japanese language …. 'Natsukashii. Cham, natsukashii. Sā, uri chip e ikimashō.'" This particular woman whom Chang was quoting spoke in a hybrid language—half-Japanese and half-Korean—as she welcomed Chang into her home and expressed the nostalgia she felt upon meeting someone from Japan.[36] If hybridity had been an important cultural theme during the US Occupation—a way for Japan to embrace the culture of her occupier but still maintain her distance from it—Chang Hyŏk-chu was here evoking a more abject form of hybridity, one that suggested what some former colonists had lost with Japan's defeat in the Second World War, which is to say their very identity as Japanese.[37] In a later piece, published in the leading *Yomiuri* newspaper, Chang tells the tragic story of a Japanese woman working on a cargo ship off the coast of Korea, making deliveries to Kŏje Island, the location of a famous camp reserved for communist prisoners of war. Desperate to return to Japan to find her elderly mother, this Japanese woman was stuck working as a cleaner on the cargo ship, where she had also been forced to become the "shared mistress" of all the sailors on board.[38] In addition to these journalistic accounts,

Chang would eventually publish three fictional stories about Japanese women trapped in Pusan, the closest Korean city to Japan. A port city brimming with war refugees, many of whom had fled there after the North Korean army had quickly made its way down the peninsula in the summer of 1950, Pusan had a special refugee center for ethnic-Japanese women and their children, whose immigration status and suitability for repatriation to Japan remained in limbo.

"The Blue Flower of Pusan Port" (1952), published in the widely circulated *Fun Club* (Omoshiro kurabu), is perhaps the most revealing of Chang's Pusan narratives. In it Chang tells the melodramatic tale of one Nishikawa Kyōko, a Japanese widow still living with her Korean mother-in-law, who narrowly escapes getting drawn into the prostitution industry only to fall in love with the gallant captain of a Japanese cargo ship, on which the captain plans to let Kyōko be a stow away.[39] When Kyōko's brother-in-law gets arrested for smuggling, however, Kyōko must in the end abandon her dreams of escaping back to Japan with her dashing new beau so that she can care for her husband's family. Sacrificing her own personal happiness for the sake of her new Korean family, Kyōko remains a good mother and daughter-in-law to the very end of the story. Chang himself, however, weaves into the work a collage of stereotypes and distortions that draw on enduring anxieties about the presence of loose women in the colonies, and the potential for illegal immigration from the Korean peninsula. Editors at the magazine *Fun Club*, too, preferred to market Chang's story in terms of prevailing stereotypes, suggesting that it was the Korean government, rather than family ties, that was keeping women like Kyōko trapped in the country. "Hunger! Spies! Piracy! Fornication! War!" So began the extra-large captions attached to Chang's work. They continued: "In the agonizing Korean port of Pusan, there are Japanese women still being detained, gazing out with nostalgic tears across the Straits to their home country." Notwithstanding the many trials faced by the protagonist, Chang's short story finds its sad but respectable resolution in the unimpeachable character of the ethnic-Japanese daughter-in-law, who foregoes the chance to return to her home country for the ultimate, filial duty of womanhood by remaining in Korea to take care of her Korean mother-in-law.

"The Female Spies of Pusan" (1952), published in the prestigious literary journal *Literary Chronicle* (Bungei shunjū) alongside other works of "documentary fiction," shows Chang shifting registers from melodrama to spy drama and pressing deeper into the realm of Cold War anxieties by offering portraits of Japanese women whose re-entry into Japan is hampered primarily by the North Korean spies rumored to be among them.[40] The piece focuses on a woman named Toshiko, a second-generation Japanese born in Pusan, who has lost both her Korean husband and her only child, and who is pressured by South Korean army intelligence to sniff out a suspected spy named Omi-san among the potential returnees. Toshiko ends up interacting with a variety of Japanese women, some of whom have fully assimilated into Korean culture and language in order to expressly escape the Korean hatred of their former Japanese occupiers, while others like Omi-san have apparently become "UN Madames," servicing American GIs to make ends meet. Each of these encounters gives Chang the opportunity to have someone lament the loss of stable Japanese rule, to repeat tiresome tropes of "soldiers stinking of garlic," or to point out the hypocrisy of anti-colonial communists—apparently North Korean female prisoners, for example, only use Japanese brands of makeup such as Kurabu and Shiseido. The twists and turns of Chang's story itself led Toshiko into a napalm explosion at a South Korean barracks, to a re-encounter with the evil South Korean soldier who killed her husband, and to accusations of her own loyalties which then followed her to jail. She is then beaten by South Korean soldiers, nursed back to health by North Korean medical staff working at an internment camp, and paraded in front of a UN committee, who eventually determine her fate. One of the female Korean judges, however, who speaks not only English but also flawless Korean, turns out to be Omi-san, the very woman Toshiko had been tasked with searching for in the first place. It now dawns on Toshiko that Omi-san is in fact a double agent, though she does not turn her in. Once Toshiko is released from jail she receives a letter from Omi-san, which she burns in an act of solidarity to keep secret this story of a fellow ethnic-Japanese woman, also raised in Korea, and forced to work as a spy for the North. The reader is left with a sense of the fortitude these women all demonstrate as model Japanese citizens, who are willing to do whatever it takes to survive, to support their families, and in some cases to return to Japan—especially when placed under the direst of circumstances.

Scholars have pointed out how the figure of the spy became central to narratives about Koreans in Japan in this period.[41] The Korean War helped add fuel to the fire of this increasingly prominent narrative as the media latched on to the story of North Korean spies rooted deeply in the ethnic Korean community and of "terrorists" working in organizations such as the Zainichi Koreans' United People's Front (*Minsen*), who were in fact conducting acts of sabotage against Japan's direct and indirect support of the Korean War.[42] What made Chang's story particularly unique was the implication of former Japanese colonists—women at that—in these broader espionage rings.[43] The questionable allegiance of former Japanese soldiers, held for years in Soviet forced labor and re-education camps, was a precursor to these new suspicions of possibly "red" women returning from Korea, which occupied but a small space in Japan's literary imagination—doubts that in the long term lingered only when it came to members of the Korean community. When it came to the figure of the Japanese widow, however—willing as we see in Chang's story to even become a North Korean spy in order to secure her passage to Japan—Chang for his part seems willing to harbor a deep sympathy for them, a sympathy in line with a broader narrative of Japanese victimization that no doubt helped Japan heal the wounds of it own defeat in the Second World War and cope with the indignities of US Occupation. Indeed, what connects Chang's 1949 story "Clearing the Clouds of Her Sorrow" and these later works of Korean War fiction about Japanese women is their contribution to a broader discourse on the oppressed innocence of ordinary Japanese caught up in war—an innocence that proved crucial to maintaining the myth of Japan's neutrality and perhaps also to suppressing a deeper reflection on its own historical culpability for the Korean War.

After the publication of Chang's 1952 novel "Alas Korea!" (*Aa Chōsen*), his voice came to carry the authority of someone in a strong position to understand the complexities of war-torn Korea—an ethnic Korean whose background gave him both the expertise and neutrality needed to speak about the Korean War in a trustworthy way. As Yang Hŭi-suk notes, Chang's reportage about the Korean War, published after trips sponsored by the *Mainichi shimbun* and *Women's Club*, contained a good deal of "objective information" about the Korean War that was not yet widely known in Japan.[44] When reviewed in the press, Chang's journalistic work in fact received accolades precisely for its "objectivity," a term that had become newly heralded as the hallmark of proper journalism.[45] Referring to the early release of an extract from Chang Hyŏk-chu's "Alas Korea!," Usui Yoshimi wrote in the *Yomiuri* newspaper that "Chang's work deftly expresses [Korean] suffering, and bears witness to an objectivity and poignancy that appeals to people worldwide."[46]

If it is hardly surprising that a notorious Second World War collaborator like Chang Hyŏkchu was later able to find success as a writer in Japan during the US Occupation, Chang did so in a curious way, by composing a body of work that on the one hand could be celebrated for its objectivity—by a Japanese press corps largely purged of its more progressive journalists—and on the other hand drew audaciously on melodramatic tactics as a means of grappling with the transition from Japanese to American Empire, tactics which downplayed the adverse effects of Japanese imperialism on Korea. Chang's popularity in the early 1950s is certainly testament to the ways in which Japanese letters during the Korean War were reconfigured to accord with new Cold War priorities and also broadly committed to rearticulating a postwar identity. Much the same might be said for the work of early *zainichi* writer Kim Tal-su and others when it came to negotiating the new ideological territory of the US Occupation and the interdependency of discourses on gender and nationalism in the post-Second World War era. But compared to the work of more progressive writers such as Kim, whose readership was more limited, and in stark contrast to the voices of ordinary Japanese citizens printed on the pages on the *Women's Democratic News*, Chang's work carries little remorse for the horrors of Japanese imperialism or the dire consequences that Japan's involvement in the Second World War had on Korea.

The coexistence of this extremely wide range of narratives about the Korean War demonstrates the kind of contestation one might expect to find in occupied Japan, given the multiple communities who felt in one way or another a strong connection to Korea: not only those ethnic Koreans who had migrated from the Korean Peninsula, but also those Japanese returnees who had themselves been born there as well as anti-war activists, colonial apologists, and other Japanese, who may have seen in the Korean War echoes of their own Second World War experiences. Japanese culture under US Occupation responded to the onset of the Korean War by producing a body of works that often grappled with Japan's responsibilities to its former colony when it came to understanding itself as an imperial power and translating its postwar constitution into a meaningful reflection on the legacies of that past. But as we have seen in highbrow journals such as the *Women's Review* and in the popular fiction and journalism of writers such as Chang Hyŏk-chu it also celebrated works that avoided all discussion of these responsibilities and sought to smooth over the contradictions of a postwar Japan in what was effectively a trans-war reality. One might call the growing gap between what was happening on the ground in Japan's former colony and the Japanese imagination of its part of that process of "historical amnesia," which many historians have seen as instrumental in the construction of a "postwar" ideology. One might also follow the pages of the *Women's Democratic News* by calling it an "indifference" on the part of ordinary Japanese, many of whom benefited materially from Japan's participation in the Korean war even as they rejected Japan's participation in it. Either way, Japan's diverse experiences of the Korean War were bound to the ways in which public perception was being shaped through the privileging of narratives which may have seemed truthful and self-evident at the time but were in fact politically and culturally constructed.

Notes

1 Kitade Akira, *Fuzan-kō monogatari: Zaikan Nihonjin tsuma wo sasaeta Ch'oe Pyŏn-de no hachijūnen* (Shakai hyōron, 2009).

2 Lori Watt, *When Empire Comes Home: Repatriation and Reintegration in Postwar Japan* (Cambridge, MA: Harvard East Asian Monographs, 2009), p. 195; Tessa Morris-Suzuki, "Guarding the Borders of Japan: Occupation, Korean War and Frontier Controls," *Asia-Pacific Journal* 9, issue 8, no. 3 (February 21, 2011).

3 For recent studies of Japan's Korean War, see Tessa Morris-Suzuki, "Lavish are the Dead: Re-envisioning Japan's Korean War," *Asia-Pacific Journal* 11, no. 52 (December 30, 2013); Masuda Hajimu, "Fear of World War III: Social Politics of Japan's Rearmament and Peace Movements," *Journal of Contemporary History* 47, no. 3 (2012), pp. 551–571; Ashida Shigeru, "Chosen sensō to Nihon: Nihon no yakuwari to Nihon e no eikyō," *Senshi kenkyū nempo* 8 (March 2005), pp. 103–126.

4 See *Life* (August 28, 1950).

5 Toyoda Minoru, *Chōsen sensō to reddo pāji: erosu no urei* (Kōdansha, 1986), pp. 170, 172.

6 See Bruce Cumings, *The Korean War: A History* (New York: Modern Library, 2011), p. 161.

7 Wolfgang Schivelbusch, *The Culture of Defeat: On National Trauma, Mourning, and Recovery*, trans. Jefferson Chase (New York: Picador, 2003).

8 Ko Youngran examines the Japanese myth of "the postwar" as a broader modern phenomenon dating back to the early twentieth century. Ko Youngran, "*Sengo*" *to iu ideorogii: rekishi, kioku, bunka* (Fujiwara shoten, 2010).

9 For an account of the US role in reconstructing a postwar Japanese military, see Col. Frank Kowalski, *An Inoffensive Rearmament: The Making of the Postwar Japanese Army* (Annapolis, MD: Naval Institute Press, 2013).

10 Nishimura Hideki, *Ōsaka de tatakatta Chōsen sensō* (Iwanami shoten, 2004).

11 Hiratsuka Raichō, *Shinjoen* (September 1950), reprinted in *Hiratsuka Raichō chosakushū* 7 (Ōtsuki shoten, 1984), p. 111.

12 See "Sensō hantai ni noridasu fujinkai no chōrōtachi: Gauntlett, Hiratsuka, Jōdai, Nogami, Makimura no go joshi," *Fujin minshu shimbun* (July 8, 1950).

13 Tani Toshiko, "Chōsen no koto – watashi no furusato," *Fujin minshu shimbun* (July 1, 1951).

14 "Su tatsu kora ni nobiru sensō no shokushu," *Fujin minshū shimbun* (February 25, 1951).

15 For details on the bombing of North Korea, see chapter 6 of Bruce Cumings, *The Korean War* (New York: Modern Library, 2010), pp. 148–161.

16 Mark Selden, "Living with the Bomb: The Atomic Bomb in Japanese Consciousness," *Asia Pacific Journal* 3, no. 8 (August 3, 2005).

17 "Gakusei okorasu 'shūshin yōryō' – Keiō de mondai to naru," *Fujin minshu shimbun* (July 8, 1951), p. 2.

18 See, for example, Mōri Fumie, "Hokusen dasshutsuki: Sei to shi no sanjū hachi sendō," *Kingu* (November 1950).

19 See, for example, "Machiwabiru kokoro," *Kingu* (October, 1950), pp. 170–175; and "Anunteimei no Fukuoka-shi," *Fuji* 3, no. 12 (December, 1951), pp. 40–45.

20 For a study of the Japanese red purge, see Hirata Tetsuo, *Reddo pāji no shiteki kyūmei* (Shin Nihon shuppan, 2002).

21 Kim Tal-su "Kanashimi to okori to," *Fujin minshu shimbun* (July 15, 1950).

22 Kim had co-translated, with Pak Wŏn-sun, Yi Ki-yong's novel *Ttang* (Earth) and its follow-up *Kaekan* (Cultivation) as a single novel entitled *Yomigaeru daichi* (A Great Land, Resurrected) (Nauka, 1951). For an even earlier postcolonial story, see also Sata Ineko, "Shiro to murasaki" (1950), available in translation: "White and Purple," in Sata Ineko, *Five Faces of Feminism: Crimson and Other Works*, trans. Samuel Perry (Honolulu: University of Hawai'i Press, 2016).

23 Kim Tal-su, "Hye-sun no negai," *Fujin minushu shimbun* (October 12, 1952–January 1, 1953).

24 This paragraph is closely adapted from Samuel Perry, "Article Review of Simon Nantais, 'Race to Subversion: Nationality and Koreans in Occupied Japan, 1945–1952,'" *H-Diplo Article Review*, no. 611 (April 28, 2016). For policies toward Koreans in US-occupied Japan, see Kim T'ae-gi *Sengo Nihon seiji to zainichi Chōsenjin mondai: SCAP to tai-zainichi Chōsenjin seisaku 1945–1952* (Keisō Shobō, 1997).

25 For a translation of this work, see Chang Hyŏk-chu, "Hell of the Starving," translated by Samuel Perry, in Heather Bowen-Struyk and Norma Field, eds., *For Dignity, Justice, and Revolution: An Anthology of Japanese Proletarian Literature* (Chicago: University of Chicago Press, 2016).

26 For a recent study of Chang's wartime work, see T. Fujitani, *Race for Empire: Koreans as Japanese and Japanese as Americans during World War II* (Berkeley: University of California Press, 2011).

27 John Whittier Treat, "Chang Hyŏkchu and the Short Twentieth Century," in *The Affect of Difference: Representations of Race in East Asian Empire*, eds. Christopher P. Hanscom and Dennis C. Washburn (Honolulu: University of Hawai'i Press, 2016), p. 256.

28 Chang Hyŏk-chu "Simchŏng monogatari," *Shōjo kurabu* (December 1953), pp. 255–267; Chang Hyŏkchu, *Ri ōke hishi: Hien no hana* (Sekaisha, 1950).

29 Chang Hyŏk-chu "Urei ga harete," *Shōjo sekai* 2, no. 1 (January 1949), pp. 26–35.

30 Yoshikuni Igarashi, *Bodies of Memory: Narratives of War in Postwar Japanese Culture, 1945–1970* (Princeton, NJ: Princeton University Press, 2000).

31 For shifting attitudes to war crimes in the 1950s, see Barak Kushner, *Men to Devils, Devils to Men: Japanese War Crimes and Chinese Justice* (Cambridge, MA: Harvard University Press, 2015).

32 Pak Chŏng-wŏn, *Chōsen sensō: Nihon wa kono sensō ni dō kakawatta ka* (San'ichi shobō, 2013), p. 313.

33 "Chang Hyŏk-chu-shi ga kika – Nanboku ryōsen ni irerarezu – tai-Nichi nijū-nen shukugan no tetsuzuki," *Yomiuri shimbun*, Morning edition (October 12, 1952), p. 3.

34 Watt, *When Empire Comes Home*, p. 99.

35 See, again, Mōri, "Hokusen dasshutsuki."

36 Chang Hyŏk-chu, "Chōsen no dōkoku," *Fujin kurabu* 34, no. 1 (January 1952), p. 240.

37 Igarashi notes this hybrid character of occupation culture. See Igarashi, *Bodies of Memory*, p. 82.

38 "Mite kita higeki no Chōsen," *Yomiuri shimbun*, Morning edition (October 29, 1952), p. 3.

39 Chang Hyŏk-chu, "Fuzan-kō no aoi hana," *Omoshiro kurabu* 5, no. 10 (September, 1952), pp. 48–72.

40 Chang Hyŏk-chu, "Fūzan no onna kancho," *Bessatu Bungei shunjū*, no. 31 (December 1952), pp. 162–181.

41 See, for example, Christopher Donal Scott, "Invisible Men: The Zainichi Korean Presence in Postwar Japanese Culture," PhD diss., Stanford University, 2006.

42 Park Jung Jin, "North Korean Nation Building and Japanese Imperialism: People's Nation, People's Diplomacy, and the Japanese Technicians," in *The Dismantling of Japan's Empire in East Asia: Deimperialization, Postwar Legitimation and Imperial Afterlife*, trans. Sherzod Muminov, eds. Barak Kushner and Sherzod Muminov (London: Routledge, 2016), pp. 199–219.

43 See, for example, "Anunteimei no Fukuoka-shi."

44 Yang Hŭi-suk, "Chō Kakuchū [Chang Hyŏk-chu] sengō no shuppatsu – zainichi Chōsenjin minzoku dantai to no kakawari wo chūshin ni," *Shakai bungaku* no. 38 (2013), pp. 90–103.

45 See Steven Casey, *Selling the Korean War* (Oxford: Oxford University Press, 2008).

46 Chang Hyŏk-chu, "Aa Chōsen," *Shincho* 49, no. 2 (February 1952), pp. 172–212; Usui Yoshimi, "February's Top 4," *Yomiuri shimbun* (January 28, 1952).

Chapter 4

RECONSTRUCTING ARCHITECTURAL MEMORIES OF THE JAPANESE EMPIRE IN SOUTH KOREA

Hyun Kyung Lee

Korea's Japanese colonial architecture: Roots in a problematic past

From the Meiji Restoration in 1868 to the end of the Second World War in 1945, Japan expanded its imperial reach from East Asia (Taiwan, Korea, Manchuria, and China) throughout Southeast Asia and to the islands of the Pacific Ocean. As a component of this imperial expansion, newly built colonial cities underwent a radical transformation of their urban landscape and architectural styles. Japanese authorities attempted to signify their imperial power through new forms of urban design and imperial architecture.[1] In these processes, the Japanese colonizers transplanted modernity along with industrialism and capitalism, and "old" historic sites in colonial cities were frequently replaced with "new" modern Japanese buildings.[2]

These tendencies are illustrated well in the history of the Japanese Empire in Korea. Japan's colonial occupation of Korea (1910–1945) brought about a critical turning point not only in Korean history and in the Korean national identity but also in the nation's urban landscape and its architectural style. A new political, economic, social, and cultural system under the Japanese colonial regime supplanted the traditional systems of Joseon (1392–1910, as Korea was formerly known); this brought about dramatic spatial and visual distinctions between Korean traditional buildings and Japanese modern architecture. A clear illustration can be found in the construction of the Japanese Government-General Building (the headquarters of the Japanese colonial administration) on the site of Gyeongbokgung Palace, which had been the first palace of Joseon: this symbolized the shift of power from Joseon to Japanese imperialism.[3]

After liberation in 1945, new South Korean official narratives began to cast Japanese colonial architecture in a different light and to open a new chapter in its history. The South Korean government considered some monumental Japanese architectural sites, such as the Japanese Government-General Building, to positively instantiate the conflict between Korean tradition and Japanese modernization. From this perspective, in South Korean society, Japanese architectural sites were frequently interpreted as loci of a rupture in Korean history and tradition, as places that the Japanese colonial authorities had deliberately targeted in an effort to transplant their imperial power. Such views, though they were by no means held uniformly by all in Korean society, frequently triggered nationwide debates about the fate of Japanese colonial architecture and in particular about whether it should be destroyed or preserved.

These debates on how to treat Japanese colonial architecture can be understood through a theoretical framework concerning the interrelationship between architecture and urban design, political power and nation building. Significant works in the existing literature set out clearly how architecture and urban design have been manipulated in the service of politics.[4] Hence, these modes are frequently used to express political power and to promote a version of identity that can support and help legitimize rule.[5] In addition, from the perspective of Heritage Studies, buildings and places are considered to be both "symbol[s] and repositories of memory" and "containers of meaning and history" due to the human activities, experiences, and events that are associated with them.[6]

With this point of view, this chapter takes architecture to be a significant element for examining political power and intention in nation building. It also examines the ways in which South Korea from 1945 to 1965 reconstructed its national narratives as a way to reverse the impact of Japanese colonial efforts, through its treatment of Japanese architecture. Considering that the architectural legacy of the post-colonial period is closely related to what occurred in the colonial period, this chapter deals in some detail with the colonial period, despite its predominant focus on the post-colonial period. Finally, this chapter questions whether these processes were intended primarily to overcome the colonial past or to legitimize the new political powers in South Korea.

The agents both of building the empire and of dealing with its aftermath were of course diverse, and should not be treated as homogeneous. The main focus in this chapter is on mainstream, mass, and popular discourses on colonial architecture's construction and de- or reconstruction, and interesting scope remains for future research to explore dissenting and diverging views from individual perspectives.

In order to provide an in-depth analysis, this chapter investigates two difficult heritage sites built by the Japanese in Korea: Seodaemun Prison and the Grand Shrine of Joseon (see Figure 4.1). Seodaemun Prison, established in 1908 by the Japanese authorities, was Korea's first modern prison; the Grand Shrine of Joseon, built in 1925, was the largest and highest-status Shinto shrine built in Korea.

The rationale for choosing these two architectural sites concerns their significance in the formation of South Korea's official narratives of Japanese colonial rule. As mentioned before, the majority of South Koreans are educated and socialized into perceiving the Japanese colonial period as "a shaming past" and Japan as "a national foe."[7] Major components in the operation of these narratives about Japanese brutality, enmity, and shame concern the history of the Korean independence movements and the politics of shrine worship. Seodaemun Prison is often invoked to illustrate how the Japanese colonial authorities brutally and harshly oppressed independence activists, and the Grand Shrine of Joseon

Figure 4.1 Seodaemun Prison (left, source: photo taken by the author in 2012) and the Grand Shrine of Joseon (right, source: Seoul Museum of History).

is presented as a showcase for how Japanese colonial power forced Koreans to worship Shinto in order to discipline them as dutiful subjects of the Japanese emperor. That is, these two sites are specifically employed to strengthen South Korean official narratives and evoke South Koreans' national sentiment against Japan. In addition, the treatment of the two sites since the end of the colonial period presents both general and particular trends regarding how Japanese colonial architecture has been dealt with since liberation in the (re)construction of a new nation.

Seodaemun Prison: A symbol of fear and violence

Seodaemun Prison, Korea's first modern prison and a key colonial building, offers us clear illustrations of shifts in the geopolitical meaning of Japanese colonial architectural sites and in its post-colonial history, and understanding of how post-liberation memories were rewritten according to shifts of political power in South Korea's nation-building processes.

After signing a Protectorate Treaty with Japan in 1905, rebellions against Japanese power burgeoned throughout Korea.[8] Eager to prevent these riots, the Japanese authorities tightened their system for suppressing the Korean independence movement.[9] The colonial control system had its ultimate embodiment in Seodaemun Prison, opened in 1908 as the first modern prison in Korea to mark the start of a centralized Japanese judicial system.

The name "Seodaemun" indicated the new prison's location close to Seoul's West Gate (*Seodaemun*). Although not regarded then as the center of Korea's capital, this site entailed significant meanings: it had been used to promote the nation's sovereign independence and to reassert the power of the throne immediately before the Japanese annexation of Korea.[10] During the Joseon Dynasty, this area had been designated for the use of Chinese envoys and represented Korea's servile position relative to China. However, the nearby erection in 1897 of the Independence Gate had shifted the area's symbolism to now connote Joseon's independence from

China, as from other foreign interventions. In a geopolitical sense, the major communicative flows that passed through this area cemented it as a prime site for exhibiting Korea's political status both domestically and internationally.[11]

Korean sociologist Lee Jong-min and Korean journalist Gwon Gi-bong have argued that the Japanese imperial powers seem to have understood the significance of this gate as a sign of the end of Chinese influence upon Korea, and that in situating the first and ultimately largest modern prison in Korea next to it they seem to have intended to signify both their new power over Korea and the expansion of their empire.[12] From the case of Taipei Prison in Japan's new colony of Taiwan, which was built out of materials from a wall that the Chinese Qing Dynasty had constructed, there exists evidence of the Japanese Empire seeming to emphasize its victory over China through the construction of colonial prisons.[13] Although original documents detailing the Japanese authorities' rationale in selecting the prison's location have not surfaced, Seodaemun Prison's location crucially made visible the locus of Japanese imperial power.

Seodaemun Prison's architecture reflected a German brick style, popular from the late nineteenth to early twentieth century, that had been imported to Japan and now appeared in its colonies.[14] The building reflected a German medievalist style, of a type used for Catholic churches, intended to have an imposing effect both on prisoners and passersby.[15] In a similar vein, the physical presence of such an enormous prison in central Seoul served to instill a sense of the power and authority of Japanese rule in the Korean population.[16] Korean sociologist Yang Byeol-il has argued that this grand architecture might have stimulated the imaginations of those who passed by regarding what happened inside, breeding fear in the face of Japanese imperial power.[17]

Seodaemun Prison's interior structure represents the new prison system that the Meiji government adopted. The Meiji government adopted a practice from modern Western prisons (e.g., Eastern State Penitentiary in the United States and a *maison centrale* in France), whereby "dangerous figures," such as political offenders, were imprisoned to separate them from society.[18] Whilst the traditional prison was a holding facility for convicts awaiting actual punishment (e.g., flogging or execution), the modern prison was changed into a living space for the prisoners under 24-hour-a-day control, subject to a strict daily schedule (and labor).[19] The Meiji government built modern prisons in similar styles not only in Japan but also in its colonies (Taiwan, Korea, and Port Arthur in China) to administer the correction and control of political offenders.[20] Accordingly, Seodaemun's internal structure used Jeremy "panopticon" model: the "all-seeing" prison had a radial structure, with cells along three corridors fanning out like spokes of a wheel from a central inspection "hub," where prison officers were stationed. Cells were kept bright while the inspection house remained dim, allowing prison officers to keep a close watch on the prisoners without being seen themselves: the prisoners, therefore, never fully knew whether they were being watched or not. Michel Foucault, among others, has explained how such a layout meant that prisoners in such institutions become unconsciously self-surveillant, behaving always as if they were being watched.[21] In the specific context of Korea, many Korean scholars have observed that the fear of being watched meant that inmates in such prisons became ever more subdued, limiting their actions and ultimately obeying the Japanese authorities.[22]

The prison underwent repeated expansion and redevelopment during the colonial period, with a particular focus on accommodating rising numbers of independence activists (see Figures 4.2 and 4.3). Additional solitary confinement cells were built, and the prison reached its peak population, 2,670 prisoners, in

Figure 4.2 Photo of Seodaemun Prison in 1908 (source: Seodaemun Prison History Hall).

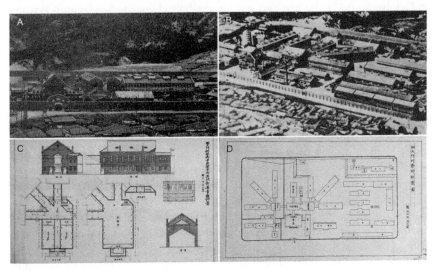

Figure 4.3 Photos of Seodaemun Prison in 1923 (A) and in 1934 (B); the floor maps of Seodaemun Prison in 1923 (C) and 1934 (D) (source: Seodaemun Prison History Hall).

1937.[23] Thus, throughout the colonial period, that is to say up until the end of the Second World War, Seodaemun Prison symbolized a place of fear and violence associated with Japanese imperial power as exercised against Korean independence activists. It became also a site associated with heroic stories in the official history of the Korean independence movement. Then, with the end of the Asia-Pacific War in 1945, the prison entered a new phase.

After Korea's liberation from Japanese rule in 1945, Seodaemun Prison remained in use as a prison until 1987, when physical deterioration led to its closure. The prison's physical structure remained little changed from the liberation until its closure: however, the post-colonial narratives attached to the Seodaemun Prison developed, deeply interwoven with contemporary Korean political history.[24] In the shift from the colonial to the post-colonial period, we see with the case of this prison the development of complex memories and heritage concerning not only the colonial period but the period thereafter, too.

The period following Japan's defeat in the Pacific War on August 15, 1945, saw intense upheaval on the Korean peninsula. In less than a decade Korea underwent the country's division at the thirty-eighth parallel (1945), US military rule (1945–1948), the establishment of the Republic of Korea (1948), and the Korean War (1950–1953). After the war's end, successive Korean presidents—particularly, Syngman Rhee (1948–1960) and Park Chung-hee (1963–1979)—added further trauma by pursuing political courses that hindered the development of Korean democracy. Throughout this political turmoil and economic crisis, the post-colonial stories of Seodaemun Prison provided a lens for understanding the power relationship between those who were imprisoned and those who oppressed the prisoners—a relationship that changed rapidly as political circumstances changed.

Following liberation (and lasting until the start of the US military occupation on October 9, 1945), the first and most immediate change to Seodaemun Prison's meaning from a mainstream Korean perspective was a dramatic shift from a symbol of fear and violence to one of emancipation. Anticipating defeat in the war, the Japanese Government-General of Korea had on August 10, 1945, begun preparing for surrender and withdrawal from Korea: as part of this, they had classified prisoners into two groups (political prisoners and common criminals relating to murder, robbery, and rape).[25] The political prisoners were released from Seodaemun at 9:00 a.m. on August 16, 1945, following an agreement made between Japanese government-general official Endō Ryūsaku and Korean independence leader Mongyang Lyuh Woon-hyung.[26] According to Korean independence activist Song Nam-heon's recollections, crowds of Koreans watched the release, lining the main road from Seodaemun Prison to the Independence Gate. Waving Korean flags and chanting "*Daehanminguk Manse!*" (Korea, everlasting), all of them then marched together on Jong-ro street. From this point, Seodaemun Prison and its surroundings were embedded in the concept of emancipation and independence from Japanese colonial rule.

The release of the political prisoners to this rapturous reception left common criminals behind in the prison, but not for long: a day later, a riot broke out among the still-incarcerated condemned and long-term prisoners: they broke the cell doors and main gate, releasing themselves. Beside the chaos of the riots, according to the account of a chief guard, Moon Chi-yeon, members of the public attacked Seodaemun Prison in a public outpouring of formerly suppressed frustration, taking the prison as a symbol of Japanese sovereignty over Korean society.[27] Moon notes that amid the confusion and vengeful atmosphere, some civilians assaulted prison officers; other officers hence left their jobs due to their fear of Korean vengeance.[28] Therefore, for two months immediately after the liberation, Seodaemun Prison became a place for the expression of jubilant feelings, for released prisoners and ordinary Koreans alike—and a fearful space from which Japanese prison officers wanted to escape. Then, however, once the US military power arrived, it immediately turned into a battlefield for ideological conflicts.

During the years of US rule (1945–1948), the political climate of the Korean peninsula shifted from one of imperialism to a Cold War footing, and the country became a different type of contested area. South Korea's communists mounted a strong resistance to military rule, while the US military government and Korean pro-American politicians ranged themselves against both the Soviet Union and North Korea.[29] Due to these left–right ideological conflicts, this period saw a surging number of assassinations, acts of terrorism, and public uprisings.[30] Consequently, the number of prisoners of conscience, who were mainly communists, rose dramatically. Seodaemun Prison reached a new maximum capacity, growing from 2,521 inmates immediately after the liberation to 2,963 in early 1947. The prison during these years maintained the exact same system that had operated there during Japanese rule, simply replacing the Japanese prison officers with Korean counterparts who had worked as prison officers during the colonial era.[31] What is interesting is that some prisoners who had been independence activists during the colonial period were now again imprisoned due to their ideology (including, for example, those involved in the Jeju April 3 Uprising, which was an attempted insurgency on Jeju Island followed by an anti-communist suppression campaign from April 1948, to May 1949).[32] The end of Japanese colonial rule thus did not mean an end to the generation of negative memories concerning the prison for some sections of Korean society.

Amid intensified ideological struggles between North and South Korea, the government of the Republic of Korea was established on August 15, 1948, relinquishing, at least for the time being, the objective of re-founding a unified Korea that would incorporate the North. In October 1948, the Constitutional Assembly formed a Task Force on Traitorous Activities and began to put pro-Japanese collaborators on trial.[33] Consequently, under Rhee's regime, Seodaemun Prison served initially for the imprisonment of pro-Japanese collaborators. For example, the Task Force, on January 12, 1949, arrested Chunwon Yi Kwang-su, a famous writer and pro-Japanese collaborator.[34] As an influential intellectual, he actively promoted Japanese assimilation policy through newspaper articles and public lectures, such as the policy whereby Korean names were replaced with mandatory Japanese alternatives and military conscription for the Asia-Pacific War.[35] While the Task Force examined his pro-Japanese activities in February 1948, he was detained in Seodaemun Prison in March 1948.[36] In this site, where once those who stood against the Japanese had been constrained and controlled, now those who had collaborated with them were incarcerated.

However, since many pro-Japanese collaborators had worked with Rhee's regime following liberation, the prison terms they served were mostly only brief. Rhee needed the former collaborators' support to retain his political power and ultimately disbanded the Task Force in August 1949.[37] Seodaemun Prison was full of Japanese collaborators for only a short while, and for some it thus also holds a memory of a failure to judge these collaborators properly and to build South Korea's legitimacy, as a consequence of deliberate sabotage by Rhee's regime.[38]

A major component in Rhee's loss of interest in the treatment of former collaborators was his new focus on anti-communist policy rather than anti-colonial policy. To this end, Rhee's regime, on December 1, 1948, enacted a National Security Law aimed at controlling anti-governmental activities. The law was applied mostly to members of North Korea's communist party and its supporters in South Korea, and produced an increase in the number of political offenders. Seodaemun Prison now became overcrowded with prisoners convicted under the National Security Law, finally reaching a total population of 8,782 in 1950.[39]

Against the backdrop of this upsurge in anti-communist sentiment in South Korea, the Korean War broke out on June 25, 1950. President Rhee fled Seoul on June 26, 1950, leaving a rupture in administrative functioning wherein significant political and economic affairs were neglected.[40] No provisions were left for the treatment of political offenders in Seodaemun Prison, and in the chaos immediately after the war, the Seodaemun prisoners were freed. Debate continues on who released them: either civilian rioters or the North Korean People's Army (NKPA) opened Seodaemun Prison's main gate, allowing political offenders to depart.[41]

For the remainder of the war the profile of inmates in the prison vacillated dramatically as control of Seoul shifted. While the NKPA held the city, the prison was filled with anti-communists; when the South's army retook it they executed NKPA captives in the prison.[42] In the aftermath of the Korean War, the Republic of Korea entered seven years of one-man rule under Syngman Rhee. While Rhee's regime held power, political offenders who stood against his politics were oppressed in Seodaemun Prison. But a new period in the prison's history began with the April 19 Revolution of 1960, when protestors rejected the results of the so-called March 15 rigged election, regarded as the acme of the corruption of Rhee's regime.[43] In demonstrations led by thousands of students and labor groups, and at a cost of 186 protestor deaths, this revolution successfully brought Rhee's dictatorship to an end.[44] Now, prominent political figures and political gangsters who had presided over the March 15 election, and officials who shot April 19 protesters, came to be imprisoned in Seodaemun Prison, including Home Affairs Minister Choi In-gyu and the ninth minister of justice, Hong Jin-gi.[45] Now that Rhee had lost power, his supporters suffered in Seodaemun Prison as his opponents had under his tenure. Clearly, memories of Seodaemun Prison track the rise and fall of political power in South Korea.

While Rhee's officials languished in Seodaemun Prison, Park Chung-hee seized power through a coup d'etat on May 16, 1961. The new profile of political prisoners at Seodaemun now reflected his passage of an Anti-Communism Law in 1963: victims included thirteen politicians of the Reformist Group in 1965 as part of the first People's Revolutionary Party Incident, a legal case in which the South Korean government accused individuals of socialist inclinations. Others imprisoned under Park were opponents of his regime in the 1970s who advocated for modern democracy, including President Moon Jae-in, who was imprisoned in Seodaemun Prison in the 1970s. Consequently, Seodaemun Prison bears not only narratives documenting Park's oppression of his political opponents but also the stories of democratic protests against Park's military dictatorship.

Throughout this post-liberation period, South Korean authorities then sought to defend the country against a new political and ideological enemy, communist North Korea, as well as against the ghosts of the Japanese legacy. In order to repress those who stood in opposition to government policy, the regimes reactivated the fear and intimidation that had been attached to Seodaemun Prison by the Japanese authorities. While the regimes officially proclaimed themselves hostile to the Japanese legacy, they nevertheless adopted Japanese methods of control over those who opposed them. Fear and intimidation were instilled during the post-conflict period in ways reminiscent of the colonial occupation period. Both during the colonial period and thereafter, Seodaemun Prison constituted a site for imprisoning political offenders specifically Jeju island for separating them from ordinary people Jeju island and a center of cruel oppression and punishment.

Following the prison's closure in 1987, the site was partly converted to form the Seodaemun Independence Park in 1992 and further developed to open the Seodaemun Prison History Hall in 1998. Through these transformations, this site has been used not only to commemorate the history of Seodaemun Prison but also to support the official narratives of South Korea, to glorify the heroic stories of Korean independence activists. Hence, the site has emerged as a "dark tourism" attraction and has subsequently gained additional connotations as a "holy site" due to stories of the sacrifice of the independence activists. As a result, this is now one of the most important heritage sites in Korea. However, it is important to note that the main storytelling at the site focuses on remembering its *colonial* history. Despite the recent efforts of the director and curators in the Seodaemun Prison History Hall to include post-colonial stories, the site's post-colonial history barely features, appearing briefly and understatedly in a single section installed in 2008. The democratic activists' stories remain problematic, as they may receive diverse interpretations depending on political orientation while conservatives intend to hide them, liberals seek to glorify them. Hence, although Seodaemun Prison has a longer post-colonial history (forty-two years) than its colonial tenure (thirty-seven years), the former stories still remain hidden to visitors.

The Grand Shrine of Joseon: A center of spiritual assimilation

Having traced the formation of Japanese colonial/post-colonial memories of Seodaemun Prison, a representation of the Japanese modern control system, we turn now to the second case: the site of the Grand Shrine of Joseon (*Chōsen Jingū* in Japanese). In order to understand how and why the Grand Shrine of Joseon functioned in post-colonial South Korea, it is essential to understand its background and formation during the colonial era.

Shinto stems from indigenous Japanese folk beliefs concerning the worship of a multitude of gods (*kami*).[46] After the Meiji Restoration, State Shinto emerged as the new Meiji government's ideological rendering of traditional Shinto. While Shinto was made into an established religion in 1882, State Shinto functioned as a non-religious moral, traditional, and patriotic practice.[47] In order to cement its establishment of a powerful and centralized government, the Meiji government emphasized the Japanese emperor as a divine being, originating from Amaterasu Ōmikami (goddess of the Sun); the State Shrine was used as a site to worship the emperor as an absolute power whom people should obey.[48] Promoting such worship of the emperor, the Meiji government made political use of State Shinto not only to control its domestic Japanese population but also to assimilate the colonized in the Japanese Empire.[49] Hence, establishing Shinto shrines was a typical phenomenon in the founding of Japanese ruling systems in the expansion of Japan's empire (i.e., in Taiwan, Manchuria, Sakhalin, China, and Southeast Asian countries).[50]

State Shinto was also a component of the Japanese assimilation policy in Korea. As clearly stated in the book *History of Gyeongseongbu* (*Gyeongseongbusa*), written by the Japanese Government-General of Korea in 1934, the assimilation policy was the foundation of administration in colonial Korea after the Japanese annexation of Korea, and building Shinto shrines throughout Korea, designated as centers of national reverence, was the root measure in transplanting Japanese national customs into colonial Korea.[51] Based on its belief that State Shinto facilitated the assimilation policy, the Japanese Government-General of Korea promulgated the Regulations on Shrines and Temples on August 16, 1915, as the 82nd ordinance of the Japanese Government-General of Korea.[52] By this measure, State Shinto was officially inaugurated into the Korean religious sphere, along with Buddhism and Christianity, and the establishment and control of shrines in Korea was arrogated to the Japanese Government-General of Korea. This legislation regularized the role of small, private shrines, and State Shinto was publicly brought into Korean daily life under colonial rule.

In the 1930s, under a policy called "Japan and Korea as a single body" (*naisen ittai*), State Shinto was rather aggressively promoted in the wartime context.[53] In order to discipline the Korean populace, cultivating absolute obedience to the emperor as a loyal military force during wartime, Minami Jirō (1936–1942) and other Japanese Governors-General of Korea, sought to fundamentally transform Koreans into "dutiful subject[s] to an imperial community."[54] In August 1936, through the Revision on the Regulations of Shrines of the Japanese Government-General of Korea, every shrine in Korea was ranked according to a system that sought to assist the completion of state rituals.[55] On this solid legal footing, the *Japanization* policy brought about a massive expansion in the number of shrines throughout colonial Korea.[56] By the time of the empire's defeat, the total number of shrines in Korea reached 1,140 (including eighty-two Shinto shrines), illustrating how State Shinto was deeply implicated in the lives of the colonized.[57]

At the onset of the State Shinto assimilation policy, the Grand Shrine of Joseon was built in 1925 on Mt. Nam, becoming the top shrine in the religious hierarchy in Korea. This was the first Shinto Shrine that would be used not only by the Japanese but also by Koreans (Shinto Shrines built only for Japanese settlers had already existed in Korea before the start of the colonial period).[58] This religious space thus was the starting point and the center in the Japanese "spiritual assimilation" of the Korean people.[59]

It was through the colonial education system at schools that visiting and paying one's respect at the Grand Shrine of Joseon was institutionalized as a Korean daily practice. In particular, from the 1930s, shrine worship was strongly emphasized in education, as can be seen in the book *Principles and Practices of the Education of Subjects of the Japanese Empire*, published by the Educational Association of Joseon Citizens.[60] School events relating to Shinto Shrine worship took place daily, weekly, and monthly, and Korean students had to participate in worship at the Grand Shrine of Joseon.[61] Therefore, the number of Korean students who made a pilgrimage to the Grand Shrine of Joseon dramatically increased, from 55,797 in 1928 to 672,760 in 1943.[62] These figures indirectly reflect how Shinto Shrine worship was emphasized in Korean education. Beside these school trips, ordinary Koreans also had to pay their respects at the Grand Shrine of Joseon, in particular, at the New Year's celebration and during the war period.[63]

Those Koreans who sought to resist Shinto worship were punished by the Japanese Government-General of Korea under the Maintenance of the Public Order Act issued on May 8, 1925 (which set out sanctions for those who refused, including the expulsion of school students and principals).[64] In particular, the Korean Christian movement that strongly resisted the worship provisions was strictly controlled under the 1940 law "Arrest of the Japanese Empire against the Disturbing Elements of Joseon Christianity" (which led to the arrest of 2,000 Korean Christians and closure of 200 churches, and the death of 50 Korean Christians in colonial prisons).[65] The Grand Shrine of Joseon was developed as a powerful medium to suffuse Japanese spiritual assimilation into Koreans' daily lives.

The plan for the construction of the Grand Shrine of Joseon had first been launched in 1912, with a budget requisitioned by the Japanese Government-General of Korea. On March 22, 1918, Hanyang Park in the middle of Mt. Nam was selected as its location. On July 18, 1919, the shrine's rank and the gods that would be enshrined there were confirmed, and construction started on May 27, 1920. Finally, the Grand Shrine of Joseon was completed on October 15, 1925.[66] It is noteworthy that this shrine took fifteen years to complete following the Japanese annexation of Korea in 1910, whereas Shinto shrines of the same rank in other Japanese colonies were established immediately after Japanese colonization (e.g., the Sapporo Shinto Shrine in Hokkaido in 1871, Taiwan Shinto Shrine in Taiwan in 1901, and the Karafuto Shinto Shrine in Sakhalin in 1911).[67] This was the result in part of long debates in 1918 and 1919 on the shrine's location, with its designers seeking to combine convenience and visual effect upon the formation of the colonial landscape.[68] Another long debate from 1920 to 1925 concerned the selection of a god whom the Koreans could obey rather easily: it should be one that would not evoke any particular anti-Japanese sentiment.[69] Regarding this long construction period, Korean sociologist Kim Baek-yeong pointed out that the Japanese Government-General of Korea seemed to devote particular care and attention to the construction of the Grand Shrine of Joseon as compared to other cases.[70] It is true too, though, that a lack of budget was also an important factor in delaying the shrine's construction.[71]

With this grounding in the use and policies of the Grand Shrine of Joseon, we now turn to the spatial impact upon colonial Korea of the construction of the Grand Shrine of Joseon. Itō Chūta, a Japanese architect and an expert on the construction of Shinto shrines, was appointed in 1918 as the project advisor for the Grand Shrine of Joseon.[72] Based on his previous experiences of constructing symbolic Shinto shrines in both Japan and its colonies (e.g., the Meiji Shinto Shrine in Japan, and the Taiwan and Karafuto Shinto Shrines), Itō paid much attention to the selection of the location for the Grand Shrine of Joseon.[73] Itō's report shows that he examined eight proposed sites according to twelve criteria, also factoring in cost.[74] This report helps us understand how he valued the environment, landscape, and view of the Grand Shrine of Joseon.[75] Korean historian Choi Jin-seong notes an interesting distinction between the shrines the Japanese built at home and in Korea: over 90 percent of the shrines established in colonial Korea were located on hills, with their façades facing toward urban areas, while shrines in Japan were surrounded by forests to emphasize their sacred character.[76] In other words, shrines in Korea were situated so as to be visible to the whole city, and so people could see them from any vantage point. This spatial effect seemed to be weighed more highly by the Japanese shrine builders in colonial Korea rather than concerns to do with enhancing the religious atmosphere.

Itō ultimately selected Hanyang Park (the current Hoehyeon area) on Mt. Nam. According to an interview in 1925, Itō believed that "this Shinto Shrine could express its dignity only when people recognize[d] clearly where it was."[77] Hanyang Park was one of the most conspicuous places in Seoul; placing the shrine there established a visual connection between the shrine and the whole city.[78] The fact that the land was nationally owned also helped reduce construction costs.[79] In addition, this location in Yongsan District was useful due to its geographical proximity to the extensive Imperial Army Base and Japanese community.[80]

To place it in its wider context, the Grand Shrine construction project formed part of the "Great Gyeongseong Project" to reconfigure the city's urban structure during Japanese rule. The focus of the Great Gyeongseong Project was to construct a major north–south axis through the city, constructing a new Japanese Government-General Building, a symbol of Japanese imperial power at the start of the north end, and the Grand Shrine of Joseon at the end of the south end, supplanting the main east–west axis formed during the Joseon Dynasty.[81] The Japanese historian Aoi Akihito points out that the completion of the Japanese

Government-General Building and the Grand Shrine of Joseon exhibited Japanese sovereignty and gave visual expression to the unity of religion and politics (*saisei-itchi*) under Japanese rule.[82]

Of particular interest is the architectural style of the Grand Shrine of Joseon. Most Japanese colonial architecture built for public and official uses, including Seodaemun Prison, followed Western architectural styles, such as the neo-classical (i.e., Joseon Bank) or neo-renaissance (i.e., Gyeongseong Court), and was made of stone.[83] This Shinto Shrine, however, adopted the *shinmei-zukuri* style of Ise Shrine, considered to be the holiest of Japan's Shinto shrines.[84] Built of wood, shinmei-zukuri as an ancient Japanese architectural style is regarded as the pinnacle of Japanese traditional architecture, characterized by an extreme simplicity. Itō admired its pure Japanese style, free from admixture with foreign cultures and representing the essence of the Japanese native character.[85] Hence, building a structure in this style on the giant scale of the Grand Shrine of Joseon looked like transplanting Japanese tradition in one of the most visible places in Seoul. This establishment, as a major part of the Grand Gyeongseong Project, brought about dramatic changes to the colonial cityscape, giving clear visual representation to the aim of the colonial policy of *Japanization* (see Figure 4.4).

This massive and prominent religious site brought about changes not only to the colonial landscape but also in the spatial meaning of its location. Many Korean historians have pointed out that the establishment of the Grand Shrine of Joseon implied a replacement of Korean traditional religion with a new religious order.[86] A traditional Korean Shamanic Shrine, Guksadang (also called *Mokmyeok Sinsa*),

Figure 4.4 The Great Shrine of Joseon in 1929 (left, source: Seoul Museum of History).

had been located at the summit of Mt. Nam (or Mt. Mokmyeok) from the beginning of the Joseon Dynasty to the mid-1920s. This site was a popular place of daily worship for Joseon people and shamans, and along with its religious connotations and the endurance of a mountain worship tradition, Mt. Nam was regarded as an auspicious and sacred place in the Joseon Dynasty.[87] Although during the earlier colonial period part of Mt. Nam was converted into public parks or given over to Japanese settlement, for a time this Korean shrine continued to function as a significant Korean folk worship place.

However, in late 1924, with the Grand Shrine of Joseon nearly completed, the Guksadang was at risk of demolition, along with other Korean Confucian shrines (Dongmyo Shrine and Bukmyo Shrine).[88] Ultimately, the Japanese Government-General of Korea decided not to demolish it, fearing potential riots among folk believers if they did so.[89] Instead, they announced in 1924 that the Guksadang would move to Mt. Inwang. The rationale for the move was that the high number of Korean shamans and folk believers who came to the Guksadang for daily worship harmed the site's scenic beauty, according to the daily newspaper the *Maeil Sinbo*, which was the organ of the Japanese Government-General of Korea.[90]

Regarding this decision, many Korean historians currently insist that a major consideration in the announcement of this move concerned the Guksadang's location: it was situated on the site of the current Palgakjeong Pavilion on Mt. Nam, and thus at a higher elevation than Hanyang Park, where the Grand Shrine of Joseon was erected.[91] These historians argue that the Japanese authorities saw this higher elevation as a threat to the visual status of the Japanese Shinto shrine and felt that two different national gods should not be permitted to coexist; therefore, the Japanese government decreed that Guksadang must be lowered to a height beneath that of the Grand Shrine of Joseon. In July 1925, Guksadang was moved halfway down Mt. Inwang, located to the west of the capital.[92] Korean historians view the move negatively: the establishment of the Grand Shrine of Joseon seemed to be related to high-handed Japanese treatment of Korean tradition, and the Korean tradition was sacrificed.

A lack of surviving data makes it difficult to determine ordinary Koreans' reactions to the Guksadang's transplant. It is also unclear to what extent the Guksadang's movement influenced Korean people's minds toward the construction of the Grand Shrine of Joseon. However, some emotional traces can be found in records of public responses to the shrine. A report sent on September 28, 1925, by the chief of police in the Honchō branch to the director of police affairs mentioned that Kō Shin college students planned demonstrations against this celebration, arguing that the Koreans had their own gods that they worshipped.[93] In addition, the officer of the Grand Shrine of Joseon, Tedzuka Michio, described feeling afraid of being attacked by the Koreans during the inauguration while he led the procession bringing the sacred object symbolizing the spirits of the gods from Gyeongseong Station to the Grand Shrine of Joseon.[94] During the ceremony, the entire Gyeongseong police force was present and on high alert. This suggests that the Japanese colonial authorities recognized the strength of negative feeling toward the Grand Shrine among the Korean populace.

In addition, according to the testimony of a Japanese bystander who watched the inauguration ceremony for an hour, Korean attendees did not worship at the shrine, merely "visiting" it, while the Japanese paid respects to Amaterasu Ōmikami.[95] Moreover, in a magazine article published in February 1932, the Governor-General of Korea, Ugaki Kazunari, pointed out a similar attitude among Koreans: most answered that they visited the Grand Shrine of Joseon in order to enjoy its beautiful landscape and to take exercise, whilst Japanese visitors prayed reverently at the shrine.[96] Japanese colonial authorities might have intended this shrine to serve as a center for the spiritual assimilation of Korea, but the Korean people did not seem to seriously worship the Japanese gods.

It should be noted that there were some Koreans who sponsored the construction of the Japanese shrines and supported the expansion of such shrines across Korea. Most of them were local governors who voluntarily changed their Korean names to Japanese alternatives before the enactment of the name-changing system, and who actively collaborated with Japanese colonial policies.[97] Throughout the colonial period, such Japanese collaborators occupied exalted positions and took advantage of the educational and economic opportunities they conferred. Nevertheless, resistance movements opposing daily worship in the Grand Shrine of Joseon also continued, in particular among Christian and student groups. The fierce and systematic Korean Christian resistance movement led by pastor Ju Ki-cheol expanded in late 1930 and the 1940s, despite repression by the Japanese Government-General of Korea; mandatory daily worship persisted nonetheless.[98] Some Koreans' memoirs document attending the Shrine to collect rations from the Japanese Government-General of Korea while inwardly praying that the Japanese Empire would quickly collapse.[99] Others recall putting linens distributed by the Japanese administration at the Grand Shrine deep in the back of their closets.[100] Although anyone who profaned the Japanese shrines was subject to strict punishment in accordance with the provision of Article 74, "Crime against the Japanese Imperial House," some Koreans stole the ancestral tablets from the shrines or damaged the shrines themselves (e.g., the Japanese shrine in the West Gate in 1925).[101] For many historians, such accounts are evidence that the majority of Koreans, apart from the Japanese collaborators, pretended superficially to obey the Japanese gods in the Grand Shrine of Joseon but nurtured an internal hostility toward it.[102] In other words, in the official narratives of Korean history, the Grand Shrine of Joseon has been remembered with negative connotations interwoven with the spiritual assimilation policy.

Immediately after liberation on August 15, 1945, members of the Korean public expressed their feelings toward the Japanese Empire by attacking and damaging not only Japanese public and official buildings but the Shinto shrines too. According to the book *Chosenn syusenn no kiroku: Beiso ryogunn no sinchuuto Nihonnzinn no hikiage* (The Record of Joseon after the End of the War), written by Morita Yoshio, formerly an officer of the Japanese Government-General of Korea and later in charge of the relationship between Japan and Korea in the Ministry of Foreign Affairs, a total of 136 Shinto shrines and small shrines were damaged and set on fire in the eight days following the liberation.[103] The events here bear clear parallels to the attacks and riots at Seodaemun Prison, as documented in the previous section. The frequency of shrine attacks was greater than on Japanese administrative buildings and lower than the 146 cases at police offices.[104] As many Korean historians point out, these violent actions against the shrines can be seen as the revenge of the Koreans against Japanese spiritual policy.[105]

Afterwards, a project to complete the demolition of the remains of State Shinto shrines and small local shrines alike was planned in 1946 by a Preparatory Committee for the Celebration of the August 15 Peace and Liberation under the US Military Government, demonstrating the rather systematic nature of these buildings' removal.[106] Newspapers, which throughout 1946 reported frequently on the complete demolition of such shrines, tended to dub them "idols of the Japanese empire."[107] These records reflect how the Korean public, media, and leaders endeavored to erase Japanese religious legacies that were negatively understood.[108]

In parallel, the Japanese Government-General of Korea endeavored to protect the Grand Shrine of Joseon, considered most significant by the Japanese authorities, against both popular riots and the arrival of US troops.[109] In the morning of August 16, 1945, the Japanese Government-General of Korea and the officers of the Grand Shrine of Joseon held a meeting about the fate of the Shinto and other shrines in Korea.[110] They decided to hold a ceremony to cause the ascension of the spirits of the gods enshrined in the Grand Shrine of Joseon.[111] They believed that after the ceremony, the spirits of the gods, which were the most important element in the shrine, could not be damaged even if physical damage occurred. At 5:00 p.m. on August 16, 1945, this ceremony was held, with the entire officer complement of the Grand Shrine of Joseon in attendance as well as Honda Takeo (the local section chief at the Secretariat of the Japanese Government-General of Korea) and Takamatsu Tadakiyo (the head officer in charge of religious work in the Japanese Government-General of Korea, as proxy for the Governor-General of Korea).[112] Subsequently, the sacred object symbolizing the spirits of the gods and the sword of state, which the gods of the Grand Shrine of Joseon dwelled in, were taken to the Imperial House of Japan by plane on August 24, and the shrine's treasures and a funeral oration (*saibun*) were incinerated on August 25. As US military rule was imminent, under the US authorities' permission, the Koreans dismantled the throne hall and many buildings in September, and the hall in which the spirits of the gods were enshrined was incinerated by the Japanese authorities in October 1945.[113] After two years, surviving buildings on the site were completely destroyed, led by the aforementioned Korean committee under the auspices of the US military government in early July 1947.[114]

The fate of its physical structure notwithstanding, the significance and symbolic meanings of the Shrine were immediately altered after liberation. During US military rule (1945–1948) Hanyang Park, the location of the shrine, was renamed "Namsan Park" and was converted from a site of Japanese spiritual assimilation into a public site that belonged to every man and woman in modern Korea, with capacity to hold massive rallies and demonstrations.[115] According to the *Dong-a ilbo* newspaper on March 4, 1946, it was a "miracle of miracles" that those who had compulsorily worshipped at the Grand Shrine of Joseon were finally able to celebrate the Korean pro-independence movement at this site on March 1, 1946.[116] This was a commemoration of the wide-scale protests that had broken out across the nation on March 1, 1919, when Koreans had rallied for independence from Japanese occupation, but which had been brutally suppressed by the Japanese authorities. Today it is a national holiday known as March First Independence Movement Day. On March 1, 1946, the Koreans who joined the celebrations would have been free to shout for independence at a site at which the Japanese authorities had tried to integrate Koreans into a Japanese identity.

On April 20, 1948, Kim Yang-seon, a pastor and an archaeologist, obtained permission from the US Army Military Government in Korea (USAMGIK)[117] to establish a Museum of Christianity and the Maesan Archaeological Museum at the site of the Grand Shrine of Joseon, in accordance with a US guideline "Principle of Dealing with Enemy Property."[118] According to Korean historian Ahn Jong-cheol, the site of the Grand Shrine of Joseon was built on nationally owned land so it could not be taken over by any Korean individual.[119] Since the shrine was classified as a religious facility, the principle meant that it could be handed over to Korean religious groups. This also explains why many former Shinto shrines were converted into churches.[120]

After the period of US military rule, the Museum of Christianity was severely damaged during the Korean War, and finally closed on February 28, 1958, on the order of President Rhee. Rhee's motive was to establish a building to house the National Assembly of the Republic of Korea at this very site, thus replacing a sacred Japanese place with a site symbolic of Korean democracy.[121] Korean sociologist Kim Baek-yeong perceives this idea as stemming from a desire for vengeance against Japanese colonial rule in South Korea.[122] Regardless, Rhee's regime postponed the plan due to the limitations of the site, and the idea was eventually abandoned by Rhee's successor Park Chung-hee.

Instead, a statue was installed at the site, continuing its overlaying with yet more significance in a changing political landscape. Rather than building a symbol of Korean democracy, President Rhee ultimately prioritized hagiography to glorify his own achievements and political power: on Liberation Day in 1956, a statue of Rhee was erected at the site of the Grand Shrine of Joseon, celebrating the President's eighty-first birthday as well as his presidential inauguration.[123] Representing Rhee's age, the statue stood at roughly eighty-one *cheok* (Korean feet, 24.5 meters) high, making it one of the tallest statues in the world at the time. Moreover, to build a new national narrative, Rhee presented himself as a symbolic "strong national father" who had founded a democratic country and "saved" South Korea from communism.[124] Although the object of encouraged worship and admiration at the site had changed from Japanese imperial power to Korean presidential power, this site on Mt. Nam thus continued to be used to direct Korean public respect toward the highest power in the nation. Yet Rhee's endeavor to idolize himself has received a generally negative appraisal in South Korea among those who have evaluated him as an unpopular pro-American politician who made little effort to lead Korea and was simply invited to do so by the United States.[125]

Rhee's statue was torn down in 1960 during the April 19 Revolution, in a rebellious act revealing the people's anger against Rhee's regime.[126] Mt. Nam was then made over yet again during the military dictatorship of Rhee's successor, Park Chung-hee, following the May 16th military coup, this time through installing memorials and statues depicting Korean independence activists and the resistance movement. Intent on legitimizing his political power, Park sought at Mt. Nam to cultivate robust national narratives, inspiring patriotic nationalism and emphasizing the restoration of Korean tradition. On the site of the former Grand Shrine of Joseon, he constructed two new squares commemorating renowned Korean independence figures (Baekbeom Plaza and Ahn Jung-geun Plaza), with statues of their namesakes: a memorial hall to Ahn Jung-geun followed in 1971.[127] Mt. Nam was used to restore national power and identity through the creation of memorials and statues for national heroes, erasing any memories of the Japanese occupation. In 1973 Guksadang was nationally designated as a Korean folk heritage site, reversing its position under Japanese rule in 1925 when Korean folk beliefs had been prohibited as superstitions impeding the development of modernity.[128]

President Park's handling of both the Guksadang and former Grand Shrine sites seem to lack a specific interest in handling Japanese legacies per se. But it was symbolically important that, from the 1960s onwards, this site once used to symbolize the figures of mandatory worship during the Japanese occupation was now occupied by the figures of Korean patriots, who played an important role in the rhetoric used to construct a heroic national narrative of South Korea that relied upon casting Japan as a significant other. Park's policy rehabilitated the Guksadang, denigrated under Japanese rule, restoring recognition of the Korean folk tradition's value.

This site's history, though, has an interesting coda: immediately after liberation, the site of the former Grand Shrine of Joseon was a hotspot for the expression of many Koreans' anger against Japanese colonial oppression. However, despite Rhee's and Park's subsequent efforts to cultivate nationalistic sentiments at the site through new place-making initiatives, the colonial memories of this place are today largely forgotten: contemporary Koreans seem to remember little about the Japanese assimilation policy, and this site is of little public interest. Nor has Guksadang escaped the same fate. Despite receiving national protection as a key site for Korean folk traditions, Guksadang today is an unpopular and neglected place, in sharp contrast with its intense popularity during the colonial period.

The treatment of Japanese colonial heritage in the reconstruction of post-colonial South Korea

These two sites, manifest how Japanese imperial power constructed new spatial meanings relating to their traditional Korean meanings, and how political shifts shaped the sites' fates in the deconstruction of the Japanese Empire and reconstruction of South Korean national identity. We turn now to the broader context of South Korea's construction of national identity after the liberation, these sites' significance within it and their influence on the nation's reconciliation of its traumatic past.

The two weeks between the Japanese surrender and US troops' arrival on September 4, 1945, were a time of intense chaos in South Korea. Many Japanese officials fled to Japan; those Japanese who remained in Korea feared reprisal attacks from Koreans. Many Koreans who felt that they suffered under the Japanese occupation celebrated their newfound independence, displaying their repressed sorrow and anger by rioting and attacking Japanese religious buildings (Japanese temples and Shinto shrines), police offices, administrative buildings, and prisons. From many Koreans' perspectives, these places connoted Japanese oppression not only of Korean independence activists but also of ordinary Koreans.

Under US military occupation (1945–1948) key aspects of the architecture (both figurative and literal) of the Japanese colonial administration in Korea were retained. Japan's military and bureaucratic structures were kept, now with US military officials in charge, and many Japanese collaborators continued to work for the new administration.[129] Most of the buildings representing the Japanese colonial social and political system retained their former uses, simply undergoing superficial renaming: the Japanese Government-General Building and Japanese military camp became the US Military Government Office and US military camp, respectively.

Meanwhile, the Japanese legacy was further managed by renaming streets and districts.[130] The South Korean capital was renamed Seoul (from Gyeongseong/ Keijō) on September 14, 1945, in order to change the city's status from a Japanese colonial capital to a South Korean one.[131] Restoring the city's identity as the capital of South Korea, the Name Amendment Committee endeavored to revert Japanese district and street names to their original appellations during the Joseon Dynasty (i.e., Gwanghwamuntong to Yukjo-ga).[132] In the Sogong-dong District, the committee chose new street names commemorating famous Korean generals. As this area had historically been the main base of the Japanese and Chinese presences in the city, the government believed that the new names, such as Eulji (after a general who had fought against China) and Chungmu (Yi Sun-sin's nom de plume for a general who had opposed Japan), would protect Korea against foreign countries.[133] This renaming reflected the Korean traditional belief that invoking a figure's name would cause their spirit to occupy the associated place.[134] In this mood, many remaining Japanese colonial architectural sites were renamed to reflect the end of Japanese rule: Joseon Bank was renamed the Bank of Korea, Gyeongseong Station became Seoul Station, and Gyeongseong Imperial University became Seoul National University. In Korean traditional belief, naming has considerable significance: a name has influential power to determine an entity's identity and future.[135] From this point of view, these renaming processes can be seen as the independent South Korea's efforts to restore their identity in subtle ways.

With the end of US military rule in 1948, Syngman Rhee became the first South Korean president (1948–1960). As a pro-American patriot, Rhee maintained the existing social and political system, working with the pro-Japanese collaborators that the US military government had inherited from the Japanese Empire. In turn, most Japanese colonial public architecture remained in use in the Republic of Korea, as it had under the US military government. Such buildings received no particular special treatment under Rhee, either to preserve or condemn them: if many remained in use, many others that were damaged during the Korean War were allowed to fall into disrepair, with lack of budget cited.

Although Rhee's main focus during a tenure that included the Korean War was anti-communist, we can nonetheless see anti-colonial sentiments expressed in his rule. Refusing a "sport diplomacy" initiative by Japan, Rhee banned Japanese football players from entering Korea.[136] Further, a cultural property protection policy that Rhee enacted in 1956 excluded cultural heritage related specifically to the Japanese colonial period.[137] These examples demonstrate the attitude of Rhee's regime to dealing with Japanese colonial legacies: as it battled extreme national poverty, ideological conflicts, and the economic crisis precipitated by the division of national territory and the Korean War (1950–1953), Rhee's regime lacked the scope to dismantle and replace the entire physical, social, political, and urban structure that the Japanese Empire had constructed. It was scarcely surprising that Rhee's hard-pressed regime would reuse what the Japanese Empire left behind in the beginning of this new nation, showing its anti-colonial sentiment more passively.

Rhee's successor, Park Chung-hee (1963–1979), remains one of the most controversial political leaders in Korean history, characterized by commentators as, Janus-like, both the builder of the nation and a military dictator. After Rhee's presidency collapsed with the April 19 Revolution in 1960, Park capitalized on the ensuing political instability to stage the May 16 military coup in 1961 and seized power. As a strong state director, Park focused on protecting the Republic of Korea as an independent country, mainly through anti-communist rhetoric and a program of economic development.[138] Park endeavored to build a strong nation with a consolidated sense of national identity, emphasizing the protection of Korean tradition and national spirit.[139] Under Park's political umbrella, three different aspects interfering with Japanese colonial legacies emerge especially clearly: 91) the restoration of Korean traditions that had been in conflict with Japanese modernization; 92) the erection of statues of Korean patriotic heroes associated with anti-colonial sentiment; and 93) the reuse of Japanese architecture under the "economy first" policy.

In the 1960s President Park designated as historic sites several symbolic locations that embodied the political structures of the Joseon Dynasty and had been changed or damaged by the Japanese colonial authorities. He launched a project to restore the Hangyang City Wall, acknowledging the significance of its value as a symbol of Korean culture and of national security against North Korea.[140] Hanyang City Wall had been built as a boundary of the Joseon capital but was extensively damaged from 1907 by the Japanese Government-General of Korea's "City Wall Processing Committee." With a major anti-communist focus, this project does not seem directly focused on restoring a Korean tradition damaged by Japanese colonial policy. But here again, as seen in the case of Guksadang, Park indirectly helped to protect and rebuild Korean traditions that had been in sharp conflict with Japanese modernization.

Second, Park allocated space for enhancing national identity and patriotic sentiments, by erecting monuments, memorials, and statues of Korean national heroes relating to Japan: besides the aforementioned statues of independence activists at the former Grand Shrine of Joseon, these included a statue of Admiral Yi Sun-Sin, Korea's defender during the Japanese invasion of 1592, in Sejong-ro Street in 1968. Park believed these figures' patriotic spirits helped keep Korea safe and secure. Park himself had served as an officer in the Japanese Kwangtung Army in 1940, and many historians point out that he did not emphasize anti-colonialist sentiments during his regime.[141] However, many have also noted Park's practical use of national heroic images as an effort to identify himself with them.[142] Through borrowing heroic images, he tried to attenuate his own image as a Japanese collaborator and to justify his own military power.[143]

Finally, while building a new Korean national identity, Park and the Korean government accelerated the nation's economic development in the 1960s and 1970s. Most of the Japanese colonial architecture created for public and official use was repurposed; many such buildings were absorbed into Seoul's urban structure and the fact that they were part of the Japanese legacy was gradually forgotten. Due to rapid urbanization and industrialization, some significant Japanese colonial sites (i.e., the Joseon Military Police Headquarters, the Joseon Oriental Colonial Company, the Joseon Industrial Bank, and the Joseon Railway Hotel) were demolished, but these acts reflected expediency rather than particular anti-Japanese sentiment.[144] Under the "economy first" policy, Park did not perceive the Japanese colonial architecture as part of a negative Japanese legacy per se, but as economic resources that could be readily reused or demolished.

The Japanese colonial sites, nonetheless, experienced differing fortunes throughout the 1980s. Due to rapid economic development, South Korea shed its status as one of the world's poorest countries, gaining financial stability in the 1980s. Accordingly, interest in the value of cultural heritage increased; this trend influenced the treatment of the Japanese colonial architectural sites. For example, acknowledging their architectural value, three Japanese colonial buildings were designated as national historic sites in 1981: Joseon Bank (the Bank of Korea), Gyeongseong Station (Seoul Station), and the old administration building of Gyeongseong Imperial University (Seoul National University). These buildings were designated under their post-liberation names rather than their original Japanese colonial era ones; this illustrates the Korean government's claim on these sites as "our" heritage, by emphasizing their post-colonial uses.

However, other Japanese colonial sites faced risks precipitated by anti-Japanese sentiment in the wake of the "textbook controversies" in 1982, in which the Japanese authorities were accused of whitewashing Japan's colonial past through the use of soft-pedalled terminology in officially produced textbooks.[145] This first "textbook controversy" provoked a storm of Korean protest, emotional mass media commentary, and fierce street demonstrations.[146] With strong support from the Korean public, the response included the construction of memorial halls commemorating the Korean independence movement against the Japanese authorities: these were the first active anti-colonial memorial works in South Korea. This was also connected to the decision to preserve Seodaemun Prison in 1987 in the debates between its demolition and preservation. Most of the Japanese colonial architecture that remained in use was by this time deteriorating, and processes began to determine whether it would be preserved or destroyed. Against this backdrop of anti-Japanese sentiment, the decision was frequently to destroy them. Hence, the 1980s represent a milestone era in which the public started to connect Japanese colonial architecture to the traumatic memories of Japanese colonial rule, just as the expediency of retaining former colonial buildings declined.

After a long succession of military regimes, President Kim Young-sam was, in 1993, the first civil president elected by a popular vote. In order to distinguish his government from those of his predecessors, he identified his presidency with establishing a real democratic nation and rectifying Korean history. He tried to erase the Japanese colonial legacy and to secure Korean legitimacy through the reorganization and refurbishment of public buildings and spaces relating to the Japanese colonial period. Under his administration, the Japanese Government-General Building, a key symbol of Japanese colonial sovereignty still used as a Capital Hall (1962–1983) and national museum (1986–1995) during the military dictatorships, was demolished in 1995 after long debates between those advocating conservation and demolition.[147] Meanwhile, reflecting the trend for the restoration of tradition, the Joseon Military Police Headquarters site was recreated as a traditional housing village. The Namsangol Traditional Housing Village, a pseudo-folk village reminiscent of the Joseon Dynasty, was constructed in its place in 1998 as a tourist attraction. The Japanese colonial architectural sites that had continued in their occupation-era usages were now often converted for new purposes.

Since the 2000s, public awareness of Japanese colonial architecture has increased and many Japanese colonial buildings have been protected for educational purposes under a Registered Cultural Heritage Law enacted in 2001. In addition, those Japanese architectural structures designated as heritage sites have in many cases been converted into public spaces, such as galleries, museums, and libraries. Some smaller port cities such as Gunsan and Pohang, famous during the colonial period, promote their surviving colonial architecture as tourist attractions (Table 4.1). Although negative perspectives on Japanese colonial legacies still persist, diverse views and understandings of these legacies exist in contemporary Korean society.

This brief outline of the post-colonial treatment of Japanese colonial legacies illustrates how they have been diversely managed in nation building. In particular, from liberation to the 1970s, Japanese colonial architecture was either reused or demolished. In some cases where Japanese colonial buildings belonged to the South Korean government, the government seemed to perceive these buildings as essential to the functioning of the Korean political/social system. Where ownership was private, individual owners saw economic benefit in reusing rather than destroying them.

Table 4.1 Trends in the treatment of Japanese colonial architecture[148]

Period	1945–1960	1960s–1970s	1980s	1990s	2000s
Trends in the treatment of Japanese colonial architecture	Ignorance and reuse (erasure of religious buildings)	Lack of awareness and reuse	Anti-Japanese sentiments and Japanese colonial architecture at risk	Liquidation of the vestiges of Japanese imperialism; erasure and transformation of Japanese colonial architecture	The increased awareness and protection of Japanese colonial architecture

However, from the 1980s to the 2000s, with an increase in civic participation and civic consciousness around deciding the fates of colonial buildings, more varied and complex debates ensued. When a major stakeholder perceived the architecture as emblematic of a painful and traumatic past, they could sometimes press their case successfully and have the building demolished to "purify" Korean identity.[149] Other demolitions were less emotive and more pragmatic, where former Japanese sites were viewed as obstacles in the context of urbanization and redevelopment policy. In other cases, colonial architecture was designated as a cultural heritage site for educational purposes, to help people understand the colonial past. This idea stemmed from the increasingly popular view that Japanese colonial legacies should not be erased from Korean society as though the occupation had never taken place, but needed to be protected so they would not be forgotten by the next generation. Still other colonial buildings remain in use without any particular debate: their colonial identity is effectively ignored, and these buildings have been reabsorbed into Korean society.

Seodaemun Prison and the Grand Shrine of Joseon trace differing paths in this context of post-conflict heritage. The riots and attacks immediately after the liberation illustrate how many members of the public identified these two sites with the Japanese colonial power that oppressed their lives. However, from 1945 to 1965, the US military government and successive South Korean presidents viewed Seodaemun Prison as a modern punitive system, but not necessarily an erasure of the previous Joseon punitive system. Hence, this system continued its function post-liberation.

The Grand Shrine of Joseon, for its part, was partly dismantled at the very dawn of the post-liberation era: for the Japanese imperial authorities it was the sacred and precious dwelling of their imperial spirit, so they deliberately disassembled some important parts of the Shrine to preempt attacks in the wake of Japan's withdrawal. After the Japanese were gone, many Korean people endeavored to completely obliterate the remaining religious architecture, viewing their own actions as a representation of the end of the Japanese Empire. The distinctive Japanese religious character and architectural style of the Grand Shrine of Joseon denied this shrine the pretext of representing any kind of Western modernization that might have served to justify its survival in subsequent Korean society.

While the Grand Shrine site was by the 1970s completely transformed into a site for memorializing the spirits of Korean independence figures, Seodaemun Prison's transformation started only in the late 1980s. Debates on this site's fate weighed the value of stories concerning both the heroic efforts of Korean independence fighters and the tales of their victimization as tortured and repressed prisoners of the Japanese. Heroic narratives today help visitors appreciate the sacrifice of the independence activists and cultivate a sense of pride. But at the same time, narratives of victimhood at the site can stir up a view of Japan as Korea's national foe, narrowing visitors' focus onto the painful and traumatic colonial past. This may limit the opportunities for Korean visitors to reconcile the past and present relationship with Japan.

It is interesting to note, then, that despite the considerable effort poured into managing these two specific sites by presidents and heritage committees alike, neither seems today to play a positive role in reconciling Korea's relationship with Japan at the national level. Seodaemun Prison cultivates Korean national identity with a lively telling of colonial history but does not actively promote sentiments of rapprochement or accord, while the former Grand Shrine site is generally forgotten.

Conclusion: The future role of Japanese colonial architecture in nation-building

With regard to nation-building, the post-colonial treatment of Japanese colonial architecture demonstrates how South Korea's perception of Japanese colonial legacies has changed through the passage of time and, in turn, how these sites' roles have been diversely constructed. Also, the architecture's post-colonial treatment partly illustrates South Korea's struggles in overcoming its contemporary national tragedies. More specifically, in the period directly after liberation, South Korea chose to ignore and thus "seal in" traumatic colonial memories, focusing its efforts on overcoming economic difficulties and fighting against communism. Japanese colonial architecture was managed more with the objective of healing colonial wounds at a domestic level than of building a new and peaceful relationship with Japan.

The two sites of Seodaemun Prison and the Grand Shrine of Joseon show diametrically opposing cases of post-conflict treatment: conservation as a heritage site and complete demolition. Hence, Seodaemun Prison survives as living evidence of the Japanese colonial period and actively contributes to the formation of the official narratives, whereby the South Korean government today frequently casts Japan as a significant "other"—sometimes an "arch-enemy." However, the Grand Shrine of Joseon was completely demolished in the mid-1940s, and memories relating to the sites are gradually fading away. Yet although the treatment of these sites might differ, both serve the aim of nation-building according to the climate of the periods in which their transformations took place. Even before the establishment of the Republic of Korea, the intentional demolition of the Grand Shrine of Joseon symbolized Korean independence through erasing colonial memories and legacies. The case of Seodaemun Prison represents the late post-colonial treatment style of converting the space into "living evidence," again though symbolizing Korean independence.

At present, we need to consider the future role of Japanese colonial architecture not only in South Korean nation-building but also in building the relationship between Japan and Korea. When focused on nation-building, the official handling of Japanese colonial architecture has tended to invoke a Japan-as-perpetrator/Korea-as-victim dichotomy. Yet we see signs that South Korea's interpretation of Japanese colonial architecture has diversified, with sites cast variously as negative symbols of Japanese imperialism, as one type of modern architecture, and as interesting resources for tourism, with different stakeholders holding diverse perceptions and views. Although such varied interpretation may generate political dissonances, Japanese colonial architecture can open a channel of communication between groups with conflicting memories, ultimately becoming a peacemaker reconciling the traumatic past with the present—both within Korea and with Japan.[150]

Notes

"Part of this chapter appeared in author's book *'Difficult Heritage' in Nation Building: South Korea and Post-Conflict Japanese Colonial Architecture* (London and New York: Palgrave Macmillan, 2019)."

1   Hiroshi Hashiya, *Ilbon Jegukjuui,Sikminji Dosiruel Geonseolhada*, trans. Jae Jeong Kim (Seoul: Motive, 2005).

2   Chu-joe Hasia, a Taiwanese scholar of urban planning writing on colonial Taiwan, has called these dramatic changes "creative destruction" from the colonizer's perspectives, and "destructive creation" from the colonized people's perspectives. Please see Chu-joe Hsia, "Theorizing Colonial Architecture and Urbanism: Building Colonial Modernity in Taiwan," *Inter-Asia Cultural Studies* 3, no. 1 (2002), pp. 7–23.

3   For details, please see Jong-heon Jin, "Demolishing Colony: The Demilition of the Old Government-General Building of Chosŏn," in *Sitings: Critical Approaches to Korean Geography*, eds. Timothy R. Tangherlini and Sallie Yea (Honolulu: University of Hawai'i Press; Centre for Korean Studies, 2008), pp. 39–60.

4   Lawrence Vale, *Architecture, Power and National Identity* (New York: Routledge, 2014).

5   David Harvey, *The Urban Experience* (Baltimore: JHU Press, 1989).

6   Brian Ladd, *The Ghosts of Berlin: Confronting German History in the Urban Landscape* (Chicago: University of Chicago Press, 1997), p. 4; Robert Bevan, *The Destruction of Memory: Architecture at War* (London: Reaktion, 2007), p. 15.

7   Mi-young Oh, "'Eternal Other' Japan: South Koreans' Postcolonial Identity," *International Journal of the History of Sport* 26, no. 3 (2009), pp. 371–389.

8   Park Kyeong-Mok, "Daehan Jegukmalgi Iljeui Gyeongseong Gamok Seolchiwa Bongam, Bungamje Sihaeng" (The Construction of Gyeongseong Prison and the Enforcement of the New System called "Bongam" and "Bungam" during the late period of the Daehan Empire), *Hanguk Geunhyundaesa Yeongu (Study on Modern and Contemporary Korean History)* 46 (2008), p. 88.

9   Ibid., p. 92.

10   Todd A. Henry, *Assimilating Seoul: Japanese Rule and the Politics of Public Space in Colonial Korea, 1910–1945*, (Berkeley, CA University of California Press, 2014), p. 25.

11   Park, "Daehan Jegukmalgi Iljeui Gyeongseong Gamok Seolchiwa Bongam, Bungamje Sihaeng," p. 97.

12   Jong-min Lee, "Jeguk Ilbonui 'Mobeom' Gamok – Tokyo, Taipei, Gyeongseongui Gamok Saryereul jungsimeuro" (The "Exemplary" Prisons of Imperial Japan: Focusing on the Cases of Tokyo, Taipei, and Keijo), *Dongbanghakji* 17, no. 12 (2016), pp. 271–309.

13   Ibid., p. 293.

14   Seok-jae Im, *Seoul, geonchukui dosiruel guekda 1* (Seoul, Walking the City of Architecture 1) (Seoul: Inmulgwa Sasangsa, 2010), p. 186.

15   Hyun-kyung Lee, "Miguk Geundae Gamokui Teukseong: Dongbu Jurip Gamokeul Jungsimeuro" (The Characteristics of Modern Prisons in the U.S.: A Case of Eastern State Penitentiary), in *The Annual Symposium proceeding: Geundae Gamukui Gachiwa Hwaryong (The value and use of modern prison)*, ed. Seodaemun Prison History Hall (Seoul: Seodaemun Prison History Hall, 2017).

16   Hyun-kyung Lee, *Difficult Heritage' in Nation Building: South Korea and Post-conflict Japanese Colonial Occupation Architecture* (New York: Palgrave Macmillan, 2018).

17   Byung-il Yang, "Seodaemun hyeongmusoui sangjing ikgi" (Reading Symbol in Meanings of Seodaemun Prison), *Sahoegyoyukak (Social Studies Education)* 45, no. 4 (2006), pp. 59–82.

18   Lee, "Jeguk Ilbonui 'Mobeom' Gamok," p. 272.

19   Ibid., p. 272.

20   Shu-Mei Huang, "Ethics of Heritage: Locating the Punitive State in the Historical Penal Landscape of Taipei," *International Journal of Heritage Studies* 23, no. 2 (2017), pp. 111–124.

21   As Foucault observed, the panopticon is like a theater that creates an "illusion of surveillance." Michel Foucault, *Discipline and Punish: The Birth of the Prison* (New York: Pantheon Books, 1979), p. 195.

22   Yang, "Seodaemun hyeongmusoui sangjing ikgi."

23   Joseon Chongdokbu (The Japanese Government-General of Korea), *Joseon Chongdukbuyeonbo 1937 (Statistics annual report of the Japanese Government-General of Korea)* (Gyeongseong: Joseon Chongdokbu, 1939), p. 360. Kyeong-mok Park, "Ilje Gangjeomgi Seodaemun Hyeongmuso Yeongu" (The Study on Seodaemun Prison during Japanese colonial period) (Unpublished PhD thesis, Chungnam University, 2015), p. 53.

24   Kim Tae-dong, Interview with author, March 29, 2017.

25   Park, *"Ilje Gangjeomgi Seodaemun Hyeongmuso Yeongu,"* p. 187.

26   For the details on their agreements, please see ibid., p. 188.

27   Chi-yeon Moon, "Gwadogiui Suhyeongjaui Dongtae" (Prisoners' Movement during the Transition Period.), *Penal Administration 1 (Hyeongjeong 1)* (Chihyeong Hyeopoe (Penal Administration Association), 1947, p. 18.

28   Ibid., p. 18.

29   Kim Sam-wung, "1948–1959 nyeonui Seodaemun Hyeongmuso" (Seodaemun Prison from 1948 to 1959), in *The 13th Academic Symposium Proceeding: Rhee Syngman Jipgwongiui Seodaemun Hyeongmuso* (Seodaemun Prison during Rhee Syngman Regime), ed. Seodaemun Prison History Hall (Seoul: Seodaemun Prison History Hall, 2012), p. 21.

30   Ibid., p. 19.

31   Shim Ji-Yeon, *Heo Heon Yeongu* (The Study on Heo Heon) (Seoul: Yeoksabipyeong, 1994), p. 405.

32   *Joseon Ilbo*, August 20, 1950.

33   Banminjokaengwiteukbyeoljosawiwonhoe (in short, Banminteugwi).

34   Kim, "1948–1959 nyeonui Seodaemun Hyeongmuso," p. 12.

35   *Maeil Shinbo*, January 15, 1940.

36   Kim "1948–1959 nyeonui Seodaemun Hyeongmuso," p. 12.

37   Ibid., pp. 5–38.

38   Ibid.

39   Chung-sok Suh, *Cho Bong-amgwa 1950yeondae (Ha)* (Cho Bong-am and the 1950s (2)) (Seoul: Yeoksa Bipyeongsa, 1999), p. 584.

40   Kim, "1948–1959 nyeonui Seodaemun Hyeongmuso," p. 31.

41   For details, Seong-cheol Kim, *Yoeksa Apeseo: Han Sahakjaui 6.25 ilgi* (In Front of History: A Diary of the Korean War Written by a Historian) (Seoul: Changjakgwa Bipyeongsa, 1993), p. 71; Yeong-bok Ju, *Naega Gyeokkeun Joseonjeonjaeng 1* (The Joseon War that I experienced 1) (Seoul: Gyoryewon, 1990), pp. 191–193.

42   Kim, "1948–1959 nyeonui Seodaemun Hyeongmuso," p. 37.

43   Jun-sik Lee, "Bujeongseongeowa Seodaemun Hyeongmuso" (Rigged Election and Seodaemun Prison), in *The 15th Academic Symposium Proceeding: 4.19 Hyeongmyeonggi Seodaemun Hyeongmuso* (Seodaemun Prison during the period of April 19 Revolution), ed. Seodaemun Prison History Hall (Seoul: Seodaemun Prison History Hall, 2013), pp. 25–32.

44   Kim, "1948–1959 nyeonui Seodaemun Hyeongmuso," p. 4.

45   In-gyu Choe, *Myeongin okjunggi* (A Master's Diary Written in Prison) (Seoul: Huimang Chulpansa, 1996), p. 268.

46   Seon-ja Yoon, "Iljeui Sinsa Seollipgwa Joseoninui Sinsa Insik, Yeoksahak Yeongu" (The Establishment of Japanese Shrines and the Recognition of Koreans about Shrines), *Yeoksahakyeongu* (*Chonnam Historical Review*) 42 (2008), p. 107.

47   Baek-yeong Kim, "Sikminji Donghwajuui Gongganjeongchi: Joseon Singungui Geonseolgwa Hwaryongeul Jungsimeuro" (C'onial Assimilationism and Urban Space – Joseon Shrine in Colonial Seoul, 1920~30s), *Incheonhakyeongu* (*Journal of Incheon Studies*) 11 (2009), p. 60.

48   Ibid., p. 62.

49   Seung-tae Kim, "Ilbon Sindoui Chimtuwa 1910, 1920 nyeondaeui (Sinsamunje)" (Inroad of Japanese Shinto to Korea and the Arguments of the Shinto Shrine in the 1910s and the 1920s), *Hanguksaron* (Argument of Korean History) 16 (1987), pp. 277–278.

50   Kim, "Sikminji Donghwajuui Gongganjeongchi," p. 60.

51   Ki-bbcum Yoo, "Namsanui Geunhyeondae Sunansa: Jonggyojeok Sangjingui Isikgwa Gonganhwa Gwajeong" (The History of Exploiting Namsan in Modern and Contemporary Korea: From Religious Symbol to Empty Space), *Jonggyomunhwayeongu* (*Journal of Religion and Culture*) 21 (2013), p. 245.

52   Ibid., p. 245. *Sinsasawon Gyuchik*.

53   Kim, "Sikminji Donghwajuui Gongganjeongchi," p. 73.

54   Todd. A. Henry, "Respatializing Chosŏn's Royal Capital: The Politics of Japanese Urban Reforms in Early Colonial Seoul, 1905–1919," in *Sitings: Critical Approaches to Korean Geography*, eds. Timothy R. Tangherlini and Sallie Yea (Honolulu: University of Hawai'i Press, 2008), p. 16.

55   Yoo, "Namsanui Geunhyeondae Sunansa," p. 245.

56   Kim, "Sikminji Donghwajuui Gongganjeongchi," p. 73.
57   Sung-ha Kook, "Ilje Gangjeomgi Sudaneuroseoui 'Joseonsingung' ui Geollipgwa unyeong" ("Chosun Shrine" as a Method of an Assimilation Policy in Japanese Colonization), *Hangukgyoyuksahak (Korean Society for History of Education)* 26, no. 1 (2004), p. 36.
58   Henry, *Assimilating Seoul.*
59   Dae-ho Kim, "20segi Namsan Heoihyeon Jarakui Byeonhyeong, Sigakjeok Jibaewa Gieokui Jeonjaeng: Gongwon, Shinsa, Dongdangui Geonribul Jungsimeuro" (The Change in the Northwest Mt. Nam, the Design of Prospect and the Maintenance of Memory in the Twentieth Century: Focusing on the Parks, Shrines, and the Construction of the Statue), *Doshi Yeongu (Korean Journal of Urban History)* 13 (2015), pp. 7–59.
60   Kook, "Ilje Gangjeomgi Sudaneuroseoui 'Joseonsingung' ui Geollipgwa unyeong," p. 45.
61   Joseongongmingyoyukhoe (Joseon Citizen Educational Association, 1933), pp. 122–124, quoted in Kook, "Ilje Gangjeomgi Sudaneuroseoui 'Joseonsingung' ui Geollipgwa unyeong," p. 47.
62   Ibid., p. 43.
63   *Maeil Sinbo* on January 3, 1940.
64   *Donga ilbo* on January 21, 1936, *Donga ilbo* on October 21, 1937.
65   The Academy of Korean Studies, "Sinsachambae Geobuundong" (Resistance to the Shinto Worship), in *Encyclopedia of Korean Culture*, available online: http://terms.naver.com/entry.nhn?docId=560276&cid=46623&categoryId=46623, accessed December 15, 2017.
66   Yoo, "Namsanui Geunhyeondae Sunansa: Jonggyojeok Sangjingui Isikgwa Gongganhwa Gwajeong," p. 244.
67   Kim, "Sikminji Donghwajuui Gongganjeongchi," p. 71.
68   Ibid., p. 70.
69   Kim, "20segi Namsan Hoehyeon Jaragui Byeonhyeong, Sigakjeok Jibaewa Gieogui Jeonjaeng," p. 18.
70   Kim, "Sikminji Donghwajuui Gongganjeongchi," p. 71.
71   Kim, "20segi Namsan Hoehyeon Jaragui Byeonhyeong, Sigakjeok Jibaewa Gieogui Jeonjaeng," p. 26.
72   Akihito Aoi, "Shinto Shrines and Urban Reconstruction of Seoul Focusing on Chosen Jingu Project," *Journal of Seoul Studies* 32 (2008), p. 47.
73   Ibid., pp. 47–48.
74   Quoted in Kim, "20segi Namsan Heoihyeon Jarakui Byeonhyeong, Sigakjeok Jibaewa Gieokui Jeonjaeng," pp. 20–24.
75   Aoi, "Shinto Shrines and Urban Reconstruction of Seoul Focusing on Chosen Jingu Project," p. 20.
76   Young-im Chi, "Jeonhu Hangugeseoui Gukgasindosiseolui Beonyong: Guknae Geollipdoen Sinsawa Sinsateoreul Jungsimeuro"(A Study on Transformation of the State Shinto Facilities in Postwar Korea – Focusing on Shinto Shrine and Shinto Shrine Site Erected in Korea), *Ireoinmunhak (Japan Language and Literature)* 69 (2016), p. 355.
77   Aoi, "Shinto Shrines and Urban Reconstruction of Seoul Focusing on Chosen Jingu Project," p. 52.
78   Kim, "20segi Namsan Hoehyeon Jaragui Byeonhyeong, Sigakjeok Jibaewa Gieogui Jeonjaeng," p. 21.

79 Aoi, "Shinto Shrines and Urban Reconstruction of Seoul Focusing on Chosen Jingu Project," pp. 51–53.

80 Ibid., p. 52.

81 Ibid., p. 53.

82 For more details, see Jang Gyu-Sik, *Seoul, Gongganuro bon Yeoksa* (Seoul, which History is Seen by its Space) (Seoul: Hyean, 2004), p. 68.

83 Seok-jae Im, *Seoul, geonchukui dosiruel guekda 1* (Seoul, Walking the City of Architecture 1), pp. 42–56.

84 Kim, "20segi Namsan Hoehyeon Jaragui Byeonhyeong, Sigakjeok Jibaewa Gieogui Jeonjaeng," pp. 23–24.

85 Ibid., pp. 23–24.

86 For example, Kim, "Sikminji Donghwajuuiui Gonggan Jeongchi"; Yoo, "Namsanui Geunhyeondae Sunansa"; Yoon, "Iljeui Sinsa Seollipgwa Joseoninui Sinsa Insik, Yeoksahak Yeongu."

87 Kim, "Sikminji Donghwajuuiui Gonggan Jeongchi," p. 70.

88 Ibid.

89 Ibid.

90 *Maeil Sinbo* on November 24, 1924.

91 Yoo, "Namsanui Geunhyeondae Sunansa: Jonggyojeok Sangjingui Isikgwa Gongganhwa Gwajeong," p. 252.

92 Jeong Jae-Jeong, Yeom In-Ho, and Jang Gyu-Sik, *Gaehyeok, Chimryak, Jeohang, Geungukui Jachuirul chakaganuen Seoul Geunhyeundaesa Yeoksa Giheng* (Reformation, Invasion, and Resistance: Modern and Contemporary History Trip to Follow the Trace of Founding a Country in Seoul) (Seoul: Seoul City University Press, 1998), p. 160.

93 Yoon, "Iljeui Sinsa Seollipgwa Joseoninui Sinsa Insik, Yeoksahak Yeongu," p. 129.

94 Ibid., p. 129.

95 Kook, "Ilje Gangjeomgi Sudaneuroseoui 'Joseonsingung' ui Geollipgwa unyeong," p. 38.

96 Seok-yeong Choi, *Iljeha Musokrongwa Sikminji Gwollyeok* (Discourse of Shamanism and Colonial Authorities under Japanese Colonial Rule) (Seoul: Seokeongmunhwasa, 1999), p. 123.

97 Yoon, "Iljeui Sinsa Seollipgwa Joseoninui Sinsa Insik, Yeoksahak Yeongu," p. 124.

98 Kook, "Ilje Gangjeomgi Sudaneuroseoui 'Joseonsingung' ui Geollipgwa unyeong," p. 48.

99 Ibid., p. 48.

100 Ibid.

101 *Maeil Sinbo* on October 22, 1925.

102 For example, Hea-jin Moon, "Iljesikminsigi Gyeongseongbu Sinsa: Sinsa mit Jesinui Sigibyeol Seonggyeongeul Jungsimeuro" (Japanese Shinto Shrines in Keijyo(Seoul) during the Japanese Colonial Period: Focused on Time-Variant Characteristics of Japanese Shinto Shrines and Gods), *Jeongsinmunhwayeongu* (*Korean Studies Quarterly*) 36, no. 3 (2013), pp. 369–396; Kook, "Ilje Gangjeomgi Sudaneuroseoui 'Joseonsingung' ui Geollipgwa unyeong"; Yoon, "Iljeui Sinsa Seollipgwa Joseoninui Sinsa Insik, Yeoksahak Yeongu."

103 Morita Yoshio, *Chosenn syusenn no kiroku: Beiso ryogunn no sinchuuto Nihonnzinn no hikiage* (Shouwa: Gannandou-shoten, 1964), pp. 107–110.

104 Ibid., pp. 107–110.

105   For example, Choi, *Iljeha Musokrongwa Sikminji Gwollyeok*; Young-im Chi, "Jeonhu Hangugeseoui Gukgasindosiseolui Beonyong: Guknaee Geollipdeon Sinsawa Sinsateoreul Jungsimeuro" (A Study on Transformation of the State Shinto facilities in Post-War Korea – Focusing on Shinto Shrine and Shinto Shrine Site erected in Korea), *Ireoinmunhak (Japan Language and Literature)* 69 (2016), pp. 349–365.

106   *Donga ilbo* on August 9, 1946.

107   For example, *Donga ilbo* on January 19, 1946; *Gyeonghyang Sinmun* on November 22, 1946.

108   The destruction of Japanese Shinto shrines was a common phenomenon throughout Japan's former colonies. This contrasts with the treatment of colonial churches, which tended to be reused and turned into heritage sites (Hashiya, *Ilbon Jegukjuui, Sikminji Dosiruel Geonseolhada*, p. 98).

109   Chi, "Jeonhu Hangukeseoui Gukgashindo Siseolui Beonyong," p. 356.

110   Chang-su Kim, "Haebanggwa Hamkke 'Sumeun Sin' Amateras" ("Hidden Goddess" Amateras with liberation), *Kyeongin ilbo*, August 17, 2011, available online: www.kyeongin.com/main/view.php?key=600199, accessed December 2, 2017.

111   The Japanese Government-General of Korea phoned each shrine to hold the ceremony (Choi, *Iljeha Musokrongwa Sikminji Gwollyeok*, p. 125).

112   Morita, *Chosenn syusenn no kiroku: Beiso ryogunn no sinchuuto Nihonnzinn no hikiage*, pp. 107–110.

113   Kim, "20segi Namsan Heoihyeon Jarakui Byeonhyeong, Sigakjeok Jibaewa Gieokui Jeonjaeng," p. 35.

114   Ibid., p. 36.

115   Ho-gi Jeong, "Gukgaui Hyeongseonggwa Gwangjangui Jeongchi" (The Formation of a Nation and Politics of Agora), *Sahoewa Yeoksa (Society and History)* 77 (2008), pp. 179–181.

116   Kim, "20segi Namsan Heoihyeon Jarakui Byeonhyeong, Sigakjeok Jibaewa Gieokui Jeonjaeng," p. 36.

117   Yoo, "Namsanui Geun, Hyeondae Sunansa," p. 263.

118   *Jeoksancheriwonchik.*

119   Jong-cheol Ahn, "1930–40 nyeondae Namsan Sojae Gyeongseong Hoguk Shinsaui Geonrib, Hwalyong, geurigo Haebank Hu Byeonhwa" (The Founding, Usage, and the Postwar Change of the Seoul National Patriotic Shrine during the 1930–40s), *Journal of Seoul Studies* 42 (2011), p. 66.

120   Yoo, "Namsanui Geun, Hyeondae Sunansa," p. 263.

121   Kim, "Sikminji Donghwajuuiui Gonggan Jeongchi," pp. 70–75.

122   Ibid., p. 70.

123   Jae-jeong, In-ho, and Gyu-sik, *Gaehyeok, Chimryak, Jeohang, Geungukui Jachuirul chakaganeun Seoul Geunhyeundaesa Yeoksa Giheng*, p. 231.

124   Guy Podoler, "Seoul: City, Identity and the Construction of the Past," in *Remembering, Forgetting and City Builders*, eds. Tovi Fenster and Haim Yacobi (Farnham: Ashgate, 2010), p. 130.

125   For example, The Academy of Korean Studies, ed., *Hanguk Hyeondaesaui Jaeinsik 1* (Rethinking Modern Korean History. vol. 1.) (Seoul: Oreum, 1998).

126   Kim, "20segi Namsan Heoihyeon Jarakui Byeonhyeong, Sigakjeok Jibaewa Gieokui Jeonjaeng," p. 40.

127   Gwon Gi-Bong, *Seoulul geonilmye sarajeganun Yeoksarul Mannada* (I Meet a Disappearing History When Walking around Seoul) (Paju: Alma, 2011), pp. 68–70.

128 You-jin Jung, "Park Chung-hee Jeongbugi Munhwajaejeongchaekgwa Minsokshinang: Guksadanggwa Bamseombugundangeul jungsimeuro" (Policy of Cultural Assets and folk beliefs in the Period of Park Jung-hee- Focused on the Guksadang and Bamseom Bugundan), *Yeoksaminsokhak (Journal of Korean Historical-folklife)* 39 (2012), pp. 180–183.

129 Bruce Cumings, "The Legacy of Japanese Colonialism in Korea," in *The Japanese Colonial Empire, 1895–1945*, eds. Ramon H. Mayers and Mark R. Peattie (Princeton, NJ: Princeton University Press, 1984), pp. 478–496.

130 Jae-jeong, In-ho, and Gyu-sik, *Gaehyeok, Chimryak, Jeohang, Geungukui Jachuirul chakaganuen Seoul Geunhyeundaesa Yeoksa Giheng*, p. 138.

131 Ibid., 138.

132 *Seoul Sinmun* on November 24, 1945.

133 Gwon, *Seoulul geonilmye sarajeganun Yeoksarul Mannada*, p. 207.

134 Jae-jeong, In-ho, and Gyu-sik, *Gaehyeok, Chimryak, Jeohang, Geungukui Jachuirul chakaganuen Seoul Geunhyeundaesa Yeoksa Giheng*, p. 138.

135 Ibid., p. 138.

136 Guy Podoler, "Nation, State and Football: The Korean Case," *International Journal of the History of Sport* 27, no. 1 (2008), pp. 1–17.

137 Jeong-tae Eun, "Park Chung-hee Sidae Seongyeokhwa Saupui Chuiwa Sunggeok" (The Development and Characters of the Sanctification Project during Park Chung-hee's Era), *Yeoksamunjeyeongu (Korean Historic Studies)* 15 (2005), p. 244. Cultural Heritage Sites relating to North Korea were also excluded.

138 Jin, "Demolishing Colony," pp. 45–47. For details of Park's governing mythology as regards anti-communist rhetoric, see Andre Schmid, *Korea between Empires, 1895–1919* (New York: Columbia University Press, 2002), p. 272. His Yushin movement was modeled on the Meiji Restoration and Saemaul movement, and was similar to a movement seen in colonial Manchuria.

139 Podoler, "Seoul: City, Identity and the Construction of the Past," p. 133.

140 Yu Seung-Hun, *Hyeonjang Sokui Munhwajae Jeongchaek* (Cultural Heritage Policy in the Field) (Seoul: Minsokwon, 2004), pp. 65–67.

141 Podoler, "Seoul: City, Identity and the Construction of the Past," pp. 133–134.

142 For example, Jae-ho Jeon, *Bandongjeok Geundaejuuija Park Chung-hee* (A Reactionary Modernist, Park Chung-hee) (Seoul: Chaeksesang, 2000); Hyeong-jin Gwon and Jong-hun Lee, *Daejung Dokjaeui Youngwoong Mandeulgi* (Making a Hero for Public Dictatorship) (Seoul: Humanist, 2005).

143 For example, Eun, "Park Chung-hee Sidae Seongyeokhwa Saupui Chuiwa Sunggeok."

144 Due to this "economy first" policy, even examples of Korean traditional architecture had to be relocated, losing their original places despite being under legal protection (e.g., the Gate of Sajikdan Altar in 1968; the Independence Gate in 1979).

145 Podoler, "Seoul: City, Identity and the Construction of the Past," p. 135.

146 Ibid., p. 135.

147 Ministry of Culture and Sports, *Gu Joseonchongdokbu Geunmul Silcheuk mit Cheolgeo Bogoseo Sang* (The Report Regarding the Survey and Demolition of the Former Japanese Government-General Building, vol. 1) (Seoul: Ministry of Culture and Sports and the National Museum of Korea, 1997), p. 344.

148 Hyung Kyung, Lee, *"Difficult Heritage" in Nation Building: South Korea and Post-Conflict Japanese Colonial Architecture* (London and New York: Palgrave Macmillan, 2019), p. 279.

149   This was the case for the Japanese Government-General Building; see Lee, *"Difficult Heritage" in Nation Building: South Korea and Post-conflict Japanese Colonial Occupation Architecture.*

150   Lee, *'Difficult Heritage' in Nation Building*, p. 279.

Chapter 5

THE CINEMATIC RECONSTRUCTION OF EAST ASIA IN POSTWAR JAPANESE WAR FILMS

Dick Stegewerns

In the aftermath of the Second World War, the countries and regions that had been part of the former Japanese Empire were often too preoccupied by the need simply to survive and to rebuild to be able to address issues that pertained to the colonial rule and wartime occupation by the Japanese. In Japan itself the Cold War structure and other factors also meant that Japan's colonial and wartime past was not in full focus, and a social consensus on the nature of the war and Japan's role in it was not established.[1] This situation in most cases also left unaddressed issues such as responsibility, guilt, and compensation, resulting in a shaky basis for Japan's relations with its East Asian neighbors and a continuation of Japan's modern mindset ever since the Meiji period in the sense of emphasizing the distinction between the national self and the Asian other.

Cinema was one of the most popular and influential formats of popular culture in the postwar period. The mainly American forces implementing the Allied occupation of Japan were keenly aware of the power of the medium of film and enforced a policy of strict censorship on one hand, while on the other hand certain subjects were endorsed: democracy, emphasis on the individual, equal role of women, and some kissing and baseball.[2] During the occupation period the American interpretation of the war as a Pacific War was prescribed and especially the wartime military leadership was characterized as evil. However, the recent war in general was not very much in focus and many facets of the war were completely obscured. Once the occupation was lifted, the silver screen became a major site for the expression of competing visions of Japan's collective war memory. The genre of the war movie was firmly reinstated within most big studios, and related subgenres were created and re-created during the 1950s.[3]

The end of Japan's empire, the temporary lack of sovereignty and diplomatic relations during the occupation period, the division of Asia under the Cold War, and anti-Japanese feelings due to Japan's colonial and wartime occupation implied that Japan to a large extent was cut off from the Asian continent during the first two decades after the Second World War. During this period war films were the major genre to project Japan's East Asian neighbors on the cinema screen. In subgenres such as the combat film, the war hero film, the war crime trials film, the Asian brotherhood film, and the wartime comedy, the venue of the East Asian continent was reintroduced and Japanese relations with its inhabitants were re-enacted.[4] The representations of war could be vastly different, depending on the differing views on the war held by filmmakers and producers, and their equally competing views of the reconstruction of Japan's position in the postwar world. However, both in what they showed and what they ignored there are often striking similarities encompassing all competing camps.[5]

As yet there is no overview and overall analysis of postwar Japanese war films, let alone a categorization of the various subgenres. This essay is a first attempt, although limited to the time span of the two postwar decades, to analyze the depiction of Asia in Japanese war films. Accordingly, in this chapter I will only analyze Japanese war films, including films dealing with the aftermath of war, from the period 1945–1965, that depict the countries and regions formerly included in Japan's colonial or wartime empire. On the basis of this limited analysis, I propose four main categories of depicting Asia in Japanese films: (1) Asia as a horrendous war zone where the Japanese were killed, (2) Asia as an Orientalist stage for exotic love affairs, (3) Asia as a boundless and adventurous Wild East, and (4) Asia as an instrument to whitewash Japan's wartime history into an anti-colonial pro-Asian liberating mission. In the first category, I make a further distinction of three subcategories, on the basis of whether the Japanese soldiers were killed by their officers, by enemy armies, or by the native population.

The dominant trends I discern on the basis of my analysis for this chapter go beyond the small number of postwar films that depict the countries and regions formerly included in Japan's colonial or wartime empire. The tendency to deal with Asia as if it has no content and the cover-up of Japan's former empire are representative of the large majority of Japanese postwar war films. Moreover, the lack of interest for the Asian other and the more or less explicit notion that Japan is not part of Asia link directly to Japan's modern mindset, in which the country— before and after the period discussed here—looked down upon Asia.

The invisible or unattractive Asia of the Occupation period

In his book on transnational film culture in Imperial Japan, Michael Baskett has argued that Japan's empire in Asia possessed a particularly compelling "filmic attractiveness," and that this attractiveness continued after the war until the present day.[6] Even so, I find it difficult to make the case that Japanese cinema in the postwar period started out by providing an attractive picture of the continent.

First of all, Asia was hardly shown during the Occupation period. The Occupation authorities were keen to foster a harmonious relationship between the occupation forces and the Japanese people. Thus they wanted as much as possible to avoid opening fresh wounds and chose to refrain from providing the Japanese audiences with scenes of the recent war, especially if this involved fighting between the Japanese and American armies. Accordingly, films made in the occupation period and dealing with the war did not include battle scenes, and in this way the screen on Asia, the venue of the war, was turned empty.[7] In a way, such a development was perhaps inevitable, as it was in sync with Japan being returned to the scope of its late Edo period size, disconnected even from the southern archipelago of Okinawa. Moreover, in the immediate postwar period of upheaval and severe food shortages, the people were too obsessed with daily survival to have the opportunity to consider the loss of their Asian empire.[8]

During the last stage of the Occupation, when control and censorship by the Occupation bureaucracy had relaxed considerably, the first postwar war films showing Asia were made. However, as these were still products of the Occupation period, there was not much leeway to stray away from the official interpretation of the war as a Pacific War, in which Japan was looked upon as an evil entity, characterized by such traits as militarism, feudalism, imperialism, aggression, inequality, and a complete lack of democracy and individualism. The postwar depiction of wartime Asia started out with a relatively limited number of scenes of Japan's military presence on the various Asian battlefields, with all the related negative symptoms up front. It introduced the main image of Asia in war films during the period 1945–1965 as an unattractive place where the Japanese were killed.

In this chapter, I will discuss this most common, negative depiction of Asia in postwar Japanese war films, divided in three subcategories on the basis of who killed the Japanese soldiers and presented in chronological order.

Asia as the war theater where we killed each other

The very first films made under the Occupation that dealt with the wartime period, such as *Who is a Criminal* (Hanzaisha wa dare ka, 1945), *The Morning of the Ōsone Family* (Ōsone-ke no asu, 1946), *People's Enemy* (Minshū no teki, 1946), *No Regrets for Our Youth* (Waga seishun ni kui nashi, 1946), *Once More* (Ima hitotabi no, 1947), *Between War and Peace* (Sensō to heiwa, 1947), and *A Flower Blooms* (Hana hiraku), were set on the home front. All carried a strong anti-war message. In these films, the Japanese people were represented by anti-war liberal parliamentarians, journalists, and factory workers, oppressed by the military and their capitalist henchmen. The military, and especially the military police (kempeitai), were the "criminals" and "the people's enemy" mentioned in the titles of these films, and especially the 1952 *A Secret Tale of the War's End - The Dawn of August 15* (Shūsen hiwa - Reimei hachigatsu jūgonichi, 1952) stands out for its overwhelming anti-kempeitai character. The films of the late Occupation period that brought us the first postwar scenes of Japan's military presence in Asia during the wartime period merely linked to the already established image of the military in the anti-war home front films from the early Occupation days onwards. However, since there was no realistic place for parliamentarians, journalists, and factory workers on the war front, the role of the good, moral, and heroic protagonist was given to the regular foot soldier. The bad guys were now no longer enacted by the military police but by army (often lower- or middle-rank) officers. And like the oppression of civilians by the military police on the home front sometimes could escalate into the military causing the death of innocent and/or resisting civilians, in the anti-war films located in Asia an identical tradition was created in the form of the sadistic Japanese military officer killing by himself the heroically resisting regular soldier under his command.

This pattern was introduced in the film *Desertion at Dawn* (Akatsuki no dassō, 1950) of 1950, located on the central China front. The unforgettable final scene shows commander Ozawa Sakae almost ecstatically mowing down with a machine gun the love couple of the deserting soldier Ikebe Ryō and singer Yamaguchi Yoshiko.[9] Ozawa's impressive role established the standard image of the Japanese middle-rank officer as a corrupt and sadistic rapist, who tried to cover his shortcomings and frustrations by taking bloody revenge on intellectually or morally superior (and sometimes more romantically successful) subordinates. On the Burma front of *Listen to the Voices of the Sea* (Nihon senbotsu gakusei no shuki - Kike wadatsumi no koe, 1950) of the same year, no women are involved, but the intraregiment killing is equally rampant. However, in this film based upon the writings of conscripted students who died in battle, there is the added divide between the career soldiers and the conscripts, the former treating the latter with contempt and abuse, and eventually using them as gun fodder.

This divide is also focused upon in the first postwar kamikaze movie, *Beyond the Clouds* (Kumo nagaruru hate ni, 1953). In the final scene of this movie, the commanding officers, confronted with the complete failure of the kamikaze missions of the squad, coolly comment that these young boys were immature—the next batch will do better. This first postwar film dealing with the kamikaze was ironically also the last to be outspokenly negative in its depiction of the kamikaze project. The subsequent productions in this particular war film subgenre, which have been highly popular until this very day, have misrepresented the true face of the war. The kamikaze missions are only a very small and minor part of the war, during its very last stages, and the number of casualties is negligible when compared to those on the Chinese front and Pacific islands. In the last case most soldiers died of illness and starvation – a most unromantic variety of death during wartime. This cinematic misrepresentation has contributed to what I term 'the kamikaze taboo', which have elevated the young kamikaze pilots and their mission to a sacred and inviolable level beyond rational criticism. In their urge to eulogize the sacrifice and bravery of the innocent young men (often impersonated by good-looking actors), these films have consciously hushed-up crucial but unwelcome facts. They usually depict the young soldiers as your average boy-next-door, whereas the overwhelming majority of the kamikaze pilots were drafted elite students. Moreover, many of them hated the war, the army, and the emperor, and were hardly able to make any sense of their "holy mission." However, in contrast to the professional pilots, they did not have the freedom to reject the request to go out on a suicide mission.[10]

From the end of the Occupation onwards the kamikaze pilots have been treated in an increasingly favorable way, which has resulted in their present-day untouchable status of almost holy purity and patriotism. However, this status is unique and does not extend to their Kaiten submarine equivalents, or victims of identically (coerced) suicidal missions. Accordingly, there are not many films eulogizing the central army policy of forbidding their troops to surrender in the face of inevitable defeat and instead forcing them into such irrational and cruel actions as conducting a final futile attack (*totsugeki*) or committing collective suicide (euphemistically termed *gyokusai*, or shattering diamonds). In sharp contrast to the lack of films critically dealing with the kamikaze, there are quite a few (anti-)war films such as *The Last Charge* (Saigo no totsugeki, 1957) and *Fires on the Plan* (Nobi, 1959), condemning the cruelty and insaneness in the Field Service Code (*senjinkun*) ideology of not being allowed to surrender. The film *The Last Women* (Saigo no onnatachi, 1954) extended its focus, uniquely, to the army-enforced collective suicide of civilians involved in the fall of Saipan (although there are identical depictions in films on the battle of Okinawa, which I excluded from this chapter on non-Japanese Asia).

Neither should we forget a few even more extreme examples of Japanese soldiers killing one another on the Asian front, although these were not dictated by army hierarchy and ideology and thus were more "spontaneous." In the early 1950s the Japanese media, and thus also cinema, went wild over the astounding story of two dozen Japanese shipwrecked soldiers killing each other in their competition for one woman, that was re-enacted in the films *This is the Truth of Anatahan* (Anatahan-tō no shinsō wa kore da!, 1953) and *Anatahan* (Anatahan, 1953) (the first had the remarkable selling point that they had found the woman willing to act herself, the second boasted foreign maestro Joseph von Sternberg as director).[11] Another extreme form of Japanese-on-Japanese killing was explored in the film *Fires on the Plain* (Nobi, 1959) an adaptation of the novel by Ōoka Shōhei. Although it did not result in a media spectacle, the film had a particularly strong impact and turned into an anti-war classic. Written on the basis of his own experiences at the end of the war in the Philippines, Ōoka's novel testified how the emperor's army in a protracted state of chaos, fatigue, and hunger let go of all humaneness and completely debased itself by resorting to cannibalism.

The hierarchy and brutality of life in the army barracks on the China front also provided the framework for many army comedy series of the late 1950s and early 1960s, such as *Buck Privates* (Nitōhei monogatari, 1955–1961), *Soldier Kingorō* (Kingorō no heitai, 1956–1959) and *Dear Mr. Emperor* (Haikei tennō heika-sama, 1963–1964). The fun was mainly in showing how the cunning privates were able to evade the deprivation and brutality of army life and outwit their officers, although the last of these three series is rather different in the sense that the protagonist is just so good-hearted and innocent that he does not even understand that his superiors are trying to bully him. The comic heroes in these series sporadically resist their commanders, but never with overly violent or fatal consequences.[12] A more cathartic effect was offered by the army outlaw series of *Desperado Outpost* (Dokuritsu gurentai, 1959–1964) and *Yakuza Soldier* (Heitai yakuza, 1965–1968, 1972), which showed lower-class and yakuza outcasts of Japanese society on the Wild West-like North China war front exacting revenge upon the corrupt and brutal officers who had caused the deaths of their comrades. However, all this was part of a rather less than realistic framework colored by adventure, comedy, and male bravura.[13] In the more realistic genre of (anti-)war films, where there was little comic relief, attempts at resistance were invariably shown as futile. And in the few cases where violent subordination is depicted, as in the classic anti-war series *The*

Human Condition (Ningen no jōken, 1959–1961), in which the heroically struggling protagonist (played by Nakadai Tatsuya) in growing desperation successfully kills his bully-commander, the hero is not allowed to walk away unscathed and ultimately dies on the battlefield. Anti-war films almost always focus on the horror and ultimate futility of the human loss involved in warfare, and accordingly do not often allow the survival of the main protagonist or any other happy ending.

The enemy camp was sometimes depicted as a place of comfort and even freedom for the suffering common soldier. In Between War and Peace, a Japanese soldier retreating from the front is saved from drowning by a Chinese fishing boat and ends up being treated with respect and understanding by his captors. And in Desertion at Dawn (and its 1965 remake *Story of a Prostitute* (Shunpuden, 1965)), the capture of the two protagonists (a man and a woman, the latter played by Yamaguchi Yoshiko) by the Chinese army provides them with the only opportunity for their love to blossom. In this last film in particular, China is shown as a benign, almost idyllic, paradise: Yamaguchi dons Chinese dress, speaks the local language, and confides to her lover that they have been caught by "an enemy whom we cannot hate." All this, however, was not allowed to obscure the dominant message, which had to be that Asia was hell.

Asia as the war theater where we were killed by the enemy

As discussed in the previous section, from the last phase of the Occupation onwards Asia was reconfigured as a scene of horror, where pure and good Japanese soldiers were tortured and killed by their brutal sadistic officers. This new trend cannot be seen as separate from the anti-militaristic message emanating from the occupation forces and the related interpretation that the responsibility for the war and Japanese war crimes lay predominantly with the leaders of Japan's Imperial Army (with a certain leniency extended toward the more high-brow and Anglophile Imperial Navy, who often are characterized as merely having done their job while in essence being against the war). Under the occupation forces' drastic control of the media it was forbidden to show any Americans in Japanese films, let alone to portray them in a negative way. Since scenes of battle and the atomic bombing of Hiroshima and Nagasaki would inevitably link to the erstwhile picture of the United States as the enemy of Japan, these were also forbidden. However, already before the end of the occupation this strict media control gradually gave way. In 1950 and 1951 films were produced that dealt with the after effects of the atomic bombs, and in the anti-war films *Desertion at Dawn, Listen to the Voices of the Sea*, and *Bengawan River* (Bungawan soro, 1951), the Imperial Army and Japan's empire were shown again, although the battlefields and occupied territories were strategically chosen in the sense that these did not directly involve an American enemy.[14]

With the formal end of the Occupation in April 1952 no formal restrictions remained about showing or referring to an American enemy. Conveniently, one of the last films made under the Occupation gave an indication of the way in which the American–Japanese war legacy had best be treated. *Oath of Heaven* (Ōzora no chikai, 1951) was the first installment in a Cold War-inspired series depicting two pilots, one Japanese and one American, who landed on a desert island somewhere in the Pacific, eventually becoming inseparable friends. In this series, there is a clear depiction of the war that is taking place between the United States and Japan, and we see for the first time an actor who plays the American enemy. In very little time, however, the two former enemies start to demonstrate a friendship, one that is clearly extended to American–Japanese friendship at large.[15]

Due to the demands of the Cold War structure, in the postwar period Hollywood no longer provided detailed scenes of Japanese wartime atrocities, as it had been prone to do during the war years.[16] War was still hell, and as before American soldiers heroically and sometimes tragically gave their everything to end this hell, but they were seldom confronted by the evil Japanese.[17] In a comparable way, after the Occupation ended the Japanese film industry returned to its wartime tradition of focusing on the hardships of, and sacrifices by, a brotherhood of simple and like-minded men in the face of an invisible and amorphous enemy that was most often represented in the soulless formats of bullets, bombs, aircraft, and battleships. Thus, although there are numerous Japanese war films in which the brothers-in-arms (*senyū*) fall one by one under enemy fire, scenes that present us with a fighting enemy that has a body, a soul, and a face are absent.[18] This is true of the first instalments in the major war film subgenres dealing with the Lilly Corps (*Himeyuri-tai*) during the battle of Okinawa, the kamikaze pilots, the battleship *Yamato*, the atomic bombing of Hiroshima, and Admiral Yamamoto Isoroku, which all flooded the screen in 1953.

Although (Pacific) Asia from the end of the Occupation onwards thus gradually evolved from an unattractive war zone where Japanese soldiers were killed by their officers into an equally horrendous place where they were killed by enemy forces, the Asian character of the venue was not sustained. This is to a considerable extent due to the advent of what I term "anti-anti-war films," which were revisionist in the sense that they consciously rejected the negative depiction of Japan's involvement in the Second World War in the way that the anti-war films did. As these films do not celebrate war in itself, nor advocate a continuation of the fighting, "pro-war films" is probably too strong a wording. However, some of these films reintroduced wartime propaganda terms such as "military gods" and "Greater East Asian War" and thus openly rejected the American-coined "Pacific War" interpretation of the war and the verdicts of the Tokyo Tribunal. In their zeal to highlight the purity and bravery of Japanese soldiers and/or to emphasize the bilateral American-Japanese nature of the war, the backdrop of anti-anti-war films is seldom outspokenly Asian, and almost without exception the enemy is non-Asian.[19]

Anti-war films have a stronger predilection to firmly place themselves in mainland China or at one of the Pacific venues of the American island-hopping strategy, but the focus is rather inward and the enemy often remains amorphous. An exception to this rule is *Songs on the Battlefield* (Senjō ni nagareru uta, 1965), in which we, together with an army marching band, are first taken to north China and next to the Philippines, both of which are depicted in detail and are populated by many local inhabitants. This film also stands out in that it presents a scene in which Japanese soldiers in army trucks are caught by Chinese guerillas on horseback, and a large share of the military marching band members are killed.

In the previous section we noticed how with the relaxation of censorship during the final years of the Occupation, the depiction of the war front, and thus of

Asia, became possible. In this section we have seen how the end of the Occupation resulted in the lifting of the ban on showing or mentioning the United States as Japan's wartime enemy. This resulted in a shift in postwar Japanese war films from scenes showing the Japanese killing one another to scenes showing the Japanese being killed by (American) enemy fire. However, there was no inherent change in the trend of mainly depicting Asia as a horrendous war front that, moreover, was often void of clear Asian elements or inhabitants.

Asia as the war theater where we killed the natives and the natives killed us

Anti-anti-war films, which appeared at the end of the Occupation and before long outnumbered anti-war films to become the overwhelmingly dominant type of war film, usually provide at most an amorphous enemy in the Asian war theater and hardly ever show local inhabitants, let alone combatants.[20] However, a few anti-war films have delved somewhat deeper into the relations between the Japanese occupying armies and the local population, in order to point out that these relations were anything but cordial. These films also include scenes of Japanese killing one another or Japanese being killed by an amorphous American enemy, and thus are not entirely different from the two types discussed in the previous sections, but they provided a new element: the Japanese killing, and being killed by, local inhabitants.

In this section, I will briefly discuss three films, all anti-war films. The anti-war classic Fires on the Plain provides two scenes involving Filipinos that, although few in number, are strong in impact. In the first scene the good but emaciated private Tamura, on his solitary odyssey through the jungle, in a lakeside village bumps into a young couple who are terrified by him, and he ends up inadvertently killing the girl. This is echoed by a scene at the end of the film where a Japanese soldier surrendering to the American troops is shot down by a vengeful Filipino female soldier. The plot of To the End of the Sun (Hi no hate, 1954) is too complex and far-fetched to explain briefly, but here also the native love interest of a deserted Japanese army doctor shoots the benign protagonist Lieutenant Uji, upon which his crazy militarist subordinate shoots the native woman. The well-intentioned members of the army marching band in Songs on the Battlefield are taught the same lesson in China and the Philippines: that there is an unbridgeable gap between them and the locals, which may easily lead to fatal incidents. Although they themselves do not support the killing of Chinese guerillas and locals by their army superiors, there is no way they can avoid seeing anti-Japanese slogans wherever they go and becoming victims of local resistance. And even when in the middle of nowhere they think they have come upon a kindred soul in the form of an elderly Peking Opera actor and musician, their hopes of finding some common ground are dashed by mentions of the Nanjing Massacre and the kind requests to clear out as soon as possible. A shift of scene to the Philippines does not provide any opportunity for Asian fraternity either. Although the local Americanized citizens willingly dance to some of the Japanese marching band's jazzy tunes, eventually they end up going through the same motions of the Japanese killing the natives and the natives killing the Japanese. Even sharper is the contrast with the ending scene, where the remaining members of the decimated Japanese marching band, defeated, starving, in rags, and doing forced labor, finally find some consolation and fraternity in playing *Auld Lang Syne* (Hotaru no hikari) with an impeccable American army orchestra.

Many films of the two types discussed in the previous two sections more or less consciously left open the question whether there was any truth to the wartime propaganda of Japan bringing about an Asian brotherhood, often merely by not showing any local inhabitants. However, the three anti-war films that present us with clear examples of the local population mercilessly show the bankruptcy of such Asianist dreams and instead add the local Asian people to the camps of those being killed by, or killing, the Japanese.

Asia as the tropical paradise (and ultimate hell) of our exotic love affairs

The postwar depictions of Asia and Japan's involvement in the region were not all bleak. The new postwar image of Asia as a theater of animosity, hatred, horror, and death could not completely do away with its exotic Orientalist attraction, which had been the feature of many prewar and wartime songs, books, and films.

The first Asia-focused genre with wartime roots to reappear on the postwar scene was that of the so-called goodwill movie (*shinzen eiga*). This genre, most famously represented by the so-called "three continental films" starring Ri Kō-ran (the Chinese cover-up name of the Japanese actress Yamaguchi Yoshiko) and Hasegawa Kazuo, was part and parcel of the wartime government policy to "pacify" Asia, in most cases China.[21] These invariably showed how a male, strong, and kind-hearted Japan confronted the anti-Japanese opposition of a female, weak Asia and due to his superior moral qualities succeeded in winning her trust and love. It is quaint that the Chinese in occupied territories in spite of the abstruse propaganda message flocked to the cinemas to admire Ri Kō-ran. However, it is even more astonishing that the first postwar instalment in the wartime propaganda film type of the goodwill movie was made during the Occupation period.

The film Bengawan River, named after an Indonesian song well familiar amongst the Japanese, concentrates on a wartime love affair between a Japanese officer and an Indonesian woman, although the latter was impersonated by a Japanese actress whose face had been given a darker color. The setting is that of an exotic premodern paradise: beaches, palm trees, and bananas galore. Instead of the well-organized modern colonial metropole of Batavia (present-day Jakarta) or the oil fields that largely inspired the Japanese invasion of Indonesia, the country is represented by the outspokenly premodern (no car or electricity) and rural setting of a tiny Javanese village. And, to make the Orientalist dream complete, the Asian other which populated this exotic setting is mainly personified by local female beauties who show themselves quite moved and impressed by the male Japanese intruders into their hitherto undisturbed lives. The female protagonist Sariya, repeating a stereotype present in almost all goodwill films, at first shows herself hostile to the Japanese because of the Japan-inflicted death of her brother. However, before long she offers herself to officer Fukami, in highly sexualized scenes. Unsurprisingly, her love is reciprocated and in the end she even risks her life for her foreign lover, but due to a twist of fate she lives and he dies, and their love remains unconsummated.[22]

One would be inclined to slight Bengawan River and the almost identical *Terang Boelan – The Light of the Moon* (Toran būran – tsuki no hikari, 1954), this time named after a well-known Malaysian song, as a run-of-the-mill melodrama. And although the former film incorporated elements of the anti-war film located in Asia, such as the evil Japanese superior killing the good soldier, it is clear that the general mood and message of these films were pointing in a completely different direction, derivative of the wartime genre of goodwill films. It was no coincidence that these two films were produced by Shin-Tōhō, the studio that started out with, and during its brief existence remained most active in, the mission to undermine the interpretation of the war forced upon Japan by the Occupation.[23]

Regardless of such political intentions, the other studios Daiei, Nikkatsu, Shōchiku, Tōei, and Tōhō were not loath to join in using the out of the ordinary backdrop of exotic wartime circumstances to heighten the passion and drama of a tragic love affair. The list of such films includes *Desertion at Dawn, Fragrance of the Night* (Ieraishan, 1951), *Woman of Shanghai* (Shanhai no onna, 1952), *Military Police* (Kempei, 1953), *Farewell Rabaul* (Saraba Rabauru, 1954), *Princess of Asia under War Clouds* (Senun ajia no jōo, 1957), *Floating Clouds* (Ukigumo, 1955), *Songs on the Battlefield, Story of a Prostitute, Ku-Nyan and the Five Assault Soldiers* (Kūnyan to gonin no totsugekihei, 1958), and many more. The common denominator was that the female lead role was either Japanese or ambiguously Japanese (i.e., Chinese appearance but Japanese ancestry or upbringing) and that in most cases both protagonists, but at least one of the two, tragically died. A happy ending was out of the question.

As ever, it was Shin-Tōhō that took the genre in extraordinary directions. Almost continually looking for a way out of bankruptcy, it was not loath to cover a terrain that other studios feared to tread. It used the exotic setting of a warfront hospital in China to provide a story of lesbian romance and drama in *Battlefield Nurses* (Yasen kangofu, 1953); nor did it show any qualms in using the tragedy of nurses forced to become comfort women in *Broken Blossoms* (Senjō no nadeshiko, 1959) in order to show young actresses unbuttoning their nurse uniforms readying themselves for a shower scene. However, it could be argued that this was well within the boundaries of "historic reality" when compared to the mind-boggling pieces of fantasy the studio unleashed upon its audiences in the days before its bankruptcy in 1961. Its most creative eruption was unquestionably *Female Slave Ship* (Onna doreibune, 1960), which starts out in Rabaul, in Papua New Guinea, with the actor Sugawara Bunta as a man on a sacred military mission, whose plane is shot down but who—unlike Admiral Yamamoto Isoroku—survives this plight only to find himself rescued by a ship packed with female slaves, many of them prostitutes. Here the exotic wartime island setting is nothing but a lame excuse to enact a battle between pirates and prostitutes, which in turn is nothing but the forgettable framework in order to show as much of Mihara Yōko's voluptuous body as the censors would allow.

Asia as the boundless space where we were free: Japan's Wild East

There was yet another way in which Asia was depicted in postwar war films, although this was limited to the setting of Manchuria (nowadays China's three northeastern provinces). In the prewar and wartime periods Manchuria was invariably promoted in all media as the land of unlimited resources and opportunities. Although there was also a modern urban side to the Manchurian dream, the standard image was that of a paradise (*rakudo*) with endless plains and horizons. The film industry was also used to support this government propaganda, and during the 1930s and early 1940s setting off to Manchuria to try out one's luck in this newly opened Japan-controlled region became a stereotypical happy ending to many films.[24]

In the postwar setting the Manchurian dream did not lose all its former luster, as its modern urban multiracial setting was often used—like Shanghai—for spy stories, often involving romantic interludes with Chinese or Japanese/Chinese women. However, in these films of the postwar period the vast horizons of the Manchurian countryside had vanished. It was not until the famous "army outlaw" series' of the 1960s that these horizons filled the wide cinemascope screens again. The Manchurian plains formed the background of one installment of the *Desperado Outpost* series—in the other installments the North China front featured in an identical way—and in almost all episodes of the *Yakuza Soldier* series. However, in contrast to wartime images stressing the limitless opportunities of a fruitful countryside, now the setting was presented as a zone of freedom and lawlessness, where the hierarchy of army life could be turned upside down and desperados could release their male energy without any restraint. In other words, in a very conscious endeavor by some Japanese film studios to create an equivalent to the American genre of the Western, Manchuria was used as Japan's Wild East, where small bands of highly individualistic soldiers roamed as cowboys, with or without a mission. Every once in a while their paths crossed, or they were ambushed by the Chinese Communist Eighth Route Army or guerilas—who thus held similar functions to the "Indians" of the Wild West movies in America.[25]

Somewhat surprisingly, these Second World War comedy and adventure Westerns were not merely more realistic in the sense of clearly showing an enemy but, in sharp contrast to most war films, also provided a picture of a war front populated by many civilian non-combatants, including women. The presence of women can be explained if one remembers that every film that starred the charismatic actor Katsu Shintarō would necessarily require a female love interest or two. However, the *Desperado Outpost* series also feature a fair number of Japanese, Chinese, and Korean comfort women, prostitutes, and other women. Moreover, in what is often a somewhat farcical style, many of the films in this genre of comedy and adventure Westerns provide insights into the irrational, dirty, brutal, and ugly faces of the war, which in this sense rather linked them to anti-war films.

Foreign-colonized Asia as the source of our war legitimacy

While anti-war films staged outside Japan are often set in China, anti-anti-war films preferred to focus on the (losing) battle against American warships and airplanes in a non-distinct Pacific area during the latter part of the war.[26] However, from the late 1950s onward a few films were made that can exceptionally be termed "pro-war films," in the sense that these outspokenly challenged the negative depiction of Japan's involvement in the Second World War within the American framework of the Pacific War, and instead advocated a positive reappreciation in terms of the Japanese wartime propaganda framework of the Greater East Asian War. Some of these films actively sought otherwise almost completely under-represented outposts such as Malaysia, Indonesia, and Burma.

Set in Asian outposts, strategically located in (former) Western colonies, these films were also part of the genre of "goodwill films." Most of the postwar sequels of this wartime genre did not go much further than indulging in tragic love affairs between Japanese soldiers and native women. However, the outspokenly pro-war films in this genre focused on pan-Asian collaborative resistance against a Western enemy (and/or a Western-influenced Chinese enemy) and were located in war theaters that were or had been Western colonies. One may argue whether *Terang Boelan - The Light of the Moon* fully fits into this category, as its political message is not very outspoken, although the native female love interest and her brother eventually help out in infiltrating an anti-Japanese guerilla group. But in the case of *The Silent Battlefield at Dawn* (Shizuka nari – akatsuki no senjō, 1959), predictably also a Shin-Tōhō production, there is no doubt about the politically motivated content whatsoever. The film is in the same mold as wartime "Asian brotherhood" propaganda films such as *The Tiger of Malaya* (Marai no tora, 1943), *Forward, Flag of Independence* (Susume dokuritsuki, 1943), *Fire on That Flag!* (Ano hata o ute, 1944), *Storm over Bengal* (Bengaru no arashi, 1944), and many uncompleted wartime projects like Ozu Yasujirō's *Operation Burma – Faraway Motherland* (Biruma sakusen – haruka nari fūbo no kuni). The "Asian brotherhood" films took the regular format of the "goodwill film," in which two individuals in love enacted Sino-Japanese understanding, to the level of Asian collective armed resistance against the West.

In *The Silent Battlefield at Dawn* a group of Indian prisoners of war gradually grow sympathetic to Japan's lofty goals, turn against their English colonial masters, and eventually join the Japanese army. This may look like a mere extension of a "goodwill film" scenario. However, as a postwar film this is not about focusing on a true story from the wartime period but rather about going full-force against the postwar order, symbolized by the American interpretation of the war as a Pacific War and the related verdicts of the Tokyo Tribunal. Although the neutral term "the Second World War" is used to refer to the war in the language of the film, and the Japanese and Indian protagonists with a few exceptions are presented as benign and likable people, the underlying radical political motivation is clear: to celebrate and relive the idea of Japan's Greater East Asian War as if the Tokyo Tribunal never happened. A few quotes from this film should be sufficiently telling. The Indian actors have lines such as "Asia for the Asians, that is what Japan is fighting for," "The Japanese do not look down upon Indians, we are Asian brothers," "For the freedom and liberation of Asia, we must collaborate with Japan," etc. The film, which professes to be based on a true story, ends with the written statement that thanks to the Japanese "the Indian independence army formed and rapidly expanded. Through their battles on the Malaysian and Burmese front it formed the foundation stone of Indian independence." This film provided an early precedent for films produced several decades later such as *Pride – The Fateful Moment* (Puraido – unmei no toki, 1998) and *Merdeka 17805* (Murudeka 17805, 2001), which also focused in a highly selective manner on parts of Asia formerly colonized by Western powers in order to tell tales of a legitimate war by the Japanese armed forces waged for the liberation of Asia.[27]

These pro-war films thus featured Asia in a very prominent way, both in terms of the setting and the actors. However, the strong political motivation behind these films made sure that the Asia presented was limited to the parts colonized by the Western powers, and the former Japanese Empire in Asia was completely ignored, as if it never existed. One must also note that the Asians portrayed in these films are not autonomous and are merely shown in their relation to the West and Japan. On the one hand they function as the victims of Western suppression and on the other hand as beneficiaries of Japanese support. Their main role is to sing the praise of Japan and the Asian brotherhood, and thus legitimize Japan's war effort in terms of ridding the continent of Western colonialism and creating a Greater East Asian Co-Prosperity Sphere.

The dominant trend of an invisible Asia

In the first two decades of the postwar period, the aforementioned *The Silent Battlefield at Dawn* stands out as one of the very few outspoken remakes of wartime "Asian brotherhood" propaganda films. However, among the large body of postwar Japanese war films it also stands out in the sense of giving a prominent role to non-Japanese Asians, in this case even impersonated by Indian actors. The 1998 film *Pride – The Fateful Moment*, which explores Tōjō Hideki's proud and heroic struggle at the Tokyo Tribunal, involves an important secondary storyline of a Japanese youngster traveling to India to support the independence movement. However, in the 1959 film *The Greater East Asian War and the International Tribunal* (Dai tōa sensō to kokusai saiban), the first film to eulogize Tōjō and which also focused on the Tokyo Tribunal, Asia was all but absent, despite the fact that it was mentioned in the title.

The words with which Tōjō in this latter film resolves to take upon himself the responsibility for defeat in the war are telling: "I will gladly die as a soldier, in the sense of an apology (*shazai*) toward the emperor and the people." Interestingly, the producers of this film were bold enough to use the taboo word "Greater East Asian War" in the title of their film, rejecting the official line that the term "Pacific War" should be used; but they somehow forgot to include this "Greater East Asia" in the film itself. However, this is nothing but a reflection of the common pattern in postwar Japanese war films that Asia is used as a concept with no content, and is at most a stage without indigenous actors. In a similar vein, one will be hard pressed to find any local Asians in regular postwar Japanese war films that include words such as Southern Isles, Rabaul, or the Pacific in their titles.

In the case of the war films made by Shin-Tōhō from 1951 up until 1961, the regular Japanese anti-anti-war films tend to focus on the latter stages of the war and rarely show or discuss the causes of the war.[28] And even where the film has a more outspoken pro-war political message with the war being drawn in terms that accord with the wartime propaganda discourse of "the Greater East Asian War," it is still highly unusual to find a mention of the Greater East Asia when it comes to the justification of or motivation for war. In the end, all the brave kamikaze pilots and human torpedoes go down for the sake of their nation, as signified by the constantly repeated "on behalf of the country" (*okuni no tame ni*), which is sometimes combined with a call for the greater glory of the Imperial Navy. However, these battle cries never include a reference to territory outside the homeland. In the lines spoken in the film by General Tōjō mentioned earlier, there is not one reference to Asia as an object of responsibility and guilt. The objects of responsibility and guilt are of a strictly Japanese nature. Another understated political message in many anti-anti-war films that should not be overlooked is that Asia becomes invisible due to the focus on the Japanese–American part of the war. There simply is no Asian enemy and, accordingly, no defeat by Asia. Thus, whether as an ally, enemy, cause, or victim, Asia stands out by its invisibility and absence.

Another telling fact that reflects postwar Japanese views of Asia is that the annexed and colonized parts of Japan's empire—Taiwan and Korea—were equally absent. This reveals a continuity between the prewar and wartime periods. Whereas the Korean peninsula was the focus of Japan's foreign policy, even leading up to the First Sino-Japanese War (1894–1895) and the Russo-Japanese War (1904–1905), it faded from Japanese minds after its annexation in 1910. And within the anti-colonialist wartime propaganda it was opportune to keep Japan's own colonies relatively out of sight. Nonetheless, Korea and Taiwan were shown in the wartime cinemas through productions such as *Suicide Troops of the Watchtower* (Bōrō no kesshitai, 1943) and *Sayon's Bell* (Sayon no kane, 1943), and a series of films made in Korea but also screened in Japan.[29] After the war, however, these two former colonies no longer featured on the silver screen. Whereas Japan's informal colony in Manchuria retained—and continues to contain—a nostalgic or exotic image in Japanese minds and is accordingly featured in urban spy mysteries and Western-like adventures, Japan's relatively lengthy colonial experience in Taiwan and Korea seems to have been completely forgotten. To the best of my knowledge, the 1975 film *When We Were Young* (Waga seishun no toki) is the first postwar Japanese film to be staged in colonial/wartime Korea, and I cannot think of one example dealing with colonial/wartime Taiwan.

Considering the various wartime productions and the many Japanese film industry people involved in film production, distribution, and screening in the former colonies, this marked absence has to be seen as a conscious break with the past. In the prewar and wartime days, Japanese calls for resistance to Western colonialism and in favor of pan-Asianism and racial equality always sounded hollow, since these hardly ever addressed the actual situation of Japan's colonial policies toward its neighboring countries and regions, which clearly contradicted this apparent support for independence. This not terribly illustrious legacy of Japanese prewar and wartime debate continued in an apparently unreflective manner by the postwar film industry in Japan, either completely eliding this important page of Japan's recent history or, especially by film studios such as Shin-Tōhō, showing no qualms in criticizing Western colonialism while covering up Japan's colonial exploits in Taiwan, Korea, and Manchuria.

Conclusion

After its defeat in the Second World War Japan lost its foothold on the Asian mainland and experienced a period of hardship during which left it little leeway to focus on its recent history on the Asian continent. The end of the Allied Occupation and the restoration of autonomy in 1952 did not make a fundamental change in this situation, since the Cold War created a structure of two ideologically antagonistic camps that continued to isolate the country from large parts of Asia. The anti-war films made during and after the Occupation period presented a view of the world in which Japan occupied a humble position, not one higher than other Asian countries. Many of these films urged the nation to reflect on Japan's misdeeds during the recent war and to show remorse. In some of these films the Chinese were presented as more humane than the Japanese, but the overall impression of Asia was that of a stage where the Japanese killed each other or were killed by an amorphous enemy. However, starting from the late 1950s less critical war films, which I have chosen to call anti-anti-war films, took the main stage, toppling this humble view of Japan and its position in Asia, and re-establishing more confident views familiar to Japanese society since the Meiji period. These, in some cases, revived prewar and wartime images of an exotic and attractive Asian empire, but mostly focused on the part of the war that was waged from 1941 against the United States. Accordingly, they mainly provided images of an indistinct Asia with few if any local inhabitants, or even completely erased Asia from view. The tendency to make invisible or forget Asia is especially prominent in the case of Japan's former colonies Taiwan and Korea. In this way, the postwar nation was allowed to return to what I have termed "Japan's Modern Mindset," in which Japan positioned itself in between the East and the West, looking up to the leading countries of the West but simultaneously looking down upon and not including itself in the inferior category of Asia.[30]

Notes

1   See for instance Yoshikuni Igarashi, *Bodies of Memory: Narratives of War in Postwar Japanese Culture, 1945–1970* (Princeton, NJ: Princeton University Press, 2000); Franziska Seraphim, *War Memory and Social Politics in Japan, 1945–2005* (Cambridge, MA: Harvard University Press, 2006); Fukuma Yoshiaki, *Shōdo no kioku: Okinawa, Hiroshima, Nagasaki ni utsuru sengo* (Shinyōsha, 2011).

2 Kyoko Hirano, *Mr. Smith Goes to Tokyo: Japanese Cinema under the American Occupation, 1945–1952* (Washington, DC: Smithsonian Institution Press, 1992); Inoue Masao, *Bunka to tōsō: Tōhō sōgi, 1946–1948* (Shinyōsha, 2007); Hiroshi Kitamura, *Screening Enlightenment: Hollywood and the Cultural Reconstruction of Defeated Japan* (Ithaca, NY: Cornell University Press, 2010).

3 Dick Stegewerns, "Establishing the Genre of the Revisionist War Film: The Shin-Tōhō Body of Post-Occupation War Films in Japan," in *Chinese and Japanese Films on the Second World War*, eds. Timothy Y. Tsu King-Fai Tam and Sandra Wilson (London: Routledge, 2015), pp. 93–106. For a Japanese translation, see Stegewerns, "Shūseishugiteki sensō eiga no kakuritsu: Senryōki-go no sensō eiga," in *Shinryōiki/jisedai no Nihon kenkyū*, eds. Hosokawa Shūhei, Yamada Shōji, and Sano Mayuko (Kyoto: Kokusai Nihon Bunka Kenkyū Sentaa, 2016), pp. 9–21.

4 Michael Baskett, *The Attractive Empire: Transnational Film Culture in Imperial Japan* (Honolulu: University of Hawai'i Press, 2008), pp. 132–154.

5 Stegewerns, "Establishing the Genre of the Revisionist War Film."

6 Baskett, *The Attractive Empire*, pp. 132–154.

7 For the various prohibited subjects, see Hirano, *Mr. Smith Goes to Tokyo*, pp. 47–103.

8 For a detailed analysis of the Japanese mindset under the Occupation, see John W. Dower, *Embracing Defeat: Japan in the Wake of World War II* (New York: W. W. Norton, 1999).

9 It is relatively well-known that this film project was held up for two years by the lengthy process of censure by the occupation forces and that within this process the scriptwriters Taniguchi Senkichi and Kurosawa Akira had to change the prostitute in the original 1947 short novel *The Story of a Prostitute (Shunpuden)* by Tamura Taijirō into a singer. What is less known is that in the original the prostitute is a Korean comfort woman, that her relationship with the soldier is mainly driven by her feelings of revenge toward the officer, and that the couple die as a result of the soldier's attempt to commit suicide. Tamura, who became extremely popular as the rising star of Japanese literature during the early Occupation years, advocated "the literature of the body," depicting protagonists who were principally motivated by their bodily desires. He had spent five years as a soldier in China, and during his stay he had two chance meetings with Yamaguchi Yoshiko, who at the time was used by the Manchurian Film Company as a propaganda tool and sold to the outside world as the Chinese singer Li Xianglan, fluent in Japanese and loyal to the foreign occupier. Tamura was mainly impressed by her bodily presence and wrote *The Story of a Prostitute* with her in mind. This made her the natural candidate for the female lead role in the film version, and her eroticism—quite new to Japanese cinema—was a large factor in the film's commercial success. Yomota Inuhiko, *Ri Kō-ran to Hara Setsuko* (Iwanami Shoten, 2011), pp. 357–398.

10 Fukuma Yoshiaki, *Junkoku to Hangyaku: [Tokkō] no katari no sengoshi* (Seikyūsha, 2007); Yoshikuni Igarashi, "Kamikaze Today: The Search for National Heroes in Contemporary Japan," in *Ruptured Histories: War Memory and the Post-Cold War in Asia*, eds. Sheila Miyoshi Jager and Rana Mitter (Cambridge, MA: Harvard University Press, 2007), pp. 99–121; Emiko Ohnuki-Tierney, *Kamikaze Diaries: Reflections of Japanese Student Soldiers* (Chicago: University of Chicago Press, 2006).

11 For the Von Sternberg film, see Dick Stegewerns, "The Physical and Mental Criteria of Japanese Identity: Can Foreigners Make an Authentic Japanese Movie?," in *Japanese Studies Around the World: Observing Japan from Within*, ed. James C. Baxter (Kyoto: International Research Center for Japanese Studies, 2004), pp. 304–305.

12   Michael Baskett, "Dying for a Laugh: Japanese post-1945 Service Comedies,"
     Historical Journal of Film, Radio & Television 23, no. 4 (October 2003), pp. 291–310.

13   Hiroshi Kitamura, "Wild, Wild War: Okamoto Kihachi and the Politics of the
     Desperado Films," in *Chinese and Japanese Films on the Second World War*, eds. Timothy
     Y. Tsu King-Fai Tam and Sandra Wilson (London: Routledge, 2015), pp. 107–120.

14   For an overview of Japanese films on the atomic bombings, see Mick Broderick, ed.,
     Hibakusha Cinema: Hiroshima, Nagasaki and the Nuclear Image in Japanese Film
     (London: Kegan Paul International, 1996). For an analysis of European attitudes to
     Japanese and Western films on the atomic bombings, see Dick Stegewerns, "Kyori,
     seigi, tabū: Nichi-Ō [Hiroshima] imeiji no kakuzetsu," in *Fukusū no [Hiroshima]:
     Kioku no sengoshi to media no rikigaku*, eds. Fukuma Yoshiaki, Yamaguchi Makoto,
     and Yoshimura Kazuma (Seikyūsha, 2012), pp. 311–324.

15   Stegewerns, "The Physical and Mental Criteria of Japanese Identity," pp. 300–304. For
     an identical bonding of the former enemies in which Japan is feminized, see Naoko
     Shibusawa, *America's Geisha Ally: Re-Imagining the Japanese Enemy* (Cambridge, MA:
     Harvard University Press, 2010).

16   John W. Dower, *War Without Mercy* (New York: Pantheon Books, 1986), pp. 77–190.

17   For a short analysis of American films on the Asia Pacific War, see Monma Takashi,
     Ō-Bei eiga ni miru Nihon (Shakai Hyōronsha, 1995), pp. 65–73. For an overview of
     non-Japanese films on the Asia Pacific War, see Tōmon Jinni and Yunoki Hiroshi,
     Gaikoku eiga ni miru Ajia-Taiheiyō sensō (San-ichi Shobō, 1995).

18   Stegewerns, "Establishing the Genre of the Revisionist War Film," pp. 100–101.

19   Ibid., pp. 102–103.

20   Ibid., p. 103.

21   See Peter B. High, *The Imperial Screen: Japanese Film Culture in the Fifteen Years' War,
     1931–1945* (Madison: University of Wisconsin Press, 2003), pp. 271–285;
     Freda Freiberg, "China Nights (Japan, 1940): The Sustaining Romance of Japan at
     War," in *World War Two: Film and History*, eds. John Whiteclay Chambers II and
     David Culbert (Oxford: Oxford University Press), pp. 31–46.

22   See also Baskett, *The Attractive Empire*, pp. 139–142.

23   Stegewerns, "Establishing the Genre of the Revisionist War Film," pp. 95–104.

24   High, *The Imperial Screen*, pp. 268–271. Manchuria was the "new earth" of *New Earth*
     (Atarashiki tsuchi), the Itami Mansaku version of the 1937 Japanese-German co-
     production that because of a fall-out between the two directors spawned two almost-
     identical films, although the other version by Arnold Fanck came with the completely
     different title of *Die Tochter der Samurai*. Ozu Yasujirō's *The Brothers and Sisters of
     the Toda Family* (Toda-ke no kyōdai, 1941) and Shimazu Yasujirō's *A Brother and His
     Younger Sister* (Ani to sono imōto, 1939) featured Manchuria as the deus-ex-machina
     to solve family problems. Toyoda Shirō's *Ōhinata Village* (Ōhinata-mura, 1940) and
     Kurata Bunjin's *A Vast and Fertile Land* (Yokudo banri, 1940) are focused on the
     theme of emigration to Manchuria, just like many documentaries.

25   Hiroshi Kitamura, "Wild, Wild War." Interestingly, the cinema of the equally
     mountainous South Korea has used these same Northeast Chinese plains for the
     "Manchurian Western" genre. See Hye Seung Chung, "The Man with No Home/
     Musukja (1968): *Shane* Comes Back in a Korean 'Manchurian Western,'" *Journal of
     Popular Film and Television* 39, no. 2 (June 2011), pp. 71–83; and Mark Morris, "On
     the Trail of the Manchurian Western," *Korea: Politics, Economy and Society* 4 (2010),
     pp. 217–246.

26   Stegewerns, "Establishing the Genre of the Revisionist War Film," pp. 101–102.

27   For the background of these latter two films, see Luk van Haute, "Dealing with the Identity Crisis: Japanese Cinema Lefty and Right," *Asian Cinema* 16, no. 1 (Spring/ Summer 2005), pp. 125–134.

28   Stegewerns, "Establishing the Genre of the Revisionist War Film," pp. 101–102.

29   For the films made in colonial Korea, see the Korea-related contributions to the special issue on "Transcolonial Film Coproductions in the Japanese Empire: Antinomies in the Colonial Archive," *Cross-Currents: East Asian History and Culture Review*, E-Journal no. 5 (December 2012), and the various texts by Chonghwa Chung for the DVD releases by the Korean Film Archive of films from colonial Korea.

30   Dick Stegewerns, "From Chinese World Order to Japan's Modern Mindset: Japanese Views of the Outside World from the Early Modern Period until the Present Day," in *Japan – Past and Present*, ed. Kurt Almqvist (Stockholm: Bokforlaget Stolpe, 2019), pp. 55–72.

Chapter 6

ANTI-IMPERIALISM AS STRATEGY: MASKING THE EDGES OF FOREIGN ENTANGLEMENTS IN CIVIL WAR-ERA CHINA, 1945–1948

Matthew D. Johnson

The unraveling of Japan's empire in China did not occur immediately, but in media terms its disappearance was swift. Reporting on the trials of people accused as traitors and collaborators was perhaps the most visible evidence of the shedding of imperial legacies.[1] Military participants in the struggle against imperialism such as the Nationalist Party (KMT) of Chiang Kai-shek and Chinese Communist Party (CCP) of Mao Zedong also used anniversaries, first-hand accounts, and other forms of official and unofficial remembrance to portray themselves as authentic champions of the Chinese people and saviors of the nation.[2] These public *aides-mémoires* also had international currency: they served to shame a reindustrializing Japan and to delegitimize domestic political rivals accused of having resisted or avoided participating in the national salvation effort.[3] Nonetheless, the rapid forgetting of the war of resistance was an observable and widespread phenomenon even prior to the CCP victory over the KMT for control of the Chinese mainland in 1949.[4]

Yet disappointingly for many patriots in China, the empire's unraveling did not bring an end to the longstanding situation of powerful external actors—foremost among them the United States of America (USA) and the Union of Soviet Socialist Republics (Soviet Union)—involving themselves in China's insecure state of internal affairs. While China's war of resistance faded as a reality, it was quickly replaced by the KMT–CCP civil war, which had continued even during the years of total war against the Japanese Occupation. The dilemma was that Chiang, Mao, and others had to grapple with the reality of international alliances of necessity, at the same time making sure that they were not being perceived as mere tools of new imperialist forces. This chapter examines the strategies and rhetoric through which the USA and Soviet Union sought to play an influential role in the postwar landscape of a de-imperializing East Asia through political stagecraft, networks, and media. In revisiting propaganda in this way, my goal is to read statements about the impact of international forces on China not as ideology in the narrow sense of reflecting actors' systematic beliefs but as part of carefully constructed "masks" by which the CCP, KMT, USA, Soviet Union, and other lesser-known (and comparatively far weaker) political forces such as the Democratic League attempted to build up popular support through appeals to anti-imperialism, all the while pursuing supranational agendas of accommodation and coalition-building.

The chapter's primary argument, which complements the findings of other work in this volume on the reconstruction of postwar East Asia, is that creating systems of postwar order and control—in this case, control over public opinion—not only engaged many of the same powerful approaches and actors that had characterized the 1937 to 1945 wartime period but also necessitated engagement with new, quasi-imperial "edges" in the form of American and Soviet interests. The result of this contradictory state of affairs, which has remained relatively unexplored in the histories of the Chinese Civil War (1945–1949) to date, was that political ideology on both sides was characterized by sharply anti-imperialist politics which mirrored popular dissatisfaction with the nation's perceived international weakness and inability to independently resolve its internal and external crises. If the history of postwar East Asia has been written from a mainly US-centered perspective, it can also be argued that this perspective includes overlooking the degree to which not just anti-imperialism but also anti-Americanism became a cornerstone of postwar Chinese politics from 1945 onward, anticipating the emergence of the Asian non-aligned movement by nearly a decade.

Coming to terms with this legacy has not been easy for historians. The idea that shared opposition to foreign forces has been central to post-imperial, and post-colonial, state-building is not particularly new, nor is the proposition that international forces play pivotal roles in the process of state formation.[5] However, historians of the Chinese Civil War in particular have tended to emphasize opposition to the KMT, anti-war sentiment, and feelings ranging from "futility and incomprehension" to passivity and acceptance as the dominant attitudes found in the print media (primarily newspapers and magazines) and among the wider populace.[6] Anti-imperialism as a broader concern and political paradigm has yet to be systematically explored. By drawing on the personal papers of John F. Melby (1913–1992; collection hereafter referred to as JMCF), a former US diplomat and political analyst active in China during the 1940s; US military and political reports from the era gathered and catalogued by the Digital National Security Archive project (hereafter DNSA); and published internal documents from the CCP Central Propaganda Department, it is possible to begin reconstructing how anti-imperialism and anti-Americanism were strategically conceived, spread, and accepted by the public as legitimacy-enhancing political platforms during the "postwar" Chinese Civil War period.

The information ecology of post-1945 China

The negative space created by imperial collapse and reordering of political information networks in China was quickly filled by multiple media, and media producers, whose presence made effective governance over mass opinion a difficult task. During the period of June to July 1946, more than twenty different Chinese newspapers were published in Shanghai alone, in addition to foreign newspapers; analysis of the information contained in these publications was one of the main activities which diplomats such as Melby undertook in their daily work as political officers.[7] The city was also home to twenty-six Chinese magazines focusing on political, economic, and general news. Counting short-run and low-budget "mosquito sheets," national totals reached 1,384 newspapers, 566 news agencies, and 1,448 magazines registered with the Ministry of the Interior in September 23, 1947, according to the Government Information Office.[8] Many of these sources of information were concentrated in a fairly limited number of cities (Nanjing, Shanghai, Beijing, Chongqing, and Canton) and provinces (Jiangsu, Zhejiang, Fujian, Hunan, and Jiangxi). An additional band of activity stretched from Northwest China to the northeast.

During the first year after the war, this robust vernacular press exhibited a range of opinions and expressions. Even under areas dominated by the KMT government, Communist, liberal, and independent (or "opposition") newspapers were all tolerated.[9] The number of newspapers in Shanghai, including those operating without a government license, was believed by American embassy observers to reach into the hundreds. Of these, many were "small fly-by-night or yellow scandal sheets which exercised little influence on public opinion," though such judgments must be treated cautiously. During the winter of 1946/7, the government began to show more concern with control, leading to raids and closures throughout the country, particularly of those newspapers associated with anti-government viewpoints; those allied with the Democratic League; or those controlled by the CCP. Independent conservative newspapers, such as the Nanjing *Dagong bao* were also closed and reorganized. In April 1947, when the KMT announced an end to political tutelage—meaning that the government and KMT were no longer one and the same—official government newspapers such as the *Central Daily News* (*Zhongyang ribao*) were nonetheless controlled primarily by the KMT "CC Clique" leader, Chen Li-fu. Liberal and independent media support for student strikes led to further repressive consequences, leaving only two licensed independent newspapers by July 1947: the conservative but critical *Xinmin bao*, published in Shanghai, and the intellectual and "progressive" though still somewhat KMT-leaning *Dagong bao*, published in Tianjin, Chongqing, and Hong Kong, and which served as a "bulwark" to the CCP-friendly Democratic League. (Established in 1941, the Democratic League was originally a "third way" wartime political organization that subsequently became closer to the CCP.) Despite government efforts to drive it out of existence, a mimeographed two-page newspaper was also produced in Shanghai by the CCP.

The print media was one critical channel of information and opinion in postwar, post-imperial China; the radio was another. By December 1947 officials estimated that approximately one million radio receivers were in use in China, a dramatic increase over the war years. Takeover of Japanese military and Occupation government radio stations began immediately in August 1945, with private activity quickly restored in KMT-controlled areas.[10] The principal service, the Central Broadcasting Service (CBS), was directly managed by the KMT government. Emergency regulations (*Guangbo fuyuan jinji cuoshi banfa*), promulgated by central broadcasting authorities (the *Zhongyang guangbo shiye guanlichu*), were issued with the aim of regaining complete control over national airwaves. Following intensification of the KMT–CCP civil conflict in 1946, the Ministry of Communications (*Jiaotongbu*) further prohibited foreign citizens from engaging in broadcast activity.[11]

As in the case of newspapers, these regulations were not effective in establishing central government authority. United States and Soviet broadcasts continued; while a solution to the "Soviet problem" of broadcast within China may have been reached in early 1947, US military stations remained active in Nanjing, Tianjin, and Qingdao with the tacit acceptance of the KMT government.[12] Forty-three private stations were in legal operation in March 1943, but these numbers fluctuated dramatically. In May 1946, central broadcasting authorities and the Ministry of Communications closed 54 of an estimated 106 registered stations in Shanghai, many of which lacked equipment or were no longer functioning.[13] One of these stations had been secretly established and operated by underground CCP members. Several former "enemy" stations in North China had also been taken over by the Eighth Route Army; additional CCP and Soviet seizures of broadcasting facilities and equipment took place in Manchuria, with the CCP broadcasting legally from Dalian, which remained under Soviet military control after August 1945. CCP broadcasting from Yan'an, though inconsistent during the war, resumed in September 1946 with retransmission taking place from Zhangjiakou. (CCP sources claim that, though intermittent, the reach of these stations potentially covered the entire Pacific region, and broadcasts were carried out in multiple languages. Such claims, however, are difficult to verify.)

A third source of information and opinion, rarely discussed in the major newspaper-based accounts of 1940s popular attitudes, was clandestine intelligence and propaganda networks. Former Office of Strategic Studies (OSS) personnel returned to China under business and economic cover to engage in peacetime intelligence work.[14] A new American organization, the Strategic Services Unit (SSU), was responsible for quasi-military and clandestine operations in the China Theater, and was "active [in] collecting intelligence against Japanese and Germans" in the areas surrounding Shanghai, Canton, Hankou, Qingdao, Tianjin, and Beiping.[15] Counter-intelligence (X-2) operatives identified British "traitor propagandists" in Shanghai and Indian Independence League members in Canton, reported on German and Japanese activity in coastal China, and documented a secret Japanese organization's attempts to foment civil war.[16] SSU personnel further investigated "safe haven" activities in Shanghai, including CCP attempts—some successful—to recruit Japanese still in China.[17]

Investigation of enemy and rival intelligence agencies revealed more specific propaganda-related activity, such as Soviet campaigns to "discredit" American personnel in Shanghai carried out by the TASS news agency.[18] This activity was implemented through Russian and Russian-controlled Chinese newspapers and in cafés, where cartoons ("Uncle Sam, with ape-like arms, encircling the Pacific Ocean") were given to American sailors and soldiers by bargirls and prostitutes. Soviet intelligence operatives also allegedly enlisted non-Russians in disseminating anti-American rumors and instructed some to seek employment in US Army offices and military facilities. In December 1945, the SSU also reported on more than twenty members of the New Fourth Army political section operating in Shanghai's Hongkew district, where they recruited former Japanese soldiers and ex-Municipal Police officers. Russian Orthodox Church leaders were observed urging White Russians in Manchuria to apply for Soviet citizenship; in Beijing, recruitment took place through the Soviet consulate.

Soviet propaganda and Japanese "subversion" continued into 1946. A Soviet organization (referred to as "CDL") was reported to be carrying out propaganda among Japanese and Chinese laborers for recruitment and training purposes. Soviet operatives also focused on German and Jewish groups in China, aiming to "bring together" the European community in China under an anti-US umbrella; intelligence and propaganda groups were most noticeably active in Shanghai, Qingdao, and Tianjin. KMT counter-intelligence and reports from the Bureau of Statistics and Investigation confirmed that Soviet propaganda was "considerable," to which was further added anti-American propaganda from Japanese organizations still in China.[19] (One uniting factor appeared to be actual liaisons between Russian and Japanese communists.) CCP networks, political training centers, and newspapers gained strength in Shanghai and, quickly, Canton.[20]

Japan's imperial edge had receded, but not completely. With respect to media and other forces capable of shaping public opinion, conditions were made more complex by a proliferation of national and non-national actors: Chinese, American, Soviet, Japanese, and other European and Asian groups. Many of these expressed views that had direct bearing on the post-1945 political situation. Along with being critical of the KMT government, anti-Americanism was one of the most widely shared standpoints. Primarily observed in dense, relatively internationalized urban settings, it circulated via print media, radio, and clandestine political organizations, making its potential reach both broad and difficult for authorities to track.

CCP anti-Americanism: Masking the Soviet "edge" and preparation for war

The most effective transmitter of anti-Americanism was undoubtedly the CCP and its Soviet allies. During the War of Resistance, the CCP under Mao Zedong had maintained a policy of cooperating with the allies to overthrow the forces of Occupation while at the same time fanning the flames of popular dissatisfaction with the KMT. The CCP Central Committee's Chongqing Bureau and Southern Bureau, whose activities were loosely coordinated by Zhou Enlai, emphasized opposition to the KMT's "reactionary propaganda" immediately from August 16, 1945, onward.[21] The basis of the CCP platform against the KMT was opposition to the civil war, advocacy of peace (while preparing for, and waging, war), and advocacy of democracy. According to the OSS Research and Analysis Branch, the CCP also sought to minimize the risk of a rapid increase in American intervention by appearing to seek a closer relationship with the United States.[22] While Soviet commitment to siding wholly with Mao and his supporters was not certain, there was confidence that the CCP, its military forces, and its political coalition, which included parties in the Democratic League alongside other anti-KMT "liberal elements," would ultimately prevail. (Likewise, one of Zhou's key strategies in opposing the KMT in words was the recruitment of democratic "personages" [*renshi*], meaning non-CCP public figures.)

Prior to the Japanese Empire's end, CCP propaganda against Chiang Kai-shek and his party sought to show that the KMT, dominated by "reactionaries, monopolists, and big landlords," had created a "police-ridden, corrupt, and populace-fearing regime," had failed to mobilize the Chinese people for war against Japan and had connived with puppet officials to secure Japanese aid in the war against the CCP prior to Japanese defeat. In June 1945, Yan'an broadcasts transmitted the request that the USA discontinue providing lend-lease to Chongqing, as these were being used to fight the CCP not the Japanese.[23] The CCP also sought to portray US support for the KMT as the main reason why Chiang had not already sought a unified political solution to the civil crisis. At the same time, warm relations between the CCP and the Soviet Union were already observable in Yan'an and Manchuria; in the case of the latter, the USSR had been seen to "welcome" CCP forces in exchange for the use of port and transportation facilities, despite Stalin also working toward a peace treaty with the KMT that lasted until 1950. Nonetheless, the extent to which the CCP would adopt an anti-American position did not seem entirely decided.

The presence of large numbers of US troops in China and their cooperation with the forces of Chiang Kai-shek, however, further hardened the CCP position. Publications like the *Liberation Daily* (*Jiefang ribao*) routinely contained top CCP leaders' criticisms of American intervention, local telegrams and letters requesting US military withdrawal, and news on global and domestic support for the pro-withdrawal position, including within the USA itself.[24] From late 1945 onward, a constant stream of allegations against US Army forces was published in CCP newspapers to support perceptions of the USA as an invader resented by an angered populace, while CCP policies were portrayed as favoring political and peaceful solutions to the internal crisis. Chiang Kai-shek's forces were, by contrast, tarnished with accusations that they colluded with Americans in attacking civilians and that large numbers of Japanese troops had joined the KMT side to attack the army of the CCP. Credible stories also circulated in the *Jiefang ribao* of CCP victories over remaining Japanese and puppet forces; that American and Japanese forces had jointly occupied Tianjin; and that Japanese and puppet forces were still "oppressing" people in Shanxi, Suiyuan, and other parts of China. By contrast, it was reported that Soviet forces remaining in Manchuria had postponed their withdrawal only at the request of the Chinese government. On the occasion of US ambassador Patrick J. Hurley's resignation, the *Xinhua ribao* reported that the Chinese people were "grateful to the United States for their help during the war against Japan"; however, there was never any question that the continued presence of US forces was seen as "counter to the wishes and interests of the Chinese people."[25]

CCP propaganda starkly described the United States as an "imperialistic world power" whose only true rival, in terms of military might, was the Soviet Union.[26] The Truman government used America's postwar "mighty attacking force" as the backbone of its foreign policy while the Soviets, in line with global trends, stood for peace. Such outward pronouncements did not mesh with the realities on the ground, such as Soviet augmentation of CCP military operations—training, supplies, and assistance with patrols and destruction of railroads and airfields— in Manchuria and North China, but this of course was not the point.[27] The main propaganda objective was to convince audiences that the American military did not belong in China and that the presence of Soviet forces could be explained by the need for political and military order in the northeast (where, as was noted by US intelligence forces, "the Chinese hate and fear the Soviet Army").[28] By spring 1946 constant radio and transportation contact between Yan'an and Moscow could be observed by the Yan'an [Yenan] Observer Group stationed there.[29]

Strategically, the logic ran deeper. The true enemy of the CCP, and thus of the Chinese people, was the "reactionary clique" of Chiang Kai-shek ("China belongs to the Chinese people, not to the reactionaries," exhorted Mao).[30] Newspapers, broadcasts, and networks of influence reaching across and outside of China were all enlisted in the effort to strike back against, and discredit, the KMT.[31] As Zhou Enlai instructed the CCP Central Committee Southern Bureau Work Group:

> In order to expose Chiang's deceiving plot [to frame the CCP as responsible for civil war and scare the people], we must concentrate our propaganda on opposing civil war, opposing dictatorship, advocating peace, advocating democracy—these four slogans ... in order to put pressure on Chiang's reactionary propaganda, we must push [these slogans] in all directions.[32]

Establishing Xinhua news agencies across the north and northeast was one strategy as the war with Japan drew to a close; another was contacting foreign embassies and journalists to mount the CCP's case. In order to further widen the space for anti-Chiang criticism, the *New China Daily* (*Xinhua ribao*) also put pressure on the KMT Propaganda [Publicity, Information] Department to eliminate the news censorship system.[33] Beyond the CCP influence campaign of interviews, high-level networking, and formation of social and cultural organizations, the Southern Bureau also extended contacts in "external organizations" such as student groups and China aid organizations, mobilizing letter-writing campaigns and spreading news and opinion by word of mouth.

The KMT responded with frustration and hostility, closing down news agencies in Chongqing and Kunming in October.[34] However, CCP radio activity continued, with the beginnings of a nascent trans-regional network emerging in the northeast and northern Rehe Province the following month. Propaganda war complemented an overall strategy of "political attack, military self-defense" in negotiations with the KMT in December.[35] Reorganization of the New China News Agency (*Xinhuashe*) followed in May 1946, in order to strengthen coordination of editorial line and content; radio activity, rather than newspaper circulation, remained the primary CCP means of circulating anti-American and anti-KMT propaganda throughout the civil war period, with one station, in Handan, used exclusively for broadcasting within KMT-controlled areas.[36]

Within CCP propaganda outlines, Japan was almost never mentioned: the past eight years of total war were irrelevant to broader goals of ending one-party KMT government and eradicating enemy and puppet forces in areas whose "nationalization" and "democratization" was being carried out under CCP political-military authority.[37] In addition, local CCP organizations were to document and publicize KMT and "puppet-traitor" counterattacks on CCP forces as well as "illegal" US military behavior. In the northeast, the emphasized themes concerned local self-government, the withdrawal of Soviet forces, and opposition to the entrance of KMT forces into Manchuria.[38] Overall, the "exposure" of American armed intervention into the conflict took top priority, along with positive propaganda concerning CCP victories; CCP leaders also hoped that by portraying the KMT as having initiated the civil war, Chiang Kai-shek's government would lose legitimacy in front of the entire world while also bolstering the case for CCP counter attacks as "self-defense."[39] Targets included both Chinese and foreign audiences; Americans themselves, including those within the military, were believed to oppose involvement in the war between the KMT and CCP.

CCP propagandists also made use of non-attributed (gray) methods. Propaganda circulated in the northeast was initially not to mention the CCP by name.[40] Other approaches included circulation within KMT armies.[41] Foreign reporters were not to be treated "like intelligence and secret service personnel" (who were actively prevented from directly observing the military situation) but instead to be given help and their "free" role accommodated.[42] CCP Central Committee Propaganda Department head Lu Dingyi was aware that by 1946, the effect of anti-American propaganda was increasingly to make Americans angry and that foreign audiences generally were unfamiliar with CCP political programs, history, organization, and leadership—there was, in other words, a softer side to propaganda activity which was less obviously anti-American in tone and content.[43] Moreover, the revelation in February 1946 that the KMT was beginning to split into two factions likewise instigated a trend toward more "cooperative" messages.[44] In both cases, the main line of reasoning maintained that attacks on leaders, not people and parties, and identification and criticism of "imperialist" (American) and "fascist" (KMT) factions within the government itself were the most effective ways of waging propaganda war.

The CCP used the paired images of a hostile Truman government and a reactionary Chiang-led KMT faction to blame conflict on the enemy while distracting from the highly sensitive northeast situation, where Soviet policy and conditions on the ground changed constantly. By design, the CCP's own military prowess and successes in social policy remained largely unknown to both domestic and international audiences during the years immediately following

Japanese surrender.[45] After 1947, propaganda focus shifted almost entirely to outspoken broadcasts and articles emphasizing the "imperialist" and "fascist" course of US policy and KMT outrages against the Chinese people, reportedly carried out in collusion with US forces. American imperialists were the "leaders of world reaction," whose aim was to rule the world; anti-Soviet propaganda was dismissed as a smokescreen for imperialism, and an indication of the likelihood of future war between the United States and the Soviet Union—"the most progressive country in the world."[46] In the struggle between democratic and anti-democratic forces, including within capitalist countries themselves, the forces of democracy, and anti-fascism, would prevail.[47] In this sense, the war with Japan had simply been part of a longer sequence of events unfolding both globally and within China, and had no special significance of its own other than the role which CCP leaders feared that residual Japanese and Occupation government forces might play in supporting the KMT.

KMT independent nationalism: Masking disunity and isolation

The Chiang Kai-shek-led KMT central government in 1945 was a fractured organization politically and militarily. The loyalty of civil and military officials in south and southwest China was questionable.[48] "Liberals" both inside and outside the KMT seemed largely CCP-leaning. Building a strong post-imperial central state would require resolving these and other internal tensions, such as those between the various factions (CC, Whampoa, Sun Fo's "liberal business" clique) and external organizations (in particular, the Federation of Democratic Parties and Democracy [Democratic] League) which impeded creation of an effective single ruling bloc.[49] In addition to the existence of the CCP itself, which controlled much of China north of the Yellow River already in April 1945, the KMT was also constrained by fears concerning the possibility of prolonged foreign intervention by the Soviet Union and US forces.

US policy, in particular, was maddeningly ambiguous. The replacement by US president Harry Truman of Patrick J. Hurley with George C. Marshall as the primary diplomatic figure in China in early December 1945 did little to change the basic scenario: that the United States was unable and perhaps unwilling to resolve the internal crisis in Chiang's favor.[50] For this reason, KMT propaganda focused mainly on highlighting a program of independent nation-building. China would become "modern" through adherence to the Three People's Principles established by Sun Yat-sen: by becoming rich, powerful, and prosperous; as the outcome of the KMT-led revolution and national reconstruction; and by eliminating communist influence. By February 1946, the stance was clearer where the Soviet Union was concerned. The Chen Li-fu-led KMT organized anti-Soviet demonstrations of more than 10,000 students in Manchuria, demanding immediate evacuation of all troops and denouncing Joseph Stalin as the "Satan of Asia."[51] Incited by organizers from the Three People's Principles Youth Corps, protesters ransacked the offices of the *Xinhua ribao* (published by the CCP) and *Minzhu ribao* (published by the

Democratic League). Anti-Soviet activity was tacitly, though rarely openly, endorsed as part of the central government's broader anti-CCP and anti-communist platform.

While anti-Soviet demonstrations had apparently diminished by 1947, this did not mean that the KMT necessarily "leaned" toward the USA. As the Chiang government struggled to regain control over the media environment through tightening of restrictions on the press, fighting communism was portrayed mainly as part of a nationally focused struggle for unity, peace, and democracy.[52] National reconstruction was dependent on internal order and stability, not US aid. The activities of non-KMT groups, such as the Democratic League, were to be kept within narrow limits. Where possible, the CCP was to be hounded out of existence and militarily crushed. To this end, KMT propaganda also maintained a tireless anti-CCP campaign which emphasized its inability to compromise in peace negotiations or give up independent military forces. This latter line of propaganda was viewed with skepticism by political independents within China, who still held out a hope that the future might lie in a coalition government.[53] The military, however, supported the KMT by publicly maintaining an anti-CCP line. In general, the political atmosphere became increasingly polarized in ways that paralleled the changing military situation.

For Chiang, however, the problem lay not in the lack of constant US assistance but rather in "too much reliance on foreign help." In a September 22, 1947, speech at the KMT Fourth Plenary Session, he declared that if the country was able to "stand on [its] own 'two feet'" in restoring the economy while eradicating communism, neither the Soviet Union *nor* the US would "come out in open opposition against us."[54] Pessimism concerning the internal situation was a result of propaganda and was thus unwarranted. Where the CCP was superior to the KMT, however, was in organization and party discipline. By contrast, Chiang lambasted KMT media organs, including the China News Agency, Central Broadcasting Station, and China Motion Picture Studio, for their inability to keep members and the country united. Similar points had been made nearly a month earlier, when KMT secretary general Wu Te-chen wrote in an August 29, 1947, statement titled "A Correct Interpretation of China's Current Problems" and published by the *Nanjing Daily News* that China had the right to ask for assistance from allies in order to overcome hardships.[55]

With respect to the KMT's anti-communist wing, which, headed by Chen Li-fu, aligned closely with Chiang Kai-shek and controlled the party propaganda apparatus, these allies were unlikely to include the Soviet Union. Chen was a frequent visitor to US diplomatic offices, where he was known as the "main proponent of the extermination of Chinese Communism."[56] For Chen and Chiang, however, the vision of China's foreign relations was somewhat perilously balanced between trying to draw the United States more deeply into the civil conflict in order to counterbalance the Soviet Union, while simultaneously hewing to an independent path of "saving China" without reliance on one external source of aid only. According to Chiang in 1948, the "problem of China was a problem of the world," and the "center of endeavor in Asia must be in China."[57] While Chiang pinned his hopes foremost upon "the American people and their statesmen …

[dedicating] their lives to this task," he also depicted the CCP and Soviet presence in Manchuria as the start of a "third world war"—an issue of significance to all of the world's nations. This perspective came partly from frustration with the United States, even on the KMT "right," which had emerged publicly in 1947 when articles in the *Shen bao* (CC Clique) and *Yi shi bao* (conservative-Catholic) criticized the American "Europe-first" policy. The China mission figurehead lieutenant general Alfred C. Wedemeyer also took criticism for failing to "understand China properly" and adopting an "inappropriate attitude" in forcing "suggestive will"— likely a reference to a push for compromise and a coalition government solution —on China without proper regard for Chinese dignity.[58]

To the extent that an anti-American anti-imperialist coalition existed within Chinese politics, it was overwhelmingly nationalist, secondarily anti-Japan, and overall Soviet-neutral. Both the KMT and liberal-independent organizations (and their media) evidenced concern first and foremost for China's autonomy, with the main foreign threat still viewed as US intrusion in Asia as manifested by a reindustrializing Japan. In contrast, rather than being purely undesirable, Soviet involvement in China's politics and territorial transition was viewed as a necessary, if suboptimal, counter to that threat.[59] National business and commercial leader Sun Fo gave a series of "sensational interviews" in September 1947 to the effect that if a US–China agreement acceptable to China failed to materialize, China would have to seek closer rapprochement with the Soviet Union.[60] The viewpoint that China would have to solve internal problems without American help, and that the American line was "not firm and proper … [and] acceptable to Chinese sensibilities," was also echoed in the independent and CCP press. American observers noted considerable uniformity across the press, from the CC Clique to the CCP ends of the spectrum, that Americans were "self-interested," had failed to understand China, and were unable to propose workable solutions to the conflict. The predominant view was also that all Chinese people should support the cause of nationalism; Soviet involvement in China's internal affairs was not necessarily bad for China (coverage ranged from mute to positive); and that the Soviet, not American, policy toward Japan was the correct one.

With the return of a Soviet ambassador to Nanjing it was further noted, with some alarm in the case of the US diplomatic community, that rumors were circulating that high-ranking KMT officials and military intelligence officers had established themselves as "channels" for a more conciliatory Soviet policy toward China.[61] (One such figure was alleged to be Chiang Kai-shek's son, Chiang Ching-kuo.) This clique was, moreover, believed to represent more widespread sentiment at the upper levels of Chinese society, which appeared more open to the prospect of settlement with the CCP and closer cooperation with the Soviet Union as the only "desirable and necessary option" given internal problems faced by the Chiang-led KMT and its government. It seems that members of this same political cluster might even have been willing to concede Manchuria to the Soviet Union, as had already been agreed concerning Mongolia.[62] During the post-1945 period, it therefore appears that the KMT was, overall, a far less US-aligned and far more eclectic organization in both propaganda and foreign policy terms than its apparent dependence on American aid would seem to suggest. While Chiang and intermediaries regularly approached Washington for support, their public propaganda was extremely cautious in highlighting ties to the United States except where these might rally faith in the faltering KMT cause. Instead, KMT and external groups of all ideological positions seemed to mainly play up frustration with the pace and direction of US policy, while at the same time remaining mute—except perhaps in the case of anti-communist loyalists—on the subject of China's likely future relationship with the Soviet Union and the role to be played by the CCP.

Creating psychological defense: US information as a mask for national interests and global strategy

The official position of the US government toward China during and after 1945 was that a "united and democratic" China was important to world peace. As articulated by US president Harry S. Truman on December 19, 1946, political unity further required economic recovery.[63] Subsequent statements, such as that issued by the Marshall mission in 1947, further emphasized a "positive and realistic policy toward China which is based on full respect for her national sovereignty." Respect for sovereignty, of course, was not equivalent to winding up the wartime emergency systems of information gathering and dissemination which had supported US military action in China in years prior. Further work conducted under the auspices of the United States Information Service (USIS) from 1945 onward, following disbandment of the Office of War Information (OWI), relied on offices scattered throughout major Chinese cities (Shanghai, Chengdu) and, less publicly, on the old OWI radio network and stations in Shanghai, Nanjing, Kunming, and Tianjin.[64] The USIS also ran English classes in Manchuria, in addition to arranging for movies, concerts, and poster exhibits, and its administrators supported other initiatives, such as the Fulbright grant program, intended to positively impact cultural and educational ties.

For several years these programs aimed to produce a "full and fair" picture of the United States abroad.[65] Only by 1948 did the overall policy orientation begin to turn toward more directly countering anti-American propaganda campaigns, based on the realization—though evidence had already abounded for years—that China's politically active population had become largely critical of the US; not for reasons of CCP propaganda alone (if at all), but because of economic deprivation and "international fear" based on the concern that American policy might again turn China into a battleground, this time in a conflict between the United States and the Soviet Union. Since 1947, US Embassy officials in Nanjing had been advocating a policy of depicting the Soviet policy as imperialist in an effort to relieve pressure caused by similar charges against the USA. However, official government policy was to avoid using the same methods as communist organizations; the Voice of America did not refute public statements by other governments but instead rebroadcast news items from the American media that were believed to be of interest to foreign audiences.

The intended targets for the new policy were the estimated 50 million Chinese citizens who were literate and "politically conscious," and not already committed to either party. These included school groups (students and teachers), those in banking business and trade as well as government officials and civil servants.[66] The primary goal was to refute anti-American propaganda themes used by both the CCP and Soviet Union: that the United States was the world's "number one imperialist power" with an intention of dominating the world and threatening and enslaving other nations. Revealingly, it was noted by the policy drafters that audience receptivity for this propaganda was based not only on suspicion of American commercial and cultural-educational activities abroad but also on the fear of Japan, out of concern that the USA was rebuilding Japan for its own expansionist purposes in Asia. A similar line of critique was observed to emanate from the KMT: that, in addition to failing to appreciate the threat posed by communism, US policy threatened China's interests and industrial ambitions by facilitating the economic recovery of Japan. The point at which both sides converged was on patriotic support for Chinese foreign policy, which was contrasted with US expectations that China would cater to its own imperialistic interests.

The Americans tried to push back against the growing public perception that US-fomented war represented the greatest threat to China, urging Chiang Kai-shek to comment on events in Yugoslavia that underscored the global and political destabilizing reach of the Soviet Union.[67] Chiang, however, was already known to favor a policy of conciliation, which contrasted with the stronger anti-imperialist, anti-Soviet feeling that defined the right wing within the KMT. Also considered was the possibility of more productively inflaming nationalist sentiment within China, and even within the CCP itself, by pointing out the close alignment between the CCP's leaders—Mao and others—and Moscow and the Cominform (the organization through which Soviet leaders coordinated the resurgent international communist movement immediately after 1945), highlighting that China might easily share Eastern Europe's fate.[68] Publicly, the United States praised KMT "courage" in forging ahead despite the suffering caused by the eight-year war with Japan and the internal threat of communism.[69] American analysts were aware that, for all the criticism, the Chinese press was keenly attuned to US news and policy decisions, as these had potentially important implications for domestic events.[70] For that reason they saw the need to portray US policy in the best possible light. However, and in ways which would have provided further justification for Chinese concerns, it was admitted that the "revival of Japanese trade on a peacetime basis is important for the recovery of all Far Eastern nations." The crucial objective, then, was to portray the focus on Japan as something other than a "selfish policy of the United States."[71] Yet because there was no clear agreement on what this policy was, there was no way to counter the assertion from both parties that American policymakers cared more about their own national interests and did so in ways that did not necessarily overlap with what was best for China. Europe, the Soviet Union, and reindustrializing Japan—all of these issues seemed to matter more for the USA than China. This ambivalent signaling was further compounded by the fact that USIS activity could only send messages of vague hope that a KMT-led, unified central government would somehow emerge from the conflict, reflecting real ambiguities in US policy caused by a changing calculus of where American interests truly lay with respect to Asia.

The Soviet rejoinder: Masking occupation and intervention

Soviet propaganda in China had a long history already by 1945, with networks having been established in the 1920s by the Russian Telegraph Agency (ROSTA), the forerunner to the Telegraph Agency of the Soviet Union (TASS). These networks became particularly active again after August 8, 1945, when Stalin declared war on Japan and entered Manchuria. Immediately, US military operatives in China noticed a familiar pattern and tone in Soviet pronouncements. The goals were to convince Chinese citizens of the merits of the Soviet state structure; persuade them that foreign armies should leave China as soon as possible and that the USSR desired the liberation of Asian peoples; discredit US and British armed forces by playing up misbehavior; portray CCP armies as having played the most active part in the liberation of China from Japan; and insinuate that KMT armies, by contrast, had been more interested in blockading CCP forces than in fighting the Japanese.[72] Soviet operatives were also active within White Russian communities, attempting to recruit members to return to Russia and become citizens, as Meredith Oyen also points out in Chapter 2 of this volume. (White Russian propaganda against the Soviet Union also circulated, including allegations that made use of forged documents to show that Stalin had a master military plan to use China as the first step in overthrowing US interests globally.[73]) In addition, the consulate in Beijing offered English and Chinese classes for recruitment and influence purposes, while tracking down alleged political enemies still at large in China. Soviet organizations were, furthermore, observed organizing propaganda activities among Chinese and Japanese laborers as well as other European groups within China. These campaigns were noticeably anti-US in orientation and spread southward from Manchuria into Beijing, Qingdao, Tianjin, and Shanghai.[74]

In scope and complexity, Soviet operations reached into more marginal communities still within China after the moment of Japanese surrender. This was not wholly unusual: US, CCP, and KMT militaries and intelligence services all had various degrees of contact with Japanese, Korean, Central Asian, and European émigré groups deemed to have operational and intelligence value. To this end, for example, Soviet operatives sought out liaisons with Japanese communists active in Shanghai.[75] The wide network that Soviet agencies cultivated was also useful for counter-propaganda purposes, as when poor Red Army troop discipline in Harbin and elsewhere in Manchuria required that the outrages be blamed on the CCP Eighth Route Army. As the conflict in China intensified, so did Soviet-sponsored allegations of US warmongering, which in 1947 described the Wedemeyer mission as part of a larger plan to use China, Japan, and Korea as sources for raw materials in preparation for global war against the Soviet Union.[76]

To a certain extent, these accusatory campaigns served as cover and distraction while Soviet military forces built up economic and strategic control over

Manchuria and, further west, Mongolia and Xinjiang. By portraying the United States as avaricious and "power-mad," Soviet propaganda was also able to play on Chinese insecurities concerning Japan by making the Americans appear bent on creating their own Asian empire in Japan's stead (including through the reindustrialization and rearming of post-surrender Japan).[77] Here the anti-American propaganda campaign was not entirely effective. Popularly, American observers noted, and particularly following the Czech "coup d'etat," public opinion within China concerning the Soviet Union had grown increasingly skeptical. However, more threatening than Soviet control and the disasters it might unleash was the "major threat" of the destruction of China by a war between a US-backed KMT and Soviet-backed CCP. Because the KMT was so deeply discredited already, US interference in China's affairs was therefore the greater problem. For this reason, Soviet propaganda strategy did not ultimately deny the looting of Manchuria and de facto control over Dalian and Port Arthur, but rather it insisted that these were legal and legitimate actions.[78] The Americans, by contrast, were made to appear as uninvited and illegitimate interlopers. Anti-American anti-imperialism thus became a means of drawing attention away from unpopular Soviet policies and military behavior, while at the same time providing an alternative to the necessity of having to hide or lie about interests in Northeast and Northwest China, where Russian influence was rapidly overwhelming the Chinese government's claims to effective sovereignty.

Constitutional democrats, liberals, and popular opinion: Masking despair

Even in 1945, the production of anti-American news and propaganda in China was not solely attributable to CCP and Soviet machinations. Newspapers and rumors in northern China and Shanghai carried less politically motivated accusations of rapes and robberies by the US forces, and US military intervention on both sides of the conflict between the CCP and KMT.[79] "Mosquito press" reports played to anti-American sentiment by sensationalizing these stories. Moreover, Japanese organizations still within China also contributed to a general sense that the United States might be drawing China and Asia into yet another global conflict, this time with the USSR.[80]

This did not mean that anti-Americanism was the sole, or even the dominant, frame through which ordinary people in China experienced the events of the war. Tillman Durden of the *New York Times* related to John Melby impressions that in Kalgan, there was "tension and no great love for Communists," along with the fear of KMT troops and of being seen as a Japanese collaborator or sympathizer, especially by the CCP, whose program against puppet leaders was being "vigorously prosecuted" through arrests and executions.[81] Manchurians felt "considerable bitterness over the renewal of hostilities … [and that] they had been abandoned by everyone." CCP forces were observed to be fatigued and unwilling to fight. Beijing was disorganized, with students politically active and increasingly pro-CCP, at least partly out of desperation and disgust with the national government.

As a group, students may have been among the most anti-American political forces within China, due mainly to their association of US forces with the KMT government, which they believed was emboldened in its efforts to tame social criticism as a result of tacit American support.[82] In addition to student groups and newspapers, members of the Democratic League also opined that civil conflict in China would only be exacerbated, not ended, by foreign interference, as symbolized by the presence of US Marines.[83] By 1947, the intensity of the conflict and obvious fact of foreign involvement on both sides meant that Chinese newspapers of all political hues focused mainly on international events. By then it was clear that few foreign powers had an immediate interest in Chinese unity except on terms which favored one side or the other. Because the United States was identified with the most unpopular domestic alternative, the KMT, even "middle-of-the-road" viewpoints were almost indistinguishable from the CCP on the issue of getting the United States out of China's political and military conflict.[84] KMT "fascism" supported by the United States was far more unpalatable than a CCP aligned with the Soviet Union.

Across the press, the presence of foreign troops was decried as an affront to Chinese sovereignty but, here again, the Soviet presence remained largely invisible and was deemed less objectionable. The United States by contrast, was associated straightforwardly with imperialism: "in Formosa (Taiwan) and (by virtue of connection to the British) in Hong Kong as well."[85] Both the left (the *Wenhui bao* and *Xinmin bao*) and the right (the *Xinwen bao* and *Xinsheng bao*) were critical of US policy, and published news from around Asia alongside opposition opinions from within the USA itself to highlight Americans as the major perpetrators of "foreign interference." (The government and KMT party press, however, tended to be more opposed to the Soviet position, particularly in Dalian, for the reason that it was seen as benefiting the CCP.) In Mukden (present day Shenyang), student complaints were recorded which included the opinion that conditions in China were hopeless, and education had been better under the Japanese.[86]

Liberal positions in China were primarily nationalistic. If liberalism connoted anything specific, it was opposition to the KMT government and criticism of China's "supine" policy toward both the United States and Soviet Union.[87] Government interference in everyday life was a powerful source of dissatisfaction, even among the wealthy and powerful; by contrast, a kind of abstract admiration for the USA persisted, even if the American policy and government were seen as "wicked." The presence of American goods, culture, military personnel, and "incidents" involving American soldiers fanned denouncements of American imperialism; feelings toward the Soviet Union, by contrast, were a mixture of suspicion of Soviet motives and acceptance of a social policy based on socialism. The overarching goal was to solve national problems and, ultimately, restore China to a position of greatness and strength. Yet of all of these issues, US support for Japan was possibly seen as the most egregious, especially in 1948, when China's economy was spiraling downward and repercussions of war were being more widely felt across China.[88]

Internal CCP perspectives also suggest another experience of the period: political indifference and unwillingness to enter mass organizations. An uncertain military situation, political assassinations and terror, and lack of local media interest in carrying political propaganda were identified in 1946 as "common and serious problems" with respect to winning support in northern China.[89] In the fluid 1940s, however, one did not have to be a party supporter to be a patriot. The "basic attitudes" observed by American analysts included: firm support of China's independence and territorial sovereignty; nationalism, which referred to the belief that China possessed an honorable, superior civilization and culture; anxiety to see China become equal with the world's great powers; hope for improvement of the general welfare; and, overwhelmingly, criticism of KMT weaknesses, particularly in foreign relations.[90] By 1948, it was widely understood that, deplorable as the KMT leadership might be, the CCP was also to blame for the war. However, both the CCP and a Soviet-backed new government were seen as preferable to a situation of prolonged warfare and devastation, with general openness to socialism and the belief that the Soviet Union was not an imperialist power prevalent among educated and politically active citizens. There was also widespread agreement that the United States was the primary source of China's troubles, as its government had prolonged the survival of an irredeemably flawed political clique, and that American leaders planned to dominate East Asia, thus making the Soviet "option" unavoidable. In both cases, entanglement with external actors was seen as ultimately undesirable but, where the CCP–Soviet alliance was concerned, necessary.

Conclusion

Histories of postwar East Asian politics have tended to focus primarily on the entangled themes of modernization and nation-building. However, new transnational archives and modes of scholarship have made it possible to discern overarching patterns of shared political ideology and other forms of what is often loosely characterized as "interaction" (cultural flows, technology- and information-sharing, proxy conflict, and social mobilization) stretching across these national divides.[91] Using the case of China, this chapter has highlighted the existence of anti-imperialist and anti-American political configurations which primarily involved Chinese, American, and Soviet actors and their related media but, at the same time, stretched further outward (and in more elusive ways) to reach Europe, Korea, Japan, and other global political centers and publics. While such evidence is not particularly heartening from a perspective of, say, US public history, it does provide some context and precedent for opposition to American policy that has characterized the global peace movement seemingly from the moment of its postwar inception.

The irony, of course, is that in promoting a politics of independence from "imperialist" US forces the KMT was forced to mask the degree of its dependence on the US for survival. The CCP and Soviet Union, in turn, were forced to mask the depth of their political interconnection and territorial concessions which Chinese politicians on both sides had already made to Soviet interests. And the United States itself was forced—too late—to adopt an information policy which stressed its respect for the dignity and virtue of a KMT government whose failure became inevitable in the eyes of American leaders before the Chinese Civil War had even been concluded. Liberal Chinese political groups and the politically active public, in a similar-yet-opposite reversal, justified their dislike for American policies mainly in terms of the CCP–Soviet alternative being less repugnant. Where Japan reappeared amid this tangled thicket of news, opinion, and belief was primarily as evidence of US government war preparations (reindustrialization, rearmament)— in other words as an augur of a Third World War—or as a residual threat to China's long sought-after independence. (Realists knew better, and by 1949 there was little doubt concerning the CCP–Soviet relationship or the nature of Soviet power in East Asia.) Anti-imperialist anti-Americanism thus became, it might be argued, part of the ideology of the postwar Asian state independence and nonalignment movements.[92] While Japan was no longer the primary target, the pattern of political alliance-building and mass mobilization around the issue of a common enemy of civilization and peace remained firmly intact.

Notes

1   See Charles D. Musgrove, "Cheering the Traitor: The Post-War Trial of Chen Bijun, April 1946," *Twentieth-Century China* 30, no. 2 (April 2005), pp. 3–27; Barak Kushner, *Men to Devils, Devils to Men: Japanese War Crimes and Chinese Justice* (Cambridge, MA: Harvard University Press, 2015).

2   See, for example, CCP Central Committee, "Guanyu Dongbei xuanchuan wenti gei Dongbei ju de zhishi" [Directive to the Northeast Bureau Concerning the Northeast Propaganda Issue], March 6, 1946, in *Zhongguo Gongchandang xuanchuan gongzuo wenxian xuanbian, 1939–1945* [Selected and Edited Documents on Chinese Communist Party Propaganda Work, 1937–1945] (hereafter *ZGDXGWX*), eds. Zhong-Gong Zhongyang Xuanchuan Bu Bangongting, and Zhongyang Dang'an Guan Bianyan Bu (Beijing: Study Press, 1996), p. 618.

3   JMCF, Box 1, General, 1946 (June–December), "Manifesto of the Central Committee of the Chinese Communist Party on the Occasion of the Ninth Anniversary of the War of Resistance," July 7, 1946.

4   He Yinan, "Remembering and Forgetting the War: Elite Mythmaking, Mass Reaction, and Sino-Japanese Relations, 1950–2006," *History & Memory* 19, no. 2 (Fall 2007), pp. 43–74; Rana Mitter, "Old Ghosts, New Memories: Changing China's War History in the Era of Post-Mao Politics," *Journal of Contemporary History* 38, no. 1 (January 2003), pp. 117–131.

5   One definitive statement on this theme, with broad application to China, is Theda Skocpol, *States and Social Revolutions* (Cambridge: Cambridge University Press, 1979). See also J. Yasushi Yamanouchi, Victor Koschmann, and Ryūichi Narita, eds., *Total War and "Modernization"* (Ithaca, NY: East Asia Program, Cornell University, 1998); Rana Mitter, "Modernity, Internationalisation, and War in the History of Modern China," *The Historical Journal* 48, no. 2 (June 2005), pp. 431–446; Ja Ian Chong, *External Intervention and the Politics of State Formation: China, Indonesia, and Thailand, 1893–1952* (Cambridge: Cambridge University Press, 2012).

6 Suzanne Pepper, *Civil War in China: The Political Struggle 1945–1949* (Berkeley: University of California Press, 1978); Lloyd Eastman, *Seeds of Destruction: Nationalist China in War and Revolution, 1937–1949* (Stanford, CA: Stanford University Press, 1984); Odd Arne Westad, *Decisive Encounters: The Chinese Civil War, 1946–1950* (Stanford, CA: Stanford University Press, 2003); Diana Lary, *China's Civil War: A Social History, 1945–1949* (Cambridge: Cambridge University Press, 1949).

7 JMCF, Box 2, General, 1947 (June–December), airgram no. A-193 from American Embassy, Nanking to Secretary of State, Washington, DC, October 3, 1947.

8 Ibid.

9 JMCF, Box 2, Situation of the Chinese Vernacular Press, July 1947, Melby, "Situation of the Chinese Vernacular Press," n.d. [*c*. July 1947].

10 Zhao Yuming, *Zhongguo xiandai guangbo jianshi* [Concise History of China's Modern Broadcasting] (Beijing: China Broadcasting and Television Press, 1987), pp. 79–81.

11 Ibid., p. 82.

12 Ibid., pp. 83–84.

13 Ibid.

14 DNSA, CI00016, "Peacetime Intelligence Requirements," September 14, 1945; DNSA, CI00023, "Reassignment of Responsibility for Quasi-military and Clandestine Activities," September 22, 1945.

15 DNSA, CI00038, "Present Status and Future Plans of the Strategic Services Unit, China Theater," December 28, 1945; DNSA, CCI00050, "SSU Activities: October 1945," January 25, 1946.

16 DNSA, CI00051, "Summary of SSU Activities during November, 1945," January 25, 1946.

17 DNSA, CI00052, "Summary of SSU Activities during December 1945," February 6, 1946.

18 DNSA, CI00055, "Summary of SSU Activities during January 1946," February 11, 1946.

19 DNSA, CI00068, "Chinese Intelligence Reports," March 10, 1946; DNSA, CI00082, "Monthly Progress Report – Counter Espionage Section," March 31, 1946.

20 DNSA, CI00109, "Monthly Progress Report, April 1946," May 1, 1946; DNSA, CI00134, "Monthly Progress Report, May 1946," June 1, 1946.

21 Zhou Enlai, "Jiji xuanchuan fan neizhan fan ducai, jiechuan Jiang Jieshi de qipian yinmou" [Enthusiastically Propagandize Anti-Civil War Anti-Dictatorship (Messages), Expose Chiang Kai-shek's Cheating Plots], August 16, 1945, in *ZGDXGWX*, pp. 590–591.

22 DNSA, CCI00009, "Chinese Communist Preparations for Civil Crisis in China (Current Intelligence Study Number 32)," July 27, 1945.

23 Ibid.

24 JMCF, Box 1, General, 1938–1945, "Analysis of Geifang [sic] (from Young, Yenan)," December 7, 1945.

25 JMCF, Box 1, General, 1938–1945, "Chungking Press Reaction over Ambassador Hurley's Resignation," December 7, 1945; JMCF, Box 1, General, 1938–1945, "Protest to the US Forces on Their Intervention in Chinese Domestic Affairs," November 8, 1945; JMCF, Box 1, General, 1938–1945, "Letter of San Min Chu I Comrades Union to American People," n.d.

26 JMCF, Box 1, 1938–1945, "Turmoil – A Comment on World Affairs," translation, November 3, 1945.

27 See DNSA, CI00048, "Chinese Meeting with Soviet Union in Mukden,"
    January 22, 1946.

28 DNSA, CI00083, "Military Information: Russian Activities," April 3, 1946.

29 DNSA, CI00093, "Final Report of Yenan Observer Group," April 15, 1946.

30 Lin Zhida, *Zhongguo Gongchandang xuanchuan shi* [History of Chinese Communist
    Party Propaganda] (Chengdu: Sichuan People's Press, 1990), p. 217.

31 Zhou, "Jiji xuanchuan," pp. 590–591.

32 Lin, *Zhongguo Gongchandang*, p. 220.

33 Chen Qingquan and Song Guangwei, *Lu Dingyi zhuan* [Biography of Lu Dingyi]
    (Beijing: Chinese Communist Party History Press, 1999), p. 294.

34 Ibid., p. 299.

35 Wang Jianying, *Zhong-Gong Zhongyang jiguan lishi yanbian kaoshi (1921–1949)*
    [Inquiry into the History and Evolution of CCP Central Institutions (1921–1949)]
    (Beijing: Communist Party History Press, 2004), p. 489.

36 Ibid; Chen Qingquan, *Zai Zhong-Gong gaoceng 50 nian: Lu Dingyi chuanqi rensheng*
    [Fifty Years at the Upper Levels of the CCP: The Extraordinary Life of Lu Dingyi]
    (Beijing: People's Press, 2006), p. 141.

37 CCP Central Propaganda Department, "Guanyu muqian xuanchuan fangzhen wenti
    de tongzhi" [Circular Concerning Issues in the Current Propaganda Plan], September
    29, 1945, *ZGDXGWX*, pp. 592–593.

38 "Zhongyang guanyu zuzhi yezhanjun he jiaqiang Dongbei renmin zizhi de xuanchuan
    jiaoyu gongzuo gei Peng Zhen, Lin Biao de zhishi" [Directive Given to Peng Zhen,
    Lin Biao by the CCP Central Committee Concerning Field Army Organization and
    Strengthening Propaganda and Education Work for People's Self-Government in the
    Northeast], November 4, 1945, *ZGDXGWX*, p. 596.

39 CCP Central Propaganda Department, "Guanyu kaizhan jielu Mei-Jiang jingong
    jiefang qu de xuanchuan gongshi zhi ge zhongyang ju, ge qu dangwei dian" [Telegram
    to Every Central Bureau and Regional Committee Concerning Propaganda Offensive
    to Develop Exposure of US-Chiang Attacks on Liberated Areas], November 4, 1945,
    ZGDXGWX, pp. 597–598.

40 CCP Central Committee, "Guanyu zan bu yi Gongchandang zhongyang ju mingyi
    fabiao xuanyan gangling gei Dongbei ju de zhishi" [Directive to Northeast Bureau
    Concerning Temporarily not Issuing Statements and Outlines Using the Name of
    CCP Central Bureaus], November 16, 1945, *ZGDXGWX*, p. 604.

41 CCP Central Committee, "Guanyu dui Guomindang jundui jinxing xuanchuan
    gongshi de zhishi" [Directive Concerning Advancing the Propaganda Offensive
    against Nationalist Forces], November 17, 1945, *ZGDXGWX*, pp. 605–607.

42 CCP Central Propaganda Department, "Guanyu dui waiguo jizhe ying yu qingbao,
    tewu renyuan qubie kandai gei Jin-Cha-Ji zhongyang ju de zhishi" [Directive to the
    Jin-Cha-Ji Central Bureau Concerning Treating Foreign Reporters Differently than
    Intelligence and Special Forces Personnel], November 30, 1945, *ZGDXGWX*, p. 608.

43 Lu Dingyi, "Guanyu Jiang dang de gaikuang bianxie cheng ce yiji Mei guangbo deng
    qingkuang xiang Zhongyang de zhishi" [Directive to the [CCP] Central [Committee]
    Concerning Compilation and Writing of Handbooks on Party General Conditions
    and Conditions with Regard to Broadcasting Aimed at America], January 6, 1946,
    ZGDXGWX, p. 613.

44 CCP Central Committee, "Guanyu zhengqu Jiang Jieshi Guomindang xiang minzhu
    fangmian zhuanbian zanshi tingzhi xuanchuan gongshi de zhishi" [Directive
    Concerning Temporarily Stopping the Propaganda Offensive to Seize the Turn

toward a Democratic Direction from Chiang Kai-shek's KMT], February 7, 1946, *ZGDXGWX*, pp. 615–617.

45 CCP Central Propaganda Department, "Guanyu guangbo, baozhi, xuanchuan fangzhen de tongzhi" [Circular Concerning (Our) Orientation in Broadcasting, Newspapers and Propaganda], March 8, 1946, *ZGDXGWX*, p. 619.

46 JMCF, Box 2, Lu Ting-yi [Lu Dingyi], "Explanation of Several Basic Questions Concerning Post-War Situation," Supplementary English News Service, New China News Agency, Nanking, January 21, 1947.

47 JMCF, Box 2, General, 1947 (June–December), American Embassy, Nanking, "Analysis of Certain Factors in Current World Problems by Lu Ting-yi, Head of the Department of Information of the Chinese Communist Party," *c.* June 1947.

48 DNSA, CI00005, "Political Conflict in China (Current Intelligence Study Number 12)," April 20, 1945.

49 Ibid; see also JMCF, Box 2, General, 1947 (January–May), "Special & Feature Articles, Various Cliques of Chinese Army," *c.* January 7, 1947.

50 JMCF, Box 1, 1938–1945, memorandum, "Chungking Press Reaction over Ambassador Hurley's Resignation," December 7, 1945.

51 JMCF, Box 1, General, 1946 (January–May), John F. Melby, "Memorandum," February 23, 1946.

52 JMCF, Box 2, General, 1947 (January–May), incoming telegram no. 558 from Nanking to Secretary of State, March 14, 1947.

53 Ibid.

54 JMCF, Box 2, General, 1947 (June–December), "Excerpts from Generalissimo's Speech at Fourth Plenary Session of the Kuomintang Central Executive Committee," September 22, 1947.

55 JMCF, Box 2, General, 1947 (June–December), American Embassy, Nanking, "Statement by Dr. Wu Te-chen, Secretary-General of the Kuomintang," September 10, 1947.

56 JMCF, Box 2, General, 1947 (June–December), J. Leighton Stuart, "Memorandum," *c.* August 1947.

57 JMCF, Box 3, General, 1948 (June–December), American Embassy, Nanking, November 5, 1948. Text released by Central News Agency of interview with Arthur T. Steele of *New York Herald Tribune*. Statements repeated in *Zhongyang ribao* (KMT) and *Heping ribao* (Army).

58 JMCF, Box 2, General, 1947 (June–December), incoming telegram no. 1963, from Nanking to Secretary of State, September 19, 1947.

59 Ibid. Article in *Da gong bao*.

60 JMCF, Box 2, General, 1947 (June–December), incoming telegram no. 1990, from Nanking to Secretary of State, September 26, 1947.

61 JMCF, Box 2, General, 1947 (June–December), airgram no. 275, from American Embassy, Nanking to Secretary of State, Washington DC, December 19, 1947.

62 JMCF, Box 3, General, 1948 (June–December), airgram no. 283, from American Embassy, Nanking to Secretary of State, Washington DC, November 22, 1948.

63 JMCF, Box 1, General, 1946 (June–December), American Embassy, Nanking, "Press Release – President Truman Issues Statement on China," December 19, 1946.

64 JMCF, Box 1, 1938–1945, memorandum, "USIS Emergency Program in China till [sic] June 30, 1946," December 12, 1945.

65 JMCF, Box 3, General, 1948 (January–May), instruction to J. Leighton Stuart, Ambassador, Nanking from Department of State, March 4, 1948.

66 JMCF, Box 3, General, 1948 (January–May), "Working Paper on US Information Policy for China," March 1, 1948.

67 JMCF, Box 3, General, 1948 (June–December), airgram A-203 from American Embassy, Nanjing to Secretary of State, Washington, August 6, 1948.

68 JMCF, Box 3, General, 1948 (June–December), memorandum of conversation between Li Wei-kuo and John F. Melby, "Propaganda in China," July 19, 1948.

69 JMCF, Box 3, General, 1948 (January–May), United States Information Service, "Daily News Bulletin – Special Supplement," *c.* March 30, 1948.

70 JMCF, Box 3, Press Review, 1948 (September–December), from David N. Rowe, "Conclusions to be drawn from Press Survey thus far," October 11, 1948.

71 JMCF, Box 3, General, 1948 (June–December), "Publicity Campaign on Japanese Foreign Trade," June 3, 1948.

72 DNSA, CCI00055, "Summary of SSU Activities during January 1946," February 11, 1946.

73 JMCF, Box 3, General, 1948 (June–December), American Embassy, Nanking, "Memorandum for the Ambassador," September 2, 1948.

74 DNSA, CI00068, "Chinese Intelligence Reports," March 10, 1946.

75 DNSA, CI00109, "Monthly Progress Report, April 1946," May 1, 1946.

76 JMCF, Box 2, General, 1947 (June–December), J. Leighton Stuart, "Memorandum," *c.* August 1947.

77 JMCF, Box 1, General, 1946 (January–May), John F. Melby, "Memorandum," February 23, 1946; JMCF, Box 3, General, 1948 (June–December), American Embassy, Nanking, "Proposed Information Directive," June 9, 1948.

78 JMCF, Box 3, General, 1948 (June–December), American Embassy, Nanking, "Soviet Propaganda in China," August 11, 1948.

79 DNSA, CI00065, report from William S. Crawford to H. Ben Smith, February 28, 1946.

80 DNSA, CI00082, "Monthly Progress Report – Counter Espionage Section," March 31, 1946.

81 JMCF, Box 1, 1938–1945, "Memorandum," November 9, 1945.

82 JMCF, Box 1, 1938–1945, "Copy of Letter from USIS, Kunming," December 1, 1945.

83 JMCF, Box 1, 1938–1945, "Copy of Statement Presented to United States Military Authorities in North China," November 15, 1945.

84 JMCF, Box 2, General, 1947 (June–December), "Subject: Democratic League Attitude Toward Chinese Situation," December 17, [1947].

85 JMCF, 1947, Box 2, General, 1947 (January–May), from Nanking to Secretary of State, April 19, 1947.

86 JMCF, Box 1, General, 1946 (June–December), "Transmission of Excerpts from Letter Written by Public Affairs Officer, Mukden," October 1946.

87 JMCF, Box 2, General, 1947 (June–December), "Political Attitudes of Nanjing Students," from Bennett, Josiah W. to American Embassy, October 2, 1947; JMCF, Box 3, General, 1948, (January–May), "Mukden Students Winter Camps," from American Consulate General, Mukden, February 25, 1948.

88 JMCF, Box 3, General, 1948 (June–December), airgram no. 189, from American Embassy, Nanking to Secretary of State, Washington, DC, July 19, 1948.

89 CCP Central Propaganda Department, "Guanyu guangbo, baozhi, xuanchuan fangzhen de tongzhi" [Circular Concerning (Our) Orientation in Broadcasting, Newspapers and Propaganda], March 8, 1946, *ZGDXGWX*, p. 619.

90 JMCF, Box 3, General, 1948 (January–May), "Working Paper on US Information Policy for China," March 1, 1948.

91 A related form of transnational interaction is the "imaginary." See Robeson Taj Frazer, *The East Is Black: Cold War China in the Black Radical Imagination* (Durham, NC: Duke University Press, 2014); Masuda Hajimu, *Cold War Crucible: The Korean Conflict and the Postwar World* (Cambridge, MA: Harvard University Press, 2015).

92 On anti-imperialism and the politics of Asian unity, see Ramachandra Guha, ed., *Makers of Modern Asia* (Cambridge, MA: Harvard University Press, 2014), passim.

Chapter 7

FROM THE ASHES OF EMPIRE: THE RECONSTRUCTION OF MANCHUKUO'S ENTERPRISES AND THE MAKING OF CHINA'S NORTHEASTERN INDUSTRIAL BASE, 1948–1952

Koji Hirata

Anshan Iron and Steel Works (*Angang* in Chinese) is situated in the city of Anshan, Liaoning Province in Northeast China, which was historically called Manchuria.[1] Today, Angang is often referred to as a prime example of the archaic and inefficient state-owned enterprises (SOEs) endemic to China's northeastern "Rust Belt." During the Mao period (1949–1976), however, heavy industry, including the steel industry, and the SOEs were regarded as the core of "socialist industrialization," which was to bring China to a higher stage of history along the Marxist predetermined route. The Northeast was considered the most "advanced" region, with the highest concentration of heavy industry and SOEs in the country.

Importantly, Angang was originally established by a Japanese colonial company rather than by the Chinese state. Japan's South Manchurian Railway Company, or *Mantetsu*, established the Anshan Ironworks in 1918, and in 1933 it was reorganized and renamed the Shōwa Steelworks under the Japanese puppet regime of Manchukuo (1932–1945).[2] Following Japan's surrender in the Second World War, the enterprise was taken over first by the KMT and then by the Chinese Communist Party (CCP). Of the twenty work units that make up Angang today, four were established during the Japanese period. Moreover, the story of conversion from a Japanese colonial enterprise into a Chinese SOE is not unique to Angang. Many, if not all, of the major heavy-industry SOEs in Northeast China share a similar background. The Fushun Colliery was first developed by the Russians around the *fin de siècle* and was then expanded by Mantetsu after the Russo-Japanese War (1904–1905). The Benxihu Iron and Steel Works was established by a Japanese business conglomerate, Ōkura-gumi, beginning in 1905.

Until recently, scholars paid scant attention to the Chinese takeover of Japanese industrial enterprises in Manchuria. This was partly due to disciplinary boundaries that left Manchukuo almost exclusively for Japan scholars rather than China scholars.[3] For scholars of modern Japan, the major issue concerning post-Second World War Manchuria was how and whether the Japanese were repatriated from Manchuria to Japan, rather than what the remaining Japanese did in Manchuria, now reintegrated into the Chinese nation-state.[4] The study of the legacy of Manchukuo's industrial development as an influential force during the early construction of the People's Republic of China (PRC) was initiated only recently.[5] However, scholars set their research questions squarely within the confines of the history of the Japanese Empire or Sino-Japanese relations rather than discussing broader questions about the origins of the Chinese socialist planned economy. In the field of modern Chinese history, discussion of the continuities across the Communist Revolution of 1949 focuses overwhelmingly on the KMT inheritances in the early PRC.[6] This focus elides more or less completely Northeast China and the Japanese influence there from the narrative, which also reflects the disciplinary divide between the Chinese and Japanese studies. This omission of the Northeast is problematic, given that the region, in fact, became China's largest heavy industrial base under Japanese Occupation, producing 49 percent of coal, 89 percent of pig iron, 91 percent of steel, 67 percent of electricity, and 66 percent of cement in the whole of China in 1943.[7]

This chapter situates Manchuria's industrial legacy within the *longue durée* of state-led heavy industrialization in twentieth-century China. Drawing upon primary sources in Chinese, Japanese, and Russian, I tell the story of the CCP reconstruction of former Japanese-owned factories and mines in Northeast China between 1948 and 1952, and the role of Japanese engineers in this process. I argue that the Manchurian industrial base, which a 1952 *Time* magazine article called "one of the richest areas in Asia" and "Red China's Ruhr," was built upon the legacy of industrialization under Japan's puppet regime of Manchukuo as well as China's KMT government (1928–1949).[8] I also posit that the expertise of Japanese engineers played a critical role in the CCP's reconstruction of the region's industry, given the CCP's lack of technological experts at the time. Formed under the Japanese and KMT regimes, industrial Manchuria played a decisive role in the development of the early PRC's industrial economy, the main priorities of which were investment in heavy industry, economic planning, and the SOE system. By narrating the story in this manner, I situate Mao-era China within the context of the longer history of war and empire building in China before 1949.

The chapter begins with a discussion of the CCP reconstruction of Manchuria's industrial enterprises after they conquered the region in 1948. The following section focuses on the role of Japanese engineers in CCP-controlled Manchuria. I conclude by exploring life in the community of the Japanese under CCP control.

Cradle of the communist industrial economy

After the Second Sino-Japanese War (1937–1945), Northeast China became the first industrial region that fell under the control of the CCP in the Chinese Civil War (1945–1949). In August 1945, Soviet forces began their invasion of Northeast China, then under Japanese Occupation, quickly defeated the

Japanese military forces there and occupied the entire region. Thanks to the Soviet military presence, which hindered KMT military control, the CCP first became dominant in village areas and the Soviet-controlled port city of Dalian before going on to occupy other cities. Following the Soviet retreat from the Northeast (with the exception of Dalian) in the spring of 1946, the KMT took control of many of the urban areas in southern Manchuria. However, by 1948, the CCP's military advantage was so substantial that it effectively held most of the Northeast and took over the former-Manchukuo enterprises previously controlled by the Nationalists.[9]

The industrial base of the Northeast was crucial; the CCP, hitherto largely focused on the countryside, had recognized during the war with Japan the significance of industrialization as a major policy goal. During the Sino-Japanese War, Mao decried China's lack of modern industry as the chief reason for its backwardness and thus helplessness at the hands of foreign aggression: "Japanese imperialism bullies China in this way because China does not have strong industry. They bully us because of our backwardness [*luohou*]."[10] By the end of the war, the Northeast had developed into China's largest heavy-industry region under the Japanese Occupation. Two months before the end of the Sino-Japanese War, Mao stressed the importance of the region's industry for his future Communist Revolution:

> The Northeast is very important ... even if we lose all the current liberated areas, the foundations for the Chinese revolution will be firm as long as we keep the Northeast ... For now, our foundations are not firm. Why are they not firm? Because the economy of our current liberated areas is still handicraft economy, and there is no large-scale industry, nor heavy industry.[11]

The CCP's experience in Manchuria during the Civil War was thus pivotal to its transformation from rural guerrilla forces into a bureaucratic organization committed to heavy industrialization.[12]

Most of the CCP cadres who became the new masters of the Northeastern industrial sites, however, lacked experience in managing modern high-tech industries. Having been based in the countryside since the late 1920s, the CCP had few technologically competent cadres. Back then, the CCP cadres were

Table 7.1 Production in Northeast China in 1949 (10,000 tons). *Source*: Report by the Northeastern Department of Industry (January 1950), DJCZ, vol. 2, pp. 255–268

Product	1944	1949
Coal	2,199	1,123.90
Pig iron	118	17.25
Steel	28	7.8
Cement	875	213.8

largely labor movement organizers, experts in rural land reform, and guerrilla fighters—not factory managers or industrial engineers. A March 1947 report by the industry and mining department of the CCP's regional authority in the Northeast admitted as much, noting that "cadres are lacking, technology cadres are more lacking. Nobody has experience in leading and managing large factories and mines."[13]

However, even though few of the CCP cadres had any experience in modern industry, the reconstruction of enterprises, which had suffered serious damage during the Soviet Occupation and the Civil War, nevertheless kept up an impressive pace. According to a 1949 report by the Industry Department of the CCP Northeast Administration Committee, "a vast majority of the enterprises that we took over from the enemies and puppets had suffered prolonged destruction with only a few exceptions where the destruction was comparatively light." Still, "the reconstruction work of 1948 progressed thanks to the efforts and courage to overcome difficulty on the part of the comrades who participated in the reconstruction work."[14] In April 1949, of the 323 mines and factories under CCP control in the Northeast, 234 (72.5 percent) were reopened and 58 (18 percent) were under reconstruction.[15] In 1949 many heavy industries were showing signs of recovery: they had achieved 51.1 percent of their coal production in 1944, the last full year of the Japanese occupation of the region, 14.6 percent of pig iron production, 27.9 percent of steel production, and 24.4 percent of cement production (see Figure 7.1). While not obviously impressive, these figures are significant given that most industries in Northeast China had been devastated by Soviet occupation forces, and then by the CCP and Nationalist forces, and had also been stripped clean by local residents who robbed materials from factories.

In reconstructing industry and experimenting with economic planning, the CCP authorities in Manchuria also began an economic partnership with the Soviet Union. In September 1948, the CCP authority in the region contacted the Soviet consulate-general in Harbin to request that the USSR share with them their materials and books on the five-year plans of the USSR so that they could learn from them.[16] In October, Gao Gang, the highest-ranking CCP leader in the Northeast, telegraphed Stalin asking him to export cotton to Manchuria so that they could restore the region's textile industry.[17] In December 1948, Chen Yun, the CCP leader who was in command of the economic policy in the Northeast, asked the Soviet Union to send five or six planning experts to assist the CCP's economic planning in the region.[18]

The ongoing Chinese Civil War between 1945 and 1949 made the reconstruction of Northeast China's industry all the more urgent, as CCP leaders informed the Soviets of their intention to make the region a "crucible of national defensive capacity."[19] According to the memoir of a CCP cadre in Anshan, Angang produced 3,000 explosive shells between February and October 1948.[20] The industrial products, manpower, and grain from the Northeastern industrial base contributed to the CCP victory over the Nationalist forces in China proper. On October 1, 1949, Chairman Mao proclaimed the establishment of the People's Republic of China from atop Tian'anmen, the main gate to the Forbidden City.[21]

One year after the establishment of the PRC, China assisted North Korea by entering the war on the Korean Peninsula (1950–1953). Faced with major battles with the US military in Korea, the PRC leaders further continued to stress the importance of heavy industry, and therefore of the Northeast, which was the nation's heavy-industry center. In the First National Industrial Meeting in February and March 1951, the PRC economic policymakers decided that 52.2 percent of state investment in industry was to be allocated to heavy industry. In particular, the iron and steel industry was allocated 32.9 percent of state investment.[22] This policy demonstrated a continued focus on industrial Manchuria, the largest heavy industry region in the early PRC.

During the Korean War, the regional government of Manchuria continued the reconstruction of the region's industrial enterprises, which were the main providers of military-related goods to the PRC forces fighting in the peninsula. In 1952 the region was producing 40.6 percent of electricity, 33.2 percent of coal, 39.4 percent of cement, 69.9 percent of steel, and 55.1 percent of petroleum in China.[23] According to a 1950 government report, "most of our industry is concentrated in the Northeast and Shanghai. The former is a heavy-industry region, and the latter is a light-industry region." Such an unbalanced regional allocation arose from "the influence of imperialism." As the report explained, "industry in the Northeast is a leftover from construction during occupation by Japanese imperialism; much of the industry in Shanghai relies upon raw materials inherited from the imperial period."[24]

The Northeast shaped the early PRC's industrial economy in several other important ways. First, the early PRC's economic bureaucracy was dominated by cadres who had experimented with the planned economy in the Northeast during the Civil War, in particular, the leaders of the Northeastern Economic Planning Committee. In 1951, two of the four members of the PRC Finance and Economy Committee had gained experience in Manchuria. In November 1952, seven of the seventeen members of the PRC National Planning Commission had experience in the Northeast.[25] Second, the CCP cadres who had worked in the Northeast during the Civil War also took a leading role in early PRC–Soviet economic relations. Indeed, many of the Sino–Soviet joint projects in the early PRC were the continuation of projects that had begun in the Northeast before 1949.[26] When China and the Soviet Union formulated a protocol on the reconstruction of Angang in February 1952, the party representing the Chinese side was the Northeastern regional government in Shenyang rather than the national government in Beijing.[27] Finally, the Northeast also played an important role in the formation of the SOE management system in the country. Even before the drive to nationalize private enterprises that started in 1953, the Northeast's industrial economy was already dominated by the state sector. In 1949, of the entire industrial output in the region, the output produced by the public sector occupied 87.5 percent, while the private sector produced only 12.5 percent.[28] The management methods of the SOEs in Manchuria, which the CCP's regional authority had developed during the Civil War, thereafter spread to other parts of China seeking improvements in output.[29]

From devils to comrades

The achievement of the CCP's industrial reconstruction of the Northeast is all the more impressive given that there were few experts who had the knowledge necessary for managing modern industrial enterprises. The CCP overcame its lack of expertise by working with its former enemies—the Chinese who had been associated with the nationalist regime and the Japanese.

Regarding the Chinese Nationalist managers, the CCP Northeast Department resolved in late 1948 that "even if these managers have problems in thought and behavior, their skills and knowledge of management are needed for economic construction and people's enterprises, now and in the future. Many of us CCP members still need to seriously learn such knowledge and skills from them."[30] Thus, when the Communist cadres took over offices and factories, they kept the original staff, including the managers, in their posts. As the Communist leaders later described, most notable in their 1948 conquest of Shenyang was the fact that "high-level staff of so many factories, companies, organizations and schools ... all registered and went to work. For now the personnel has not seen any changes."[31] A Japanese mining engineer working in the Communist-ruled part of the Northeast witnessed how Communist cadres took over the management power from the original managers in the workplace without any halt in the work:

> The [Communist] cadres who were ordered to enter the workplace were either from the intelligentsia or the military. They were studious and serious, but they probably saw the mines and factories for the first time in their lives. ... Only after they realized the production mechanisms, they instigated the workers to clear the old boss out.[32]

The CCP's use of the human resources of the Nationalist regime followed a nationwide pattern in the early Communist years, as noted in many recent historical studies, including Chang Chihyun's examination of post-imperial uses of Customs Services in chapter eight.[33]

What distinguished the CCP takeover of Northeast China from that of other regions of China was that the CCP sought to cooperate with the relatively large number of imperial Japanese experts who had remained in the region. The Nationalist authorities had already allowed a considerable number of the Japanese to repatriate before the CCP takeover, which made the remaining Japanese engineers all the more important to the CCP.[34] In June 1948, a CCP official in the Northeast suggested that one way of overcoming the problem of the lack of engineers was to avail themselves of Japanese human resources. As he put it, "many of the first-rate technicians in the puppet-Manchukuo period were Japanese. Although a vast majority of them have already been repatriated, still many of them remain. [We should] take measures to gather the technical talent who were dispersed to different places during the two years of the [civil] war, and make use of them."[35] Accordingly, the CCP authority in Manchuria created a Committee for the Management of Japanese in October 1948.[36] In April 1950, it was renamed the Committee for the Management of Japanese in the Northeast.[37] A report by the committee argued that "[Japanese] technicians have been working in the Northeast for the last two to three decades, and today the economic recovery of the Northeast region really requires the help of Japanese technicians."[38]

The committee estimated the number of Japanese in Northeast China at 20,797 in June 1950.[39] According to its categorization, 12 percent of the Japanese in the region were "technicians" (*jishuzhe*), 23 percent "skilled workers" (*jishu gongren*), 23 percent "ordinary workers" (*yiban gongren*), 4 percent "office workers" (*zhiyuan*), and the remaining 38 percent "family members" (*jiazu*).[40] This means that there were roughly 2,500 Japanese technicians and 4,800 skilled workers in Manchuria. This is no small number, given that the number of Soviet specialists working in China in the peak year of 1956 is estimated at only about 4,000.[41]

The occupations of the Japanese who worked for the CCP varied, covering almost all the jobs that needed special training. Some remained there voluntarily, while others were not given the choice to repatriate. A number of Japanese doctors and nurses worked with the CCP during and after the Civil War. Japanese engineers maintained the existing factories and mines, and designed new ones. Japanese scientists continued their research, and some taught at universities after the end of the Civil War. Chemist Marusawa Tsuneya, who had once been a professor at Osaka Imperial University, served as the director of Mantetsu's Central Research Center in the city of Dalian during the Manchukuo era. After Japan's surrender, he continued research in Dalian for the CCP until he was repatriated to Japan in 1955.[42] Even the first pilots of the CCP air force were trained by a former Kwantung Army pilot, Hayashi Yaichirō. At the request of Lin Biao, who was then the highest CCP military commander in Northeast China, Hayashi, together with other Japanese pilots, trained 160 young Chinese Communist soldiers on old fighter planes left by Japan's Kwantung Army.[43] There were also Japanese filmmakers and actresses who made propaganda films under the CCP in the Northeast. Among them were two famous film directors: Uchida Tomu and Kimura Sotoji.[44]

Sasakura Masao was one of those Japanese engineers who was forced to remain in China in the early People's Republic. His memoir vividly depicts the life of a Japanese engineer in the Communist Northeast. A geologist educated at Kyoto Imperial University, he entered Mantetsu in 1933 and engaged in research on the mineral resources of China. After Japan surrendered, he first worked under the Soviet occupation authorities in Dalian until he moved to join the newly founded Association for Economic Construction of China in the spring of 1946. Not long afterwards, the representative of the Association, a Chinese man fluent in Japanese, asked him to join a two-month inspection trip to the Communist-ruled zone of northern Manchuria with other Japanese engineers. Twenty Japanese engineers including Sasakura arrived in Harbin via North Korea. Unexpectedly, the CCP authorities in Harbin then forcibly detained these Japanese engineers. They protested, but to no avail, and the Chinese man who brought them there did not come to their aid. Forced to remain in the CCP-controlled part of Manchuria, Sasakura worked as a mining engineer first in Jixi and then in Jiapigou. After the whole Northeast fell under Communist rule, he was moved to Shenyang in March

1949, and there he became the deputy chief of the Office of Geological Research of the Department of Non-Ferrous Metals of the Northeast.[45]

Sasakura's most important resource was his knowledge and experience as a geologist, but part of his work in the northeastern mines involved the transfer of Japanese research output to the Chinese. His first work under the CCP was to help translate Japanese-language reports such as "Gold mines of the Northeast," "Coal of the Northeast," and "Iron mines of the Northeast" into Chinese. In Jixi, Sasakura and two other Japanese engineers made a catalogue of the vast number of Japanese-language books, reports, and maps that the CCP had brought from Changchun when they lost the city to the Nationalists. In Jiapigou, the mining maps that the Japanese researchers had left helped him do his own research in the mine.[46]

The use of the "leftovers" of Japan's colonial industry seemed to be a common practice in the early People's Republic. According to Wakasa Sueo, a railway engineer, while constructing new railway lines in Chongqing and other inland areas, the Chinese did not build new tracks but moved old tracks from the Northeast to these areas. In designing a new locomotive for China, he recycled a Mantetsu plan. Of the 1,500 pages in the original manual, he revised only fifty pages and kept the remaining pages intact.[47]

Educating and training Chinese youths was also an important task that the CCP deferred to the Japanese experts. In Jiapigou the CCP cadres asked Sasakura to train twenty-three Chinese youths in subjects related to geology. Even though most of them were not well educated in sciences, the students were serious about their study and respectful toward their teacher, calling him *laoshi* (teacher). In the morning Sasakura did his research in the mine with his students, and in the afternoon he gave lectures on geology for two to four hours. He wove discussion sections into his lectures to make them more compelling for students. After dinner Sasakura wrote lecture notes until midnight and often as late as two in the morning. The students' progress made Sasakura feel "the sense of satisfaction that one can rarely experience in life." Even after he returned to Japan, the days spent with students remained "a happy memory" for him. His lecture notes were later published as two textbooks. When the Department of Non-Ferrous Metals of the Northeast researched the mineral-rich district of Dongchuan in Yunnan Province in 1952, his students were sent on a research trip there. He recalled "It made me truly happy that the youths I had trained went on a research trip to China's biggest copper mine."[48]

An insulated community—Japanese among Chinese

How was it possible that just a few years after all the bloodshed and humiliation of the Second Sino-Japanese War Japanese and Chinese were cooperating? The CCP leaders attributed the success to the ideological transformation of the Japanese that it saw as having occurred at its instigation.[49] In a 1950 internal memo, cadres of the CCP regional authority in Northeast China discussed their success in instilling socialist ideas in the Japanese: "It is a tremendously difficult task to transform the thoughts of the Japanese and to enable them to become democratic and to embrace revolution. However ... our work experience has proved that transforming their thoughts is not only possible, but also in reality very fruitful."[50] The CCP was a regime that at its core believed it could remake people's minds through ideological education. In the 1950s, it even believed that it could transform Japanese war criminals through education.[51] How much easier it would be to re-educate engineers! However, the picture becomes more complex at the level of individual factories and towns.

The CCP chose to control the Japanese in Northeast China indirectly, through a group of Japanese cadres, rather using the Chinese bureaucracy. Some of these Japanese cadres were former Japanese soldiers who had been captured and re-educated in Yan'an by the CCP during the Sino-Japanese War. Others were Japanese Communist Party members who had been in Manchuria before 1945. Still others were people who had been recruited and trained by the CCP immediately after 1945.[52]

The Japanese who were thus employed found themselves being treated fairly well in daily life. For example, there was a distinction between the canteens that CCP cadres could frequent and those open to non-cadre ordinary citizens; but Sasakura Masao and his fellow Japanese engineers were allowed to eat in the better one for cadres.[53] Many Japanese experts testified too that they were seldom harassed by the locals. A Japanese art director, Sei Mitsuo, who worked for a filmmaking company in the Communist Northeast, remembered that when he expressed an apologetic feeling toward the Chinese people, his Chinese colleagues chided him for his "narrow-minded ethnic notions." As he reported, one of these Chinese colleagues told him:

> We make a clear distinction between you and our companions and the imperialists of the period when Japan was invading China. I used to live in the countryside in Shandong Province. I saw my parents and brothers slaughtered by Japanese soldiers. I still have an unforgettable hatred toward those devils. But you are now working hard as filmmakers for the people of China. We do not see you as any different from us, nor do we have ethnic prejudice toward you. Rather, we are grateful to you. Why do you have such ridiculous restraint?[54]

At least some of the Japanese began to feel sympathy with the Communist revolutionaries under whom they were working. In Jiaxi, Sasakura Masao was forced to join a political study group with some thirty other Japanese people twice a week. The study group was led by a young Japanese communist who had been in Yan'an during the war. Sasakura and other Japanese engineers often challenged the party line taught by the group leader and engaged in free discussion. Still, he noted at the time, "if you join in and discuss the same topics repeatedly, the arguments begin to strongly affect you. ... Your brain gradually gets used to the slogans that come up in the study group, and you find yourself gradually adapting to the views and ideas of the Communist Party." Sasakura considered the Communist cadres who worked with him to be kind and respectable people: "I was affected despite myself by the cadres like Dong, Lin, Sun and Yuan. I responded to their unselfish character and enthusiasm. I came to have a pure desire to do something useful for these people."[55]

Such appreciation for the principles and devotion of the moral and work ethic of CCP cadres was fairly common among Japanese people in Northeast China. In some cases, they openly showed their gratitude. In a round table discussion for the general-affairs magazine *Chūō kōron* held after his return from China, the Japanese film director Kimura Sotoji eagerly seized his chance to express his thanks to the Communist Party: "I am wholeheartedly grateful to the cadres of the Chinese Communist Party for not treating us Japanese differently, and for letting us participate in the project of building New China together with the Chinese people."[56] Kimura wrote an essay for the same magazine, to rebuff the "wrong" impression conveyed by the Japanese media regarding Communist China and to explain how Chinese people had become happier, richer, cleaner, and freer under CCP rule.[57] Given that they expressed these feelings after repatriation to Japan, not under the watchful eyes of the CCP, it seems that we can take their respect for the CCP as genuine.

Some Japanese specialists later moved on from the Northeast to other parts of China, to serve the need for industrial construction in those regions. In October 1950, the PRC authorities ordered railway engineers in the Northeast, who had been repairing railways and training Chinese technicians, to move to the city of Tianshui in Gansu Province, for the construction of railways there. Eight hundred Japanese, including their family members, doctors, nurses, and teachers, moved from the Northeast to Tianshui. The engineers were ordered to help with the extension of a railway line from Tianshui to Lanzhou at the beginning of 1951. "Thanks to the undefeatable spirit of the Chinese people," one of their memoirs reports, "and the hard work of the Japanese engineers and others," the Tianshui–Lanzhou line was finished on August 23, 1952. Its completion was celebrated by Chairman Mao. When the Japanese in Tianshui were allowed to return home in March 1953, the railway authorities there paid them a retirement allowance. The Japanese left the city on a train, to the locals' adulation: "Despite the bad weather in which yellow dust was flying, the platform was filled with frenzied cheers from a great number of officials, citizens, musicians and dancers."[58]

The tolerant attitudes of Chinese people witnessed by the Japanese specialists, however, should be treated with some reservation. CCP cadres seem to have spent much energy in convincing, or "educating," Chinese workers that the Japanese experts working in China were different from the Japanese imperialists. Sasakura Masao recalls:

> When I sat in on speeches by Chinese people, I often heard the words "Japanese invaders" and "Japanese devils." At first I felt somehow uncomfortable when I heard these words. Some Chinese people nearby glanced at us, looking at our faces when these words were uttered. Their expression was not that of hatred. Rather, it seemed that they were trying to see how we would react: they felt pity for us. The cadres then educated them, telling them that the Japanese comrades

here were different, that the engineers cooperating with them were comrades. After that, nobody glanced at us. We got used to it, and no longer had any reaction to the words.[59]

Takashima Kojirō, a sound engineer, recalls the day when he joined the filming of a public meeting celebrating the liberation of Changchun, which had served as Manchukuo capital under the Japanese name of Shinkyō:

40,000–50,000 people had gathered at that place. Before going there, the Chinese comrades worried about us so much. They told us that they had made every effort to assure our security and that we should go there with no anxiety. We did have some stones thrown at us, but they did their very best to defend us.[60]

For the vast majority of the crowd, it was probably impossible to distinguish one nationality from another; nevertheless there was clear residual hostility toward the Japanese. Quite understandably, anti-Japanese feeling among ordinary Chinese people was very strong at that time. CCP cadres expended energy in arranging workplaces for Japanese specialists where they would not feel threatened.

Indeed, one of the ways in which they attempted to reduce the risk of tension between the two peoples seems to have been by ethnic segregation: the Japanese resided in different areas to the Chinese. In Anshan, the Japanese resided in one neighborhood, and their social lives were lived mostly within the Japanese community—with limited contact with local Chinese in everyday life. Moreover, most of the Japanese engineers could speak no Chinese and relied upon interpreters (usually, Chinese people who had learnt Japanese) for their interaction at work.[61] In Communist Anshan, the Japanese engineers and their families lived as a community insulated from the local Chinese population.

Even if they succeeded in motivating Japanese and Nationalist experts to work for them, the need to rely on these people made the CCP leaders uncomfortable. Whether intentionally or not, the insularity of the Japanese community must have made it easier for the CCP to keep them invisible. A CCP internal report on northeastern industry noted that the Japanese engineers were "neither serious nor loyal" and that they were hired only because there was no alternative.[62] Contemporary CCP media reports on the reconstruction of northeastern industrial enterprises made no mention of these Japanese and Nationalists, but they did stress the contribution of Soviet experts, even though the number of Soviet experts was dwarfed by their Japanese and Nationalist counterparts at that time. In February 1949, CCP leaders were telling Soviet officials that they were reluctant to use the Japanese engineers in Anshan and that they would much prefer Soviet experts if only they were available.[63] Shortly after the establishment of the PRC, Chen Yun told the Soviet ambassador in Beijing:

A serious obstacle on the matter of restoration of national economy is the lack of skilled technical cadres who are devoted to the People's Government. From the Guomindang [the Nationalists] the new government inherited a total of

20,000 engineers and specialists, the majority of whom are reactionary and pro-American in their political beliefs. … A typical example showing the lack of technical cadres in China is the fact that at the largest steel industrial complex in Anshan (Manchuria) sixty-two out of seventy engineers are Japanese, and they have hostile attitudes toward the Chinese in general and toward the Chinese Communists particularly.[64]

Industrial enterprises in the Northeast had thus become a bizarre space where Japanese engineers and former Nationalist engineers worked together for the shared goal of industrial reconstruction under CCP cadres who never ceased to be suspicious of them.

Most of these Japanese were allowed to return home only after 1953, when the Soviet Union began sending specialists, although a few stayed on even after that. Highly skilled people like Sasakura or Marusawa found their places in business or academia in Japan. Uchida Tomu and Kimura Sotoji made their names as film directors, the latter eventually joining the Japanese Communist Party. Hayashi Yaichirō served as president of the Society for Japan–China Friendship. Others found it difficult to resettle in Japanese society, however.

Conclusion

The legacy of Japanese industrial construction in occupied Northeast China was considerable in the early PRC. Many of the major SOEs in the region had their origins in the Japanese colonial developmental state. The Japanese became responsible for an enormous amount of economic construction in the region, even though their original purpose had been to support Japan's war efforts in other regions of China. The legacies were human as well as institutional: some Japanese citizens continued to work in the same workplaces during the Manchukuo period, through the Soviet occupation, the Chinese Civil War, and into the early PRC. Their expertise was indispensable to the new People's Republic, even though their presence was hardly known outside their workplace.

Today, there is a new consensus among historians that the early People's Republic of China had much continuity with the period before 1949.[65] In terms of the economy, scholars stress that Nationalist China, especially its National Resources Commission, strengthened state control of the economy and developed heavy industry in preparation for and during the war with Japan, thus laying the foundation for the planned economy of the Maoist period.[66] This argument makes sense, but it is also perhaps incomplete. Nationalist-controlled regions centered on Chongqing were simply much smaller than those in the Northeast in terms of industrial capacity. In order to fully comprehend the pre-1949 origins of China's socialist economy, it is critical to bring into perspective the Japanese occupiers' involvement in the wartime economy of the Northeast and other occupied regions and the two successive Chinese governments' efforts to reintegrate these regions into China's national economy after Japan's surrender.[67]

The continuities and similarities between the Mao government and its predecessors also point to the necessity of re-examining these regimes within a transnational context and over a longer time frame. Despite major differences in political ideology between the CCP, the Japanese Empire, and Nationalist China, the three regimes shared certain visions about economic development, including the need for state-coordinated economic planning, the centrality of heavy industry, and the preference for SOEs. Beginning in the 1920s, political leaders, civil servants, business leaders, scientists, and intellectuals in both China and Japan enthusiastically studied political-economic models abroad, such as Stalin's Socialism, Hitler's National Socialism, Mussolini's Corporatism, and Roosevelt's New Deal, all of which stressed the state's positive role in regulating the economy and society. These Soviet and Western models were more or less the products of their common experience of the First World War and the Great Depression. All of which seems only to confirm the validity of attention to the considerable degree of similarity between the CCP, the Japanese Empire, and the Nationalists. They were all part of a wider global trend toward state-led industrial modernity.

Notes

1 Northeast China (which is also simply called "the Northeast" in English, literally translated from the Chinese designation, *dongbei*) today consists of the three provinces of Liaoning, Jilin, and Heilongjiang. This region was historically called "Manchuria," and was regarded as the homeland of the Manchu, the ruling group of China's last dynasty, the Qing, who were ethnically different from the Han, China's ethnic majority. The Japanese occupied the region between 1931 and 1945, and ruled it through a puppet state of Manchukuo (1932–1945). Because of this historical context, the name Manchuria (*Manzhou* in Chinese) is barely used as the designation of the region in China today. See Mark Elliot, "The Limits of Tartary: Manchuria in Imperial and National Geographies," *Journal of Asian Studies* 59, no. 3 (2000), pp. 603–646. In this chapter, I refer to the region as "Northeast China" or "the Northeast."

2 I trace Anshan's local history in depth in my dissertation that is inprogress, "Steel Metropolis: Industrial Manchuria and the Making of Chinese Socialism, 1909–1964."

3 For example, see Louise Young, *Japan's Total Empire: Manchuria and the Culture of Wartime Imperialism* (Berkeley: University of California Press, 1998). There exist a small number of studies of Manchukuo by China scholars. For example, see Rana Mitter, *The Manchurian Myth: Nationalism, Resistance, and Collaboration in Modern China* (Berkeley: University of California Press, 2000); Prasenjit Duara, *Sovereignty and Authenticity: Manchukuo and the East Asian Modern* (Lanham, MD: Rowman & Littlefield, 2003).

4 For example, see Lori Watt, *When Empire Comes Home: Repatriation and Reintegration in Postwar Japan* (Cambridge, MA: Harvard University Press, 2009); Andrew Barshay, *The Gods Left First: The Captivity and Repatriation of Japanese POWs in Northeast Asia, 1945–1956* (Berkeley: University of California Press, 2013).

5 Matsumoto Toshirō, "*Manshūkoku*" *kara shin Chūgoku e: Anzan tekkōgyō kara mita Chūgoku tōhoku no saihen katei, 1940–1954* (Nagoya: Nagoya daigaku shuppankai, 2000); Mine Takeshi, *Chūgoku ni keishō sareta Manshūkoku no sangyō: Kagaku kogyō*

wo chūshin ni mita keishō no jittai (Ochanomizu shobō, 2009); Iizuka Yasushi, "Senji Manshū to sengo Tōhoku no keizaishi," in *Chūgoku Keizaishi Nyūmon*, ed. Kubo Toru (Tokyō daigaku shuppankai, 2012), pp. 149–162; Amy King, *China–Japan Relations after World War Two: Empire, Industry and War, 1949–1971* (Cambridge: Cambridge University Press, 2016), pp. 58–65.

6 William C. Kirby, "Continuity and Change in Modern China: Economic Planning on the Mainland and on Taiwan, 1943–1958," *Australian Journal of Chinese Affairs* 24 (1990), pp. 121–141; Joseph W. Esherick, "War and Revolution: Chinese Society during the 1940s," *Twentieth-Century China* 27, no. 1 (November 2001), pp. 1–37; Morris L. Bian, *The Making of the State Enterprise System in Modern China: The Dynamics of Institutional Change* (Cambridge, MA: Harvard University Press, 2005).

7 Dongbei wuzi tiaojie weiyuanhui, *Dongbei Jingji Xiaocongshu*, 20 vols. (Beiping and Shenyang, 1947–1948), vol. 9, p. 32.

8 "North of the Great Wall," *Time*, 59, no. 20 (May 19, 1952), pp. 42–43. Ruhr was the major industrial area of Germany.

9 Steven I. Levine, *Anvil of Victory: The Communist Revolution in Manchuria, 1945–1948* (New York: Columbia University Press, 1987).

10 Mao Zedong, "Mao Zedong tongzhi haozhao fazhan gongye dadao Rikou," May 22, 1944, Takeuchi Minoru, ed., *Mō Takutō shū*, 2nd edn., 10 vols. (Sōsō sha, 1983) vol. 9, p. 98.

11 Mao Zedong, "Guanyu diqijie houbu zhongyang weiyuan xuanju wenti," June 10, 1945, in *Mao Zedong wenji*, 8 vols., ed. Zhonggong zhongyang Wenxian Yanjiushi (Beijing: Renmin chubanshe, 1993–1999) vol. 3, p. 426.

12 Past scholarship has stressed Manchuria's strategic position and agricultural output during the Chinese Civil War. See Levine, *Anvil of Victory*, pp. 175–196.

13 Report by the Department of Industry (March 1947), Dongbei jiefangqu caizheng jingji shi bianxiezu et al., *Dongbei jiefangqu caizheng jingji shi ziliao xuanbian* [Collection of Historical Materials on Financial Affairs and Economy in the Northeastern Liberated Zone], 4 vols. (Ha'erbin: Heilongjiang renmin chubanshe, 1988) [hereafter, *DJCZ*], vol. 2, pp. 11–22 (citation from p. 21).

14 Report by the CCP Northeast Administration Committee (April 20, 1949), *DJCZ*, vol. 2, pp. 139–152 (quote from p. 144).

15 Table by the Northeastern Finance and Economy Committee (April 1949), *DJCZ*, vol. 2, pp. 162–163.

16 V. Zorin to A. D. Panov (September 20, 1948), Archive of the Foreign Policy of the Russian Federation (Moscow, Russia), fond 0100/opis' 41/delo 277/s.48.

17 Gao Gang's telegram to Stalin (copy), October 16, 1948, Archive of the Foreign Policy of the Russian Federation (Moscow, Russia), fond 0100/opis' 41/delo 277/s. 48.

18 Memorandum by N. T. Fedorenko, the head of the first far-eastern department of the USSR Ministry of Foreign Affairs, for A. A. Gromyko, USSR foreign minister, December 22, 1948, No. 389, in *Russko-kitaiskie otnoshenii v XX veke: materialy i dokumenty*, ed. Andrei Ledovskii (Moscow: Pamiatniki istoricheskoi mysli, 2000–2010) [hereafter, *RKOVXX*], vol. 1, pp. 491–492.

19 Page 55 of No. 432, Note of conversation between A. I. Mikoyan and Ren Bishi and Zhude, February 2, 1949, *RKOVXX*, vol. 2, pp. 52–56.

20 Wang Qun, "Huiyi Angang 'qi jiu' kaigong," in *Anshan shuguang*, pp. 274–283 (esp. p. 278).

21 Tian'anmen Square, which was built in the 1950s in front of the gate, was named after the gate.

22 Li Fuchun, "diyici quanguo gongye huiyi jielun" (March 6, 1951), Zhonghua Renmin Gongheguo guojia jingji maoyi weiyuanhui, *Zhongguo gongye wushinian* (Beijing: Zhongguo jingji chubanshe, 2000), pt. 1, vol. 2, pp. 1167–1173 (quote from p. 1169).

23 Gongye jiaotong wuzi tongji si, *Zhongguo gongye jingji tongji ziliao* (Beijing: Zhongguo tongji chubanshe, 1985), pp. 166–168, 170, 172.

24 Kang Yan, "Gongye quwei peizhi wenti" (September 1950), *Zhongguo gongye wushinian*, pt. 1, vol. 1, pp. 1821–1824 (quote from pp. 1823 and 1824).

25 Kokubun Ryōsei, *Gendai Chūgoku no seiji to kanryōsei* (Keiō gijuku daigaku shuppankai, 2004), pp. 31–36, 69–75.

26 M. Saburov's report to Molotov, received on January 25, 1950, Russian State Archives of Social and Political History (Moscow, Russia), V. M. Molotov papers, fond 82/opis' 2/delo 1246/ss. 12–15.

27 Protocol on examination of preliminary allocation between the Soviet and Chinese sides of supply of equipment necessary for the restoration and reconstruction of Angang, February 26, 1952, Russian State Archives of Economy (Moscow, Russia), fond 8875/opis' 1/delo 3298.

28 Dongbei gongyebu, "Dongbei siying gongye ziben bizhong wenti" (1950), *DJCZ*, vol. 2, pp. 339–341.

29 Kawai Shin'ichi, *Chūgoku kigyō to Soren moderu: itchōsei no shiteki kenkyū* (Ajia seikei gakkai, 1991).

30 Resolution by the Northeastern Bureau (August 1, 1948), *DJCZ*, vol. 2, pp. 63–69 (quote from p. 67).

31 Chen Yun, Tao Zhu, and Wu Xiuquan, report on the takeover of Shenyang (November 11, 1948), Zhongyang Zhonggong Wenxian Yanjiushi, ed., *Chen Yun wenji* (Beijing: Zhongyang wenxian chubanshe, 2005), vol. 1, pp. 658–664 (citation from p. 660).

32 Sasakura Masao, *Jinminfuku nikki* (Banmachi shobō, 1973), pp. 183–184.

33 For example, the entire leadership of the Nationalist government's National Resources Commission remained on Mainland China, continuing working for the CCP. See Kirby, "Continuity and Change in Modern China."

34 Report by the Northeastern Department of Industry (February 22, 1949), *DJCZ*, vol. 2, pp. 118–132 (esp. pp. 130, 131).

35 Chao Zhuohua, report on industry in Southern Manchuria (June 18, 1948), *DJCZ*, vol. 2, pp. 56–62 (quote from p. 59).

36 Report by the Committee for the Management of Japanese, August 11, 1949, PRC Foreign Ministry Archives (Beijing), 105–00224-02 (1), p. 10, note taken by Amy King.

37 Report by the Committee for the Management of Japanese in the Northeast, June 15, 1950, PRC Foreign Ministry Archives, 118–00086-01 (1), note taken by Amy King.

38 The PRC Foreign Ministry Archives (Beijing), 105–00224-02, pp. 4, 14, note taken by Amy King.

39 The PRC Foreign Ministry Archives, 118–00118-02, Dongbei Ribenren qingkuang he chuli yijian [Views on the Situation and How to Deal with the Japanese in Northeast China], August 1–November 30, 1951, p. 1, note taken by Amy King. Meanwhile, a report by Japan's foreign ministry estimated that about 37,000 Japanese were living in Manchuria in November 1951. See Report by Japan Ministry of Foreign Affairs, November 5, 1951 (Japan, Diplomatic Record Office, K.7.1.2.2–3-1).

40 The PRC Foreign Ministry Archives, 105–00224-02, p. 20, note taken by Amy King.

41 Shen Zhihua, *Sulian zhuanjia zai Zhongguo* (Beijing: Xinhua chubanshe, 2009), p. 144.

42　Marusawa Tsuneya, *Shin Chūgoku kensetsu to Mantetsu Chūō shikenjo* (Nigatsusha, 1979).

43　NHK "Ryūyōsareta Nihonjin" shuzaihan, *"Ryūyō" sareta Nihonjin: watashitachi wa Chūgoku kenkoku wo sasaeta* (Nihon hōsō shuppan kyōkai, 2003), pp. 142–216.

44　"Watashitachi wa shin Chūgoku de Eiga wo tsukuttekita: zadankai," *Chūō kōron* 69, no. 2 (February 1954), pp. 138–148.

45　My description of Sasakura's career in China is based on his memoir: Sasakura, *Jinminfuku nikki*. One important question is how the CCP treated these Japanese who refused to work for it, but I have not yet found sources related to such cases.

46　Sasakura, *Jinminfuku nikki*, pp. 28, 29, 40–43, 127.

47　"Gijutsusha no mita shin Chūgoku: zadankai," *Ekonomisuto* 31, no. 28 (July 1953), pp. 52–61 (especially 57–58).

48　Sasakura, *Jinminfuku nikki*, pp. 160–165, 174, 287 (quotes from pp. 161, 164, 165, 287).

49　It seems that, at this point, Japanese war crimes during the Sino-Japanese War were not among the major themes of the CCP ideological education toward the Japanese remaining in China.

50　A report by the Committee for the Management of Japanese in the Northeast (copy), October 15, 1950, PRC Foreign Ministry Archives, 118–00118-02 (1), pp. 8–16 (quotes from pp. 8, 9, and 16), note taken by Amy King.

51　Barak Kushner, *Men to Devils, Devils to Men: Japanese War Crimes and Chinese Justice* (Cambridge, MA: Harvard University Press, 2015), pp. 248–299.

52　A report by the Committee for the Management of Japanese in the Northeast, June 1950, PRC Foreign Ministry Archives, 118–00086-02 (1), pp. 16–17, note taken by Amy King. The number of these Japanese cadres is unclear.

53　Sasakura, *Jinminfuku nikki*, p. 118.

54　"Watashitachi wa shin Chūgoku de eiga wo tsukuttekita," p. 140.

55　Sasakura, *Jinminfuku nikki*, pp. 59–60, 136 (quotes from pp. 60 and 136).

56　"Watashitachi wa shin Chūgoku de eiga wo tsukuttekita," p. 148.

57　Kimura Sotoji, "Chūgoku dewa tanoshikatta," *Chūō kōron* 68, no. 5 (1953), pp. 183–192.

58　Tensuikai, "Sengo Chūgoku hondo (Kanshuku shō Tensui) ryūyō ki"; Mantetsukai, *Mantetsu shain shūsen kiroku* (Mantetsukai, 1996), pp. 668–674 (quote from p. 673).

59　Sasakura, *Jinminfuku nikki*, p. 105.

60　"Watashitachi wa shin Chūgoku de eiga wo tsukuttekita," p. 139.

61　Interview with SN and FS, February 29, 2016. They both lived in CCP-controlled Anshan through the early 1950s as their fathers were Japanese engineers employed by Angang.

62　Chen Yun, "Dongbei zhonggongye jianshe de wenti" (January 10, 1949), *Chen Yun wenji*, 667.

63　Record of conversation between A. Y. Mikoyan, Ren Bishi, and Zhu De, February 2, 1949, *RKOVXX*, vol. 2, pp. 52–56.

64　Note of conversation between N. V. Roshin, USSR ambassador to the PRC, and Chen Yun, vice prime minister and chairman of the financial and economic committee, No. 524, October 28, 1949, *RKOVXX*, vol. 2, pp. 204–206.

65　Esherick, "War and Revolution."

66　Kirby, "Continuity and Change in Modern China"; Bian, *The Making of the State Enterprise System in Modern China*.

67　Kubo Tōru, "Sōron: 1949nen kakumei no rekishiteki ichi," in Kubo, *1949nen zengo no Chūgoku* (Kyūko shoin, 2006), pp. 3–27, mentions the Northeast as well.

Chapter 8

EMPIRES AND CONTINUITY: THE CHINESE MARITIME CUSTOMS SERVICE IN EAST ASIA, 1950–1955

Chihyun Chang

The modern history of East Asia is intertwined with the Manchu (Qing), British and Japanese empires' rise and decline. The First Sino-Japanese War of 1894 to 1895 resulted in the Manchu Empire's decline, the outbreak of the Pacific War led to the Japanese Empire's replacing the British Empire as the dominant force in East Asia, and the end of the Second World War marked the ultimate collapse of the Japanese Empire. It seems that in 1945 the three empires had already given up their control of East Asia but there was an agency which carried on the three empires' characteristics, and which continuously maintained an influence in China, Taiwan, and Japan after 1945. This agency was the Chinese Maritime Customs Service (CMCS). The three empires' fight for control over the CMCS was over the all important customs revenues fundamental for a functioning government. During the Second World War, all East Asian countries' customs revenues from international trade were seriously hampered by the Pacific War, so the financial contributions to states from the CMCS became less important. However, after the Second World War, customs revenues grew even more important than during the pre-Second World War period because they became a crucial financial pillar for war debt securities. They also helped rehabilitation funds, protected domestic industries, and acted as a generator of external aid. As the East Asian states suffered from post-Second World War civil wars and the Cold War, the Taiwanese Maritime Customs Service (TMCS), Peoples' Maritime Customs Service (PMCS), and Japanese Maritime Customs Service (JMCS) also became priority institutions for postwar rehabilitation. This chapter aims to explore the three empires' influence on the CMCS and the CMCS's impact on the economic well-being of postwar East Asia.[1]

The CMCS and the Manchu Empire, British Empire, and Japanese Empire

Historians tend to consider the CMCS as a synarchic agency, that is, a "joint administration by a mixed Chinese and non-Chinese bureaucracy" (the non-Chinese bureaucratic actors being Britain and Japan).[2] They credit the success of this joint administration to Robert Hart's (second head of the CMCS, 1883–1911) "bicultural achievement."[3] This term, coined by the Harvard historian John Fairbank, means that Robert Hart successfully created a Sino-foreign cultural hybrid system in the CMCS. However, in the eyes of Fairbank, the role of China should be analyzed further, because in his understanding the Chinese side should be separated into the Han and Manchu ethnic groups.[4] The characteristics of the Manchu Empire can be observed in the following two points: (1) institutional linkage: most of the customs revenues were controlled by the Imperial Household Department in charge of the internal affairs of the Manchu imperial family and the activities of the Forbidden Palace; and (2) personal linkage: the superintendents of the CMCS were all Manchu royals, such as Prince Gong, Wenxiang, etc. Due to the two linkages, British employees in the CMCS were considered loyal servants to the Manchu Empire.

Customs revenues continuously supported the rise of the Manchu Empire as the tax income increased sixty times from 1854 to 1894, and even saved the Manchu Empire from bankruptcy after 1894, following the two defeats in the First Sino-Japanese War and the Boxer Uprising in 1895 and 1901, respectively. The 1911 Revolution overthrew the Manchu Empire but this made the CMCS more independent. During the Revolution, as the Manchu and foreign governments feared the revolutionaries would seize the customs revenues from the Chinese authorities, they decided to delegate more power to the CMCS. Thus, the CMCS could levy the tariff tax and pay foreign debtors without the permission of the Chinese authorities. This independent status made both the British and Japanese empires more interested in the CMCS because control of the CMCS meant they managed not only international trade in China but also China's foreign debts as well as "China Bonds" in the global financial market.

The financial significance of the CMCS attracted the Japanese Empire's interest in the twentieth century. The Japanese Empire began to increase its influence after the First Sino-Japanese War in 1895, and the Russo-Japanese War in 1905 made Japan the biggest trading partner with Manchuria. Thus, the CMCS increased the number of Japanese staff members in all of the customs houses in Manchuria. The outbreak of the First World War forced the British Empire to focus on its affairs in Europe, allowing the Japanese Empire an opportune moment to extend its influence in the CMCS. Several capable Japanese assistants, members of the administrative staff, who were recruited by the Manchurian Custom Houses after the Russo-Japanese War, availed themselves of the chance to become leading figures in the CMCS. The most notable was Kishimoto Hirokichi, who joined the CMCS in 1905, was appointed Chief Secretary (second-in-command) of the CMCS in 1925, and became Inspector General (IG) in 1941.

Before the outbreak of the Second Sino-Japanese War in 1937, both the British and Japanese empires saw control of the CMCS as a symbol of their dominant status in China; whoever controlled the CMCS was seen as the strongest foreign power in China. Although the British Empire successfully kept one of its nationals at the head of the CMCS, the Japanese Empire was successful in taking over the Custom Houses in Taiwan and Manchuria from the CMCS. After the outbreak of the Second Sino-Japanese War in 1937, the CMCS, although still run by a Brit, was forced to recruit many more Japanese employees—269 in 1938 and an additional 200 in 1939.[5]

The struggle over control of the CMCS finally came to an end with the outbreak of the Pacific War in 1941. With the help of the collaborationist government in Nanjing, the Japanese Empire finally took over the CMCS completely in 1941, but Custom Houses under the Chongqing Nationalist government were still not under Japanese control. The Japanese chose former Chief Secretary Kishimoto Hirokichi to lead the Customs Service in Occupied China. During his tenure from 1941 to 1945, Kishimoto skilfully balanced pressure from imperial Japan and the opposition of his Chinese and European staff, who preferred an administration according to the Manchu-British tradition. As a CMCS employee for over thirty-five years, Kishimoto understood the value of this Manchu-British tradition, although some Japanized policies still had to be seen through; for example, English was removed from the list of working languages, replaced by Japanese, and staff salaries were paid in Japanese yen. However, both Chinese and Western (non-Allied) high-ranking officers still thought the CMCS operations remained the same—retaining many of the original practices of the British-controlled period.[6]

There was, probably, another, more pragmatic, reason the revenues of the two customs services under the Nationalist government and the Japanese Empire were heavily damaged by the war, but the two services preserved their financial importance under the new taxation imposition (Wartime Consumption Tax in Free China and Transit Tax in Occupied China). To ensure the efficiency of tax imposition, both the Japanese Empire and the Chinese Nationalist government decided to keep the CMCS tradition in their own customs services because the CMCS had successfully demonstrated its efficiency and incorruptibility in tax imposition since the very first day of its inception in the nineteenth century.

After the Second World War, the Nationalist government took over the three different groups' custom houses under the Japanese Empire, namely the Taiwanese, the Manchurian, and Chinese collaborationist offices. These custom houses inherited Japanized practices to different extents, in some ways following similar paths to what Hirata Koji describes in Chapter 7. In addition, after repatriation to Japan, over 4,000 former Japanese CMCS staff members served as very capable personnel for the JMCS's postwar rehabilitation. In China, some former clerks who had worked for the Customs Service in Manchukuo and Taiwan were re-hired in order to help the Nationalist government in postwar rehabilitation. The staff left by the Japanese Empire could still demonstrate their professionalism after the war.

The CMCS was officially terminated in 1949 and Communist cadres were put in charge. Under the cadres' surveillance, none of the empire's characteristics in the CMCS could continue unchanged on the Chinese mainland and the CMCS was communized and renamed the PMCS (People's Maritime Customs Service). However, peculiarly enough, the three empires' practices and legacies in the CMCS went beyond customs jurisdiction after the official closure and exerted even more influence than before. The rebuilding of the CMCS legacies in Taiwan, the elimination of the CMCS remnants in China and the extension of the CMCS experience to Japan illustrates the *realpolitik* in postwar East Asia. Nationalist Taiwan endeavored to retain its Chinese heritage by installing the Nationalist governmental framework in Taiwan, including its formerly British-controlled CMCS, Communist China deliberately cut off all its connections with pre-1949 China, and postwar Japan was forced to adopt Western models to survive through its Occupation period.

The Taiwanese maritime customs service

In its ninety-six-year history, the CMCS's relations with Taiwan were limited; it administered the two Taiwanese custom houses, Tamsui and Takow (known as Takao in Japanese, Gaoxiong in standard Chinese pinyin, or Kaohsiung in current Taiwanese pinyin), for only thirty-six years (under the Manchu Empire from 1864 to 1895 and under the Nationalist government from 1945 to 1949). The legacies of the British Empire in the two Custom Houses in Taiwan had already been expunged during its fifty-year colonization by Japan, when the Colonial Maritime Customs Service of Taiwan had been a branch of the Imperial Maritime Customs Service of Japan.

In 1946, Zhang Shenfu was appointed Acting Commissioner of the Takow Custom House and tasked with the rehabilitation of all custom houses in Taiwan.[7] Zhang immediately discovered that the practices of the Colonial Maritime Customs Service of Taiwan and the CMCS were completely different. The CMCS separated the responsibilities of the Customs Service and those of the Harbor Bureau, but the Colonial Customs Service of Taiwan "had already combined the Inspectorate and the Harbor Bureau in the end of the War," and "this made the process of rehabilitation more complicated."[8] As the CMCS was also preoccupied with other custom houses' rehabilitation, Zhang could only bring nine staff members from the Chinese mainland to Taiwan and none of them was familiar with the practice of the Colonial Customs Service. Thus, Zhang temporarily recruited twenty-eight Japanese and ten Taiwanese former clerks, and twenty miscellaneous workers.[9]

The reason Zhang did not need to ask for the Nationalist government's permission and could recruit these Taiwanese easily while the other custom houses could not, was that these Taiwanese and Japanese employees did not need to be investigated by the Staff Investigation Committee, which was established to investigate Chinese staff who might have committed treason during the Second World War. As long as these Taiwanese and the Japanese were not war criminals, their employment could be handled with more flexibility.

Japanese and Taiwanese recruits not only made the rehabilitation of Taiwanese Customs more efficient but also helped mainland staff overlook the February 28 Incident of 1947, a large-scale rebellion that arose as a result of tensions between the Taiwanese and the mainlanders. Three days after the incident, Zhang instructed every mainland Chinese staff member to arm himself and to evacuate to the Takow Custom House, and to report to the Shanghai Inspectorate for evacuation from Taiwan. However, the Incident unfolded so rapidly that some staff members in southern Taiwan could not be evacuated. They were stationed at the Budai station in Jiayi County, where the battles and collateral casualties were the most serious.[10] The mainland Chinese employees were attacked by some local Taiwanese but their Taiwanese colleagues harbored and protected them from harm.[11] In return, the mainland Chinese employees then helped their Taiwanese colleagues escape investigations after the Nationalist troops arrived.

In 1949, Lester Knox Little, the last Inspector General, brought eleven Chinese staff members from Kowloon to Taipei after the Nationalist government completely collapsed on the mainland. Little was committed to rebuilding the CMCS in Taiwan but this also meant that the practices of the British and Japanese Empires would continue in the TMCS. After his retirement, Little accepted the offer made by the Financial Commissioner of Taiwan Province Yan Jiagan's to serve as an advisor in the financial ministry until 1954; they became lifelong friends. Yan Jiagan once told Little, "You're American but you are a Chinese official. I can't talk to the American Ambassador this way; I can't talk to Chiang this way."[12]

Yan Jiagan's political career was not particularly successful before 1949 but his career skyrocketed after his move to Taiwan. He went on to serve in various capacities, including as governor of Taiwan, finance minister, premier, vice-president and, eventually, president. Yan understood the uniqueness and value of the CMCS and also agreed with Little that the CMCS's operations should remain intact in Taiwan. The TMCS continued all the practices carried out by the CMCS on the Chinese mainland before 1949. The TMCS became the only governmental unit which was independent from the Taiwanese civil service—rules defining ranks, titles, and pensions, among other things, were identical to those operated by the Manchu Empire in the nineteenth century. Most of the policies did make the TMCS as efficient and incorruptible as the CMCS but there was one policy which was a legacy of the British Empire that actually resulted in a deeper problem.

In the nineteenth century, British staff in the CMCS were superior to others in a wide range of aspects, for example, salary, rank, promotion, etc. The British Empire became the bedrock of the British staff's privileges. During the Nationalist era before 1949, most of the foreign staff's privileges were abolished, the only exception being the salaries of foreign staff members, which were much higher than those of their Chinese colleagues. This inequality was due to the Sterling Allotment in the foreign staff's salaries. The inauguration of the Sterling Allotment was a reaction to the significant decline in the Chinese currency's conversion rate to the sterling in 1931.[13] In order to ensure that foreign staff could maintain a decent retirement in the UK, half of the salary was issued in the Chinese currency and the other half in sterling.

This would not have been a particularly negative policy had the Second World War and the Chinese Civil War not broken out. These wars rendered the Chinese currency completely worthless, making the Sterling Allotment essential to ensuring the salaries of foreign staff, especially as the rate used for conversion was the official rate rather than the black market rate. Shanghai Commissioner Foster Hall recalled his daily life from 1948 to 1949:

> I was Commissioner of Customs in Shanghai and my pay, in Chinese currency, was 13 million dollars a month, the same as my Chinese colleagues. At that time a pedicab coolie on the streets could easily earn 8 or 9 million dollars! Luckily we foreigners were given a sum in sterling which went in to our banks at home.[14]

Foster Hall's Chinese colleagues, of course, resented these privileges. However, the issue of the foreign staff's privileged income became an even more serious problem to the Chinese staff after the Chinese realized that their pensions were used to pay the foreign staff's full pensions in foreign currencies.

Before he retreated to Taiwan in 1949, Little liquidated all CMCS accounts and paid off all foreign employees' pensions in US dollars and in UK sterling. Among all 20,000 Chinese employees, only eleven, who had followed Little to Taiwan in 1949, received their pensions. Even Little admitted that he knew he would get "hell from the government" if the officials knew about this "double coup."[15] Luo Manchuxiang and Fang Du, who became Little's successor, of course, received their pensions and enjoyed the IG's monthly allowance of US$500.[16]

This pension arrangement was finally revealed by the Chinese staff who arrived in Taiwan after 1949. As the TMCS was seriously understaffed and the Taipei Inspectorate could not rely on Commissioner Zhang Shenfu's staff, the Taipei Inspectorate decided to call back the Chinese staff from the mainland. However, the 1949 collapse in China forced the Nationalist government to recruit Chinese staff from the mainland much more cautiously, as some of them might have already been converted to the Communist camp. Thus, most of the Chinese staff who retreated from the mainland had to pass an investigation before they could be reinstated.[17]

Both Deputy Preventive Secretary Wang Wenju and Pakhoi Commissioner Ye Yuanzhang belonged to the 20,000 Chinese staff members abandoned by Little in 1949. Both men were instructed to stay in their posts and were not informed of the evacuation from Shanghai. They endeavored to withdraw from the People's Customs Service in 1950 and managed to flee to Taiwan. However, both of them had to wait five years for their reinstatement.[18]

Ye and Wang were reinstated in 1955 and, at the same time, Luo Manchuxiang retired, and Fang Du became the only officiating IG.[19] Fang Du was very likely to become the first Chinese Inspector General in CMCS history but the 1949 pension arrangement ruined it.

Yuan, Wang, and Ye discovered that their pensions were used to pay off the foreign staff and the eleven Chinese employees. The abandoned Chinese employees' grievances finally broke out in 1957, and the pay-off of 1949 caused a political storm in the Taipei Inspectorate. Fang Du, the successor to Little, told Little about the "unfortunate incident".

> The official impeachment [from the Control Yuan] came, principally against me and against the other ten members–including Mr. C. H. Lo [Luo Manchuxiang]–

who received the half pensions in 1949 … The impeachment tries to build up a case against us on the following "grounds":

1. The *recipients* did not have the requisite seniority to receive pensions as required by Customs pension rules. Hence a breach of Customs rules.
2. The *recipients* have *demanded* from the Inspector General for the issue of such pensions and made you approach Minister Kuan for the necessary authority to do so.
3. As pension moneys are not issuable to the Chinese staff in foreign currency according to Customs rule we broke the rules (and foreign exchange regulations) by *receiving* half of the *pro rata* pensions in US currency.
4. I was responsible for issuing the pension moneys in foreign currency *without authority*, and therefore acted *ultra vires*.[20]

Fang Du asked Little to write a letter to Minister of Finance Xu Boyuan and state that Fang Du and Luo Qingxiang had acted under instructions from Little:

I felt very strongly that something should be done to recognize the loyalty and steadfastness of this small band of Customs men who had left behind all their property and, at considerable risk, proved their faith in Free China and their devotion to the service of their Government. … The half pensions, which were issued in US dollars from "free funds" under my control, were handed personally by me to the recipients on their agreement to continue in the service of the Government. They also understood and agreed that the payments were in the nature of advances, and that the amount then issued would be deducted from the pensions they would receive when they finished their careers in the Customs. I wish to make it quite clear that the proposal to issue part pensions originated with me. If, therefore, there is any criticism, it should be directed against me and not against the men to whom I paid the pensions. [21]

Although Little tried to take all the blame, the Chinese staff were still unsatisfied because the problem was not about whether or not Fang Du had received the half pensions. The core reason for their resentment was that their pensions were used to pay off the foreign staff and eleven Chinese employees. This arrangement reflected the tradition of the CMCS, which prioritized its Western staff to the detriment of its Chinese staff. The impeachment was not against the eleven Chinese employees' pensions per se but rather protested against this imperial tradition and the Chinese employees who had become the "running dogs" of British imperialism.

After the impeachment, the first Chinese Inspector General, Fang Du, was forced to retire, leaving his post after an unprecedentedly short period of three weeks—his appointment had come into effect on June 24, 1960, but ended on July 15, 1960.[22, 23] Little wrote to Fang:

The news [of your retirement], while not unexpected, leaves me with mixed emotions, because you seem too young and too active to retire … Only last month I wrote to C. H. B. Joly [Officiating IG from 1941 to 1943 in Chong Manchu] and, *inter alia*, told him that I doubted that the foreign members of the Customs staff would ever have received their full pensions had it not been for Fang Tu [Fang Du]![24]

Ye Yuanzhang did not read this letter. However, he witnessed the whole scandal, so he commented in his memoir in 1977, "Mr. Fang was the victim of a continuous flow of accusations believed to have come indirectly from the sufferers of his self-containment policy [the pension and IG allowance Fang received]. This was evidently the reaction to the discriminatory and unfair treatment he had given to them."[25]

Since 1945, the TMCS benefited from the three empires' legacies—Zhang Shenfu hired the Japanese and Taiwanese employees back and, therefore, survived through the difficulties of postwar rehabilitation and the February 28 Incident; Luo and Fang preserved the nineteenth-century CMCS operations and, therefore, the TMCS's efficiency and incorruptibility remained intact. The Nationalist government regarded the value of these nineteenth-century operations so highly that it kept them unchanged until 1990. However, among all the virtues that the three empires may have contributed to the TMCS, a signal had to be sent—the impeachment against Fang Du—to mark the end of the foreign staff's superiority.

The People's Maritime Customs Service

Compared to the TMCS and the JMCS, the PMCS inherited most of the CMCS custom houses and staff, but the CCP's anti-imperialistic political beliefs gave rise to hostility against every aspect of the CMCS's imperial characteristics. Nevertheless, the CMCS staff's perceptions toward the CCP were completely different, as they hoped the new government could end the turmoil of the Civil War.

After Little left for Canton (Guangzhou) in 1949, the majority of the CMCS staff chose to stay in China and were led by Deputy Inspector General Ding Guitang. Most of the former CMCS employees thought that "it was not a bad idea to change the Nationalist Government" and "the CMCS's cosmopolitanism would still protect the CMCS under the Communist Government." They believed that "after they organized the returns and reports of trade, the Communist government would realize the CMCS's importance and the CMCS could remain independent."[26] It was reasonable for the Chinese staff to hold such views because the Japanese Empire had also valued the CMCS's incorruptibility and efficiency during the Second World War. Now the CCP would need the CMCS for postwar rehabilitation.

However, from the first day, the CCP did not intend to preserve even a trace of the CMCS. In August 1949, the Communist government established the Directorate General of Customs to replace the Shanghai Inspectorate. The new Directorate General convened "a roundtable discussion from 23 September to 16 October 1949" and assembled "thirty-six representatives from all Custom Houses throughout China."[27] Director-General Kong Yuan, who was a CCP intelligence worker, renamed the CMCS the PMCS. Kong indicated that the priority for the PMCS was to "protect the public and private sectors' legal foreign trade and to implement the policies of foreign trade in collaboration with other governmental units."[28]

In Kong's eyes, the Manchu Empire, British Empire, and Japanese Empire were foreign imperialist aggressors. Although the Manchu Empire was linked to the Chinese tradition, Kong was certainly not interested in preserving it because the CCP resented that tradition. The key strategy to destroy the PMCS's value was to take the "tax imposition" function away from the PMCS. The reason why the British and Japanese empires fought over control of the CMCS in the 1920s, and why the Nationalist government could tolerate the foreign staff's privileged salaries, was because the CMCS could levy enormous Customs revenues efficiently. The Kong statement clearly indicated that the most valuable part of the CMCS had now become history.

As the PMCS could not provide the CCP with the highest financial income, its staff also lost their protection, so nothing could protect the former CMCS staff who had worked for its British and/or Japanese bosses. During the Campaign to Suppress Counterrevolutionaries, some old retired staff members who had not managed to flee to Hong Kong or Taiwan were "suppressed," jailed, dismissed, or shot.

Although his colleagues suffered from political suppression, Ding appeared to secure a successful career after 1949. He was elected a National Congress Representative from Luda City in 1954.[29] He also joined the Revolutionary Committee of the Kuomintang in 1951, one of the eight permitted minority parties in the PRC, and was elected a member of the central committee in 1956.[30] However, Ding finally became a target. The CCP launched the Second Rectification Campaign in 1957, also known as the Hundred Flowers Campaign, to encourage criticism of the party and the government.[31] This Campaign was initially meant to re-examine the CCP's "three evils": formalism, sectarianism, and subjectivism. Due to this movement's open-minded attitude, Ding finally spoke out, criticizing the PMCS's formalism, sectarianism, and subjectivism, and urged the Communists to recognize the value of the former CMCS staff. Ding's open letter was then published in the *People's Daily,* and Ding listed some cases of what he saw as a lack of fairness toward the former CMCS staff after 1953.[32] Unfortunately for Ding, the CCP then suddenly changed its open-minded attitude. A leading article in the *People's Daily* fiercely labeled the people who criticized the CCP's formalism, sectarianism, and subjectivism as "bovine devils and snake demons." The original open-minded attitude was revealed to have been a strategy to let "poisonous weeds propagate." The CCP's mouthpiece, the *People's Daily*, claimed,

> People will be shocked to see these things still existed! Then we annihilated the scum ... People say this was a conspiracy. We say this is an open conspiracy because we warned our enemies in advance, then the demons and spirits came out of their cage and we destroyed them.[33]

Thereafter, the Hundred Flowers Campaign immediately became the Anti-Rightist Campaign and Ding became one of the "bovine devils, snake demons and poisonous weeds." The 1957–1958 Anti-Rightist Campaign designated over 300,000 intellectuals as "rightists," a label which would effectively ruin their careers in China. Ding was one of these rightists and, moreover, he was on "the first list of 376 persons regarded as 'Important Rightists' by the Communists."[34]

In an attempt to get himself expunged from the list, Ding recanted his position publicly, turning against the rightists in an open letter in the *People's Daily*, adding that, "China would collapse without the Chinese Communist Party." Ding claimed:

> The rightists seized the opportunity of the CCP's [second] Rectification Campaign to disseminate their anti-party, counterrevolutionary and anti-socialism fallacies. We love the party, protect the state, follow the CCP's course of socialism, and we have to strike them hard ....
>
> People should be ruthless to these rightists. "Freedom of speech" does not apply to them. We have to completely disclose their conspiracy and fight against their fallacies. We must win. Rightists! This is the time you must return to the right course of the party. The gate of socialism is still open. If you are still being counterrevolutionary and refuse to plead guilty, the people will show no mercy![35]

This was Ding's last open letter in the *People's Daily*. As a sixty-five-year-old "important rightist," Ding was old and tired. He could not easily get rid of the rightist label. At the "Give Your Heart to the Party" meeting, he admitted openly that he "had not changed his capitalistic thinking, that he had not made any progress and that he had taken advantage of the generosity of the Party and the people." Ding concluded "I am guilty of a crime against the people!"[36] After hearing these statements about Ding, Little's response was plain—"I wonder if his luck has run out."[37] For all the CMCS staff who had fled from the Chinese mainland, Ding's fate was seen as a funny story, but for the Chinese staff who stayed on the mainland, Ding's case was discouraging. None of them possessed anything like the knowledge or political status of Ding. Ding's determination to preserve the CMCS and the staff failed completely, and his demise marked the PMCS's complete rupture from the CMCS.

The Japanese Maritime Customs Service

Before 1949, exchanges between the CMCS and the JMCS only happened in Taiwan and Manchuria as their custom houses were taken over by the Japanese Empire respectively in 1895 and 1932. The structures of the CMCS and the JMCS were completely different, so Takow Commissioner Zhang Shenfu found it difficult to take over Taiwanese custom houses from 1945 to 1949.

After 1949, an unexpected opportunity helped the JMCS benefit from the Japanese Empire's legacy in the CMCS. Immediately after he stepped down from the Inspector Generalship, Little was asked to investigate with Martin G. Scott, of the "United States Customs Service, formerly Treasury Attaché in Japan," the JMCS and report to the Supreme Commander for the Allied Powers (SCAP) in Japan. SCAP might not have realized the CMCS could become a useful model to learn from but it certainly realized that (1) Little had worked with the Japanese staff from 1914 to 1941; (2) the CMCS closely interacted with the JMCS, Manchukuo Customs Service and the Colonial Taiwanese Customs Service until 1945; and (3) Little's performance as the IG at the end of Nationalist China was also highly praised by the US government and US Ambassador to China, John Leighton.[38]

The Pentagon telephoned and instructed that SCAP wanted Little to "survey Japanese Customs procedures."[39] Little's "Customs Mission" was to "assist the Headquarters in necessary SCAP review of present status of Japanese Customs procedures." The mission started in July 1950 and ended in September. Along "with officials of the Japanese Ministry of Finance and the Customs, and with representatives of Japanese and foreign commercial and shipping interests," Little inspected "the office of the Customs Division in Tokyo and of the Custom Houses at Yokohama, Kobe, Osaka and Nagoya."[40]

When Little arrived in Tokyo on July 27, 1950, he immediately discovered that, as he noted in his journal, "there is a lot of interdepartmental friction, both in the Japanese government and in the US Army Sections, with regard to the Customs. Sort of Jurisdictional dispute."[41] The nature of this jurisdictional dispute faced by Little and Japanese Finance Minister (and later prime minister) Ikeda Hayato was that the SCAP applied the US Customs model to the JMCS, so it "instructed the Japanese Government to transfer to and centralize in the Ministry of Finance the control of all Customs functions and the administration of all matters connected therewith, including Custom Houses and personnel."[42] However, the attempt failed completely and Little's CMCS experience became particularly valuable because he could easily utilize the three empires' legacies, pick up suitable parts, and fit them into the JMCS framework.

After his investigation, Little discovered two issues indicating that the US Customs model could not be applied to the JMCS. The first one was the original design of the JCS. Little explained that "although [...] the Customs Division is supposed to have jurisdiction over the whole field of Customs administration, in actual practice it is more in the nature of an advisory and research department than of an independent operating and controlling organ." The Japanese Ministry of Finance administered the Taxation Bureau, which was put in charge of revenues collections, but "the Customs Division had two sections: (1) Management, and (2) Research and Statistics." Although the US Customs model was not applicable, the Manchu Empire's original design of the CMCS was identical to the JMCS structure for three reasons. First, the Western Commissioners of Customs were the advisors for the Chinese Superintendents of Customs, sent by the Imperial Household Department. Second, before 1911, only the Chinese Ministry of Finance and its branches in local custom houses could collect the customs revenues and the CMCS could not touch these. Finally, the CMCS's Statistical Department was the most important research and statistical data center in the Manchu Empire.

The second issue that Little discovered was the overwhelming presence of the Japanese military in the JMCS: it was the Japanese military rather than the Ministry of Finance that operated the agency. Little explained that "the Customs Division exercises little actual control over the Custom Houses in the six Customs Districts, which are under the control of the Taxation Bureau" and it is to the Chief of the Japanese Gendarmerie that "the Superintendents of the Customs Districts report, and not to the Chief of the Customs Division."

Of course, the prominent presence of the Japanese Military in the JMCS was identical to its influence on the CMCS during 1940 to 1945. From 1940 to 1941, Little was the Canton (modern Guangzhou) Commissioner and had to work with the Japanese authorities. As the Canton Customs House was in Occupied China, Little had very little actual control over it. Ironically, in Japan Little met T. Fujisaki, who had been the Superintendent of Customs over the Canton Customs House and "took my place as Commissioner at Canton" after the outbreak of the Pacific War. Fujisaki had been sent by the JCS and was not a former CMCS Japanese employee, which meant that he still worked for the JCS. On August 11, 1950, he wrote to Little that "I present my compliments and hearty thanks for your task on behalf of Japanese Customs Administration."[43]

Little's feelings were, however, complicated. Before the outbreak of the Pacific War, Little was the Canton Commissioner and followed instructions from IG Frederick Maze. However, with the outbreak of the Pacific War, Japan had declared war on the US and Great Britain, so Maze, Little, and all other Allied foreign staff members were arrested by the Japanese military and put in custody. Before he was arrested, Little had surrendered charge of the Canton Custom House to Fujisaki. Little "could not forget that in the spring of 1942," while he was "locked up in the flat across the road," Fujisaki was "strolling about my garden [the Commissioner's dormitory]."[44] Little's former CMCS Japanese colleagues, however, were not as lucky as Fujisaki. Little met Kodama Toshiharu, "who had spent 25 years in the Chinese Customs," but Kodama's Chinese experience had meant that he could only "work in a steel company at a low salary" in Japan. Kodama felt "his whole work in China was wasted."[45]

As the CMCS's experiences in the Manchu and the Second World War periods were highly similar to the JCS's difficulties and the CMCS had managed to overcome all the weaknesses and rebuild its efficiency after the war, Little aimed to adapt the JMCS to the CMCS model. Little's "Report on Japanese Customs Administration and Procedures" concluded that "the existing position of the Customs in the Ministry of Finance" was "ill-defined, anomalous and submerged, and recommended reorganization at the top administration level." He further stated:

> The primary functions of every Customs Service are the application of the Customs and tariff laws, which provide for the protection and collection of Customs duties and tonnage dues, the prevention of smuggling, the control of

bonded warehouses and free ports, the entry, clearance and control of shipping and aircraft, and the compilation of statistics of trade and shipping. In addition to these primary functions, the Customs also plays a vital part in the enforcement of many other laws and regulations relating to foreign and domestic trade, economic controls, etc.

The usefulness and importance of a Customs Service cannot be judged solely by the amount of Customs revenue it collects. The Customs is much more than a "tax office," and even in countries where Customs revenue is negligible (e.g., in prewar England and post-war Japan) the Customs plays an indispensable role in a country's foreign trade, and is an important link in her international relationships.[46]

After he submitted the report, Little wrote that "if this single recommendation is accepted and implemented, the cost of the Customs Mission will be repaid a hundred times over."[47] His endeavor was repaid immediately by General Douglas MacArthur, with whom he had a meeting. Little recorded the following about this meeting:

The General asked me what we had found in the Japanese Customs, and said his information was that it was in a rather bad way. I told him that, in view of the difficulties and handicaps under which the Customs had labored, we were surprised to find how much substantial progress had been made since the Customs was re-established by SCAP in April, 1946. I added, however, that much remains to be done to bring the Customs up to the level it should occupy and the efficiency it should possess. We discussed in detail the major recommendations we are making: (1) Reorganization at top level of administration; (2) Introduction of a new tariff; and touched on several others, such as the creation of an enforcement section. The General asked about corruption, and I told him that it is much more widespread than before the war ... the opinion that one of the principal reasons was low pay ... I pointed out that there is considerable resentment in Japanese business circles because the application of the present tariff discriminates against Japanese merchants in favor of "foreign traders." The General asked us if we would be willing to come out to Japan a year from now to see how the Customs was working. We both said yes. (I think it would be difficult to say "no" to a request from Gen. MacArthur.)[48]

After his meeting with MacArthur, Little wrote that he felt "satisfied that it is a good report which, if implemented, will give Japan a good Customs Service. I fear, however, that our Mission came to Japan two – or at least one – year too late, because SCAP hesitates now to use directives to the Japanese government."[49] In order to tackle the "ill-defined position of the Customs in the Ministry of Finance," Little wrote a report titled "The position of the Customs within EES" (Economic & Scientific Section) and submitted to MacArthur. He stated:

The Japanese Customs administration has been the stepchild of the Occupation, almost an orphan because the entire burden of dealing with the rehabilitation of the Japanese Customs has fallen on one man, called "Customs Specialist," who has two men between him and the Chief of his Division. The Mission has made recommendations for what we consider are necessary and fundamental changes in Customs administration, appraisement and enforcement matters. Both these improvements, and we consider them vital, require education of the Japanese force concerned as it is doubtful that they can be effectively inaugurated without experienced counsellors. It is therefore recommended that Customs officers experienced in these fields be secured – possibly by loan from the US Customs if they cannot be secured elsewhere – for a one or two year period.[50]

Both these reports aimed to (1) "bring Japanese Customs Administration into line with that of other countries with which the Mission is familiar"; (2) "raise the Japanese Customs Administration to a Government level commensurate with its importance"; (3) "restore to the Customs in the eyes of the Government, the public, and its own employees the independent status and prestige which it requires"; and (4) "enable the Customs to carry out more efficiently its normal and recognized functions, and thus fulfil the objectives of SCAP."

Little's suggestions were to base the foundations of the JMCS on the structure of the CMCS. The postwar JMCS shared quite a few similarities with the CMCS in the mid-nineteenth century. Both imperial China and postwar Japan needed customs revenues to rebuild the state, had to follow Western trade protocols, and could not direct customs services on their own. As the CMCS had already proven its efficiency and value for almost a hundred years, the JMCS could learn from this experience. Little had already had considerable exposure in working with Japanese staff in his career and taking over JMCS's custom houses in Taiwan and Manchuria from 1945 to 1949. In addition, the installation of the CMCS model could also guarantee that the JMCS recruit a capable and sizeable staff immediately because over 5,000 former CMCS Japanese employees had returned to Japan. They had proven their value in the collaborationist government in Nanjing and became signifcant assets of the Japanese Empire's legacy in the CMCS.

After 1949, Little's advisory career in the Customs administration of MacArthur and in the Finance Ministry of Taiwan was so successful that MacArthur asked him to carry out an inspection of the Filipino Customs Service. However, Little's efforts in the Philippines were not as successful. The fact was that Little's CMCS experience could be of little service to him as none of the three empires had left any legacy in the Filipino Customs Service.

Conclusion

After 1949, the Communists were interested neither in relying on international trade nor increasing customs revenues. This was why the cosmopolitan professionalism of the CMCS and its staff was completely dismissed. It is, however, interesting to note that, because contemporary China has become a major power in international trade, the current PMCS has made great efforts to emphasize its connections with the CMCS. The Beijing Inspectorate has invited international scholars to give lectures and share primary materials every year. In the twenty-first century, the CMCS's link with the three empires is no longer seen as a source of national humiliation but as a symbol of cosmopolitan professionalism.

Judging from his diaries, Little's advisory career after 1949 was much happier compared to his stint as Inspector General between 1945 and 1949. He had compassion for the "Anti-Communist Camp" in East Asia, so he endeavored to rehabilitate the TMCS and the JMCS. In his eyes, both Taiwan (or "Free China") and Japan needed the West's help to fight against communism. The cultural hybrid in the CMCS provided the best example for the "Anti-Communist Camp" to initiate another round of westernizing projects. Both the Manchu and Japanese empires had learnt from the British Empire in the nineteenth century. After 1949, Little thought it was crucial to learn from this experience. When he looked back at his service of more than three decades in 1975, Little still felt the CMCS's cosmopolitan tradition was an asset to the world.

> The Customs in its day had a unique cosmopolitan staff. As many as twenty-three countries were represented in its service lists. These men demonstrated that individuals of all nationalities, of the most varied social, religious, and racial backgrounds, could work together harmoniously and efficiently. They strove with a considerable measure of success to maintain the highest standards of honor and probity, to be a service in deed as well as in name; and they were thus a credit both to China and to their native countries. Their record in this respect offers a lesson for today and tomorrow, as international cooperation becomes ever more necessary.[51]

The secret behind the success of the CMCS's cosmopolitan staff was that the three empires realized the importance of international trade and customs revenues, so their domination in East Asia did not impede CMCS operations but created flexibility for its functions to continue. This was why since the mid-nineteenth century Chinese, Japanese, and British employees could maintain a minimum level of cooperation. The importance of international trade and customs revenues made the CMCS the only agency that could continuously maintain its connection with the three empires and preserve its efficiency in the process. This continuous relationship with the three empires makes the CMCS history uniquely valuable in illustrating the rise and decline of the three dominant empires in East Asia. The Manchu Empire's tradition was reflected in the fact that the Taiwanese government granted a great deal of autonomy to the TMCS because the Taiwanese government considered itself the legitimate successor of the Manchu government, so it aimed to continue its bureaucratic design. The British Empire's tradition was reflected in the Communist government's hostility against the PMCS because the Communist government considered itself as the savior of the Chinese people from foreign imperialism. The Japanese Empire's tradition was reflected in the SCAP's plan to apply the CMCS experience to the JMCS because the pressure placed by the US government on Japan was similar to the one laid by the British government to Manchu China in the nineteenth century.

Notes

1   As this chapter discusses six different customs services, a clear definition of these services is needed. The Chinese Maritime Customs Service (CMCS) refers to the service administered by a foreign staff from 1854 to 1950, the People's Maritime Customs Service (PMCS) refers to the service administered by the Communist cadres in China since 1949, the Taiwanese Maritime Customs Service (TMCS) refers to the service administered by a mainland Chinese staff from 1950 to present in Taiwan, the Colonial Maritime Customs Service of Taiwan refers to the service administered by a colonial staff in Taiwan before 1945, the Japanese Maritime Customs Service (JMCS) refers to the service in Japan after 1945, and the Imperial Maritime Customs Service of Japan refers to the service in Japan before that.

   The names of these services are different from their legitimate names, for instance, the TMCS was still called the CMCS, but the changes make it easier for readers to understand this chapter.
2   John K. Fairbank, ed., *Chinese Thought & Institutions* (Chicago: University of Chicago Press, 1957), p. 205.
3   Katherine F. Bruner, John K. Fairbank, and Richard J. Smith, *Entering China's Service: Robert Hart's Journals, 1854–1863* (Cambridge, MA: Harvard University Press, 1986), p. 327.
4   Fairbank was aware of the distinction between the Chinese and Manchu imperial factors. He saw Hart and Customs as part of a Manchu–Han–Western synarchic "trinity in power" along with the Machu Empress Dowager and the Han Governor-General Li Hongzhang and British IG Robert Hart. See John Fairbank, *Trade and Diplomacy on the China Coast: The Opening of the Treaty Ports, 1842–1854* (Cambridge, MA: Harvard University Press, 1953), p. 465.
5   *Service List,* 1938–1939.
6   See, Wang Wenju, *Forty Years in the Peculiar Customs* (Taipei: Privately published, 1969), p. 56. Yeh Yuan-chang, *Recollections of a Chinese Customs Veteran* (HongKong: Longman Bookstore, 1987), p. 91. Ruan Shorong, *The Collections of Golden Ashes* (Taipei: Privately published, 1986), pp. 56–58.
7   679(1) 9897, IG Order No. 147, August 28, 1945.
8   Li Wenhuan, *The Takow Custom House History* (Gaoxiong: Takow Customs Station, 1999), pp. 181–182.
9   Ibid., pp. 189–191.
10   Lai Zehan ed., *228 Shijian Yanjiu Baogao* (The Report of the February 28 Incident) (Taipei: China Times Press, 1994), p. 105.
11   Li Wenhuan, *The Takow Custom House History,* pp. 280–284.
12   CONVERSATIONS: L/K. Little, G. E. Bunker, K. F. Bruner, Cornish, New Hampshire, December 16 and 17, 1971, p. 39.
13   679(1) 32225, Shanghai Semi-Official Correspondence, 1931, Foreign Staff's petition, January 16, 1931.

14 B. E. Foster Hall, "The Chinese Maritime Customs: An International Service, 1854–1950," National Maritime Museum, Maritime Monographs and Reports No. 26 (1977), p. 49.

15 Chihyun Chang, ed., *The Chinese Journals of L K Little, 1943–54*, vol. 2 (London: Routledge, 2017), November 12, 1949.

16 Wang Wenju, *Forty Years in the Peculiar Customs*, p. 78.

17 The only exception was Kiungchow Commissioner Lin Leming (Lam Lok-ming) because he fled to Hong Kong before the Communists took Hainan island. In October 1950, the Taipei Inspectorate "appointed him the Statistical Secretary." Lin then "reported of duty at the end of October, rebuilt the Statistical Department, and prepared to compile all Returns of Trade and Reports on Trade" (Lam Lok Ming, *Memoirs of 35-Year Service in the Chinese Maritime Customs*, pp. 38–40).

18 Wang Wenju, *Lianyu haiguan sishinian* (Taipei: Privately Published, 1969), p. 105. Former Reference Library Director Ruan Shorong (Nathan S. Y. Yuan) was the only exception. He became a refugee in Hongkong and worked as a factory laborer for two years. Then he was reinstated with the help of Soong Mei-lin (Ruan, *The Collections of Golden Ashes*, pp. 139–154.)

19 IG Circular No. 138, July 22, 1955.

20 b MS Am1999-1999.18, Lester Knox Little Paper, 1932–1964, Fang Tu to Little, March 18, 1957.

21 b MS Am1999-1999.18, Lester Knox Little Paper, 1932–1964, Little to Taiwanese Minister of Finance P. Y. Hsu.

22 Circular No. 245, June 24, 1960.

23 Circular No. 248, July 15, 1960.

24 b MS Am1999-1999.18, Lester Knox Little Paper, 1932–1964, Lester Knox Little Paper, 1932–1964, Little to Fang Tu, July 29, 1960.

25 Yeh, *Recollections of A Chinese Customs Veteran*, p. 97.

26 Ruan, *The Collections of Golden Ashes*, p. 62.

27 *People Daily*, October 26, 1949.

28 *People Daily*, October 26, 1949.

29 *People's Daily*, September 4, 1954.

30 *People's Daily*, March 2, 1956.

31 *People's Daily*, May 1, 1957.

32 *People's Daily*, May 17, 1957.

33 *People's Daily*, July 1, 1957.

34 Lester Knox Little Paper, 1932–1964, Hu Fu-sen to Little, August 18, 1957.

35 *People's Daily*, July 13, 1957.

36 b MS Am1999-1999.18, Lester Knox Little Paper, 1932–1964,Lester Knox Little Paper, 1932–1964, US Information Agency, Office of Director of Personnel, August 18, 1958.

37 b MS Am1999-1999.18, Lester Knox Little Paper, 1932–1964, Lester Knox Little Paper, 1932–1964, Little to Fang Tu, September 6, 1957.

38 CONVERSATIONS: L/K. Little, G. E. Bunker, K. F. Bruner, Cornish, New Hampshire, December 16 and 17, 1971.

39 Chang, *The Chinese Journals of L K Little, 1943–54*, vol. 3, June 30, 1950.

40 Lester Little, "Forward," "Report on Japanese Customs Administration and Procedures by the Little – Scott Mission," September 7, 1950.

41 Chang, *The Chinese Journals of L K Little, 1943–54*, vol. 3, July 27, 1950.

42 SCAPIN 941-A of April 8, 1946—Appendix I.

43 Chang, *The Chinese Journals of L K Little, 1943–54*, vol. 3, August 11, 1950.
44 Ibid.
45 Ibid.
46 Little, "Report On Japanese Customs Administration and Procedures," p. 5.
47 Chang, *The Chinese Journals of L K Little, 1943–54*, vol. 3, August 16, 1950.
48 Chang, *The Chinese Journals of L K Little, 1943–54*, vol. 3, September 6, 1950.
49 Ibid.
50 Lester Little, "The position of the Customs within Economic & Scientific Section,"
    September 10, 1950.
51 Lester Little, "Introduction," in *The IG in Peking: Letters of Robert Hart Chinese
    Maritime Customs, 1868–1907*, eds. John Fairbank, Katherine Bruner, and Elizabeth
    Matheson (Cambridge, MA: Harvard University Press, 1975), vol. 1, p. 34.

Chapter 9

INVERTED COMPENSATION: WARTIME FORCED LABOR AND POST-IMPERIAL RECKONING

Yukiko Koga*

Li Guoqiang, a 78-year-old survivor of enslavement in imperial Japan, had just returned from a trip to Chengdu, a city in central China, when I visited him in his modest lower-middle-class apartment on the outskirts of Beijing in 2008. He and his fellow remaining survivors had been guests of honor at an event held at the privately run Jianchuan Museum, a cluster of museums established in 2004 by a local millionaire, Fan Jianchuan, with one of its aims the memorialization of the "Second Sino-Japanese War (1937–1945)." Li is among the few surviving members of nearly 42,000 Chinese men who were abducted in China and forcefully shipped to wartime Japan in the 1940s to work mostly in mines, construction sites, and shipyards for brand-name Japanese corporations. The systematic capture and enslavement orchestrated by the government was to augment the significant labor shortage resulting from the conscription of Japanese men as Japan's war efforts deepened.[1] Under brutal work and living conditions, approximately one-third of these men from mostly rural China did not survive to see the Japanese defeat in 1945. While offering me watermelon to cool off from the heat of a nearly three-hour journey by local transport from the center of Beijing to his home, Li showed me the images of his trip to this unique museum.

One photograph in particular captured the moment when the museum staff took the handprints of these fragile old men to be set into the pavement of the museum plaza, along with those of other revolutionary heroes in modern Chinese history. "We are also part of China's history," Li proudly declared, showing me another image of these survivors standing among life-size statues of significant political figures of the Chinese Communist Party. The weight of this utterance became clear to me only later when he finished recounting his ordeal in Japan and his thoughts drifted back to his life back in China after repatriation.

He then invited me to his study, which was filled with books. While proudly showing me his large collection of books on the Japanese invasion of China, Li explained to me: "I left my family, my wife and six children, to learn why China was invaded by Japan, and why I almost died three times in Japan during the war." He began to explain how, after repatriation to civil war-torn China, he was recruited first by the Kuomintang Army, then eventually made his way to the Chinese Communist Liberation Army, where he built up his career, earning numerous medals for outstanding service, only to be cast out in the early 1950s, suspected of having been a spy because of his wartime experience in Japan and his subsequent repatriation to China on a US ship after the Japanese defeat.[2]

With nowhere else to go, he returned to his village to become a farmer. Li explained to me why he remained silent about his wartime experience:

> My wife didn't want me to tell my wartime story to our children because of the social stigma attached to my experience in wartime Japan. I hadn't told my story to anybody else until Japanese lawyers contacted me in the 1990s to file a lawsuit in Japan against the Japanese government and Mitsui Mining Corporation that enslaved me. It was only after being contacted by those Japanese lawyers that I learned about other survivors now living in Beijing.

After long years of silence about his experience, Li was full of appreciation that the new historical museum in Chengdu recognized his and fellow victims' wartime ordeals as an integral part of China's national history and their sacrifice as part of the Communist nation building effort. But his elation, captured in the group pictures taken at the museum, also underscores the decades of silencing that took place not only in Japan but also in China. As we shall see, the legal process since the mid-1990s, through which he and many others like him sought official apology and monetary compensation from the Japanese government and the corporations that enslaved them, not only made the survivors' voices heard but also brought this silencing mechanism to the fore.

This chapter examines how this silencing mechanism became exposed through a series of collective lawsuits filed within Japanese jurisdictions across the country by Chinese survivors represented by pro bono Japanese lawyers. These cases culminated in the landmark 2007 Supreme Court decision rejecting the victims' claims for official apology and monetary compensation for wartime enslavement. Despite formally rejecting the Chinese plaintiffs' claims, however, the Supreme Court ruling nevertheless drew attention to what can be called the Japanese imperial debt. By underscoring not only the moral and financial debt from wartime enslavement but also the new forms of debt that arose *after* the demise of the Japanese Empire, the legal process illustrated what in effect has been a debt-driven mode of the *unmaking of empire*, which perpetually defers historical redress while pursuing new forms of wealth accumulation through debts, both moral and monetary, in the economic sphere. This chapter tells the story of how the legal intervention revealed the complicity of the economy in silencing victims. I will show how the legal drama that unfolded in the courtroom has shifted the crux of the issue from accounting for wartime violence to post-imperial accountability.

While imperial Japan's use of slave labor has been discussed within the framework of Japanese responsibility for wartime violence (as epitomized in the oft-used expression, "postwar compensation lawsuits"), this chapter re-frames the issue within Japan's *imperial* debt. This reframing brings to light an underexplored and unaddressed post-imperial responsibility that escapes narrowly defined war responsibility. In so doing, the chapter aims to illuminate the expanding scope of accountability that accompanies the prolonged processes of the unmaking of the Japanese Empire, specifically how, since Japan's defeat in 1945, Japanese society has continued to accrue even more debt to the Chinese. I argue that accounting for Japanese imperial violence necessarily involves addressing not only wartime violence but also additional violence, injustice, and debt that took place through actions, inactions, and silencing *after* the Japanese Empire's demise.

I approach this underexplored question of post-imperial reckoning through the prism of "inverted compensation"—large sums of compensation that the Japanese government paid in 1946 to Japanese corporations involved in the use of Chinese slave labor, in stark contrast to the unpaid wages and unpaid compensation to the victims themselves, who were sent back to civil war-torn China without a penny. This chapter explores how the series of lawsuits have made this practice of compensating the former perpetrators a critical issue for accounting for Japanese imperial violence. The 2007 Supreme Court decision, though it denied the Chinese plaintiffs' claims for official apology and monetary compensation, highlighted the unaccounted-for imperial debts epitomized by inverted compensation. This courtroom revelation unsettles the widely shared narrative of Japanese postwar economic recovery and prosperity through diligence and innovation and instead anchors the story of prosperity in what some survivors call "blood debt."[3] This chapter tells the story of how, by exposing these compounded imperial debts, the legal process makes publicly visible the unfinished project of the unmaking of empire within the economic sphere. It is at this intersection of law and economy that our exploration begins.

Inverted compensation

Matsuda Yutaka, a former labor union organizer at one of the biggest coal mines in Japan who had later become an attorney, was the lead lawyer representing the Chinese victims in the Fukuoka Regional Court of Japan. As we shall see, Matsuda had carefully prepared a courtroom spectacle that in 2002 culminated in a landmark ruling.[4] The case marked a milestone in overcoming the statute of limitations, which was a formidable legal hurdle in the series of cases filed by Chinese victims. All of the cases, after all, were filed at least fifty years since the end of the war in 1945, decades after the twenty-year statute of limitations ran out. Rejecting the defendants' claim that the statute of limitations had run out, the judges found Mitsui Mining Corporation responsible for the wartime use of Chinese slave labor and ordered it to pay 11 million Japanese yen (approximately US$85,000 based on an exchange rate of 130 yen per dollar at the time) to each plaintiff.[5] As with all other cases involving slave labor, however, the judges denied the responsibility of the Japanese state by invoking the doctrine of sovereign immunity under the Meiji Constitution of Imperial Japan. The court determined that the Japanese state was not liable for damages resulting from actions related to its exercise of state power (*kenryoku sayō*).

But, in overcoming the statute of limitations, the Fukuoka case also exposed how the postwar Japanese economy was in fact built on a compounded debt to the Chinese victims, which has never been paid back. The Fukuoka case tells a story of how the legal intervention the effect of revealing the complicity of the economy in silencing the victims while accumulating wealth at their expense.

By the time Matsuda planned the strategy for the Fukuoka slave labor case, several other slave labor cases had already been filed in various regional courts, where the statute of limitations became the contentious issue. Matsuda knew that he had to establish not only wartime violence but also postwar injustice in order to break this legal barrier. He had a secret weapon—a set of the allegedly destroyed 1946 Japanese government archives that detailed the wartime use of Chinese slave laborers, which he would dramatically introduce to the court.[6]

In several court sessions, the Chinese plaintiffs' lawyers repeatedly requested that the government confirm and disclose the existence of this archive, while the defense lawyers consistently denied their knowledge of it or its existence. This verbal ping-pong in the courtroom was an elaborate performance of a public secret: both sides knew of the existence of this "secret" archive. In fact, the plaintiffs' lawyers even had a secret copy, to which they alluded in order to provoke the judges. Kimura Motoaki, the presiding judge, eventually lost patience and urged the plaintiffs' lawyers to submit this elusive archive to the court: "You lawyers on both sides seem to know what this 'missing' archive is all about. Yet in the past six months, *we,* the judges, have yet to see this seemingly first-class historical archive. The more we hear about it, the more we desire to see it. Instead of requesting the government side to submit these materials, would it be possible for the plaintiffs' side to submit them to the court?" This judge's utterance gave the cue for the plaintiff's lawyers to publicly disclose these documents in court.

The secret archive comprises a set of reports compiled by the Japanese government in early 1946, several months after the Japanese defeat in the Second World War. The first set of documents consists of thousands of handwritten pages of reports from thirty-five corporations that enslaved Chinese at over one hundred sites. Against the anticipated start of the Tokyo Tribunals in May 1946, the Japanese government feared prosecution by the Allied Forces and secretly ordered the affected corporate offices to produce reports on their wartime use of Chinese laborers. The Ministry of Foreign Affairs (MFA) then hired a group of seventeen social scientists to visit each site to write up detailed field reports.[7] These reports document how individual victims were captured in China and transported to Japan, how they were housed, fed, enslaved, and, often, how they died. The MFA then compiled a summary report to be used as a cover-up in the event of an Allied Forces investigation, which never took place.[8]

The government then ordered the field reports to be destroyed after the compilation of the summary reports. The field reports appeared to go "missing" immediately after their completion in 1946, yet these documents nevertheless survived through decades of the Cold War as a result of the defiant actions of those who safeguarded these archival traces of wartime violence. These archives eventually resurfaced after the end of the Cold War, first through a public television broadcast and much later through the aforementioned courtroom drama.[9] The unusual trajectory of these field reports and how they became public through legal performance in court highlights not only their importance as historical evidence but also actions and inactions that inflicted additional injustice to the victims through the process of unmaking the Japanese Empire.

We shall thus take a closer look at the political lives of this "secret" archive as they unfold through the legal process.

The plaintiff's lawyers knew about the archive because, contrary to the official story of its destruction long ago, most of it, in thousands of fragile yellowed pages, was piled up in an office closet of the Tokyo Overseas Chinese Association (*Tokyo kakyō sōkai*) in downtown Tokyo. Chen Kunwang, the director emeritus of the Association, had guarded these historical documents ever since he secretly acquired them immediately after the government ordered their destruction in 1946.

The plaintiffs' lawyers, who had heard a rumor about the presence of this supposedly disappeared archive, sought him out, and persuaded him to let them copy and use the materials for this slave labor compensation lawsuit as historical evidence. I visited Chen in this very office in 2008, and this 89-year-old man relayed to me the dramatic life of this archival material since 1946.

Chen opened the door to an office closet that was filled with hundreds of worn-out brown envelopes, and took out a large pile of documents wrapped in thick brown paper darkened with age and another set in an old manila envelope. He placed them on a large conference table and carefully took out the documents. From this pile emerged the supposedly destroyed handwritten reports compiled by one of the 135 corporate offices that benefited from the wartime use of Chinese. Another pile contained the summary reports that the Ministry of Foreign Affairs had compiled in 1946 based on the field reports.

Chen recalled how several Japanese social scientists secretly carried these thousands of pages in their backpacks in small batches, walking for miles through the burnt-down Tokyo landscape to bring them to him. These social scientists, many of whom were left-leaning intellectuals repatriated from Japan's failed puppet state of Manchukuo, defied the government order to destroy the original handwritten reports after the summary reports were compiled. Chen explained with emotion, "Despite the government order to destroy the documents, these social scientists strongly felt that it was wrong to destroy such historically important materials. These reports were brought to me in *this* very wrapping paper, and I have kept the wrapping paper as it was, because it was truly a meaningful moment for me."

In an affectionate manner, he carefully opened another envelope to show me the yellowed pages, and recounted how he became the guardian of these archives; how he strategically pressured the Japanese government in the 1950s by alluding to their existence when Sino-Japanese negotiations were underway to swap Japanese left behind in China for the remains of the Chinese slave labor victims;

and how he finally came to the decision to disclose their existence after decades of keeping them out of the public eye. With the geopolitical shift of the post-Cold War era and mounting demands across the world to seek redress for Second World War atrocities, Chen felt that the time was now ripe to make public these long-hidden traces of Japanese wartime violence. Recalling how the group of Japanese lawyers representing the Chinese war victims persuaded him to let them use these materials for the lawsuit; how these lawyers brought a portable copy machine (still a rarity at that time) to Chen's office and spent weeks copying the thousands of pages; and how these documents played a significant role in these legal cases, Chen seemed finally ready to give closure to his role as the guardian of these imperial remains. He ended our meeting by telling me about his plan in the near future to donate the documents to a museum in China.

What made these archives particularly pivotal in the lawsuit is threefold. First, they provided evidence of the systematic nature of the wartime use of slave labor. Second, and more importantly, they documented new forms of injustice that took place *after* the original violence ended in 1945 through what I am calling "inverted compensation": how in 1946 the Japanese corporations that enslaved the Chinese received large sums of compensation from the Japanese government for the "losses" incurred through wartime use and postwar loss of Chinese labor. While the original purpose of these reports was to prepare for a possible investigation by the Allied Forces, the Japanese government repurposed these records to determine the allocation of compensation to 135 corporate offices, which amounted to approximately 57 million Japanese yen.[10] This *inverted compensation* took place during the US Occupation of Japan following the Japanese defeat, indicating tacit US approval of this compensatory practice at the advent of the Cold War. The dramatic appearance of this archive through legal proceedings betrayed this inversion of the common-sense logic of compensation.[11] Third, the public disclosure of this inverted compensation was accompanied by another disclosure in the courtroom: through the defense lawyers' insistent denial of the knowledge of these archival materials, they demonstrated the Japanese government's continuous attempts to suppress their involvement in this wartime practice. The courtroom spectacle thus revealed two forms of post-imperial injustice inflicted by the Japanese government and corporations on the Chinese victims: one in the form of inverted compensation and the other in the form of persistent attempts to deny and erase their historical involvement even today.

Shortly after these archives became public at the Fukuoka trial, the government side announced that they had "discovered" a copy in the basement of a warehouse. This announcement was followed by the decision in November 2002 to declassify nearly 2,000 pages of government archives dating from 1952 to 1972.[12] These internal documents, many in the form of handwritten memos from the period between the end of the US Occupation and the start of diplomatic relations with the PRC, chronicle systematic attempts by various sections of the Japanese government—the China section of the MFA in particular—to prevent the "missing" 1946 archives from becoming public. For example, the documentation details how, after learning on March 17, 1960, about the presence of the supposedly burnt 1946 reports from Suzuki Masakatsu, who had been involved in preparing the original reports, the Ministry decided not to disclose this knowledge to the public. Instead, on May 3, 1960, Izeki Yūjirō, then head of the MFA Asia section, testified in the Special Committee on the US-Japan Security Treaty for the House of Representatives:

> I have heard that the Management Office of the Ministry of Foreign Affairs had prepared such reports. However, all the reports were burnt due to the view that such reports would affect many people (*tasū no hito ni meiwaku o kakeru*) as they could be used for prosecution of war crimes. This is how the Ministry currently does not have any reports of such nature.[13]

By publicly disclosing these documents in court, the plaintiffs' lawyers made the actions and inactions of the Japanese government an integral and critical aspect of imperial reckoning. The legal intervention thus presented the postwar compensation issue as *post-imperial* reckoning that demands accounting for both the wartime violence as well as continued injustice and accumulation of imperial debts *after* the demise of the Japanese Empire. In so doing, the Fukuoka slave labor case underscores the compounded debt that the Japanese owe to the Chinese victims. The Japanese government and corporations pursued postwar economic recovery and prosperity at the expense of compensating slave laborers, while the US turned a blind eye. By demonstrating how Japanese postwar prosperity was in part predicated precisely on redirecting funds from victims to the very companies that had enslaved them, this legal intervention has shifted the question of imperial and post-imperial debts to the center stage of belated reckoning.

(For)given time

As Li Guoqiang's story suggests, the Japanese and US governments were not the only ones complicit in this postwar structure of erasure at the expense of the victims. The Chinese Civil War that reignited after the Japanese defeat and the advent of the Cold War significantly shaped how the Chinese side approached Japan's imperial debt. In the absence of diplomatic relations between Japan and the PRC until 1972, the question of imperial debt during the 1950s and 1960s primarily revolved around victims' bodies as a quasi-currency in the form of repatriating remains of perished slave labor victims back to China. But, in 1972 on the occasion of establishing diplomatic relations, economy and the question of redress resurfaced yet again in a state-to-state agreement to confirm the silencing structure built on the economy of debt. This historical juncture is crucial to understanding the decades of silence that the victims maintained and the nature of economy that is central to the question of imperial reckoning.

The Cold War prevented both the Republic of China (ROC) and the PRC from participating in the Treaty of Peace with Japan (commonly known as the San Francisco Peace Treaty) signed in 1951 and enacted in 1952 between Japan and forty-eight countries, which ended the Allied occupation of Japan.[14] Cold War politics also deferred the establishment of diplomatic relations between Japan and the PRC until 1972. The signing of the Joint Communiqué in 1972, followed by the Peace and Friendship Treaty in 1978, then, marked the zero hour of postwar Sino–Japanese relations in which the two countries officially put the issue of Japan's war responsibility on the table but then subsequently set it aside in favor of formal economic relations through their shared goal of pursuing economic cooperation. In so doing, this state-to-state agreement ambiguously located the moral economy of accounting for Japanese imperial violence in relation to the formal economy.

By renouncing reparation claims in the Joint Communiqué, which the Japanese side feared that the Chinese would demand, the Chinese government in effect gave a "gift" to Japan. Instead of reparations, the new Sino-Japanese relations centered on Japan's Official Development Assistance (ODA) to China, at a time when other countries were reluctant to invest in China, which was just beginning to recover from the turmoil of the Cultural Revolution. It was never stated explicitly that Japanese ODA was a substitute for war reparations, and the "gift" from China came with the expectation that Japan not revert to its imperialist past.[15] As anthropological studies demonstrate, receiving a gift does not signal the end of a story but rather the beginning of it: a gift demands reciprocity and thereby becomes a debt to be repaid.[16] In 1972, Japanese received a gift—China's renunciation of reparation claims—and in turn incurred a debt that they would find difficult to repay, since it was measured in their attitude toward the past rather than in currency or concrete demands. The 1972 agreement gave the Japanese not forgiveness but the gift of time to repay this moral debt.[17] It is this *(for)given time* that set the stage for the new phase in Sino–Japanese relations: the robust development of the formal economy, initially through Japanese ODA, which started in 1979, and increasingly through Japan's direct investment in China.[18] This new and official postwar Sino–Japanese relationship, which was delayed by twenty-seven Cold War years, privileged the formal economy over the moral economy of accounting for Japanese imperial violence.

By accepting this monetary gift, the Chinese state became complicit in an amoral gift economy where, at the state-to-state level, the question of moral debt became artificially separated from and subordinated to the formal economy surrounding monetary transactions. The complicity of the Chinese state in privileging formal economy over moral economy has expressed itself in small and large gestures, ranging from their reluctance to support the victim initiatives to seek redress for Japanese atrocities to outright intimidation of those involved in the legal redress movement to the judicial refusal to accept lawsuits by its own citizens. Since 2000, the Chinese courts in various provinces had refused to accept five attempts by the victims to file compensation lawsuits until February 2014, when the Beijing No. 1 Intermediate People's Court decided to accept a slave labor case. In one of these failed cases involving a prominent Japanese corporation, after the court refused to accept the case, the lead Chinese lawyer and the leading figures among the plaintiffs were browbeaten by a high-ranking local government official, who expressed strong concerns that such a lawsuit would jeopardize ongoing negotiations with a corporation to invest in the region.

My use of parenthesis in (for)given time expresses this ambiguous location of moral debt, which the Chinese state has used as political leverage for both domestic and diplomatic maneuvering. (For)given time is a temporal framework produced through the Japanese and Chinese governments' shared project of deferring the pursuit of redress while seeking wealth accumulation. Structurally, it is a silencing mechanism that forced many Chinese victims to maintain their long years of silence.

While recurring anti-Japanese street demonstrations in China underscore this unaccounted-for moral debt, in their focus on demanding an official apology and acknowledgement of the historical facts (Japanese wartime violence) from the Japanese government, these public outcries for imperial reckoning often fail to situate what is known as Japan's "history problem" within a larger economic structure on which Sino–Japanese relations have been built after the demise of the Japanese Empire. The 2007 Supreme Court decision, as we shall see next, officially declared that, despite its formal rejection of the plaintiffs' claims for compensation, Japan still owes this double debt thanks to these latent gift relations.

Post-imperial reckoning

The Supreme Court decision on April 27, 2007, effectively put an end to the series of forced labor cases.[19] Unlike the lower court decisions, which deployed the statute of limitations or sovereign immunity to reject the plaintiffs' claims, the Supreme Court judges pointed to the 1972 Sino–Japanese agreement. Referring to the Joint Communiqué in which the Chinese government renounced its reparation claims against Japan, the court ruled that the Chinese plaintiffs did not have individual rights to claim compensation in court (*saiban-jō seikyū suru kinō o ushinatta*, literally "lost the function to claim compensation through legal means").

Despite its formal rejection of the plaintiffs' claims, the court acknowledged the violence and injustice committed by the defendant (Nishimatsu Construction) and the Japanese government not only through the wartime use of forced labor but also after this wartime practice ended with the Japanese defeat. The judges emphasized the psychological and physical suffering that the plaintiffs endured over the years against the background of the economic benefits that the defendant received through wartime slave labor *and* the inverted compensation after the war's end. The judges further reminded the defendant that the Chinese plaintiffs' lack of individual rights to claim for compensation in the court did not prohibit the defendant from making its own voluntary arrangements for redress. Repeatedly emphasizing these points in a supplementary paragraph (*fugen*) to the ruling, the court strongly encouraged Nishimatsu Construction and the Japanese government to make such efforts.

By underscoring the compounded debts—moral and monetary—that Japan owes to Chinese victims, the Supreme Court decision publicly acknowledged not only the historical fact of wartime practice but also the unfinished project of the unmaking of empire in the economic sphere, which is burdened with unaccounted-for imperial debts. By urging the defendants to repay these debts out of court, the court made the belated task of settling accounts the cornerstone of this incomplete project.

The story of inverted compensation directs us to situate the wartime slave labor issue in comparison with a parallel inverted compensation in Britain: a total of 20 million pounds sterling was paid to slave owners when colonial slavery was abolished in 1833.[20] While the so-called history problem in East Asia is often compared to postwar Germany's attempts to come to terms with the Holocaust, I suggest that we may benefit from reframing the issue as the question of post-imperial reckoning. Doing so directs our attention to the role of economy in the question of imperial reckoning. While the question of coming to terms with Japanese imperial violence often revolves around the politics of apology and historical recognition, the slave labor case points to the centrality of economy.

New legal frontier for post-imperial reckoning

In Franz Kafka's parable, "Before the Law," contained in his novel *The Trial*, the countryman eventually dies while waiting to go through the gate to stand in front of the law. This may well be the image that guides the Japanese government in its persistent deferral of the arrival of legal justice. They might be hoping that the last surviving witnesses will eventually die in front of the gate even though the gate of law remains open. Yet this is not the end of the story, for the persistence of redress is starting to shift the legal frontier itself.

In a landmark decision by the South Korean Constitutional Court in 2011, the court found it unconstitutional for the South Korean government to prohibit its own citizens from seeking compensation claims against Japan within the Korean jurisdiction. Since then, Korean plaintiffs, who had lost in the slave labor cases filed in Japan, filed and won cases in the South Korean courts, with more cases yet to come.[21] A different gate of law is now open to South Korean victims in their home country, allowing them to stand before the law.[22] This new development in South Korea spurred renewed interest among Chinese victims, lawyers, and activists to seek legal redress within the Chinese jurisdiction. Feeling the pressure, in 2014, a Beijing court officially accepted a lawsuit against Mitsubishi Materials and Mitsui Mining. Some of the forced labor victims reached a historic out-of-court settlement with Mitsubishi Materials in 2016, while others, dissatisfied with the terms of settlement, are considering further legal action.

With the emergent pressure to shift the legal frontier to the jurisdiction of the victims, the 2007 Japanese Supreme Court decision may thus not be the end of the legal redress movement, as many have suggested. Furthermore, by highlighting how South Korean and Chinese courts had previously refused to hear their cases for decades, the jurisdictional shift to victim nations ironically makes public how the victim nations had been complicit in silencing the victims. Similar to the Chinese government in 1972, the South Korean government in 1965 had renounced reparation claims from Japan in exchange for development assistance and economic cooperation. Today's regional conflicts over the "history problem" can be traced significantly to how East Asian states prioritized economic recovery and development while actively avoiding dealing with their complex pasts. In this historical context, the newly emerging legal frontier in victim jurisdictions signals a sharp turning point not only for Japan's post-imperial reckoning but also for South Korean and Chinese post-colonial reckoning.

The most recent developments in South Korea are unsettling the entire region at a magnitude unseen in recent years. On October 30, 2018, the South Korean Supreme Court ordered a leading Japanese steel company, Nippon Steel & Sumitomo Metal Corporation, to pay a cash settlement to each of the four South Korean plaintiffs. This historic decision is a watershed moment in the decades-long transnational legal redress movement in East Asia. The South Korean Supreme Court ruling, along with anticipated rulings on other slave labor cases scheduled in the same court, is jolting the region, pressuring not only the Japanese but also the South Korean and Chinese governments to reconsider their long-held positions that they had renounced reparation claims against Japan. Business communities are also scrambling to gauge this new development, while victims of Japanese imperial violence in both South Korea and China are invigorated by this ruling —not only those who participated in lawsuits filed within Japan in the past two decades but also those who had never considered such recourse until now.

At first glance, it may appear that, through this jurisdictional shift, the transnational legal redress movement has finally achieved a form of justice that they had sought over two decades, defying the 2007 Japanese Supreme Court decision that rejected the victims' claims. Yet far from giving a sense of closure, these new developments are exposing new terrains of historical accountability, with implications far beyond the responsibilities of the Japanese government and corporations alone. For example, South Korean corporations that benefited from the 1965 economic development package from Japan, in lieu of compensation for victims, are now implicated in the deferred imperial reckoning, and some in South Korea demand that these corporations join the Japanese in paying compensation for the victims. A number of South Korean victims have filed lawsuits against the South Korean government for having prevented them for decades from pursuing redress within the South Korean jurisdiction. The former chief justice of the South Korean Supreme Court was arrested in January 2019 for delaying the processing of the slave labor cases filed since 2012 at the request of then President Park Geun-hye, a daughter of Park Chung-hee, the former president and a collaborator with imperial Japan, and who signed the 1965 Treaty with Japan. Meanwhile, while watching how the recent events are opening a Pandora's box in South Korea, the Chinese government is conspicuously quiet, and its own slave labor case, once "accepted" in the Beijing lower court in 2014, remains "shelved" indefinitely.

The recent turn of events, in the form of a jurisdictional shift to victim nations, is thus calling into question these original moments of "settling accounts" in 1965 and 1972 that prioritized the wealth of nations over compensating individual victims.

(For)given time, the structure of silencing built on the economy of debt, is being challenged. In so doing, these developments have exposed the entangled processes of deimperialization and decolonization that led to decades of abandonment of the victims. The recent jurisdictional shift, therefore, demands a new accounting for inaction and abandonment in the legal, political, and economic spheres that has deferred imperial reckoning.

These new developments put East Asian cases at the forefront of a renewed reckoning through legal means between former empires and their colonies decades after the formal dissolution of empires. The cases involving former European imperial powers have taken place within the former perpetrator nation's jurisdictions or third-country jurisdictions such as US courts—examples include Britain's recent compensation paid to victims of the Kenyan Mau Mau Uprising following the 2013 ruling in a the London High Court, which in turn ignited the Caribbean nations' initiative to seek slavery compensation also in London; the Dutch government's apology, following the 2011 ruling in the Hague, to Indonesian victims of a massacre; and the ongoing class action lawsuit filed in 2017 in a New York district court by Namibian victims against Germany for apology and reparation for colonial violence.

In this larger context, where belated legal redress is reshaping relations between former empires and their colonies, the expanded scope of historical accountability in the victim jurisdictions in East Asia signals an emerging new frontier for imperial reckoning. The East Asian cases thus foreshadow the landscape of responsibility for the current generations, those of us who have no choice but to inherit losses incurred through imperialism, colonialism, and war.

Notes

*   An earlier and more extended version of this chapter was first published as "Between the Law: The Unmaking of Empire and Law's Imperial Amnesia," *Law & Social Inquiry*, vol. 41, no. 2 (Spring 2016): 402–34. Field research in China and Japan over the last fifteen-plus years was made possible by the generosity of the Chinese plaintiffs, Japanese lawyers, Chinese lawyers, and advocates and activists who allowed me to participate in and observe their involvement in the transnational legal redress movements. I would also like to thank the National Endowment for the Humanities, Japan-U.S. Friendship Commission, Association for Asian Studies Northeast Asia Council, and Hunter College for their financial support for my field research in China and Japan. Any views, findings, conclusions, or recommendations expressed in this article do not necessarily reflect those of the National Endowment for the Humanities or the Japan-U.S. Friendship Commission, or those of the Association for Asian Studies. My gratitude also goes to Waseda University in Japan for library access, and, for institutional support, to the People's Law Office in Tokyo, the University of Tokyo Interfaculty Initiative in Information Studies, Hunter College of the City University of New York, and fellowships at the Cogut Center for the Humanities and the Department of East Asian Studies at Brown University, the Harvard Academy for International and Area Studies at Harvard University, and the Program in Law and Public Affairs at Princeton University.

1   For an overview of the mobilization of Chinese slave laborers, see Nishinarita Yutaka, *Chūgokujin kyōsei renkō* (Tokyo Daigaku shuppankai, 2002). In English, see Paul H. Kratoska, ed., *Asian Labor in the Wartime Japanese Empire: Unknown Histories* (Armonk, NY: M. E. Sharpe, 2005). He Tianyi, a local Chinese historian in Shijiazhuan, where many Chinese peasants were rounded up to be shipped to work in Japan and elsewhere (some were enslaved in the Japanese puppet state Manchukuo in Northeast China), organized a project to collect oral histories of surviving victims in the early 2000s. For edited narratives from this project, see He Tianyi, ed., *Erzhan lu Ri Zhongguo laogong koushushi*, 5 vols. (Jinan, China: Qilu shushe, 2005).

2   Both the Japanese government and the Supreme Commander of the Allied Powers (which occupied Japan after the Second World War between 1945 and 1952) had growing concerns about the labor movements emerging as a result of coalitions between the Chinese, particularly CCP members, and the Japanese laborers in occupied Japan. It became in their respective interest to repatriate the Chinese, which took place from October 9 to December 11, 1945. In this period, 10,924 Chinese were sent back by the Nihon Senpaku, and 19,686 by the US-manned Landing Ships, Tank (LSTs).

3   Even the economic history of postwar Japan told through the lens of the labor movement has predominantly been told through the lens of *postwar*, with a notable lack of labor issues related to the Japanese Empire although labor unions played significant roles in bringing to light the wartime slave labor issues. For example, Andrew Gordon's exploration of the labor history of Nippon Kōkan (NKK), which was one of the Japanese corporations that enslaved the largest number of Koreans during the war, in *Wages of Affluence: Labor and Management in Postwar Japan* (Cambridge, MA: Harvard University Press, 2009), is framed within Japan's postwar. As a result, the framework of post-imperial is missing in his otherwise insightful analysis, with a notable absence of the afterlife of Korean enslavement, including the lawsuit filed in Tokyo on September 30, 1991, by one of the victims, which reached a settlement on April 6, 1999. A notable exception is Tanaka Hiroshi, an economic historian of Japan, who has exposed the post-imperial aspect of postwar Japanese economic history. See, for example, Tanaka Hiroshi, Utsumi Aiko, and Ishitobi Jin, eds., *Shiryō Chūgokujin kyōsei renkō* (Akashi shoten, 1987). As I discuss elsewhere, postwar labor relations at these affected corporate sites were as much postwar labor relations as post-imperial labor relations.

4   Heisei 12 (wa) No. 1550; Heisei 13 (wa) No. 1690; Heisei 13 (wa) No. 3862, April 26, 2002, written by Kimura Motoaki, Miyao Naoko, and Kushihashi Sayaka. The Japanese government and Mitsui Mining Corporation appealed, and Fukuoka High Court overturned the lower court decision on May 24, 2004 (Heisei 14 [ne] No. 511).

5   Article 724 of the Civil Code defines the twenty-year statute of limitations. When the Fukuoka case was filed in 2000, fifty-five years had already passed since the end of the Japanese Empire in 1945.

6   Gaimushō Kanrikyoku, *Kajin rōmusha shūrō jijō chōsa hōkokusho* (Diplomatic Record Office of the Ministry of Foreign Affairs of Japan, 1946) and *Kajin rōmusha shūrō tenmatsu hōkoku (yōshi)* (Diplomatic Record Office of the Ministry of Foreign Affairs of Japan, 1946).

7   Gaimushō kanrikyoku, *Kajin rōmusha shūrō jijō chōsa hōkokusho*.

8   Gaimushō kanrikyoku, *Kajin rōmusha shūrō tenmatsu hōkoku (yōshi)*.

9   Part of the 1946 archives became public through a Japanese public television program broadcast on August 14, 1993 (NHK Special, "Maboroshino gaimushō hōkokusho:

Chūgokujin kyōsei renkō no kiroku"), which was later published in book form
under the same title. See NHK Research Team, *Maboroshino gaimushō hōkokusho:
Chūgokujin kyōsei renkō no kiroku* (Nihon hōsō shuppan kyōkai, 1994). While
this public disclosure failed to have much traction at that time, it resulted in the
reproduction of the original archival materials. See Tanaka Hiroshi and Matsuzawa
Tetsunari, eds., *Chūgokujin kyōsei renkō shiryō: 'Gaimuhō hōkokusho' zen 5 bunsatsu
hoka)* (Gendai shokan, 1995). On the background of this government archive, see
Tanaka Hiroshi, Utsumi Aiko, and Ishitobi Jin, eds., *Shiryō Chūgokujin kyōsei renkō;*
and Tanaka Hiroshi, Utsumi Aiko, and Nīimi Takashi, eds., *Shiryō Chūgokujin kyōsei
renkō no kiroku.*

10 See Gaimushō kanrikyoku, *Kajin rōmusha shūrō tenmatsu hōkoku (yōshi)*, vol. 3,
    pp. 59–61.

11 It should be noted that my usage of the term "inverted compensation," which
    suggests an inversion of the common-sense logic of compensation, is a moral one.
    Historically, there are other cases of inverted compensation. For example, Haiti was
    required to pay 150 million francs as compensation for France and slave owners at its
    independence. Similarly, British slave owners received a total of 20 million pounds
    sterling when colonial slavery was abolished in 1833, as detailed in Nicholas Draper,
    *The Price of Emancipation: Slaver-ownership, Compensation and British Society at the
    End of Slavery* (New York: Cambridge University Press, 2010).

12 Gaimushō Kanrikyoku, *Taiheiyō sensō shūketsu ni yoru naigai jin hogo hikiage
    (gaikokujin)* (Diplomatic Record Office of the Ministry of Foreign Affairs of Japan,
    1952–1972).

13 The Chinese plaintiffs' lawyers submitted a set of these internal notes to the Fukuoka
    High Court on November 28, 2003 (Heisei 14 [ne] No. 511, Evidence No. Kō 163–46,
    51–57). The submitted memos are from the file entitled "Repatriation of Remains/
    Chinese" (Gaimushō Kanbō Sōmuka File No. 0120–2001).

14 The San Francisco Peace Treaty exempted Japan from reparations except as
    regarded the transfer of its overseas assets and compensation for POWs through the
    International Committee of the Red Cross.

15 The Chinese renunciation of reparation claims in the Communiqué was prefaced
    by and framed within the proclamation of Japanese responsibility for Chinese losses
    sustained during the war, effectively presenting China's waiver as a generous gift to
    Japan. The preamble of the Joint Communiqué of the Government of Japan and the
    Government of the People's Republic of China states that "the Japanese side is keenly
    conscious of the responsibility for the serious damage that Japan caused in the past
    to the Chinese people through war, and deeply reproaches itself." Having said that,
    article five of the Communiqué reads: "The Government of the People's Republic
    of China declares that in the interest of the friendship between the Chinese and the
    Japanese peoples, it renounces its demand for war reparation from Japan." By linking
    its renunciation of reparation claims to the promise of good deeds in the future ("in
    the interest of the friendship between the Chinese and the Japanese peoples"), the
    Chinese side expresses its expectation for reciprocity from the Japanese government,
    in the form of a return gift of "friendship" built on a "deep" sense of repentance.

16 Marcel Mauss, *The Gift: The Form and Reason for Exchange in Archaic Societies*, trans.
    W. D. Halls (New York: W. W. Norton, 1990 [1924]).

17 On the role of time in gift relations, see Jacques Derrida, *Given Time: I. Counterfeit
    Money*, trans. Peggy Kamuf (Chicago: University of Chicago Press, 1991), chs 1 and 2.

18 The Japanese government's announcement in 2007 of its plan to end ODA to China triggered an explosion of heated discussions in China, highlighting this enigmatic location of Japanese ODA in relation to Japanese moral debt to China. See, for example, Cao Haidong and Huang Xiaowei, "Riben dui hua yuanzhu san shi nian, *Nanfang zhoumo*," February 20, 2008. Available online: http://www.infzm.com/content/7707, accessed June 28, 2019.

19 Heisei 16 (ju) No. 1658, written by Nakagawa Ryōji, Imai Isao, and Furuta Yūki. For an overview of the Supreme Court decision in English, see Mark A. Levin, "Supreme Court of Japan Decision 2008/04/27: *Nishimatsu Construction Co. v. Song Jixiao et al.*," *American Journal of International Law* 102 (2008), pp. 148–154. While this Supreme Court decision concerned a forced-labor compensation case originally filed in Hiroshima, often referred to as the Nishimatsu case (as it involved Nishimatsu Construction Company), the Court used it as the basis for dismissing the appeals filed in the Fukuoka and other related cases on the same day.

20 See Draper, *The Price of Emancipation*.

21 See the South Korean Constitutional Court decision, 23–2[A] KCCR 366, *2006Hun-Ma788*, August 30, 2011, which recognized the individual rights to claim compensation in the so-called comfort women cases. Similar to the 1972 Joint Communiqué between PRC and Japan, the South Korean government renounced its right to claim reparation from Japan in exchange for future economic co-operation arrangements in the 1965 Treaty on Basic Relations between Japan and the Republic of Korea.

The landmark decision by the Supreme Court of Korea on May 24, 2012 (*2009Da22549*) echoed the 2011 South Korean Constitutional Court decision in recognizing the individual rights to claim compensation from Japan and remanded the lower court case against Mitsubishi Heavy Industries (Busan High Court decision *2007Na4288*, February 3, 2009) involved in the wartime use of forced labor. Following this Supreme Court decision, on July 10, 2013, the Seoul High Court ordered Nippon Steel & Sumitomo Metal Corporation (former Nippon Steel Corporation, which merged with Sumitomo Metal Industries in October 2012) to pay 100 million Korean won each to the four plaintiffs for the wartime use of forced labor. On July 30, 2013, the Busan High Court ordered Mitsubishi Heavy Industry to pay 80 million won each to the five plaintiffs. In addition to these cases remanded by the 2012 Supreme Court decision, the decision prompted other cases to be filed against Japanese corporations. Of those new cases, the Gwangju District Court was the first one to rule on November 1, 2013. The court ordered Mitsubishi Heavy Industries Ltd. to pay 150 million won each in compensation to four surviving Korean women who were enslaved during the war and 80 million won to the bereaved family of the two victims.

22 Through a conflict-of-laws approach, Karen Knop and Annelise Riles elucidate the heterogeneity of legal time that has played out in the South Korean comfort women case. They show how shifts in jurisdictions bring to the fore uneven terrains of temporalities. See Karen Knop and Annelise Riles, "Space, Time, and Historical Injustice: A Feminist Conflict-of-Laws Approach to the 'Comfort Women' Agreement," *Cornell Law Review*, vol. 102, issue 4 (2017), pp. 853–928.

Chapter 10

JAPAN, CHEMICAL WARFARE, AND ŌKUNOSHIMA: A POSTWAR OVERVIEW

Arnaud Doglia

From 1927 until 1944, the Japanese island of Ōkunoshima—forty-three miles southeast of the city of Hiroshima, in the Seto Inland Sea—was the main production site of toxic gas, deployed by the Imperial Japanese Army (IJA) during the Second World War. A large number of citizens, schoolchildren, volunteers, and conscripts, were employed in manufacturing these substances. Exposed to toxic fumes, many were left incapacitated or dead in the years following 1945. Taking into account the wider background of the Japanese chemical arsenal, this chapter seeks to examine the sanitation and transformation process of the island after the empire's collapse as well as the fate of the workers throughout postwar Japan. These people were the first victims of the chemical munitions developed by their own country, and the analysis of their discourse will highlight the emergence of counter-narrative memories, from the initial difficulties they faced in being acknowledged to the unexploded ordnances that have plagued the Japanese landscape for over seventy years.

At the beginning of the Second Sino-Japanese War (1937–1945), Japan was manufacturing ten different varieties of gas, color-codenamed after the German model to maintain secrecy due to the illegality of the first use of chemical warfare.[1] Immediately following surrender in 1945, the disposal of such weapons temporarily became an utmost military priority. Starting with the destruction of official documents attesting to the existence of the program, substances throughout the empire were hurriedly disposed of in a manner that would come to haunt the postwar lives of not only the Japanese population but also that of East Asia to a large extent.

Fearing American air raids, both army and navy headquarters had split factories and warehouses all over the archipelago in 1944. A consequence of this measure was that from Hokkaido in the north to Kumamoto in the south, an array of volumes of canisters, projectiles, loaded bombs, and barrels filled with toxic gas were thrown away at sea or buried hastily without any form of logistical command. By way of illustration, the navy secretly disposed of 2,000 sixty-kilo bombs in two days in Aomori Prefecture, desperate to avoid prosecution following the arrival of the Americans.[2] Testimonies also recount individual initiatives, taken locally by officers who feared being caught with illegal weapons. The lack of documents detailing the precise location of gas disposal sites thus became a critical issue in the immediate demilitarization of Japan as well as for the future of the region, and it remains so to this day.

Likewise, indiscriminate burial and dumping at sea was well under way on Ōkunoshima. Under the terms of the occupation of Japan, the Chūgoku and Shikoku areas of the country fell under the provisional administration utmost until December 31, 1945 utmost of the 10th Army Corps (composed of the 24th and 41st Divisions) of the 6th Army of the United States Armed Forces in the Pacific (USAFPAC), originally stationed in the Philippines. Headquarters were established on October 6, 1945, in the city of Kure, thirty kilometers from the island. Ten days later, the discovery of 1,844 gas masks in the Ujima district of Hiroshima City by Chemical Service Platoon 273 (41st Division) sparked the interest of the Americans. The finding was followed by a tip-off from a Japanese major, who voluntarily provided a full list, complete with locations, of army chemical materials in the Tadanoumi area.[3] On October 26, with the military occupation of the region well under way, a large stock of smoke grenades was discovered.

As early as 1941, the United States had knowledge of the existence of Japan's chemical arsenal, but the exact location of the factories and warehouses, as well as of the scope of the program, were unspecified. The first concrete discovery of gas weapons by the Americans was that of the Japanese Navy, when on September 5, 1945, troops from the 11th Airborne Unit visited the Sagami factory.[4] However, it was only following the occupation of the Ōkunoshima area that the Americans started to realize the extent of the task ahead of them. In Tadanoumi, over 1.5 million shells and smoke grenades were discovered, along with 72,600 liters of sulfur mustard (yperite).[5] On neighboring Awashima, 3,657,789 cartridges containing vomiting agents and smoke grenades were awaiting disposal. On Ōkunoshima, a "mere" 21,249 vomiting gas-filled bombs, smoke grenades, and candles were discovered, but the 4,422 tons of raw chemicals—including 3,240 tons of ready-to-use prussic acid, lewisite, yperite, and sulfuric acid—were of more immediate concern.[6] Another 1.6 million shells of varying volumes and levels of toxicity lay waiting for the Americans in the Sone factory.[7] The sheer amount of substances exposed necessitated the dispatch of reinforcements to assist Platoon 273, in the form of the 58th Chemical Warfare General Service Company.

The United States' landing on Ōkunoshima was originally a source of concern to the Allied forces. In the early days following American arrival, complete surrender and collaboration were not taken for granted, and Washington feared acts of resistance, particularly so in an area where illicit weapons were still stored. Yet the actual occupation of the island seems to have taken place in a calm and peaceful manner, albeit in an initial climate of mutual suspicion. Testimonies mention troops distributing chocolate to girls who had stayed on the island, the latter refusing the treats for fear of being poisoned. More consequentially, demobilized technicians, dreading arrest and trial, burned as many documents as they could and lied significantly about the quantities of substances left on Ōkunoshima, thus complicating the removal task.[8]

The situation was made even worse by the unwillingness of Tokyo to provide occupation forces with logistical information. For fear of reprisals and charges, the vast majority of incriminating documents had already been burned, and authorities in the capital struggled to minimize the accusations. The Japanese notably introduced a subtle differentiation between lethal and non-lethal substances. A document passed to the Americans as late as December 1945 explained that the Imperial General Headquarters (*Daihon'ei*) had never sanctioned the use of chemical warfare, because no plans were ever devised to deploy deadly weapons (blood agents and blister agents). Fumigants, vomiting, and lachrymatory agents simply did not qualify as toxic gas *stricto sensu*. Moreover, the Japanese admitted that the Narashino Army School had provided chemical warfare-related training but not to use the weapons on the battlefield.[9]

Once solely in charge, the American occupation forces started planning the demilitarization and sanitization of the Ōkunoshima area. The original strategy was to fill a tanker with 3,000 tons of lewisite and yperite—the two most dangerous substances—through a giant pipeline, before scuttling the ship in the Bingonada Sea, off the Ehime Prefecture's coast. Other ready-to-use substances, such as diphenylcyanoarsine, were to be disposed of at sea immediately south of the island. However, American hopes for prompt disposals were short lived. The Japanese military had mined the whole Seto Sea from Kure to Kobe, and to sanitize the island, the entire area had to be demined. [10]

The process, to be carried out by Japanese ships, was itself postponed by the discovery of more chemical weapons outside of Ōkunoshima. On October 17, 1945, the Americans were informed of a further logistical nightmare: 8,254 sixty-kilo yperite-loaded bombs belonging to the Japanese navy had been discovered in eastern Hiroshima, Kure, and Etashima.[11] Disposal was immediately organized. The weapons found in Etashima were transported by sea for disposal through the Bungo channel, recently demined. However, three days later, the existence of another stock of 1,548 bombs was revealed, and left intact for lack of logistical capability. The same fate awaited the 6,655 devices found in Kure. In early December, ammunitions exposed in Hiroshima were charged onto a train to Miyajima, where they would be loaded onto a ship and be disposed of at sea. However, due to the inadequacy of port infrastructure, the bombs were also returned to their original location.[12]

The impending handover of the administration of Southern Honshū and Shikoku to the British Commonwealth Occupation Force (BCOF) was planned for February 1946, and Washington demobilized the 41st Division on December 31, 1945. All remaining chemicals and weapons in the zone were left intact for the BCOF to dispose of. In January 1946, chemical components aside, Ōkunoshima was still home to over 3,000 tons of lewisite and yperite as well as several thousand loaded items of ammunition and grenades. Australian forces in charge of the area did not possess the Americans' expertise in chemical warfare and could not count on Japanese help either, since the 6th Army's first measure upon arrival had been the demobilization of all imperial armed forces in the area. The sanitization of the island—dubbed "Operation Lewisite"—therefore had to be completed by Japanese civilians, with American equipment, under BCOF command.

The original plan to first dump manufactured gases into the Pacific Ocean, south of Kōchi Prefecture and subsequently incinerate and demolish the remaining structures on the island was expected to take three years to complete.[13] Removal resumed on May 27, 1946, and all bombs and ammunitions remaining on neighboring islands were centralized on Ōkunoshima. Between June and November, Japanese citizens—under the direct supervision of Major W. E. Williamson of the United States' 8th Army Chemical Corps—in six months disposed of several thousands of tons of lewisite and yperite on ships scuttled into the Philippines Sea. Over 10,000 tons of toxic smoke canisters were hastily buried and flooded with supertropical bleach in concrete tunnels throughout Ōkunoshima.

Non-lethal components also had to be disposed of. The facility still hosted an estimated 300 million yen-worth of chemical resources as well as precious metals coveted by local industries. [14] While scrap gold and silver were sent by the BCOF to the Osaka Mint Bureau, firms started applying to occupation authorities for the acquisition of raw material, a policy encouraged by the Allies to foster economic rebuilding and commodities production.[15] Unused chemicals were to be converted into "peaceful," technologically advanced products. Throughout the country, Takeda and other medical and pharmaceutical conglomerates were given access to former military chemical facilities at competitive prices, for the sake of economic growth.[16] This mirrors the same sort of trade off that Yukiko Koga talks about in her Chapter 9. A portion of the Sone plant was acquired by industrial explosives manufacturer Nippon Kayaku for storage purposes.[17]

With factories operating in Hiroshima Prefecture as early as 1922, the Teikoku Rayon Company (*Teijin*) was ideally located to take the upper hand in the vicinity of Ōkunoshima. The firm was originally interested in developing salt production along the coastline of Mihara, but enticed by potential acquisition of chemical components, it rapidly moved to diversify its manufacturing activities to include dried foods, sweets, saccharin, synthetic sake, and, above all, a *sairōmu*-based (potassium cyanide) pesticide, *Tejiron*. In June 1946, the corporation and its subsidiaries provided Allied authorities with civilian personnel to complete the entire sanitation of the island, in exchange for unrestricted access to raw components such as 2-nitronaphthalene, phenacyl chloride, and, most importantly, potassium cyanide.[18]

An additional workforce was hired regionally to tackle the enormous task ahead. However, contrary to the belief that the end of the war would improve working conditions on the island, Teijin staff and auxiliary workers were often worse off during the disposal process than ever before. Certainly, Japanese *gendarmerie* (*kempeitai*) surveillance and child labor had been abolished.[19] But the 846 new intakes, slow and unskilled, were exposed to stringent conditions.[20] Forced to sleep on the island and working without any protective wear, they sometimes toiled day and night to handle potentially deadly chemicals. The corporation allegedly provided "gas-protection instruction," but testimonies routinely mention serious casualties and even fatalities for workers loading ships with ninety-kilo yperite bombs. [21] Flamethrowers used to disinfect laboratories equally resulted in severe wounds. Notwithstanding Williamson's lewisite poisoning, over 800 injuries were caused by mishandling, deficient logistics, or leaking pipes following a typhoon.[22]

Upon decontamination in May 1947, Ōkunoshima was handed back to the Japanese government, with Teijin granted operational rights on the island through a subsidiary company created three months later, Kunoshima sangyō. Local hopes of burying the island's tormented past were, however, very brief. In May 1948, despite local opposition, occupation authorities again requisitioned the site, this time as an ammunition storage and disposal facility. Kunoshima sangyō—whose production of *Teijiron* and lead hydrogen arsenate was being supplanted by the mass introduction of DDT—was forced to relocate to the neighboring town of Mihara, and until 1951, Japanese citizens were once more sent to work on Ōkunoshima. Beyond the scope of subcontracted Teijin employees, recruitment also took place through the local Public Employment Security Office. Jobs included the incineration of toxic containers and materials as well as the collection of metal canisters throughout the island, both resulting in several cases of explosions and burns inflicted by residues.[23] Washington wished to keep the island under its control to establish a military surveillance base, but the stakes were too high for the local population, with over 10,000 Japanese citizens actively opposing the decision. Among them, fishing communities were fighting to maintain their right to work in the area, and Ōkunoshima was officially returned to Japan in 1957.[24]

In the context of postwar reconstruction and economic growth, former Ōkunoshima laborers represented a special category of wartime victims. Unlike the majority of veterans and mobilized workers, they were both victims of wounds inflicted by their own country, and perpetrators who had contributed to Japanese aggression with the deployment of weapons of mass destruction throughout East Asia. Their situation is an interesting example of the plurality of localized wartime and postwar narratives, as I will show in the following section.

Competing for victim status, recognition, and compensations

In the 1950s, Japan's predominant image of itself was that of a victim country united in defeat. As a rule, any atrocity perpetrated by the military could only be discussed in relation to the suffering inflicted upon the Japanese people. On December 9, 1952, politician Furuya Sadao commented at the Diet on the International Military Tribunal for the Far East (Tokyo Trials) verdicts:

> It is absolutely unacceptable for us, Japanese citizens, that war criminals could be judged for minor crimes compared to the worst atrocities committed in history in Hiroshima and Nagasaki.[25]

It was impossible for a "cultured, peace-loving nation" to perceive itself solely as a perpetrator.[26] The memory of the atomic bombs was so potent that it eclipsed sufferers from other countries where war crimes had been committed, along with regional casualties and their "hidden" history. The victims of Ōkunoshima tried to (re)open the debate on Japan's participation in the Second World War as an aggressor, but their narrative went against that of a victimized country. Studies on war trauma and the constitution of memories tend to indicate that throughout the world, social groups experience their relation to the past according to rivalry and not complementarity.[27] Similarly, whereas victims are often turned into heroes or martyrs in the commemorative process, the situation of Ōkunoshima veterans was specifically problematic because the role of perpetrator they played in manufacturing chemical weapons prevented them from accessing the status of victim.[28]

The geographical localization of the former workers in Hiroshima Prefecture resulted in an inevitable form of memory competition:

> In comparison with Hiroshima victims who campaigned for the abolition of atomic weapons, almost all victims of chemical weapons kept quiet after 1945. All have endured terrible suffering, but the atomic bomb survivors (*hibakusha*) have denounced nuclear warfare and the horrors of war, whereas the survivors of the island have faded into obscurity. There is a huge difference between "the harm that we suffered because of atomic weapons" and "chemical weapons that we used." The Japanese government acknowledged "the harm we suffered," but not the "use of chemical warfare."[29]

Throughout the nation, war veterans were building narratives to make sense of the conflict. Together with discourses of atomic victimhood, 1950s popular magazines and publishers circulated heroic testimonies of the battlefield (*senkimono*), printed tales of bravery or nostalgia, to try and give meaning to the countless Japanese casualties.[30] However, documents authenticating chemical warfare were scarce, making memories of yperite and phosgene intangible, excluding them from the newly formed discourses on the past.

Any mention of suffering in the entire prefecture could only be related to the woes of the *hibakusha*, a narrative accepted nationwide and beyond. In a context of "national victimology," the experience of Hiroshima anchored the image of a defeated nation, whose memories had been nationalized.[31, 32] The trauma of chemical warfare, refuted by the Japanese government, did not belong to the realm of war memories. Even from a scientific perspective, cooperation between medical specialists of Ōkunoshima and Hiroshima victims did not commence before 1980.[33]

In the eyes of the general public, the Tokyo Trials, adjourned in 1948, had punished those responsible for making Japan plunge into total war. With very few mentions and even fewer convictions, gas warfare was passed over in silence.[34] Not a single physician or scientist was tried for the crimes committed. All men involved with Japanese biological warfare were given amnesty by the Americans (and the Soviets) in exchange for the data collected during the experiments they conducted. Since chemical warfare was intricately linked to biological weapons, the American investigation on chemical weapons—conducted by Colonel Thomas Morrow—swept the crimes under the rug, and the topic was never seriously brought up at the Tokyo Trials.

It was only at the beginning of the 1950s that the first Ōkunoshima victims began to assemble. Originally, the presence of occupation forces and biological warfare-related censorship made claims for redress impossible. More significantly, the delayed impact of toxic substances on the human body was to make the legacy of Ōkunoshima drag on for another forty years. Superficial wounds suffered during the manufacturing process had been treated throughout the war, but deeper physical sequelae from gas exposure only became evident several years later. Ailments started to develop as late as a decade after the end of the conflict. In August 1952, a man who had become completely voiceless, suffering severe respiratory problems, was transferred from Tadanoumi to the University Hospital of Hiroshima where he died twelve days later. An autopsy revealed cancer the size of a baby's fist had developed in his lungs.[35]

All over the area, former workers were left incapacitated and breathless, plagued by asthmatic coughs and abnormal fatigue. Physicians were unable to diagnose the reasons behind their suffering. A number of staff, notably nurses sent to help in the city of Hiroshima immediately after the explosion of the American bomb, were diagnosed with radiation sickness before the effects of chemical weapons on their bodies were discovered. However, those second-degree irradiated (*nyūhibakusha*) aside, the majority of former workers were neither conventional war victims nor had they been exposed to atomic radiation.[36]

Between 1945 and 1955, more than ten incidents took place across Japan involving explosions caused by chemical weapons hidden or abandoned by the military, and the list only grew over time. In July 1950, eleven fishermen were wounded in Tokushima Prefecture by a canister containing yperite. The following year, although only recognized as such in 2003, the first official fatalities took place in the city of Chōshi (Chiba Prefecture and again in 1953.[37] Shells filled with gas injured fourteen members of the Japanese Self-Defense Forces. Similar incidents followed in Kanagawa, Fukuoka, Shizuoka, and Osaka. Between 1955 and 1972, over eighty people were wounded nationwide.[38] In 1955, the Japan Maritime Self-Defense Forces threw fifty-six tons of toxic or explosive ammunition into the sea.[39] Unexploded ordnances were equally discovered on land and offshore in Chiba, where thirty people had suffered severe burns after the explosion of a device found in the nets of a fishing boat.[40] As late as 1983, 300 loaded hand grenades were exposed in Chigasaki, Kanagawa Prefecture.[41]

For fear of consequences, most Ōkunoshima victims refused to disclose information on their prior duties. They had been sworn to secrecy by the *kempeitai* military police, and the end of the war did nothing to break their silence. Social stigma equally played a significant part, as direct contact with gas had left many with indelible body stains or a permanently blackened face.[42] Incapable of offering proper diagnosis, medical experts under the direction of Wada Sunao (University of Hiroshima) distributed surveys among families, asking for identification of 210 former workers and colleagues throughout the summer of 1952. Cross-referencing ultimately encouraged others to open up; 1,632 victims, all male, were originally listed.[43] The case became a priority at the University of Hiroshima and on October 25, the first official report was published. Among Ōkunoshima personnel who had not died of natural causes, the vast majority of causes of death were imputed to cancer of the throat or lungs, or to respiratory difficulties.

In 1952, the first movement of *hibakusha* was created in the city of Hiroshima with the purpose of obtaining compensation for damages from the United States.[44] Inspired by this initiative, in April of the same year, five former workers founded the Association of Mutual Help for the Victims of Toxic Gas of Ōkunoshima, asking Tokyo for compensation. The very survival of the association was initially critical, as numbers gradually dwindled without proper treatment and financial support. Upon mutual identification, their numbers grew to over fifty members in a matter of months.[45] Among survivors, hopes were high of achieving state recognition and pecuniary compensation, since the vast majority had contracted debts. Some were even forced to sell their furniture and clothes to pay for American imported drugs.[46] Local care was unsurprisingly inadequate. The old, wooden structure of the Tadanoumi hospital—a former *kempeitai* quarters—had a leaky roof, no equipment to speak of, and remained run down until its partial renovation in 1964.[47]

With the help of their parliamentary representative, the Association of Mutual Help tried to pass a draft to formalize help for the victims. Recognition was within reach in late 1952, but the project was ultimately rejected by the Diet. The majority of representatives refused to admit that toxic gas had been manufactured, and consequently denied the existence of victims.[48] Later that year, a "Document on Special Measures to Help Overcome the Difficulties of Gas Victims" was presented at the Japanese Diet; but it was only a temporary victory for the plaintiffs, for two reasons. First, the document stipulated that veterans acknowledged as victims have their treatment paid for in the form of a pension, with a lump sum paid to the families of the deceased. Yet to benefit from this measure, former workers had to produce administrative proof of past employment on the island; measures of respiratory capacity and chest X-rays were insufficient. As most official documents regarding Ōkunoshima had been destroyed in 1945, their claims were almost impossible to substantiate.[49] Second, the ambiguous wording of the draft further confirmed Tokyo's refusal to acknowledge the existence of its chemical warfare program. The generic terms of "gas" in use throughout the text, without information clarifying its exact nature, or "difficulties" instead of "wounds," denied veterans the expected national recognition.

Moreover, this special measure only encompassed a portion of the former workers—30 people in 1954 and ultimately 202 people in 1964.[50] Teenagers forced to work on the island during the war were not included in the pension scheme; they had not received any wages and therefore did not technically qualify for financial aid or treatment. Compensation would take another twenty years, and the same applied to auxiliary personnel who sanitized the island after 1945. In 1954, former workers received additional temporary financial assistance through the "Act for Special Measures for Former Conscripts." This motion further exemplified Tokyo's obstinate denial of its responsibilities. First reserved for army veterans, compensation was granted at prefectural level, extended to Ōkunoshima workers for an additional period of three years by the Hiroshima local government.

This tale of victimhood and the quest for redress was at odds with the national narrative of the 1960s, marked by popular enthusiasm for the upcoming Olympic Games in 1964. In the context of Japan's symbolic return to the international community, an August 15, 1964, *Yomiuri shimbun* article summarized the general climate at the time:

> The war ended nineteen years ago. Last year, the United States, the United Kingdom and the Soviet Union signed the Partial Nuclear Test Ban Treaty, and because Japan decided to adopt the treaty at the end of July, war commemorations are marked by a brighter ambiance. It feels as if peace has been resurrected. This year's Olympic Games reinforce this feeling, and war memories gradually seem more distant.[51]

This "passion for peace" equally had repercussions locally. In a move to get rid once and for all of this disturbing symbol of Japan's aggression, the neighboring city of Takehara formally requested that Ōkunoshima change status. In 1960, the island was transferred from the tutelage of the Ministry of Finance to that of the Ministry of Welfare, and was to be turned into a holiday resort, at a cost of 540 million yen. Although the responsibility for this transformation is usually ascribed to local authorities, it is interesting to note that the process took place under the patronage of the Prime Minister of Japan at the time, Ikeda Hayato, himself a native of Takehara.[52]

Dubbed "Sunset Island," Ōkunoshima was incorporated into the "National Park Resorts of Japan" cooperative, a nationwide cluster of nature-oriented resorts established by the Ministry of Welfare in 1961. The facility, opened in 1963 complete with hot springs, restaurants, hotels, and tennis courts, was integrated into the district of the National Park of the Seto Sea as a nature preserve. Between 1937 and 1945, Tokyo had successfully deleted the island from maps for secrecy purposes, and Japan's return to the international scene concurred with an attempt to erase local history by assigning it a new narrative. In a climate of economic and popular euphoria, the maneuver was a success: there were over 10,000 annual visits in 1987, and ten times more a decade later.[53]

Despite the island's reinvented image and function, the inextricable connection between Ōkunoshima and the trauma of chemical warfare never truly ceased. Facilities were sanitized, but only a portion of buildings pertaining to gas weapons could be physically demolished. Entry to deeper structures, tunnels, and former storage facilities—possibly containing undisposed-of toxic ammunition—was prohibited to visitors, and the main factory buildings had become part of the landscape. However, in spite of the repeated decontaminations of Ōkunoshima, large quantities of vomiting agent-filled canisters were discovered yet again on the island, notably in 1969 and 1972.[54] This was true not only of the Hiroshima area but also throughout the country. As oral war testimonies were fading away, the national scope of the institutionalization of imperial biological warfare was beginning to resurface to inflict concrete physical damage to the Japanese population and beyond. Japan had stopped producing chemical weapons but the consequences of chemical warfare remained tangible long after the Second World War. Still partially unresolved, the issue of compensation and the costs of healthcare pushed even more veterans and their families to regroup. Between the 1960s and the 1980s, nine more victims' associations came to existence in the area, representing schoolchildren, women, and conscripted individuals The number of former workers and their relatives engaged reached a total of over 3,000 in 1986. The struggle was not limited to compensation but also triggered the local emergence of social protest. Around Ōkunoshima alone, the Japan Maritime Self-Defense Force officially carried out the demining of the area surrounding the island in 1969; however, the extent to which discarding into the sea had taken place still prevented fisheries from exploiting the area.

In 1971, deprived of resources and income, four fishing industry trade unions presented the mayor of Hiroshima with a petition asking for the complete removal of explosives and toxic substances still buried at sea. The request went unheeded, but, more significantly, the continuity of the psychological and physical traces of the use of chemical weapons started gathering attention countrywide. This is notably the case of an article published in the May issue of *Literary Chronicle* (*Bungei shunjū*) in 1956: for the first time, a journalist from the capital traveled to the island to interview ailing survivors, publicly asking why their torment had not yet become a "central problem" in Japan.[55]

The interest of the medical community in the island was manifest from the start. The first scientific writings on the topic were published in 1957, and momentum increased throughout the 1960s.[56] In 1958, the issue was brought up by Wada at the International Conference of Thoracic Medicine in Tokyo and in 1963 at a symposium in New Delhi. In 1961, Wada and three colleagues launched the Ōkunoshima Toxic Gas Victims Research Group to establish diagnoses and bring help to the victims, eventually leading to financial and scientific collaboration with the American National Institute of Health in 1967. Between 1957 and 1969, the topic was discussed in a dozen scientific journals, and biannual research seminars continue to take place.[57]

The scientists' efforts became the catalyst that propelled Ōkunoshima to the national level. Between 1966 and 1967, the topic became a nationwide issue with a large-scale analysis of the former workers' living conditions. The study, financed by Hiroshima prefecture, identified 2,200 victims (1,440 men and 760 women), of whom 229 were already deceased.[58] Exposed over time to increasing media attention, the study played a vital part in the emergence of a nationwide debate, as Japanese newspapers began to lend an ear to Ōkunoshima workers. In January 1966, the *Asahi Journal* was one of the first weeklies to publish a feature story entitled "The Unfortunate Victims of Toxic Gas." The author portrayed life on the island until 1945 through a series of interviews and vivid descriptions of the former workers' afflictions, contrasting trauma with a depiction of the lavish holiday resort:

A few minutes on foot from the Tadanoumi hospital lies the harbor, where, for fifty yen, a steamboat takes you in fifteen minutes to Ōkunoshima. On the island are luxurious housing, thermal hot springs, a carting track, camping spots, a small steam train, fishing spots and even a jukebox. I went after peak season, and it was almost deserted. I am relieved that the new generation did not experience that time when, in spite of international laws, and under the surveillance of these demons of the *kempeitai*, chemical weapons were produced on the island.[59]

The story concluded with a synecdochic metaphor on war memories, trauma and economic growth, in which Ōkunoshima perfectly embodied the situation and experience of the whole country:

The last seventy years in the history of the island are a symbol of the history of Japan. Seventy years ago, there was only a modest fishing industry, and after the war, a society based on leisure developed. Between them, [the island] was occupied by the army. One can rejoice at the development of our economy, and the successes of the welfare state, but it will not change the fate of the victims of toxic gas. This situation concerns more than just the people of Tadanoumi, and the Japanese people as a whole should think about it.[60]

In the following decade, the impact of chemical warfare on Japan was still being debated in the press, eliciting a change of tone in the media as well as civil society. In 1970, a teacher from Hiroshima Prefecture, Taniguchi Masato, popularized the cause in local schools with slides and animated cartoons for children. Developed further in 1984, "The Young Boy and the Owl, a History of Ōkunoshima" was then turned into an animated film.[61] In an article published on March 22, 1970, the Hiroshima-based *Chūgoku shimbun* newspaper criticized the government's policy toward victims as too restrictive, citing that 217 people had seen their demands for help rejected. The newspaper asked that former workers be given access to "medical care identical to that which was provided to the victims of the atomic bombings" since 1957, when healthcare for the *hibakusha* was legally implemented.[62]

Disabilities caused by toxic gas and atomic weapons in Hiroshima Prefecture are often compared because they are very specific. It must also be noted that the treatment of both afflictions was dealt with differently. Regarding the victims of the atomic bomb, it is clear that medical care is the responsibility of the state. Regarding the victims of toxic gas, however, there is no such legal disposition.[63]

The majority of the Japanese population had become aware of the seven years of censorship on the topic of gas warfare atrocities during the US Occupation, and the ongoing demand for justice and compensation prefigured public awareness in Japan that the Second World War had been a war of aggression—a topic that would soon be discussed at the international level.

Internationalization and the gradual erosion of dominant narratives

In 1972, the normalization of relations between Tokyo and Beijing began to influence the discussion of chemical weapons in the Japanese media. An article in the August issue of the magazine *Sekai* (The World) discussed the situation in Ōkunoshima, urging the remaining silent victims to break their anonymity. Until then, journalists had mainly written about the suffering of former workers, without discussing the actual use of the weapons they had manufactured. Starting the same year, newspapers also began to emphasize the purpose behind the fabrication of chemical gas. The illegality of chemical weapons and the state's responsibility were also openly mentioned in the media after the government's refusal to compensate all the victims.[64]

The image of the Second World War as an epic and idealized confrontation solely against the Anglo-Saxon enemy was starting to fade. Accounts of atrocities perpetrated in China and throughout East Asia—such as the regular columns of *Asahi shimbun* correspondent Honda Katsuichi—slowly permeated war narratives, forcing the Japanese population to endorse the role of both aggressors and victims.[65] Faced with a national level of mobilization and the support of the media for Ōkunoshima survivors, the government gradually started to change its position. The special fund established in 1954 seemed even more obsolete in the 1960s and 1970s. As early as 1961, Tokyo had agreed to pension off a portion of the workers. In 1965, it was decided that, when former Ōkunoshima personnel passed away, their families would receive financial compensation. But this measure applied only to a fraction of those affected. For instance, veterans incapacitated during the sanitation of the island had to wait until 1975 to benefit from free healthcare and allowances from the Ministry of Welfare.[66]

Tokyo's reluctance to fully acknowledge and support Ōkunoshima former personnel was resolutely in line with the official Japanese narrative vis-à-vis chemical warfare and the resolution of war atrocities at large. Until the twenty-first century, formal policies were characterized by a "two steps forward, one step back" process, which undermined governmental credibility at both national and international levels. In 1970, Japan marked a change on the international stage when it ratified the 1925 Geneva Protocol for the Prohibition of the Use in War of Asphyxiating, Poisonous or Other Gases, and of Bacteriological Methods of Warfare.[67] Four years later, Tokyo tried to go a step further and proposed the creation of an international verification agency for chemical weapons. In 1973, the Ministry of Environment commissioned a study regarding unexploded grenades and shells, and identified 138 incidents nationwide that had affected the Japanese population.[68] Hiroshima prefecture agreed in 1973 to compensate auxiliaries and conscripts who had worked on the island.[69] A further survey conducted in 2003 revealed that twenty-two prefectures had been touched since 1945, for a total of 623 incidents or discoveries of such ordnances.[70] To this day, the Ministry of Welfare provides funds for gas-related curative research.[71]

Yet these laudable efforts did not signify that the government acknowledged its responsibility for the production and use of chemical weapons. In the twelve volumes of the *History of the Greater East Asia War* published by Japan's National Defense Agency between 1967 and 1980, gas deployment by the Imperial Japanese Army was strictly passed over in silence.[72] In 1984, the Ministry of Education demanded that the mention of the use of chemical weapons against China until

1945 be withdrawn from a textbook manual due to "lack of evidence." This "double standard" stance would endure until 1984, when Tokyo publicly admitted the existence of its chemical warfare arsenal. [73]

On April 6, 1982, a document entitled "Record of the Epidemic Prevention and Water Purification Department of the Kwantung Army" was presented for the first time to the Japanese Diet by the Ministry of Welfare. The file revealed not only the creation of a research unit on bacteriological warfare in Harbin, Manchuria, on December 5, 1936, but also the pension system allocated to the former members of Unit 731, the number of people deployed, and the names of those in charge. It was irrefutable proof that Japan had set up a biological weapons program on the continent. The presentation of this evidence reflected a shift of perspectives in government circles. The state could no longer deny having created biological warfare units, first among them Unit 731, which had used— and possibly manufactured—chemical weapons jointly with the military. These changes must be understood in the broader context of Washington's admission in 1981 that it had acquired Japanese scientific data after 1945 in exchange for the absolution of the main researchers. Throughout the 1980s, Tokyo was gradually forced to officially acknowledge the reality of these war crimes—but the process was neither smooth nor simple. During the entire decade and beyond, Japanese official policies oscillated between acquiescence and denial. The latter was usually based on a supposed absence of official evidence. In a 1988 interview, a spokesman for the Japanese Embassy in Washington declared the following:

> The Japanese Government can neither confirm nor deny that experiments linked to biological warfare were ever conducted. We do not possess enough documents regarding what happened in China. Archives were totally destroyed during the war, and therefore, the only thing we can say with certainty is that we don't know what happened.[74]

The government had half-heartedly acknowledged the existence of a bacteriological warfare program, but the recurring argument of a supposed "lack of proof" was unsurprisingly applied to the search for evidence of the existence of chemical weapons used by Japan. Tokyo only admitted that lethal gases had been manufactured during the Second World War in 1995.

Japanese historiographical research into gas warfare at state level never truly stopped, even as Tokyo was simultaneously denying that such weapons had ever existed. Three volumes published in 1957 alone attest to this. The *Exposé of the Chemical Weapons Research Process of the Army Institute for Scientific Research and the 6th Army's Technical Laboratory, History of Chemical Warfare Research*, and *Historical Chronology of Japanese Chemical Warfare Techniques* were all published by the Bureau of Repatriate Welfare, a subsidiary of the Ministry of Welfare.[75] Together with tomes of recollections, testimonies, and publications of military history written by former high-ranking personnel, these volumes served as background for experiments conducted by the Japanese Self-Defense Forces.[76]

Access to these materials stored in the archives of the National Defense Agency was naturally restricted, an additional reason to explain the late emergence of the topic in the public sphere. In December 1983, the institution established a directive in order to make documents public. However, following internal reactions such as "this could be detrimental to national interests" or "such documents could provoke undesirable reactions within society," it was ultimately decided to maintain secrecy.[77] Materials pertaining to the privacy of the author (memoirs, diaries), and those that could have an "undesirable impact on society," such as biological weapons and the emperor's war responsibility, were forbidden to the public.[78] Additionally, the agency "was not in a position to comment [on the potential use of chemical weapons], because the Japanese Imperial Army and the Japanese Self-Defense Forces were completely unrelated structures."[79]

The first official archives documenting the manufacture and use of chemical weapons were uncovered in 1983 by historian Awaya Kentarō in the American archives. Specifically, a 1942 document entitled "Collection of Evidence of Gas Warfare during the China Incident" detailed the role of the Narashino Army School, but the Japanese government clung to its ambiguous attitude.[80] Two years later, historian Yoshimi Yoshiaki located a volume of archives containing more proof of the use and production of gas, but access was unsurprisingly denied. Yoshimi had to wait until 1994 and receive help from a member of parliament to access a copy.[81] Supplementary evidence was further provided from abroad, in the form of studies conducted by Chinese historians, translated into Japanese.

This ambivalence was not limited to the 1980s. In the following decade, the government started to acknowledge the existence of its former chemical arsenal by admitting the use of vomiting agents, but it also took another step backward. On November 30, 1995, Head of the Defense Agency Akiyama Masahiro declared during a parliamentary session that available documents did not allow for the conclusion that blister agents had been used during the war, even though he admitted that incapacitating gas had been deployed.[82] Likewise, in 1999, former employees of the Samukawa naval facility received reparation, but after the Ōkunoshima Historical Research Center announced the discovery of new gas canisters the same year, the Ministry of the Environment offered another response illustrating the lack of clear and coherent governmental guidelines, by insisting that such issues were "not within [their] jurisdiction."[83]

From an international standpoint, perspectives were also gradually shifting. The Imperial Japanese Army had hastily buried or dumped large quantities of chemical weapons throughout East Asia in 1945. Decades after the war, these munitions continued to resurface not only in mainland China but also in Taiwan and as far as the Chao Phraya River in Thailand, where thousands of gas shells were discharged.[84] During the 1990s, lawsuits supported by Sino–Japanese civilian associations and the signing of the Chemical Weapons Convention (CWC) in December 1993 led to collaboration between Tokyo and Beijing to eliminate the remaining projectiles on Chinese territory, a process effectively initiated in 1997.

The task was more arduous than domestic sanitization due to several factors. Not only was the sheer size of the area to be demined an issue in itself but the

1945 destruction of wartime materials documenting potential specific locations amplified the difficulty. In the larger framework, the absence of cooperation agreements outside of the Sino–Japanese convention further complicated the task, not to mention reliance on a multiplicity of national sources on a sensitive—and often classified—subject. For one, Japanese newspapers reported that postwar the Soviet Navy allegedly disposed of 30,000 tons of chemical weapons in the Sea of Japan.[85] In China alone, over two million weapons have been discovered on the continent (according to Chinese experts), and 48,000 have already been disposed of, but exact figures of remaining weapons nationwide are impossible to evaluate, let alone in the rest of East Asia and the Pacific.[86]

Politically, the stubbornness of military institutions was counterbalanced by the 1993 declaration of Prime Minister Hosokawa Morihiro, who for the first time described the Second World War as a "war of aggression" during an official speech.[87] In the process, Hosokawa presented his apologies on several occasions to China and South Korea. The specificities of chemical warfare atrocities were not explicitly mentioned, but these examples ultimately illustrate the growing role of civil society, historians, and redress associations in challenging the ambivalent narrative of the "frog in a well" and the double standard of Japanese internal politics. Another manifestation of this influence can be found in the ratification of the CWC by Tokyo, following renewed public interest in chemical weapons after the double sarin gas attacks in Matsumoto (1994) and Tokyo (1995).[88]

Starting in the mid-1980s, the Japanese state ceased to be an absolute figure of authority in terms of memorial narratives. Historian Olivier Wieviorka's description of French postwar political and historical debates apropos the Vichy government equally resonates in the Japanese case:

> The state often had to negotiate with various forces, intervening more as a regulator, sometimes as a referee trying to respond to the sometimes-conflicting solicitations of various groups and lobbies, rather than as a force of initiative defining in majesty a clear and definitive memory policy.[89]

Alongside the involvement of historians and journalists, the associations of Ōkunoshima victims played a central role in pressing the government. In 1981, 4,253 former workers were registered to benefit from a free diagnostic and healthcare service. Their number rose to 5,219 with the inclusion of those who died until that year.[90] Tokyo's obstinate rebuttal to fully admit the existence of its chemical weapons program strongly contributed to the topic's emergence in the public's consciousness.

The Second World War and its deprivations had officially ceased in 1945, but there was no end to the physical torments inflicted on the bodies of wounded citizens. In the words of a former worker: "In a present where help and assistance are not available to all those who need them, it is possible to affirm that the war is not over."[91] Veterans established associations, which grew in number as the condition of their founders deteriorated. In 1985, the number of deceased ex-personnel had reached 1,287, and was over 2,000 in 1996. Less than a decade after the end of the conflict and before the well-exposed media consequences of the Minamata disease, the continuous ailment of Ōkunoshima victims was a major factor in explaining the rapid emergence of civic movements demanding compensation from the Japanese state.

Gradual delivery of financial support to a portion of the veterans in the 1960s did not bring the case to a close. Undermined by strict eligibility criteria and limited healthcare access, those who had been forced to work on the island as children had yet to receive compensation. Taking advantage of the spotlight offered by fresh historical research and partial government acknowledgment, associations sought to ensure the continued recognition of their cause and the commemoration of the past in a concrete form. A cenotaph was erected on the island in May 1985, and petitions circulated to include the island on the UNESCO World Heritage List.[92] The concurrent establishment in 1988 of the Ōkunoshima Toxic Gas Documentation Center and the Ōkunoshima Historical Research Center managed by professional historians and volunteers further formalized a historical research framework. Guided tours of the island aimed at school children were set up as well as trips to China to facilitate financial support and communication with families of the victims. In 1996, the Ōkunoshima Toxic Gas Documentation Center organized the first historical research symposium on the topic.

Ironically, the government's refusal to consider the victims on the same level as the *hibakusha* and the premature death of the victims pushed associations to popularize their cause in the media, which in turn led to a renewed involvement of civil society to obtain reparations. Limited by the prevalence of a culture of atomic victimization, the regional discourse of Ōkunoshima originally lacked visibility, but it was also fertile ground for the development of alternative memorial narratives, both locally and internationally. The fact that a total of fourteen Japanese prefectures had been touched by such cases was clearly a factor in explaining the emergence of a national consciousness. The challenge was not simply to raise awareness inside and outside of Japan but also to continue fighting the damaging effects of what few considered a distant past.

In 1996, the water supply in Ōkunoshima still contained a level of arsenic forty-nine times higher than the legal limit. Similar manifestations equally plagued the rest of the country. In 2000, a portion of the inhabitants of the city of Kamisumachi (Ibaraki Prefecture) had to be hospitalized due to gradual limb numbness and chronic paralysis. Analysis revealed the presence of arsenic in local well water. A detailed study further showed that the substance was in fact diphenylchloroarsine, an arsenic component that did not exist in natural form. Useless beyond its military application, this product could only be a leftover from the fabrication process of vomiting agents.[93] In 2002, the unearthing of 806 canisters containing blister agents during road works near the former naval base of Samukawa (Kanagawa Prefecture)—followed by a second incident the following year in Ibaraki Prefecture —left twelve people injured. A couple of months later, a similar occurrence in the northern Chinese city of Qiqihar resulted in multiple injuries and one fatality.

These cases make for an interesting precedent in the history of compensation procedures. Historically, indemnities (including those disbursed to Ōkunoshima veterans) had been paid on an individual basis by the Federation of National Public Service Personnel Mutual Aid Association, an entity responsible for providing medical benefits, pensions, and long-term care services. Indemnification only covered healthcare costs and did not include moral or physical compensation, for example in cases where victims had lost their job. However, a policy shift under the Koizumi administration (2001–2006) resulted in the creation of specific compensation funds in 2003. Hospitalized Ibaraki victims were indemnified with 700,000 yen (300,000 yen for non-hospitalized persons) and a monthly sum of 20,000 yen for a period of three years by a special Healthcare Investigation Cooperation Fund. Tokyo paid compensation to Chinese sufferers via a direct payment of 300 million yen to the Beijing government. Those measures were nevertheless not extended retroactively to those who had previously suffered a similar fate. Damages inflicted to the victims of the 2002 Kanagawa incident were treated as occupational injuries and solely covered by individual compensation insurance. This policy shift, possibly motivated by the general election of November 2003, nonetheless coincided with the compensation of teenagers and children mobilized on the island, the final category of victims to achieve state recognition.[94]

Over five decades, the victims of Ōkunoshima managed to gain popularity nationwide and achieve compensation and state recognition. However, despite recurring media coverage and the influence of new technologies—notably of associations on the internet—the history of the island remains opaque to this day by its postwar transformation, nationally and globally. In spite of the commitment of the victims and their families, a survey conducted in August 1995 indicated that only 5.9 percent of the Japanese population answered positively to the question "Did you know that toxic gas had been manufactured on Ōkunoshima, and had then been used against the Chinese during the war?"[95]

Once erased from maps, the island ultimately blended into the postwar Japanese landscape, unable to part from its leisurely function. Indeed, internet search results for "Ōkunoshima" generally do mention chemical weapons and the wartime role played by the island, but they also return an even larger number of mentions of "Rabbit Island" (*usagi shima*). Popular myth has often pictured the approximately 700 mammals as the offspring of animals used in prewar and wartime gas experiments. This narrative allowed for the rabbits to be turned into the perfect agents of a symbolic transition from times of war and hardship to a peaceful and family-oriented prosperous resort. In reality, however, rabbits bred for experimentation on the island were treated until 1945 as another commodity by Ōkunoshima workers and eaten when food was scarce. The few remaining mammals were culled in the sanitization process, and new rabbits were reintroduced in 1971—symbolically, by local school children—to breed on the island.[96]

In line with the image of "Cool Japan" and "Kawaii Culture," numerous websites and pamphlets emphasize the recent influx of travelers and their eagerness to see the rabbits, at the expense of factory ruins and the war-related museum, often relegated to last paragraphs and secondary pages.[97] These animals have eclipsed the structure in the background, to become the most predominant symbol of the island, attracting a continued upsurge of both domestic and international tourists in search of destinations off the beaten track. Current statistics confirm this trend: foreign vacationers dramatically increased from 378 people in 2013 to over 17,000 in 2015, and Japanese tourism more modestly grew from 152,000 visits in 2010 to 186,000 four years later. Conversely, yearly calls to the Ōkunoshima Documentation Center peaked at 20,000 in the period 2004–2008, and remain a low fraction of total island holidays, despite an encouraging figure of 49,490 visits in 2014.[98] This is despite the fact that more than 2,000 people nationwide still suffer from gas-related health issues. As late as 2009, canisters filled with vomiting agents were found drifting ashore in the vicinity of Ōkunoshima, despite a subsequent government statement claiming the area did not present safety issues.[99]

The efforts of veterans to increase awareness beyond regional and national boundaries, however, leave a certain level of ambiguity in some of the narratives put forward. For instance, articles and books presenting the general background of Ōkunoshima or Japanese biological warfare recurrently discuss the issue of European concentration camps in the international context that led Japan to the war. More specifically, the use of gas by Nazi Germany is emphasized in a comparative perspective as bearing resemblance to the Japanese case. The clearest example of this can be found in the expression "toxic gas" (*doku gasu*)—a generic term that refers to blister agents as much as to zyklon—as well as in the inclusion of a photograph of Anne Frank and her diary, or pictures of children of the Holocaust.[100] In other words, Ōkunoshima memory-makers feel the need to resort to analogies in order to anchor their own war memories in world history. To be sure, it is a praiseworthy perspective if one considers that the use of biological weapons by Tokyo was virtually unknown to the rest of the world. Nonetheless, the constant reference to German war crimes discredits the process by attempting to liken two things that cannot be compared and by reducing the issues to their symbolic locations.

> There are common points between Auschwitz and Ōkunoshima regarding the sad history of the use of toxic gas against humanity. [...] First, both enterprises were kept absolutely secret by the government. Second, the horrible production process was imposed upon local populations. When considering Ōkunoshima, one should not look away from the fact that Japan waged a war of aggression, and analyze all this in perspective of what happened in Auschwitz.[101]

The invocation of Nazism as the quintessential form of evil to substantiate one's plea is not new. In the aforementioned 1966 *Asahi Journal* article, author Usami Shō emphasized that the smell on Ōkunoshima reminded him of a movie he had seen on the gas chambers of Auschwitz.[102] Yet there are numerous reasons why this parallel between Ōkunoshima and Auschwitz, let alone Japan's and Germany's use of chemical gas, is hard to sustain. First, the highest state organs in both countries reacted differently to the deployment of a chemical arsenal. Where Hirohito shared the enthusiasm of his military elites for such weapons, Hitler categorically opposed the use of biological warfare. Second, the scope of both programs must be taken into account; German experiments were less systematic than their Japanese counterparts.[103] Compared to the altogether 10,000 participants in Japan's biological weapons program, German chemical warfare mobilized approximately 1,000 military and civilian scientists alike.[104] Third, in the larger framework of biological weapons and war medicine, German and Japanese programs hardly bear any resemblance to one another. Experiments on mass sterilization and race-related genetic research were never on the agenda of Unit 731; through vivisections of live human guinea pigs of mostly Chinese or Russian origins (*maruta* "logs"), Japanese experiments focused instead on a supposed "improvement" of field surgery and the development of biological weapons to combat guerilla warfare in vast areas. Finally, a state's implementation of a policy of planned murder is not to be compared to the manufacture and use of gas during (and before) wartime. Neologisms linked to the annihilation of an entire population—"aryanized" (*arianisiert*), "de-jewed" (*entjudet*)—that concurrently appeared with the rise to power of the Third Reich never found equivalents in prewar or wartime imperial Japan since no policies were aimed at the systematic destruction of specific ethnic groups.[105] In effect, Zyklon B, developed in the 1920s, is partly composed of prussic acid, a substance mass-produced on Ōkunoshima. Nonetheless, stringent and dangerous as the working conditions on the island were, they cannot seriously be associated with the treatment and mass execution of people interned in concentration camps.

It must equally be remembered that Ōkunoshima was a military secret kept undisclosed from the start, similarly to the Pingfan facility in Manchuria where Unit 516 conducted gas experiments in the context of Japan's bacteriological warfare program. In contrast, until their transformation into Holocaust extermination camps—after which they were shrouded in secrecy—German concentration facilities played a role in terrorizing the population; people *had to* be aware of their presence. The existence of Auschwitz was known in Poland; Heinrich Himmler even called a press conference in March 1933 to announce the opening of Dachau.[106]

Conclusion

Ultimately, the concrete structures of Ōkunoshima—both as a leisure resort and as a tangible trace of the manufacture and use of chemical weapons—had contrasting influences reflecting similar issues to what Hyun Kyung Lee examines in chapter four. On the one hand, the transformation of the island into a resort allowed the victims to popularize their struggle to a growing number of visitors, resulting in an increase in public awareness. On the other hand, Ōkunoshima's makeover was the result of a governmental attempt to do away with historical facts forcibly hidden, which had yet to be acknowledged. In turn, this maneuver also triggered the veterans' commitment to gain recognition and to later win their case. The common thread to both perspectives resides in the incessant resurfacing of toxic ammunition and the wounds of former workers; physical proof of a never-ending past. These scars played a significant role in anchoring the island as the most prevalent symbol of Japan's chemical warfare program.

Seen from the perspective of memory, Ōkunoshima is unique. It is one of the very first cases of war memories nationwide to emerge publicly. In postwar Japan, the narrative of the victims has at times been discreet, unheard of, and mostly in a minority position and localized. But it is nevertheless a continuous narrative. Both as aggressors and victims, veterans were competing simultaneously with official state narratives and Hiroshima survivors. Beyond physical wounds, this factor explains their prominent role as an early vector of civil society, before the emergence of citizen movements nationwide.

Nonetheless, Ōkunoshima did not manufacture substances in a vacuum. Regardless of its size, its function was primarily the fabrication of toxic gas and not the making of chemical weapons. Failure to perceive the larger picture of the logistical process only reinforces the island's symbolic status, at the expense of other structures central to the production and deployment of gas warfare. As opposed to numerous testimonies of former Ōkunoshima workers, extremely few documents on—or witness accounts of—the Sone arsenal remain today.[107] The same is true of other locations mentioned in this chapter, for which no further archives other than a meager amount of oral testimonies exist. This situation accounts for the lack of information on the actual production process of chemical weapons, and what is true of the manufacturing is equally valid for the damages inflicted to former personnel: with very rare exceptions, no accounts recall the struggle—prewar or postwar—of staff outside of Ōkunoshima. The decontamination process of laboratories throughout the archipelago, for instance in the city of Ueda (Nagano Prefecture), presents similar shortcomings.[108]

The pioneering 1980s works of historians aside, the scarcity of official material is critical. As precious as they may be, relying solely on testimonies of fishermen and army veterans makes it difficult to paint a more precise picture of the wartime and immediate postwar history of the island. From a historiographical perspective, issues such as the development of chemical weapons by the navy, its cooperation with the army and private industries, or the activities of Unit 516 on the continent remain obscured due to the lack of archives. Similarly, reliance on contrasting sources prevents historians from painting a definitive picture of the past. Almost no Japanese documents on the American sanitization of the island remain today. Testimonies indicate that in 1945, United States forces dumped into the sea in the vicinity of the island sodium cyanide, thiodiglycol, hexachloroethane, and other hazardous components officially marked as "destroyed."[109] Chinese, Japanese, and American statistics can be self-contradictory.[110] Gas may—or may not—have also been manufactured overseas.[111] Above all, the exact locations of weapons dumped on land and offshore seventy years ago are still unavailable. Both in Japan and the East Asia-Pacific area, projectiles are resurfacing even into the twenty-first century.[112]

Ultimately, Ōkunoshima raises issues beyond the scope of memory studies and chemical warfare. The history of the island corroborates the larger picture of the transformation of modern Japan. In their haste to scientifically catch up with the Great Powers, the Meiji elites emphasized the development of Western weapons at any cost. Chemical and industrial companies contributed to the enrichment of the nation, before making Japanese gas warfare a reality. However, the concept of "research" was predominantly applied to attaining that reality with all possible haste. The critical aim of both army and navy was not technical innovation but the possession of a large-scale arsenal similar to that of the Western powers.[113]

Thus, in a global context, chemical warfare experiments and the facility of Ōkunoshima are hardly exceptional. All major powers possessed similar structures and most experimented on human subjects. To cite but one, the United States conducted tests during the Second World War with vesicant agents, selecting subjects based on racialized categories. Trials impacted 60,000 whites, Puerto Ricans, and African Americans, selected to test varying resistance to poisoning, and Japanese-American troops, enrolled to gauge potential blister agents' effects on the Japanese enemy. Similar to the case of Ōkunoshima, subjects were encouraged to enroll out of patriotism, or were lured by financial rewards, special leave, or simply to avoid combat.[114]

Throughout the Second World War and beyond, immediate production improvement, testing and the acquisition of valuable commodities took precedence over human life. In 1970, the wounds Teijin employees had suffered during the decontamination process were generally portrayed as acts of individual heroism for the sake of the company. According to the official history of the firm, employees merely "overcame with bravery" the "increased danger of contact with poison," and no further elaboration detailed their postwar fate. Across the Pacific, chemical research involving human subjects by the United States army endured until 1975.

Ōkunoshima does not possess a monopoly on suffering, but it nonetheless corroborates the unparalleled extent of the biological warfare network developed by Japan as well as the long-lasting consequences of the collapse of the empire. Secretive as they were kept, gas weapons were paramount to prewar, wartime, and postwar imperial elites. After 1945, their repercussions impacted society at large as well as the emergence of postwar counter narratives and the makeover of Japan from times of hardships to a nation of *kawaii* affluence.

Notes

1   Phosgen (blood agent, aka brown); phenacyl chloride (lachrymatory agent, aka green); diphenylcyanoarsine (vomiting agent, aka red-or blue-); lewisite (blister agent, aka yellow); arsenic trichloride (lewisite component); French, German, and frost-free yperite (blister agents); benzyl bromide (lachrymatory agent); and prussic acid (blood agent). Fumigants were codenamed "white," in Yamamoto Tatsuya and Kusanagi Daisuke, *Nihon no kagaku heiki 1, hōheiyō gasudan no hyōshiki to kōzō* (Gifu: Zen nippon gunsō kenkyūkai, 2010).

2   Matsuno Seiya, *Nihon gun no doku gasu heiki* (Gaifūsha, 2005), p. 265.

3   Ishida Masaharu, "Amerika gun no Hiroshima ken shinchū to Ōkunoshima doku gasu haiki," *Nihon rekishi* 795 (August 2014), pp. 54–71, here p. 56. Tadanoumi is the principal maritime access point from the Japanese mainland to Ōkunoshima.

4   Tsuneishi Kei'ichi, "Tokushū kenkyū kaigun no kagaku sen kenkyū kaihatsu shi," *Rekishi dokuhon* 9 (September 2010), pp. 196–201, here p. 201.

5   Exposure to 2.7 milligrams of lewisite or yperite (about 1 teaspoon) for 30 minutes is considered fatal. Similarly, a dose between 0.005 and 0.017 milligram of phosgene is estimated lethal for a human being exposed for 30 minutes, in "The National Institute for Occupational Safety and Health."

6   Headquarters 41st Division, Office of the Chemical Officer, List of Chemical Warfare Items Awaiting Disposition, December 26, 1945, 341.19.1 41st Infantry Division – Chemical Officer – Journal File (No.7), November 29–December 27, 1945, RG407, Box 10575, US National Archives at College Park, in Ishida, "Amerika gun," p. 57.

7   Matsuno, *Nihon gun*, p. 265. Ammunition and projectiles were filled at this facility— opened in Kitakyūshū in 1937—with the gas manufactured on Ōkunoshima.

8   Yukutake Masato, ed., *Hitori hitori no Ōkunoshima: doku gasu kōjō kara no shōgen* (Domes shuppan, 2012), p. 212.

9   Located in Chiba Prefecture, the Narashino Army School was specifically opened in 1933 to instruct selected officers and soldiers on the deployment of chemical weapons. The school also coordinated chemical tests and manoeuvres on the continent; Tanaka Hiroaki, "Nihon doku gasu sen no rekishi," *Kagakushi kenkyū* 4 (2011), pp. 210–220, here p. 215.

10 Mines (and typhoons) prevented the 6th army's direct landing in Kure, forcing troops to disembark in Wakayama Prefecture, before reaching Kure by land, in Sixth United States Army, ed., "Report of the Occupation of Japan 22 September 1945–30 November 1945" (8th U.S. Army Printing Plant, 1946), available online: www. memory.loc.gov/service/gdc/scd0001/2010/20101119002re/20101119002re.pdf, accessed June 28, 2019.

11 Ishida Masaharu, "Amerika rikugun dai 41 shidan no Hiroshima ken shinchū to Ōkunoshima doku gasu shori," *Chiiki akademi- kōkaikōza hōkokusho* (2013), pp. 21–25, here p. 24.

12 Ishida, "Amerika gun," p. 61.

13 Fukushima Katsuyuki, *Teijin no ayumi* (Teijin Kabushiki Gaisha, 1968), p, 199.

14 Okano Yūji, ed., *Doku gasu tō: Ōkunoshima doku gasu kōjō sono higai to kagai* (Hiroshima: Hiroshima heiwa kyōiku kenkyūjo, 1987), p. 56.

15 Fukushima, *Teijin no ayumi*, p. 208.

16 Giga Sōichirō, "Seibutsu kagaku heiki to seiyaku kigyō no rekishiteki yakuwari," *Kokumin iryō* 229 (October 1, 2006), pp. 17–24, here p. 19.

17 Hasegawa Haruyoshi, ed., *Nihon rikugun kayaku shi* (Ōhikai, 1969), p. 191.

18 Fukushima, *Teijin no ayumi*, pp. 196–197.

19 For a detailed account of wartime conditions, see Arnaud Doglia, *L'arme biologique japonaise, 1880–2010: réalités historique et anatomie de la mémoire* (Bern: Peter Lang, 2016), pp. 121–126.

20 Yoshiaki Yoshimi, ed., *Boku wa doku gasu no mura de umareta. Anata ga sensō no otoshi mono ni deattara* (Gōdō shuppan, 2007), p. 90.

21 Fukushima, *Teijin no ayumi*, pp. 201–202.

22 Takeda Eiko, *Chizu kara kesareta shima: Ōkunoshima doku gasu kōjō* (Domes shuppan, 1987), p. 175.

23 Yukutake, *Hitori hitori*, p. 234.

24 Takeda, *Chizu kara kesareta*, p. 185.

25 Yoshida Yutaka, *Nihonjin no sensō kan: sengo shi no naka no henyō* (Iwanami bunko, 2005), p. 93.

26 James J. Orr, *The Victim as Hero: Ideologies of Peace and National Identity in Postwar Japan* (Honolulu: University of Hawai'i Press, 2001), p. 2.

27 Olivier Wieviorka, *La Mémoire Désunie: Le Souvenir Politique Des Années Sombres de La Libération à Nos Jours*, L'univers Historique (Paris: Seuil, 2010), pp. 18–19.

28 Stéphane Audoin-Rouzeau and Annette Becker, *14–18, retrouver la guerre*, Collection Folio Histoire 125 (Paris: Gallimard, DL, 2003), p. 13.

29 Tatsumi Tomoji, *Kakusaretekita 'Hiroshima': doku gasu shima kara no kokuhatsu* (Nihon hyōronsha, 1993), p. 111.

30 Yoshida, *Nihonjin no sensōkan,* p. 95; *Hiroku daitōa sen shi* (Fuji shoen, 1953).

31 Fujitani Takashi, Geoffrey M. White, and Lisa Yoneyama, eds., *Perilous Memories: The Asia-Pacific War(s)* (Durham, NC: Duke University Press, 2001), p. 7.

32 Lisa Yoneyama, *Hiroshima Traces: Time, Space, and the Dialectics of Memory* (Berkeley: University of California Press, 1999), p. 13.

33 Takuso Shigenobu, "Doku gasu shōgai ni kan suru kenkyū to genjō," in *Doku gasu no shima*, ed. Higuchi Kenji (Kobushi shobō, 2015), pp. 160–175, here p. 169.

34 In 1947, a Chinese military tribunal sentenced Major-General Kajiura Ginjiro, Commander of the 231st Regiment, to a life sentence for using poison gas in combat, in Edward J. Drea, ed., *Researching Japanese War Crimes Records: Introductory Essays* (Washington, DC: Nazi War Crimes and Japanese Imperial Government Records Interagency Working Group, 2006), p. 35. In the same period, two more Japanese officers were hanged by Australian justice for conducting prussic acid experiments, *A471/1*, National Archives of Australia, ACT Regional Office, Canberra in Yoshimi Yoshiaki, *Doku gasu sen to nihon gun* (Iwanami shoten, 2004), p. 271. For a detailed account, see Doglia, *L'arme biologique japonaise, 1880–2010.*

35 Takuso, "Doku gasu," p. 160.

36 Yukutake, *Hitori hitori,* p. 180.

37 Tsuneishi Kei'ichi, "Doku gasu higai to Koizumi naikaku," *Hon* 1 (January 2004), pp. 52–54, here p. 52.

38 *Shōwa 48 nen no 'kyū gun doku gasu tama nado no zenkoku chōsa' foro-appu chōsa hōkoku sho* (Kankyōshō, 2003).

39 Yoshimi, *Doku gasu sen,* p. 104.

40 Yoshimi, *Boku wa,* p.104.

41 Matsuno, *Nihon gun,* p. 267.

42 Yukutake, *Hitori hitori,* p. 239.

43 M. Yamakido, S. Ishioka, K. Hiyama, and A. Maeda, "Former Poison Gas Workers and Cancer: Incidence and Inhibition of Tumor Formation by Treatment with Biological Response Modifier N-CWS," *Environmental Health Perspectives* 104 Suppl. 3 (May 1996), pp. 485–488, here p. 485.

44 Orr, *The Victim as Hero,* p. 142.

45 Yamauchi Masauchi, ed., *Kiroku ni nai shima, doku gasu tō rekishi kenkyūjo kaihō* (Takehara: Doku gasu tō rekishi kenkyūjo kaihō, 1996), p. 5.

46 Okano, *Doku gasu tō,* p. 57.

47 Yukutake Masato, "Tadanoumi byōin tadaima orikaeshi ten," in *Doku Gasu*, ed. Higuchi, pp. 176–187, here p. 179.

48 Tatsumi, *Kakusaretekita "Hiroshima,"* pp. 92–93.

49 Yukutake, "Tadanoumi Byōin Tadaima Orikaeshi Ten," p. 182.

50 Takeda, *Chizu kara kesareta,* pp. 200–201.

51 Yoshida, *Nihonjin no sensōkan,* p. 120.

52 The original idea to transform the island into a resort may have come from Nakajima Muratarō, vice-president of *Teijin*, in *Teijin No Ayumi*. 212. The Ministry of Welfare has been known by several names in its postwar incarnation and the author has chosen to simplify the situation for English readers and just render it as the Ministry of Welfare.

53 Takeda, *Chizu kara kesareta*, p. 204.

54 Tatsumi, *Kakusaretekita "Hiroshima,"* p. 99.

55 Sugi Yasusaburō, "Seto naikai no doku gasu shima," *Bungei shunjū* 5 (May 1956), pp. 238–251, here p. 239.

56 Nobuyoshi Manabe, "Ōkunoshima ni okeru doku gasu shōsha no haire sen shōken," *Hiroshima igakkai* 10, no. 6 (June 1957).

57 Takuso, "Doku gasu," p. 166.

58 Ibid., p. 167.

59 Usami Shō, "Kanashiki doku gasu kanjatachi," *Asahi jānaru* 2 (January 1966), pp. 103–108.

60 Ibid., p. 108.

61 Okano, *Doku gasu tō*.

62 "Saisei, Ōkunoshima no 'kage,'" *Chūgoku shimbun*, March 22, 1970, reprinted in Okano, *Doku gasu tō*; a second law was passed in 1968, Yoneyama, *Hiroshima Traces*, p. 93.

63 "Saisei, Ōkunoshima no 'kage.'"

64 Kajimura Masao, "'Doku gasu giseisha' no sengo," *Sekai*, Sequential serial number 321 (August 1972), pp. 314–316, here p. 314.

65 Honda Katsuichi, *Chūgoku no tabi* (Suzusawa shoten, 1977).

66 *Ōkunoshima doku gasu shōgai sono jissō to keishō: sengo 65 shūnen kinen jigyō* (Hiroshima: Hiroshima ken kenkō fukushi kyoku, 2011).

67 Jorma K. Miettinen, "The Chemical Arsenal: The Time to Defuse It Is Now," *Bulletin of the Atomic Scientists* 30, no. 7 (1974), pp. 37–43, here p. 41.

68 *Shōwa 48 nen no "kyū gun doku gasu tama nado no zenkoku chōsa" foro-appu chōsa hōkoku sho*, pp. 13–43. The Ministry of the Environment was initially only an agency but for sake of reading continuity the author has chosen to use its current status.

69 *Ōkunoshima doku gasu*, p. 143.

70 Matsuno, *Nihon gun*, p. 281.

71 Takuso, "Doku gasu," p. 168.

72 Yoshimi, *Doku gasu sen*, pp. 295–296.

73 Yoshida, *Nihonjin no sensōkan*, p. 149.

74 Conversation between Linda Monroe of the *Los Angeles Times*, and Imai Osamu, August 11, 1988, in Tsuneishi Kei'ichi, *Kieta saikin sen butai Kantō gun dai nana san ichi butai* (Chikuma shobō, 1993), p. 267.

75 The first volume was written by Akiyama Kanemasa, formely head of Unit 516, the Kwangtung Army chemical warfare unit. The author of the second book, Oyaizu Masao, was the director of several chemical warfare laboratories of the Japanese Imperial Army. The third volume is a compilation of collected works, in Doglia, *L'arme biologique japonaise*, p. 307.

76 Hiroaki, "Nihon doku gasu sen no rekishi," pp. 210–220, here p. 211.

77 Yoshimi, *Doku gasu sen*, pp. 295–296.

78 Hata Ikuhiko, *Gendai shi no sōten*, quoted in Matsuno, *Nihon gun*, p. 309.

79 Yoshimi, *Doku gasu sen*, p. 297.

80 Tanaka, "Nihon doku gasu," p. 211.

81   Matsuno, *Nihon gun,* pp. 304–305.

82   Yoshimi, *Doku gasu sen,* p. 296.

83   Yamauchi, *Kiroku ni nai shima,* p. 31.

84   Matsuno, *Nihon gun,* p. 273.

85   *Asahi shimbun,* May 11 and 23, 1993, cited in Bob Tadashi Wakabayashi, "Documents on Japanese Poison Gas Warfare in China," *Sino-Japanese Studies* 7 (October 1994), p. 8.

86   Ministry of Foreign Affairs of Japan Report, "Kagaku Heiki Kinshi Jōyaku," available online: www.mofa.go.jp/mofaj/gaiko/gun_hakusho/2006/pdfs/hon1_4.pdf, accessed June 28, 2019, p. 127.

87   The first official government apologies date back to Prime Minister Kishi Nobusuke's visit to Australia and Myanmar in 1957, in Jane W. Yamazaki, *Japanese Apologies for World War II: A Rhetorical Study,* Routledge Contemporary Japan Series 3 (London: Routledge, 2006), pp. 74–75.

88   Fujitani et al., *Perilous Memories,* p. 130; Kobayashi Teruki, "Tansokin dokoro deha nai akumu no sairai! Asahara, sarin, Ben Laden Ishi 731 butai to oumu shinrikyō," *Shokun* 12 (December 2001), pp. 158–169, here p. 164.

89   Wieviorka, *La Mémoire Désunie,* p. 25.

90   Takeda, *Chizu kara kesareta,* p. 218.

91   Kajimura, "Doku gasu," p. 316.

92   Ōkunoshima's application has not yet been accepted, whereas the Hiroshima Dome has been part of the World Heritage List since 1996.

93   Yoshimi, *Boku wa,* p. 97.

94   Tsuneishi, "Doku gasu higai," p. 54.

95   Yoshimi, *Boku wa,* p. 99.

96   Yamauchi Masauchi, "Doku gasu shiryōkan moto kanchō Murakami shi e no intābyū," *Kagaku to shakai o kangaeru doyō kōza ronbun shū,* no. 1 (May 1997), p. 38.

97   "National Park Resorts," National Park Resort Homepage, available online: www.qkamura.or.jp/en/ohkuno/, accessed November 11, 2017.

98   "Hiroshima Peace Media Center," Hiroshima Peace Media Center, www.hiroshimapeacemedia.jp/?p=52294, accessed November 11, 2017.

99   Ibid.

100 Yoshimi, *Boku wa,* pp. 54–55; Kamiya Noriaki, *Nagaki chinmoku: chichi ga katatta akuma no 731 butai* (Nagoya: Tsuruma hōritsu kurabu, 2001), p. vi.

101 Yamauchi, *Kiroku ni nai shima,* pp. 62–65.

102 Usami, "Kanashiki doku gasu," p. 106.

103 Gerhard Baader, Susan E. Lederer, Morris Low, Florian Schmaltz, and Alexander V. Schwerin, "Pathways to Human Experimentation, 1933–1945: Germany, Japan, and the United States," *Osiris* 20 (2005), pp. 205–231, here p. 212.

104 Ramesh Chandra Gupta, ed., *Handbook of Toxicology of Chemical Warfare Agents* (Amsterdam: Elsevier/AP, 2009), p. 19.

105 Victor Klemperer, *The Language of the Third Reich: LTI, Lingua Tertii Imperii* (London: Continuum, 2006).

106 Annette Wieviorka, *Auschwitz, 60 Ans Après* (Paris: Laffont, 2005), pp. 53, 205.

107 Yukutake, *Hitori hitori,* pp. 139–142.

108 Nakane Harushi and Arakawa Michiyo, "Shōgen kaigun doku gasu kōjō no hibi," *Chūkiren* (July 2010), pp. 50–59, here p. 59.

109 Ishida, "Amerika gun," p. 62.

110   Ibid., p. 54.

111   Matsuno, *Nihon gun,* p. 85.

112   Hagami Tarō, "Kankyōshō ga 'hōchi' shita maboroshi no 'doku gasu' jōhō futatabi kesareru? Rikugun himitsu kōjō – Hiroshima ken Ōkunoshima ga tō nihon no taishitsu," *Sandē mainichi* 9 (February 20, 2005), pp. 148–151, here p. 148.

113   Tsuneishi, "Tokushū kenkyū," p. 200.

114   Susan L. Smith, "Mustard Gas and American Race-Based Human Experimentation in World War II," *Journal of Law, Medicine & Ethics: A Journal of the American Society of Law, Medicine & Ethics* 36, no. 3 (Fall 2008), pp. 517–521, here pp. 518–519.

BIBLIOGRAPHY

Archives

Archive of the Foreign Policy of the Russian Federation, Moscow, Russia
Archive of the Ministry of Foreign Affairs, Beijing, People's Republic of China
Archives of the Ministry of Foreign Affairs, Institute of Modern History, Academia Sinica, Taipei, Taiwan (MOFA Taipei)
Hong Kong Public Record Office
Japan's Ministry of Foreign Affairs Archives
National Archives of Australia
National Archives of the United Kingdom
Number Two Historical Archive, Nanjing, People's Republic of China
Russian State Archives of Social and Political History, Moscow, Russia
Russian State Archives of Economy, Moscow, Russia
Shanghai Municipal Archive, USHMM
United Nations Archives
United States Holocaust Memorial Museum

Western language periodicals and newspapers

Asian Cinema
The American Historical Review
The Asia-Pacific Journal
The Australian Journal of Chinese Affairs
Comparative Studies in Society and History
Cross-Currents: East Asian History and Culture Review
The Daily News (Australia)
Guardian
H-Diplo Article Review
The Historical Journal
Historical Journal of Film, Radio & Television
History & Memory
History Today
Inter-Asia Cultural Studies
International Journal of Korean History
International Journal of Heritage Studies
The International Journal of the History of Sport
International Organization
Journal of Asian Studies
Journal of Contemporary History
Journal of Popular Film and Television

The Journal of Seoul Studies
Korea: Politics, Economy and Society
Life
The Mercury (Australia)
North China Daily News
South China Morning Post and the Hong Kong Telegraph (SCMPHKT)
Sydney Morning Herald
Time
Twentieth-Century China
United Nations Archives

Chinese language

Anshan shuguang
Da kung pao
Dongbei jiefangqu caizheng jingji shi ziliao xuanbian
Dongbei jingji xiaocongshu
Heping ribao
Renmin ribao
Xingdao ribao
Zhongguo gongye wushinian
Zhongyang ribao

Japanese language

Bungei shunjū
Chūō kōron
Ekonomisuto
Fuji
Fujin kurabu
Fujin minshu shinbun
Hōsō kenkyū to chōsa
Kingu
Mainichi shimbun
Omoshiro kurabu
Senshi kenkyū nempo
Shakai bungaku
Shincho
Shōjo kurabu
Shōjo sekai
Yomiuri shimbun

Korean language

Donga ilbo
Dongbanghakji
Doshi Yeongu

Encyclopedia of Korean Culture
Gyeonghyang Sinmun
Hanguk Geunhyundaesa Yeongu
Hangukgyoyuksahak
Hanguksaron
Incheonhakyeongu
Ireoinmunhak
Jeongsinmunhwayeongu
Jonggyomunhwayeongu
Joseon ilbo
Maeil shinbo
Sahoegyoyukak
Sahoewa yeoksa
Yeoksahakyeongu (Chonnam Historical Review)
Yeoksaminsokhak
Yeoksamunjeyeongu

Western language sources

Almqvist, Kurt, ed., *Japanese Self-Images*, Stockholm: Axel and Margaret Axson Johnson Foundation, 2017.

Audoin-Rouzeau, Stéphane, and Annette Becker, *14-18, retrouver la guerre*, Paris: Gallimard, DL, 2009.

Aoi Akihito, "Shinto Shrines and Urban Reconstruction of Seoul focusing on Chosen Jingu project," *Journal of Seoul Studies* 32 (2008), pp. 35–72.

Araragi Shinzo, "The Collapse of the Japanese Empire and the Great Migration: Repatriation, Assimilation, and Remaining Behind," in Barak Kushner and Sherzod Muminov, eds., *The Dismantling of Japan's Empire in East Asia: Deimperialization, Postwar Legitimation and Imperial Afterlife*, London: Routledge, 2017, pp. 66–84.

Archer, Bernice, *The Internment of Western Civilians under the Japanese, 1941-45: A Patchwork of Internment*, London: Routledge Curzon, 2004.

Audoin-Rouzeau, Stéphane, and Annette Becker, *14-18, retrouver la Guerre*, Collection Folio Histoire 125, Paris: Gallimard, 2003.

Baader, Gerhard, Susan E. Lederer, Morris Low, Florian Schmaltz, and Alexander V. Schwerin, "Pathways to Human Experimentation, 1933-1945: Germany, Japan, and the United States," *Osiris* 20 (2005), pp. 205–231.

Barshay, Andrew, *The Gods Left First: The Captivity and Repatriation of Japanese POWs in Northeast Asia, 1945-56*, Berkeley: University of California Press, 2013.

Baskett, Michael, "Dying for a Laugh: Japanese post-1945 Service Comedies," *Historical Journal of Film, Radio & Television* 23, no.4 (October 2003), pp. 291–310.

Baskett, Michael, *The Attractive Empire: Transnational Film Culture in Imperial Japan*, Honolulu: University of Hawai'i Press, 2008.

Baxter, James C., ed., *Japanese Studies Around the World: Observing Japan from Within*, Kyoto: International Research Center for Japanese Studies, 2004.

Beaumont, Joan, Ilma Martinuzzi O'Brien, and Mathew Trinca, eds., *Under Suspicion: Citizenship and Internment in Australia during the Second World War*, Canberra, ACT: National Museum of Australia Press, 2008.

Bevan, Robert, *The Destruction of Memory: Architecture at War*, London: Reaktion, 2007.

Bevege, Margaret, *Behind Barbed Wire: Internment in Australia during World War 11*, Queensland: University of Queensland Press, 1993.

Bian, Morris L., *The Making of the State Enterprise System in Modern China: The Dynamics of Institutional Change*, Cambridge, MA: Harvard University Press, 2005.

Blackburn, Kevin, and Karl Hack, eds., *Forgotten Captives in Japanese-Occupied Asia*, London: Routledge, 2007.

Bowen-Struyk, Helen, and Norma Field, eds., *For Dignity, Justice, and Revolution: An Anthology of Japanese Proletarian Literature*, Chicago: University of Chicago Press, 2016.

Broderick, Mick, ed., *Hibakusha Cinema: Hiroshima, Nagasaki and the Nuclear Image in Japanese Film*, London: Kegan Paul International, 1996.

Bruner, Katherine F., John K. Fairbank, Katherine Bruner, and Elizabeth Matheson, eds., *The IG in Peking: Letters of Robert Hart Chinese Maritime Customs, 1868-1907*, Cambridge, MA: Harvard University Press, 1975.

Bruner, Katherine F., John K. Fairbank, and Richard J. Smith, *Entering China's Service: Robert Hart's Journals, 1854-1863*, Cambridge, MA: Harvard University Press, 1986.

Calichman, Richard F., ed. and trans., *Overcoming Modernity: Cultural Identity in Wartime Japan*, New York: Columbia University Press, 2008.

Casey, Stephen, *Selling the Korean War*, Oxford: Oxford University Press, 2008.

Chang Chihyun, ed., *The Chinese Journals of L K Little, 1943-54*, vol. 2, London: Routledge, 2017.

Chang Hyŏkchu, "Hell of the Starving," trans. Samuel Perry, in Heather Bowen-Struyk and Norma Field, eds., *For Dignity, Justice, and Revolution: An Anthology of Japanese Proletarian Literature*, Chicago: University of Chicago Press, 2016.

Chong, Ja Ian, *External Intervention and the Politics of State Formation: China, Indonesia, and Thailand, 1893-1952*, Cambridge: Cambridge University Press, 2012.

Chong Young-Hwan, "The Tokyo Trial and the Question of Colonial Responsibility: *Zainichi* Korean Reactions to Allied Justice in Occupied Japan," *International Journal of Korean History* 22, no. 1 (February 2017), pp. 77–105.

Chung, Hye Seung, "The Man with No Home/Musukja (1968): *Shane* Comes Back in a Korean 'Manchurian Western'," *Journal of Popular Film and Television* 39, no. 2 (June 2011), pp. 71–83.

Cohen, Gerard Daniel, *In War's Wake: Europe's Displaced Persons in the Postwar Order*, New York: Oxford University Press, 2012.

Conrad, Sebastian, "The Dialectics of Remembrance: Memories of Empire in Cold War Japan," *Comparative Studies in Society and History* 56, no. 1 (2014), pp. 4–33.

Cumings, Bruce, "The Legacy of Japanese Colonialism in Korea," in Ramon H. Myers and Mark R. Peattie, eds., *The Japanese Colonial Empire, 1895-1945*, Princeton, NJ: Princeton University Press, 1984, pp. 478–496.

Cumings, Bruce, *The Korean War: A History*, New York: Modern Library Chronicles, 2010.

Darwin, John, *After Tamerlane: The Rise and Fall of Global Empires, 1400-2000*, London: Penguin, 2008.

Derrida, Jacques, *Given Time: I. Counterfeit Money*, trans. Peggy Kamuf, Chicago: University of Chicago Press, 1991.

Doglia, Arnaud, *L'arme biologique japonaise, 1880-2010: réalités historique et anatomie de la mémoire*, Bern: Peter Lang, 2016.

Dower, John W., *War Without Mercy*, New York: Pantheon Books, 1986.

Dower, John W., *Embracing Defeat: Japan in the Wake of World War II*, New York: W. W. Norton, 1999.

Draper, Nicholas, *The Price of Emancipation: Slaver-ownership, Compensation and British Society at the End of Slavery*, New York: Cambridge University Press, 2010.

Drea, Edward J., ed., *Researching Japanese War Crimes Records: Introductory Essays*, Washington, DC: Nazi War Crimes and Japanese Imperial Government Records Interagency Working Group, 2006.

Duara, Prasenjit, *Sovereignty and Authenticity: Manchukuo and the East Asian Modern*, Lanham: Rowman & Littlefield, 2003.

Duus, Peter, Ramon H. Myers, Mark R. Peattie, and Wanyao Zhou, eds., *The Japanese Wartime Empire, 1931-1945*, Princeton, NJ: Princeton University Press, 1996.

Eastman, Lloyd, *Seeds of Destruction: Nationalist China in War and Revolution, 1937-1949*, Stanford: Stanford University Press, 1984.

Elliot, Mark "The Limits of Tartary: Manchuria in Imperial and National Geographies," *Journal of Asian Studies* 59, no. 3 (2000), pp. 603–646.

Esherick, Joseph W., "War and Revolution: Chinese Society during the 1940s," *Twentieth-Century China* 27, no. 1 (November 2001), pp. 1–37.

Eskildsen, Robert, "Of Civilization and Savages: The Mimetic Imperialism of Japan's 1874 Expedition to Taiwan," *American Historical Review* 107, no. 2 (April 2002), pp. 388–418.

Fairbank, John K., *Trade and Diplomacy on the China Coast: The Opening of the Treaty Ports, 1842-1854*, Cambridge, MA: Harvard University Press, 1953.

Fairbank, John K., ed., *Chinese Thought & Institutions*, Chicago: University of Chicago Press, 1957.

Falbaum, Berl, ed., *Shanghai Remembered: Stories of Jews Who Escaped to Shanghai from East Europe*, Troy, MI: Momentum Books, 2005.

Fenster, Tovi, and Haim Yacobi, eds., *Remembering, Forgetting and City Builders*, Farnham: Ashgate, 2010.

Foster Hall, B. E., "The Chinese Maritime Customs: An International Service, 1854-1950," National Maritime Museum, Maritime Monographs and Reports No. 26, 1977.

Foucault, Michel, *Discipline and Punish: The Birth of the Prison*, New York: Pantheon Books, 1979.

Fraser, Robeson Taj, *The East Is Black: Cold War China in the Black Radical Imagination*, Durham, NC: Duke University Press, 2014.

Freiberg, Freda, "China Nights (Japan, 1940): The Sustaining Romance of Japan at War," in John Whiteclay Chambers II and David Culbert, eds., *World War Two: Film and History*, Oxford: Oxford University Press, 1997, pp. 31–46.

Fujitani, Takashi, *Race for Empire: Koreans as Japanese and Japanese as Americans during World War II*, Berkeley: University of California Press, 2011.

Fujitani, Takashi, Geoffrey M. White, and Lisa Yoneyama, eds., *Perilous Memories: The Asia-Pacific War(S)*, Durham, NC: Duke University Press, 2001.

Gordon, Andrew, *Wages of Affluence: Labor and Management in Postwar Japan*, Cambridge, MA: Harvard University Press, 2009.

Guha, Ramachandra, ed., *Makers of Modern Asia*, Cambridge, MA: Harvard University Press, 2014.

Gupta, Ramesh Chandra, ed., *Handbook of Toxicology of Chemical Warfare Agents*, Amsterdam: Elsevier/AP, 2009.

Hanscom, Christopher P., and Dennis Washburn, *The Affect of Difference: Representations of Race in East Asian Empire*, Honolulu: University of Hawaii Press, 2016.

Harvey, David, *The Urban Experience*, Baltimore: John Hopkins University Press, 1989.

He, Yinan, "Remembering and Forgetting the War: Elite Mythmaking, Mass Reaction, and Sino-Japanese Relations, 1950-2006," *History & Memory* 19, no. 2 (Fall 2007), pp. 43–74.

Henry, Todd A., "Respatializing Chosŏn's Royal Capital: The Politics of Japanese Urban Reforms in Early Colonial Seoul, 1905–1919," in Timothy R. Tangherlini and Sallie Yea, eds., *Sitings: Critical Approaches to Korean Geography*, Honolulu: University of Hawai'i Press, 2008, pp. 3–14.

Henry, Todd A., *Assimilating Seoul: Japanese Rule and the Politics of Public Space in Colonial Korea, 1910–1945*, Berkeley: University of California Press, 2014.

Heppner, Ernest, *Shanghai Refuge: A Memoir of the World War II Jewish Ghetto*, Lincoln: University of Nebraska Press, 1995.

High, Peter B., *The Imperial Screen: Japanese Film Culture in the Fifteen Years' War, 1931-1945*, Madison: University of Wisconsin Press, 2003.

Hirano, Kyoko, *Mr. Smith Goes to Tokyo: Japanese Cinema under the American Occupation, 1945-1952*, Washington: Smithsonian Institution Press, 1992.

Holborn, Louise W., *The International Refugee Organization: A Specialized Agency of the United Nations: Its History and Work, 1946-1952*, New York: Oxford University Press, 1956.

Hsia Chu-Joe, "Theorizing Colonial Architecture and Urbanism: Building Colonial Modernity in Taiwan," *Inter-Asia Cultural Studies* 3, no. 1 (2002), pp. 7–23.

Huang Shu-Mei, "Ethics of Heritage: Locating the Punitive State in the Historical Penal Landscape of Taipei," *International Journal of Heritage Studies* 23, no. 2 (2017), pp. 111–124.

Igarashi Yoshikuni, *Bodies of Memory: Narratives of War in Postwar Japanese Culture, 1945-1970*, Princeton, NJ: Princeton University Press, 2000.

Igarashi Yoshikuni, "Kamikaze Today: The Search for National Heroes in Contemporary Japan," in Sheila Miyoshi Jager and Rana Mitter, eds., *Ruptured Histories: War Memory and the Post-Cold War in Asia*, Cambridge, MA: Harvard University Press, 2007, pp. 99–121.

Igarashi Yoshikuni, *Homecomings: The Belated Return of Japan's Lost Soldiers*, New York: Columbia University Press, 2016.

Itoh, Mayumi, *Japanese War Orphans in Manchuria: Forgotten Victims of World War II*, New York: Palgrave Macmillan, 2010.

Jin Jong-Heon. "Demolishing Colony: The Demolition of the Old Government-General Building of Chosŏn," in Timothy R. Tangherlini and Sallie Yea, eds., *Sitings: Critical Approaches to Korean Geography*, Honolulu: University of Hawai'i Press, 2008, pp. 39–60.

Kawashima Shin, "'Deimperialization' in Early Postwar Japan: Adjusting and Transforming the Institutions of Empire," in Barak Kushner and Sherzod Muminov, eds., *The Dismantling of Japan's Empire in East Asia: Deimperialization, Postwar Legitimation and Imperial Afterlife*, London: Routledge, 2017, pp. 30–47.

King, Amy, *China–Japan Relations after World War Two: Empire, Industry and War, 1949–1971*, Cambridge: Cambridge University Press, 2016.

Kirby, William C., "Continuity and Change in Modern China: Economic Planning on the Mainland and on Taiwan, 1943-1958," *Australian Journal of Chinese Affairs* 24 (1990), pp. 121–124.

Kitamura, Hiroshi, *Screening Enlightenment: Hollywood and the Cultural Reconstruction of Defeated Japan*, Ithaca, NY: Cornell University Press, 2010.

Kitamura, Hiroshi, "Wild, Wild War: Okamoto Kihachi and the Politics of the Desperado Films," in King-fai Tam, Timothy Y. Tsu, and Sandra Wilson, eds., *Chinese and Japanese Films on the Second World War*, London: Routledge, 2015, pp. 107–120

Klemperer, Victor, *The Language of the Third Reich: LTI, Lingua Tertii Imperii*, London: Continuum, 2006.

Koga, Yukiko, "Between the Law: The Unmaking of Empire and Law's Imperial Amnesia," *Law & Social Inquiry* 41, no. 2 (Spring 2016), pp. 402–434.

Kowalski, Frank, *An Inoffensive Rearmament: The Making of the Postwar Japanese Army*, Annapolis, MD: Naval Institute Press, 2013.

Krasno, Rena, *Strangers Always: A Jewish Family in Wartime Shanghai*, Berkeley: Pacific View Press, 2000.

Kratoska, Paul H., ed., *Asian Labor in the Wartime Japanese Empire: Unknown Histories*, Armonk, NY: M. E. Sharpe, 2005.

Kushner, Barak, *Men to Devils, Devils to Men: Japanese War Crimes and Chinese Justice*, Cambridge, MA: Harvard University Press, 2015.

Kushner, Barak (Gu Ruopeng), "Chuli zhanhou de shengli: guomindang, riben yu gongchandang duiyu zhengyi de lichang" (Chen Kuan-jen fanyi), Guoli zhengzhi daxue lishi xuebao (Taiwan), di 50, November 2018, pp. 143–174.

Ladd, Brian, *The Ghosts of Berlin: Confronting German History in the Urban Landscape*, Chicago: University of Chicago Press, 1997.

Lary, Diana, *China's Civil War: A Social History, 1945-1949*, Cambridge: Cambridge University Press, 2015.

Leck, Greg, *Captives of Empire: The Japanese Internment of Allied Civilians in China, 1941–1945*, Bangor, PA: Shandy Press, 2006.

Lee Hyun-Kyung, *"Difficult Heritage" in Nation Building: South Korea and Post-Conflict Japanese Colonial Occupation Architecture*, New York: Palgrave Macmillan, 2018.

Levin, Mark A., "Supreme Court of Japan Decision 2008/04/27: *Nishimatsu Construction Co. v. Song Jixiao et al.,*" *American Journal of International Law* 102 (2008), pp. 148–154.

Levine, Steven I, *Anvil of Victory: The Communist Revolution in Manchuria, 1945–1948*, New York: Columbia University Press, 1987.

Loescher, Gil, *The UNHCR and World Politics: A Perilous Path*, New York: Oxford University Press, 2001.

Manchester, Laurie, "Repatriation to a Totalitarian Homeland: The Ambiguous Alterity of Russian Repatriates from China to the USSR," *Diaspora: A Journal of Transnational Studies* 16, no. 3 (December 2007), pp. 353–388.

Masuda, Hajimu, "Fear of World War III: Social Politics of Japan's Rearmament and Peace Movements," *Journal of Contemporary History* 47, no. 3 (2012), pp. 551–571.

Masuda, Hajimu, *Cold War Crucible: The Korean Conflict and the Postwar World*, Cambridge, MA: Harvard University Press, 2015.

Mauss, Marcel, *The Gift: The Form and Reason for Exchange in Archaic Societies*, trans. W. D. Halls, New York: W. W. Norton, [1924] 1990.

Mitter, Rana, *The Manchurian Myth: Nationalism, Resistance, and Collaboration in Modern China*, Berkeley: University of California Press, 2000.

Mitter, Rana, "Old ghosts, new memories: changing China's war history in the era of post-Mao politics," *Journal of Contemporary History* 38, no. 1 (January 2003), pp. 117–131.

Mitter, Rana, "Modernity, Internationalisation, and War in the History of Modern China," *Historical Journal* 48, no. 2 (June 2005), pp. 431–446.

Mitter, Rana, *Forgotten Ally: China's World War II, 1937-1945*, Boston, MA: Houghton Mifflin Harcourt, 2013.

Miyoshi Jager, Sheila, and Rana Mitter, eds., *Ruptured Histories: War Memory and the Post-Cold War in Asia*, Cambridge, MA: Harvard University Press, 2007.

Morris, Mark, "On the Trail of the Manchurian Western," *Korea: Politics, Economy and Society* 4 (2010), pp. 217–246.

Morris-Suzuki, Tessa, "Guarding the Borders of Japan: Occupation, Korean War and Frontier Controls," *Asia-Pacific Journal* 9, issue 8, no. 3 (February 21, 2011).

Morris-Suzuki, Tessa, "Lavish are the Dead: Re-envisioning Japan's Korean War," *Asia-Pacific Journal* 11, no. 52 (December 30, 2013).

Musgrove, Charles D., "Cheering the Traitor: The Post-War Trial of Chen Bijun, April 1946," *Twentieth-Century China* 30, no. 2 (April 2005), pp. 3–27

Myers, Ramon H., and Mark R. Peattie, eds., *The Japanese Colonial Empire, 1895–1945*, Princeton, NJ: Princeton University Press, 1984.

Nagata, Yuriko, *Unwanted Aliens: Japanese Internment in Australia*, St. Lucia, Qld: University of Queensland Press, 1996.

"National Park Resorts," National Park Resort Homepage, available online: www.qkamura.or.jp/en/ohkuno/, accessed November 11, 2017.

Neumann, Klaus, *In the Interest of National Security: Civilian Internment in Australia during World War II*, Canberra, ACT: National Archives of Australia, 2006.

Newham, Fraser, "The White Russians of Shanghai," *History Today* 55, no. 12 (December 2005), pp. 20–27.

Nish, Ian, "Regaining Confidence – Japan after the Loss of Empire," *Journal of Contemporary History* 15 (1980), pp. 181–195.

Oh, Mi-Young, "'Eternal Other' Japan: South Koreans' Postcolonial Identity," *International Journal of the History of Sport* 26, no. 3 (2009), pp. 371–389.

Ohnuki-Tierney, Emiko, *Kamikaze Diaries: Reflections of Japanese Student Soldiers*, Chicago: University of Chicago Press, 2006.

Orr, James, *The Victim as Hero: Ideologies of Peace and National Identity in Postwar Japan*, Honolulu: University of Hawai'i Press, 2001.

Oyen, Meredith, "The Right of Return: Chinese Displaced Persons and the International Refugee Organization, 1947–56," *Modern Asian Studies* 49, no. 2 (March 2015), pp. 546–571.

Park Jung Ji, "North Korean Nation Building and Japanese Imperialism: People's Nation, People's Diplomacy, and the Japanese Technicians," trans. Sherzod Muminov, in Barak Kushner and Sherzod Muminov, eds., *The Dismantling of Japan's Empire in East Asia: Deimperialization, Postwar Legitimation and Imperial Afterlife*, London: Routledge, 2016, pp. 199–219.

Pepper, Suzanne, *Civil War in China: The Political Struggle 1945-1949*, Berkeley: University of California Press, 1978.

Perry, Samuel, "Article Review of Simon Nantais, 'Race to Subversion: Nationality and Koreans in Occupied Japan, 1945–1952,'" *H-Diplo Article Review* no. 611 (April 28, 2016).

Podoler, Guy, "Nation, State and Football: The Korean Case," *International Journal of the History of Sport* 27, no. 1 (2008), pp. 1–17.

Podoler, Guy, "Seoul: City, Identity and the Construction of the Past," in Tovi Fenster and Haim Yacobi, eds., *Remembering, Forgetting and City Builders*, Farnham: Ashgate, 2010, pp. 121–140.

Saito Hiro, *The History Problem: The Politics of War Commemoration in East Asia*, Honolulu: University of Hawai'i Press, 2016.

Salomon, Kim, *Refugees in the Cold War*, Lund: Studentlitteratur, 1991.

Sata Ineko, *Five Faces of Feminism: Crimson and Other Works*, trans. Samuel Perry, Honolulu: University of Hawai'i Press, 2016.

Schivelbusch, Wolfgang, *The Culture of Defeat: On National Trauma, Mourning, and Recovery*, trans. Jefferson Chase, New York: Picador, 2003.

Schmid, Andre, *Korea between Empires, 1895-1919*, New York: Columbia University Press, 2002.

Scott, Christopher Donal, "Invisible Men: The Zainichi Korean Presence in Postwar Japanese Culture," PhD diss., Stanford University, 2006.

Seeley, John Robert, *The Expansion of England: Two Courses of Lectures*, New York: Cosimo Classics, 2005.

Selden, Mark, "Living with the Bomb: The Atomic Bomb in Japanese Consciousness," *Japan Focus: The Asia Pacific Journal*, 3, no. 8 (August 3, 2005).

Seraphim, Franziska, *War Memory and Social Politics in Japan, 1945-2005*, Cambridge, MA: Harvard University Press, 2006.

Shephard, Ben, *The Long Road Home: The Aftermath of the Second World War*, New York: Alfred A. Knopf, 2011.

Shibusawa, Naoko, *America's Geisha Ally: Re-Imagining the Japanese Enemy*, Cambridge, MA: Harvard University Press, 2010.

Sixth United States Army, ed., "Report of the Occupation of Japan 22 September 1945 – 30 November 1945," 8th US Army Printing Plant, 1946.

Skocpol, Theda, *States and Social Revolutions*, Cambridge: Cambridge University Press, 1979.

Smith, Susan L., "Mustard Gas and American Race-Based Human Experimentation in World War II," *Journal of Law, Medicine & Ethics: A Journal of the American Society of Law, Medicine & Ethics* 36, no. 3 (Fall 2008), pp. 517–521.

Snyder, Timothy, *Bloodlands: Europe between Hitler and Stalin*, London: Vintage, 2011.

Stegewerns, Dick, "The Physical and Mental Criteria of Japanese Identity: Can Foreigners Make an Authentic Japanese Movie?," in James C. Baxter, ed., *Japanese Studies Around the World: Observing Japan from Within*, Kyoto: International Research Center for Japanese Studies, 2004, pp. 304–305.

Stegewerns, Dick, "Establishing the Genre of the Revisionist War Film: The Shin-Tōhō Body of Post-Occupation War Films in Japan," in Tam King-Fai, Timothy Y. Tsu, and Sandra Wilson, eds., *Chinese and Japanese Films on the Second World War*, London: Routledge, 2015, pp. 93–106.

Stegewerns, Dick, "From Chinese World Order to Japan's Modern Mindset: Japanese Views of the Outside World from the Early Modern Period until the Present Day," in Kurt Almqvist, ed., *Japanese Self-Images*, Stockholm: Axel and Margaret Axson Johnson Foundation, 2017, pp. 41–56.

Sullivan, James T., *Beyond All Hate: The Story of a Wartime Internment Camp for Japanese in Australia, 1941-1946*, Victoria, Australia: James T. Sullivan, 2006.

Tam, King-fai, Timothy Y. Tsu, and Sandra Wilson, eds., *Chinese and Japanese Films on the Second World War*, London: Routledge, 2015.

"The National Institute for Occupational Safety and Health," Centers for Disease Control and Prevention, available online: www.cdc.gov/niosh/index.htm, accessed October 15, 2017.

Tōjō Hideki, "Inaugural Address to the Greater East Asia Conference," in *Sources of Japanese Tradition, Volume Two: 1600 to 2000, Abridged, Part Two: 1868 to 2000*, Second Edition, compiled by W. M. Theodore de Bary, Carol Gluck, and Arthur E. Tiedemann, New York: Columbia University Press, 2006.

Treat, John Whittier, "Chang Hyŏkchu and the Short Twentieth Century," in Christopher P. Hanscom and Dennis C. Washburn, eds., *The Affect of Difference: Representations of Race in East Asian Empire*, Honolulu: The University of Hawai'i Press, 2016, pp. 244–259.

Vale, Lawrence, *Architecture, Power and National Identity*, New York: Routledge, 2014.

Van de Ven, Hans, *China at War: Triumph and Tragedy in the Emergence of the New China*, Cambridge, MA: Harvard University Press, 2018.

Van Haute, Luk, "Dealing with the Identity Crisis: Japanese Cinema Lefty and Right," *Asian Cinema* 16, no. 1 (Spring/Summer 2005), pp. 125–134.

Wakabayashi, Bob Tadashi, "Documents on Japanese Poison Gas Warfare in China," *Sino-Japanese Studies* 7 (October 1994), pp. 3–33.

Watt, Lori, *When Empire Comes Home: Repatriation and Reintegration in Postwar Japan*, Cambridge, MA: Harvard University Asia Center, 2010.

Westad, Odd Arne, *Decisive Encounters: The Chinese Civil War, 1946-1950*, Stanford: Stanford University Press, 2003.

Whiteclay Chambers II, John, and David Culbert, eds., *World War Two: Film and History*, Oxford: Oxford University Press, 1997.

Wieviorka, Annette, *Auschwitz, 60 Ans Après*, Paris: Laffont, 2005.

Wieviorka, Olivier, *La Mémoire Désunie: Le Souvenir Politique Des Années Sombres de La Libération à Nos Jours*, L'univers Historique, Paris: Seuil, 2010.

Willens, Liliane, *Stateless in Shanghai*, Hong Kong: Earnshaw Books, 2010.

Woodbridge, George, *UNRRA: the History of the United Nations Relief and Rehabilitation Administration*, New York: Columbia University Press, 1950.

Xia, Yun, *Down with Traitors: Justice and Nationalism in Wartime China*, Seattle: University of Washington Press, 2017.

Yamakido, M., S. Ishioka, K. Hiyama, and A. Maeda, "Former Poison Gas Workers and Cancer: Incidence and Inhibition of Tumor Formation by Treatment with Biological Response Modifier N-CWS," *Environmental Health Perspectives* 104, Suppl 3 (May 1996), pp. 485–488.

Yamanouchi, Yasushi, J. Victor Koschmann, and Ryūichi Narita, eds., *Total War and "Modernization,"* Ithaca, NY: East Asia Program, Cornell University, 1998.

Yamazaki, Jane W., *Japanese Apologies for World War II: A Rhetorical Study*, Routledge Contemporary Japan Series 3, London: Routledge, 2006.

Yoneyama, Lisa, *Hiroshima Traces: Time, Space, and the Dialectics of Memory*, Twentieth-Century Japan, vol. 10, Berkeley: University of California Press, 1999.

Young, Louise, *Japan's Total Empire: Manchuria and the Culture of Wartime Imperialism*, Berkeley: University of California Press, 1999.

Young, Louise, "Rethinking Empire: Lessons from Imperial and Post-imperial Japan," in Martin Thomas and Andrew Thompson, eds., *The Oxford Handbook of the Ends of Empire*, Oxford: Oxford University Press, 2017. doi: 10.1093/oxfordhb/9780198713197.013.13.

Chinese language sources

Cao Haidong and Huang Xiaowei, "Riben dui hua yuanzhu san shi nian", *Nanfang zhoumo*, February 20, 2008. Available online: www.infzm.com/content/7707, accessed June 29, 2019.

Chen Qingquan, and Song Guangwei, *Lu Dingyi Zhuan*, Beijing: Chinese Communist Party History Press, 1999.

Chen Qingquan, *Zai Zhong-Gong gaoceng 50 nian: Lu Dingyi chuanqi rensheng*, Beijing: People's Press, 2006.

Chen Zhanyi, ed., *Riben ren fang Gang jianwenlu—1898-1941, xia*, Hong Kong: Sanlian shudian, 2005.

Gongye jiaotong wuzi tongji si, *Zhongguo gongye jingji tongji ziliao*, Beijing: Zhongguo tongji chubanshe, 1985.

He Tianyi, ed., *Erzhan lu Ri Zhongguo laogong koushushi*, 5 vols., Jinan, China: Qilu shushe, 2005.

Kang Yan, "Gongye quwei peizhi wenti," *Zhongguo gongye wushinian*, 1950.

Kushner, Barak (Gu Ruopeng), "Chuli zhanhou de shengli: guomindang, riben yu gongchandang duiyu zhengyi de lichang," Guoli zhengzhi daxue lishi xuebao, forthcoming.

Lai Zehan, ed., *228 Shijian Yanjiu Baogao*, Taipei: China Times Press, 1994.

Li Fuchun, "diyici quanguo gongye huiyi jielun" (March 6, 1951).

Zhonghua Renmin Gongheguo guojia jingji maoyi weiyuanhui, *Zhongguo gongye wushinian*, Beijing: Zhongguo jingji chubanshe, 2000.

Li Shufen, *Xianggang waike yisheng liushinian*, Hong Kong: The Li Shu Fan Medical Foundation Limited, 1965.

Lin Zhida, *Zhongguo Gongchandang xuanchuan shi*, Chengdu: Sichuan People's Press, 1990.

Samejima Moritaka, *Xianggang huixiang ji—Rijun zhanlingxia de Xianggang*, trans. Gong Shusen, Hong Kong: Jidujiao wenyi chubanshe, 1971.

Shen Zhihua, *Sulian zhuanjia zai Zhongguo*, Beijing: Xinhua chubanshe, 2009.

Tang Xiyong, "Huifu guoji de zhengyi: zhanhou luwai Taiwanren de fuji wenti, 1945–1947," *Renwen ji shehuikexue jikan* 17, no. 2 (2005), pp. 393–437.

Tang Xiyong, "Fenghuo hou de tongxiangqing: zhanhou Dongya Taiwan tongxianghui de chengli, zhuanbian yu jiaose," *Renwen ji shehuikexue* 19, no. 1 (2007), pp. 1–49.

Wang Jianying, *Zhong-Gong Zhongyang jiguan lishi yanbian kaoshi (1921-1949)*, Beijing: Communist Party History Press, 2004.

Wang Qun, "Huiyi Angang 'qi jiu' kaigong," in Zhonggong Anshan shiwei dangshi gongzuo weiyuanhui bangongshi (ed.), *Anshan shuguang: Anshan diqu jiefang zhanzheng shiqi dangshi ziliao huibian* (Anshan: Zhonggong Anshan shiwei dangshi bangongshi, 1992), pp. 274–283.

Xie Yongguang, *Zhanshi Rijun zai Xianggang de baoxing*, Hong Kong: Mingpao Publishing, 1991.

Xie Yongguang, *Sannian ling bageyue de kunan*, Hong Kong: Mingpao Publishing, 1994.

Zhang Jianqiu, "Tianyuan jiangwu hubugui? zhanhou Guangzhou diqu Taibao chujing ji fanji wenti," *Taiwanshi yanjiu* 6, no. 1 (1999), pp. 133–166.

Zhang Jianqiu, "Tiaotiao guixianglu: zhanhou Gang Ao diqu Taibao fanji shimo," in *Gang Ao yu jindai Zhongguo xueshu yantaohui lunwenji* (Taipei: Academia Historica, 2000), pp. 549–580.

Zhao Yuming, *Zhongguo xiandai guangbo jianzhi*, Beijing: China Broadcasting and Television Press, 1987.

Zhong Shumin, "Erzhanshiqi Taiwanren Yindu jizhongying juliuji," *Taiwanshi yanjiu* 24, no. 3 (2017), pp. 89–140.

Zhongyang Yanjiuyuan Jindaishi Yanjiusuo Koushu Lishi Bianji Wenyuanhui, ed., *Koushu lishi diwuqi: Riju shiqi Taiwanren fu dalu jingyan zhuanhao zhiyi*, Taipei: Zhongyang yanjiuyuan jindaishi yanjiusuo, 1994.

Zhonggong Zhongyang Wenxian Yanjiushi, ed., *Mao Zedong wenji*, 8 vols., Beijing: Renmin chubanshe, 1993-1999.

Zhongyang Zhonggong Wenxian Yanjiushi, ed., *Chen Yun wenji*, Beijing: Zhongyang wenxian chubanshe, 2005.

Zhonggong Zhongyang Xuanchuan Bu Bangongting, ed., *Zhongguo Gongchandang xuanchuan gongzuo wenxian xuanbian, 1939-1945*, Zhongyang dang'an guan bianyan bu, Beijing: Study Press, 1996.

Japanese language sources

Akira, Kitade, *Fuzan-kō monogatari: Zaikan Nihonjin tsuma wo sasaeta Ch'oe* Pyŏn-de *no hachijūnen*, Tokyo: Shakai hyōron, 2009.

Aramaki Hiroshi, and Kobayashi Toshiyuki, "Yoronchōsa de miru nihonjin no 'sengo': 'sengo 70 nen ni kansuru ishiki chōsa' no kekka kara," *Hōsō kenkyū to chōsa* (August 2015), pp. 2–17. Available online: www.nhk.or.jp/bunken/research/yoron/pdf/20150801_4.pdf, accessed March 21, 2018.

Chang Hyŏkchu, "Urei ga harete," *Shōjo sekai* 2, no. 1 (January 1949), pp. 26–35.

Chang Hyŏkchu, *Ri ōke hishi: Hien no hana*, Tokyo: Sekaisha, 1950.

Chang Hyŏkchu, "Chōsen no dōkoku," *Fujin kurabu* 34, no. 1 (January 1952), pp. 228–245.

Chang Hyŏkchu, "Aa Chōsen," *Shincho* 49, no. 2 (February 1952), pp. 172–212.

Chang Hyŏkchu, "Fuzan-kō no aoi hana," *Omoshiro kurabu* 5, no. 10 (September 1952), pp. 48–72.

Chang Hyŏkchu, "Fūzan no onna kancho," *Bessatu Bungei shunjū*, no. 31 (December 1952), pp. 162–181.

Chang Hyŏkchu, "Simchŏng monogatari," *Shōjo kurabu* (December 1953), pp. 255–267.

Fukuma Yoshiaki, *Junkoku to Hangyaku: [Tokkō] no katari no sengoshi*, Tokyo: Seikyūsha, 2007.

Fukuma Yoshiaki, *Shōdo no kioku: Okinawa, Hiroshima, Nagasaki ni utsuru sengo*, Tokyo: Shinyōsha, 2011.

Fukuma Yoshiaki, Yamaguchi Makoto and Yoshimura Kazuma, eds., *Fukusū no [Hiroshima]: Kioku no sengoshi to media no rikigaku*, Tokyo: Seikyūsha, 2012.

Fukushima Katsuyuki, *Teijin no ayumi*, Tokyo: Teijin Kabushiki Gaisha, 1968.

Fukushima Katsuyuki, *Teijin no ayumi*, vol. 5, Tokyo: Teijin Kabushiki Gaisha, 1970.

Gaimushō Kanrikyoku, *Kajin rōmusha shūrō jijō chōsa hōkokusho*, Tokyo: Diplomatic Record Office of the Ministry of Foreign Affairs of Japan, 1946.

Gaimushō Kanrikyoku, *Taiheiyō sensō shūketsu ni yoru naigai jin hogo hikiage (gaikokujin)*, Tokyo: Diplomatic Record Office of the Ministry of Foreign Affairs of Japan, 1952–1972.

Gaimushō Tsushōkyoku, *Benshō fukkokuban—Kaigai kakuchi zairyū honbōjin shokugyōbetsu jinkōyō: Daiichikan Meiji 40 nen—Taishō 13 nen; Dainikan Taishō 14 nen—Shōwa 4 nen*, Tokyo: Fuji shuppan, 2002.

Giga Sōichirō, "Seibutsu kagaku heiki to seiyaku kigyō no rekishiteki yakuwari," *Kokumin iryō* 229 (October 1, 2006), pp. 17–24.

Hagami Tarō, "Kankyōshō ga 'hōchi' shita maboroshi no 'doku gasu' jōhō futatabi kesareru? Rikugun himitsu kōjō – Hiroshima ken Ōkunoshima ga tō Nihon no taishitsu," *Sande- Mainichi* 9 (February 20, 2005), pp. 148–151.

Hirata Tetsuo, *Reddo pāji no shiteki kyūmei*, Tokyo: Shin Nihon shuppan, 2002.

Hiratsuka Raichō, *Shinjoen* (September 1950), reprinted in *Hiratsuka Raichō chosakushū*, vol. 7, Tokyo: Ōtsuki shoten, 1984.

"Hiroshima Peace Media Center," Hiroshima Peace Media Center. Available online: www.hiroshimapeacemedia.jp/?p=52294, accessed November 11, 2017.

Honda Katsuichi, *Chūgoku no tabi*, Tokyo: Suzusawa Shoten, 1977.

Hosokawa Shūhei, Yamada Shōji, and Sano Mayuko, eds., *Shinryōiki/jisedai no Nihon kenkyū*, Kyoto: Kokusai Nihon Bunka Kenkyū Sentaa, 2016.

Iizuka Yasushi, "Senji Manshū to sengo Tōhoku no keizaishi," in Kubo Toru, ed., *Chūgoku Keizaishi Nyūmon*, Tokyo: Tokyō daigaku shuppankai, 2012, pp. 149–162.

Inoue Masao, *Bunka to tōsō: Tōhō sōgi, 1946-1948*, Tokyo: Shinyōsha, 2007.

Ishida Masaharu, "Amerika gun no Hiroshima ken shinchū to Ōkunoshima doku gasu haiki," *Nihon rekishi*, 795 (August 2014), pp. 54–71.

Ishida Masaharu, "Amerika rikugun dai 41 shidan no Hiroshima ken shinchū to Ōkunoshima doku gasu shori," *Chiiki akademi- kōkaikōza hōkokusho* (2013), pp. 21–25.

"Kagaku heiki kinshi jōyaku," Tokyo: Gaimushō, 2006.

Kajimura Masao, "'Doku gasu giseisha' no sengo," *Sekai* (August 1972), pp. 314–316.

Kajin rōmusha shūrō tenmatsu hōkoku (yōshi), Tokyo: Diplomatic Record Office of the Ministry of Foreign Affairs of Japan, 1946.

Kamiya Noriaki, *Nagaki chinmoku: chichi ga katatta akuma no 731 butai*, Kyoto: Kamogawa Shuppan, 2017.

Kawai Shin'Ichi, *Chūgoku kigyō to Soren moderu: itchōsei no shiteki kenkyū*, Tokyo: Ajia seikei gakkai, 1991.

Kim T'ae-gi, *Sengo Nihon seiji to zainichi Chōsenjin mondai: SCAP to tai-zainichi Chōsenjin seisaku 1945-1952*, Tokyo: Keisō Shobō, 1997.

Kimura Sotoji, "Chūgoku dewa tanoshikatta," *Chūō kōron* 68, no. 5 (1953), pp. 183–192.

Knop, Karen, and Annelise Riles, "Space, Time, and Historical Injustice: A Feminist Conflict-of-Laws Approach to the 'Comfort Women' Agreement," Cornell Law Review 102, issue 4 (2017), pp. 853–928.

Ko Youngran, "*Sengo*" *to iu ideorogii: rekishi, kioku, bunka*, Tokyo: Fujiwara shoten, 2010.

Kobayashi Teruki, "Tansokin dokoro deha nai akumu no sairai! Asahara, sarin, Ben Laden Ishii 731 butai to oumu shinrikyō," *Shokun* 12 (December 2001), pp. 158–169.

Kokubun Ryōsei, *Gendai Chūgoku no seiji to kanryōsei*, Tokyo: Keiō gijuku daigaku shuppankai, 2004.

Kubo Tōru, "Sōron: 1949nen kakumei no rekishiteki ichi," in Kubo Tōru, ed., *1949nen zengo no Chūgoku*, Tokyo: Kyūko shoin, 2006.

Kubo Tōru, *Chūgoku Keizaishi Nyūmon*, Tokyo: Tokyō daigaku shuppankai, 2012.

Manabe Nobuyoshi, "Ōkunoshima ni okeru doku gasu shōsha no haire sen shōken," *Hiroshima Igakkai* 10, no. 6 (June 1957), pp. 18–20.

Marusawa Tsuneya, *Shin Chūgoku kensetsu to Mantetsu Chūō shikenjo*, Tokyo: Nigatsusha, 1979.

Matsumoto Toshirō, "*Manshūkoku" kara shin Chūgoku e: Anzan tekkōgyō kara mita Chūgoku tōhoku no saihen katei, 1940-1954*, Nagoya: Nagoya daigaku shuppankai, 2000.

Matsuno Seiya, *Nihon gun no doku gasu heiki*, Tokyo: Gaifūsha, 2005.

Mine Takeshi, *Chūgoku ni keishō sareta Manshūkoku no sangyō: Kagaku kogyō wo chūshin ni mita keishō no jittai*, Tokyo: Ochanomizu Shobō, 2009.

Minoru Takeuchi, ed., *Mō Takutō shū*, 2nd edn., 10 vols., Tokyo: Sōsō sha, 1983.

Monma Takashi, *Ō-Bei eiga ni miru Nihon*, Tokyo: Shakai Hyōronsha, 1995.

Mōri Fumie, "Hokusen dasshutsuki: Sei to shi no sanjū hachi sendō," *Kingu* (November 1950).

Morita Yoshio, *Chōsen shūsen no kiroku: beiso ryōgun no shinchū to nihonjin no hikiage*, Tokyo: Gannandō shoten, 1964.

NHK Research Team, *Maboroshino gaimushō hōkokusho: Chūgokujin kyōsei renkō no kiroku*, Tokyo: Nihon hōsō shuppan kyōkai, 1994.

NHK "Ryūyōsareta Nihonjin" shuzaihan, *"Ryūyō" sareta Nihonjin: watashitachi wa Chūgoku kenkoku wo sasaeta*, Tokyo: Nihon hōsō shuppan kyōkai, 2003.

Nakane Harushi, and Michiyo Arakawa, "Shōgen kaigun doku gasu kōjō no hibi," *Chūkiren* (July 2010), pp. 50–59.

Nihon rikugun kayaku shi, Tokyo: Ōkakai, 1969.

Nishimura Hideki, *Ōsaka de tatakatta Chōsen sensō*, Tokyo: Iwanami shoten, 2004.

Nishinarita Yutaka, *Chūgokujin kyōsei renkō*, Tokyo: Tokyo Daigaku shuppankai, 2002.

Okano Yūji, ed., *Doku gasu tō: Ōkunoshima doku gasu kōjō sono higai to kagai*, Hiroshima: Hiroshima heiwa kyōiku kenkyūjo, 1987.

Ōkunoshima doku gasu shōgai sono jissō to keishō: Sengo 65 shūnen kinen jigyō, Hiroshima: Hiroshima ken kenkō fukushi kyoku, 2011.

Pak Chŏng-wŏn, *Chōsen sensō: Nihon wa kono sensō ni dō kakawatta ka*, Tokyo: San'ichi shobo, 2013.

Sasakura Masao, *Jinminfuku nikki*, Tokyo: Banmachi shobō, 1973.

Shigeru, Ashida, "Chosen sensō to Nihon: Nihon no yakuwari to Nihon e no eikyō," *Senshi kenkyū nempo* 8 (March 2005), pp. 103–126.

Shōwa 48 nen no 'kyū gun doku gasu tama nado no zenkoku chōsa' foro-appu chōsa hōkoku sho, Tokyo: Kankyōshō, 2003.

Stegewerns, Dick, "Kyori, seigi, tabū: Nichi-Ō [Hiroshima] imeiji no kakuzetsu," in Fukuma Yoshiaki, Yamaguchi Makoto, and Yoshimura Kazuma, eds., *Fukusū no [Hiroshima]: Kioku no sengoshi to media no rikigaku*, Tokyo: Seikyūsha, 2012, pp. 311–324.

Stegewerns, Dick, "Shūseishugiteki sensō eiga no kakuritsu: Senryōki-go no sensō eiga," in Hosokawa Shūhei, Yamada Shōji, and Sano Mayuko, eds., *Shinryōiki/jisedai no Nihon kenkyū*, Kyoto: Kokusai Nihon Bunka Kenkyū Sentaa, 2016, pp. 9–21.

Sugi Yasusaburō, "Seto naikai no doku gasu shima," *Bungei Shunjū* 5 (May 1956), pp. 238–251.

Takeda Eiko, *Chizu kara kesareta shima: Ōkunoshima doku gasu kōjō*, Tokyo: Domes Shuppan, 1987.

Takuso Shigenobu, "Doku gasu shōgai ni kan suru kenkyū to genjō," in Higuchi Kenji, ed., *Doku gasu no shima*, Tokyo: Kobushi Shobō, 2015, pp. 160–175.

Tanaka Hiroaki, "Nihon doku gasu sen no rekishi," *Kagakushi kenkyū* 4 (2011), pp. 210–220.

Tanaka Hiroshi, Utsumi Aiko, and Ishitobi Jin, eds., *Shiryō chūgokujin kyōsei renkō*, Tokyo: Akashi shoten, 1987.

Tatsumi Tomoji, *Kakusaretekita "Hiroshima": Doku gasu shima kara no kokuhatsu*, Tokyo: Nihon Hyōronsha, 1993.

Tensuikai, "Sengo Chūgoku hondo (Kanshuku shō Tensui) ryūyō ki," in *Mantetsu shain shūsen kiroku*, Tokyo: Mantetsukai, 1996.

Tōmon Jinni, and YuzuKi Hiroshi, *Gaikoku eiga ni miru Ajia-Taiheiyō sensō*, Tokyo: San-ichi Shobō, 1995.

Toyoda Minoru, *Chōsen sensō to reddo pāji: erosu no urei*, Tokyo: Kōdansha, 1986.

Kei'ichi, Tsuneishi, *Kieta saikin sen butai Kantō gun dai nana san ichi butai*, Tokyo: Chikuma Shobō, 1993.

Tsuneishi Kei'ichi, "Tokushū kenkyū kaigun no kagaku sen kenkyū kaihatsu shi," *Rekishi dokuhon* 9 (September 2010), pp. 196–201.

Tsuneishi Kei'ichi, "Doku gasu higai to Koizumi naikaku," *Hon* 1 (January 2004), pp. 52–54.

Usami Shō, "Kanashiki doku gasu kanja tachi," *Asahi Ja-Naru* 2 (January 1966), pp. 103–108.

Yamamoto Tatsuya, and Daisuke Kusanagi, *Nihon no kagaku heiki 1, hōheiyō gasudan no hyōshiki to kōzō*, Gifu: Zen Nippon Gunsō Kenkyūkai, 2010, pp. 22–43.

Yamauchi Masanori, "Doku gasu shiryō kan moto kanchō Murakami shi he no intabyū-," *Kagaku to shakai wo kangaeru doyō kōza ronbun shu*, no. 1 (May 1997).

Yamauchi Masanori, ed., *Kiroku ni nai shima, doku gasu tō rekishi kenkyūjo kaihō*, Takehara: Doku gasu tō rekishi kenkyūjo kaihō, 1996.

Yang Hüisuk, "Chō Kakuchū [Chang Hyŏkchu] sengō no shuppatsu—zainichi Chōsenjin minzoku dantai to no kakawari wo chūshin ni," *Shakai bungaku*, no. 38 (2013), pp. 90–103.

Yi Kiyong, *Yomigaeru Daichi*, Tokyo: Nauka, 1951.

Yomota Inuhiko, *Ri Kō-ran to Hara Setsuko*, Tokyo: Iwanami Shoten, 2011.

Yoshida Yutaka, *Nihonjin no sensō kan: Sengo shi no naka no henyō*, Tokyo: Iwanami Bunko, 2005.

Yoshimi Yoshiaki, ed., *Boku ha doku gasu no mura de umareta. anata ga sensō no otoshi mono ni deattara*, Tokyo: Gōdō Shuppan, 2007.

Yoshimi Yoshiaki, *Doku gasu sen to nihon gun*, Tokyo: Iwanami Shoten, 2004.

Yukutake Masato, ed., *Hitori hitori no Ōkunoshima: Doku gasu kōjō kara no shōgen*, Tokyo: Domes Shuppan, 2012.

Yukutake Masato, "Tadanoumi Byōin Tadaima Orikaeshi Ten," in Higuchi Kenji, ed., *Doku gasu no shima*, Tokyo: Kobushi Shobō, 2015, pp. 176–187.

Korean language sources

Academy of Korean Studies, ed., *Hanguk Hyeondaesaui Jaeinsik 1*, Seoul: Oreum, 1998.

Ahn Jong-Cheol, "1930-40 nyeondae Namsan Sojae Gyeongseong Hoguk Shinsaui Geonrib, Hwalyong, geurigo Haebank Hu Byeonhwa," *Journal of Seoul Studies* 42 (2011), pp. 49–74.

Chi Young-Im, "Jeonhu Hangugeseoui Gukgasindosiseolui Beonyong: Guknaee Geollipdoen Sinsawa Sinsateoreul Jungsimeuro," *Ireoinmunhak* 69 (2016), pp. 349–365.

Choe In-Gyu, *Myeongin okjunggi*, Seoul: Huimang Chulpansa, 1996.

Choi Seok-Yeong, *Iljeha Musokrongwa Sikminji Gwollyeok*, Seoul: Seokeongmunhwasa, 1999.

Eun Jeong-Tae, "Park Chung-hee Sidae Seongyeokhwa Saupui Chuiwa Sunggeok," *Yeoksamunjeyeongu* 15 (2005), pp. 241–277.

Gwon Gi-Bong, *Seoulul geonilmye sarajeganun Yeoksarul Mannada*, Paju: Alma, 2011.

Gwon Hyeong-Jin, and Lee Jong-Hun, *Daejung Dokjaeui Youngwoong Mandeulgi*, Seoul: Humanist, 2005.

Hiroshi Hashiya, *Ilbon Jegukjuui, Sikminji Dosiruel Geonseolhada*, trans. Jae Jeong Kim, Seoul: Motive, 2005.

Im Seok-Jae, *Seoul, geonchukui dosiruel guekda 1*, Seoul: Inmulgwa Sasangsa, 2010.

Jang Gyu-Sik, *Seoul, Gongganuro bon Yeoksa*, Seoul: Hyean, 2004.

Jeon Jae-Ho, *Bandongjeok Geundaejuuija Park Chung-hee*, Seoul: Chaeksesang, 2000.

Jeong Ho-Gi, "Gukgaui Hyeongseonggwa Gwangjangui Jeongchi," *Sahoewa Yeoksa* 77 (2008), pp. 179–181.

Jeong Jae-Jeong, Yeom In-Ho, and Jang Gyu-Sik, *Gaehyeok, Chimryak, Jeohang, Geungukui Jachuirul chakaganuen Seoul Geunhyeundaesa Yeoksa Giheng*, Seoul: Seoul City University Press, 1998.

Joseon Chongdokbu (The Japanese Government-General of Korea), *Joseon Chongdukbuyeonbo 1937*, Gyeongseong: Joseon Chongdokbu, 1939.

Jung You-Jin, "Park Chung-hee Jeongbugi Munhwajaejeongchaekgwa Minsokshinang: Guksadanggwa Bamseombugundangeul jungsimeuro," *Yeoksaminsokhak* 39 (2012), pp. 180–183.

Kim Baek-yeong, "Sikminji Donghwajuui Gongganjeongchi: Joseon Singungui Geonseolgwa Hwaryongeul Jungsimeuro," *Incheonhakyeongu* 11 (2009), pp. 59–82.

Kim Dae-Ho, "20segi Namsan Heoihyeon Jarakui Byeonhyeong, Sigakjeok Jibaewa Gieokui Jeonjaeng: Gongwon, Shinsa, Dongdangui Geonribul Jungsimeuro," *Doshi Yeongu* 13 (2015), pp. 7–59.

Kim Sam-Wung, "1948-1959 nyeonui Seodaemun Hyeongmuso," in Seodaemun Prison History Hall, ed., *The 13th Academic Symposium Proceeding: Rhee Syngman Jipgwongiui Seodaemun Hyeongmuso*, Seoul: Seodaemun Prison History Hall, 2012.

Kim Seong-Cheol, *Yoeksa Apeseo: Han Sahakjaui 6.25 ilgi*, Seoul: Changjakgwa Bipyeongsa, 1993.

Kim Seung-Tae, "Ilbon Sindoui Chimtuwa 1910, 1920 nyeondaeui (Sinsamunje)," *Hanguksaron* 16 (1987), pp. 275–343.

Kook Sung-Ha, "Ilje Gangjeomgi Donghwajeongchaekeuroseoui Sudaneuroseoui 'Joseonsingung'ui Geollipgwa unyeong," *Hangukgyoyuksahak* 26, no. 1 (2004), pp. 31–56.

Lee Hyun-Kyung, "Miguk Geundae Gamokui Teukseong: Dongbu Jurip Gamokeul Jungsimeuro," in Seodaemun Prison History Hall, ed., *The Annual Symposium Proceeding: Geundae Gamukui Gachiwa Hwaryong*, Seoul: Seodaemun Prison History Hall, 2017.

Lee Jong-Min, "Jeguk Ilbonui 'Mobeom' Gamok – Tokyo, Taipei, Gyeongseongui Gamok Saryereul jungsimeuro," *Dongbanghakji* 17, no. 12 (2016), pp. 271–309.

Lee Jun-Sik, "Bujeongseongeowa Seodaemun Hyeongmuso," in Seodaemun Prison History Hall, ed., *The Annual Symposium proceeding: Geundae Gamukui Gachiwa Hwaryong*, Seoul: Seodaemun Prison History Hall, 2013, pp. 25–32.

Ministry of Culture and Sports of Korea, ed., *Gu Joseonchongdokbu Geunmul Silcheuk mit Cheolgeo Bogoseo Sang*, vol. 1, Seoul: Ministry of Culture and Sports and the National Museum of Korea, 1997.

Moon Chi-Yeon, "Gwadogiui Suhyeongjaui Dongtae," *Penal Administration 1 (Hyeongjeong 1)*, Chihyeong Hyeopoe (Penal Administration Association), 1947.

Moon Hea-Jin, "Iljesikminsigi Gyeongseongbu Sinsa: Sinsa mit Jesinui Sigibyeol Seonggyeongeul Jungsimeuro," *Jeongsinmunhwayeongu* 36, no. 3 (2013), pp. 369–396.

Park Kyeong-Mok, "Daehan Jegukmalgi Iljeui Gyeongseong Gamok Seolchiwa Bongam, Bungamje Sihaeng," *Hanguk Geunhyundaesa Yeongu* 46 (2008), pp. 81–104.

Park Kyeong-Mok, *Ilje Gangjeomgi Seodaemun Hyeongmuso Yeongu*, unpublished PhD diss., Chungnam University, 2015

Shim Ji-Yeon, *Heo Heon Yeongu*, Seoul: Yeoksabipyeong, 1994.

Suh Chung-Sok, *Cho Bong-amgwa 1950yeondae (Ha)*, Seoul: Yeoksa Bipyeongsa, 1999.

Yoo Ki-Bbcum, "Namsanui Geunhyeondae Sunansa: Jonggyojeok Sangjingui Isikgwa Gongganhwa Gwajeong," *Jonggyomunhwayeongu* 21 (2013), pp. 231–272.

Yang Byung-Il, "Seodaemun hyeongmusoui sangjing ikgi," *Sahoegyoyukak* 45, no. 4 (2006), pp. 59–82.

Yoon Seon-Ja, "Iljeui Sinsa Seollipgwa Joseoninui Sinsa Insik, Yeoksahak Yeongu," *Yeoksahakyeongu (Chonnam Historical Review)* 42 (2008), pp. 107–140.

Yu Seung-Hun, *Hyeonjang Sokui Munhwajae Jeongchaek*, Seoul: Minsokwon, 2004.

INDEX